P9-EMF-378

The Soviet Union Today

A Concise Handbook

THE SOVIET UNION TODAY

A Concise Handbook

REVISED EDITION

KENNETH R. WHITING

FREDERICK A. PRAEGER, *Publishers*
New York · Washington

BOOKS THAT MATTER

Published in the United States of America in 1966 by
Frederick A. Praeger, Inc., Publishers
111 Fourth Avenue, New York, N.Y. 10003

Third printing, 1968

This is a revised and expanded edition of the book published in the United States of America in 1962 by Frederick A. Praeger, Inc., Publishers.

Library of Congress Catalog Card Number: 65-15659

This book is Number 109 in the series
Praeger Publications in Russian History and World Communism.

Printed in the United States of America

Preface

Anyone bringing forth another book on the Soviet Union ought to explain his temerity, for the last decade has seen a flood of such books. Furthermore, many of them have been of high quality. This very outpouring, however, is the main justification for the present work. A single book summarizing many of the findings of numerous scholarly monographs may help answer the need of the nonspecialist, bewildered by the plethora of material on the Soviet Union.

This book, unlike many of its more scholarly brethren, breaks no new ground, advances no unique point of view, and does not attempt to treat any one subject exhaustively. It is, as its title states, a handbook. It is intended for the person seeking an introduction to things Soviet, for the busy citizen who wants a brief exposition of what makes the Soviet Union tick.

The process of condensing the many facets of Soviet life that go to make up today's Russia carries a built-in pitfall—the distortion of reality. I hope, however, that the over-all picture that emerges will be near enough to the real Soviet Union to answer the needs of the general reader.

Some readers may object to the rather large amount of history that seems to have made its way into a handbook on the Soviet Union of today. The justification is simply that Soviet institutions, ideology, and dynamism are inexplicable without some conception of the milieu within which they have evolved, and that the historical traditions of pre-Bolshevik Russia have played a leading role in the shaping of events in the last forty years. Moreover, the historical approach, by describing the relatively stable factors that move slowly beneath the bewildering changes on the surface, may help the reader to discern the more permanent aspects of Soviet life and be less impressed by the ephemeral.

I have tried to keep my distaste for the Communist brand of totalitarianism from distorting my evaluation of Soviet strengths and weaknesses, and I hope with some success. But the reader will have little trouble in detecting a distinct bias toward the democratic way of life. This is not an apology but a statement of fact.

To thank the many people who have helped in the making of this book would take many pages. But special thanks are due to my colleagues in the Air University's Research Studies Institute, and to Miss Phyllis Freeman for her careful editing.

K. R. W.

Research Studies Institute
Air University

Contents

Tables

TABLE

Figures

Figures

The Soviet Union Today

I

The Physical Setting

Although the Soviet Union today is altering in nearly every aspect—from technology to education, from food and clothing to space research—its physical setting remains immutable. It is, therefore, a logical starting point for this analysis. Many of the problems that beset the Czarist regime and now haunt its Soviet successor derive from the vast expanse of the country, the location far to the north, the continental climate, with its extremes of cold and heat, the shortage of arable land, and the inadequate rainfall. For an understanding of the Soviet Union, a physical survey of the country as a whole and of its regional characteristics provides an essential basis.

SIZE AND LOCATION

The outstanding physical factor of the U.S.S.R. is its enormous size—8.44 million square miles. Comparative statistics translate this vast territorial expanse into terms that can be understood and examined. The state of Texas would fit inside the Soviet Union some 31 times, and the Soviet Union is more than 126 times as large as the New England area. By air, the distance from Moscow to Vladivostok is about the same as from Moscow to New York. The Soviet share of the land mass of the world is also considerable. The total area of the earth that is free of water and icecaps is slightly more than 50 million square miles. The Soviet Union occupies about one-sixth of that area.

Another important physical characteristic of the Soviet Union is its extremely northern location. Simferopol, the capital of the Crimea, is in about the same latitude as Halifax, Nova Scotia; Stalino,* in the Donets Basin (Donbas) region, which is in the southern Ukraine, is in the same latitude as Great Falls, Montana; Moscow, the heart of the Soviet Union, is north of Edmonton, Alberta, or Goose Bay, Labrador; Leningrad lies in about the same latitude as Anchorage, Alaska.

North of the circle of latitude cutting through the northern edge of Edmonton live about 200,000 people of Alaska and Canada, but about 150 million people of the Soviet Union. In Canada and the United States, 99.5 per cent of the population live south of the latitude of northern Edmonton; 75 per cent of the Soviet population live to the north of it.

The very orientation of the main mass of the U.S.S.R. makes its northern location even more unfavorable. It can be schematically pictured in the form of an amphitheater, elevated in the south and the east and dropping off to the northwest. The stands and bleachers of the enormous amphitheater are the mountain ranges that run along the southern and eastern borders of the U.S.S.R.: the Caucasus, Tien Shan, Altai, Sayan, Yablonoi, Stanovoi, and Verkhoyansk ranges. In front of the stands is the floor of the amphitheater—the huge plain of European Russia and Western Siberia, spreading out toward the Arctic Ocean. There is nothing to stop the arctic air masses from moving in over this vast plain, and much of the floor of the amphitheater is so tilted toward the Arctic Ocean that many of the largest rivers flow into it. An added disadvantage is that the moderating influence of the tropical air masses and the Pacific Ocean is almost entirely cut off by the encircling mountain ranges.

These factors—vast size, northern location, and orientation toward the Arctic Ocean—have important implications in assessing the geographic setting of the Soviet Union. The deadly cold of Russia and Siberia is almost legendary. The huge land mass means that a continental climate predominates; that is, it suffers from extremes of heat and cold because of the distance

* Following the denigration of Stalin at the Twenty-second Party Congress, in October, 1961, the name was officially changed to Donetsk.

from the world's great thermostats, the open oceans. The Soviet Union does have one very long seacoast, but it is on the Arctic Ocean, a gigantic icebox.

Because of the northerly latitude and continental climate, well over 40 per cent of the U.S.S.R. (3.5 million square miles) lies within the permafrost zone, called *vechnaya merzlota* in Russian. This means that the subsurface soil is permanently frozen for a depth of from three to six feet on the lower Amur to around 2,000 feet at Nordvik. Even in summer, the surface soil thaws only to a depth of about six feet in the coniferous forests and as little as eighteen inches in the peat bogs.

The *merzlota* line begins at the White Sea about 100 miles north of Arkhangelsk, runs along the Arctic Circle to the Urals, and then swings southward. It crosses the Ob south of Berezovo and, in a curve with a definite southern bulge, reaches the Yenisei just south of Turukhansk, at which point it swings sharply south, east of the Yenisei, until it reaches Outer Mongolia. It re-enters the U.S.S.R. west of Blagoveschensk, follows the Amur to Lake Kizi and ends at the Tatar Strait, but reappears in the northeastern part of the Kamchatka Peninsula.

In Siberia, problems of building railroads, stable highways, substructures for large buildings, and airports—made difficult by the remoteness of the regions—are seriously complicated by permafrost. Agriculture and mining are also severely handicapped by this phenomenon, and until very recently, Russian industrial and agricultural development did not penetrate the *merzlota* zone.

The factors of location and terrain conspire against the U.S.S.R. in another respect, making precipitation scanty. The arctic air masses, the distance from the open oceans, and the high mountain ranges of the east and south all contribute to depriving the area of snow and rain and maintaining a low relative humidity. This lack of precipitation is especially marked in Central Asia and the arid steppes along the northern shores of the Caspian, but Eastern Siberia, too, has light snowfalls and little rain. Even the Ukraine, the most productive agricultural area of the Soviet Union, has relatively light and not entirely dependable precipitation.

Because of its location in the northern segment of the Eurasian continent, the U.S.S.R. is to a large extent landlocked. Its arctic seacoast is frozen most of the year. The warm-water seas accessible to the Soviet Union are in turn landlocked; the Caspian has no outlet, the Black Sea outlet (the Bosporus) is held by Turkey, and the Baltic outlets are controlled by Denmark and Germany. Russia's only relatively unimpeded outlet into the Atlantic is from Murmansk, on the northern coast of the Kola Peninsula. The other ice-free coast is the Far East, with its outlets on the Pacific. However, the Far East is at the rear of the amphitheater and is cut off from the rest of the U.S.S.R. by the Yablonoi and Stanovoi ranges. As a result, the Soviets have made every effort to build this region up as a self-supporting industrial and military unit.

SOIL AND VEGETATION ZONES

In dividing the U.S.S.R. into natural areas, Soviet geographers most commonly differentiate zones by soil and vegetation. The changes of climate produced by geographic latitude and distance from the ocean are very clearly reflected in the definite variations in soils and vegetation. The enormous expanses of the U.S.S.R. and the comparatively monotonous relief, however, result in wide zones of homogeneous soil and botanical types that band the country from east to west. The six basic soil and vegetation areas, moving from north to south, are the tundra zone, the forest zone, the forest-steppe zone, the chernozem-steppe zone, the arid-steppe zone, and the desert zone.

Tundra Zone

This is a vast, treeless area extending along the entire Arctic Ocean shore of the Soviet Union. The southern boundary of the tundra hovers around the Arctic Circle—above it in the Kola Peninsula and Eastern Siberia, but below it in the northeast, especially in Kamchatka. The tundra is not uniform in appearance; in the extreme north, vegetation of any type is scarce, and as the tundra extends southward, a covering of lichen mosses and dwarf shrubs develops. Much of the tundra zone is boggy because of poor drainage in the permafrost soil. Almost the only industry that flourishes in the tundra is reindeer raising, and the Soviet authorities have been devoting much time and effort to fostering it. It is estimated that the tundra zone covers 15 per cent of the U.S.S.R., or about 1.3 million square miles.

Forest Zone

The widest soil-vegetation zone of the U.S.S.R. is that of podsol and bog soils with predominantly coniferous forests, or taiga. This zone is widespread in Western and Eastern Siberia, where it extends down to the southern boundary of the U.S.S.R. In these forests, the Soviet Union has the largest timber resources in the world. This zone comprises about 4.2 million square miles, or around 50 per cent of the entire territory of the Union. Probably about 600,000 square miles of this zone, especially in Western Siberia, is swampland.

Forest-Steppe Zone

As its name implies, the forest-steppe zone is a transitional zone between the podsol-forest zone to the north and the chernozem steppe to the south. It has areas of soils peculiar to itself as well: the gray forest soils and the highly leached chernozems. The forest-steppe zone is largely confined to European Russia and Western Siberia, and there are only widely scattered islands of it east of the Yenisei; it represents about 7 per cent of the Soviet Union, or 590,000 square miles. It was in this zone that the Muscovite state arose, broke the hold of the Tatars, and gradually expanded into the present Soviet empire.

Chernozem-Steppe Zone

Although Soviet geographers distinguish as many as five different types of chernozems, by and large the term refers to rich, black soils high in organic and mineral content. These are the most fruitful soils in the Soviet Union. The zone has its widest expanse in the Ukraine, and it extends in an ever-narrowing triangle into Western Siberia. This is the basic Soviet agricultural area. There are 925,000 square miles of chernozem soils, or about 11 per cent of the Soviet Union.

Arid-Steppe Zone

This zone is at its broadest in the southern region of Western Siberia and northern Kazakhstan. These steppes are now being exploited under the program of opening up the "virgin lands"—widely discussed in the Soviet press since 1953. The entire zone is characterized by treelessness, low precipitation, and its chestnut-colored soil. In the region around the north shore of the Caspian and eastward, it becomes semidesert, good for little except limited grazing. The arid-steppe zone is estimated at 675,000 square miles, or 8 per cent of Soviet territory.

Desert Zone

The great Soviet deserts are in Central Asia (the Turkmen, Uzbek, Tadzhik, and Kirgiz republics), a region made up predominantly of sand, rocky desert, and salt flats. In this zone are located sandy deserts—the Kara Kum and Kyzyl Kum, and some smaller ones. Agriculture is feasible only in oases and along the river valleys, but where water is obtainable, the crops are abundant. Most of the Soviet cotton is grown in the river valleys and on the irrigated land of Central Asia. The desert zone occupies about 9 per cent of the U.S.S.R., or around 760,000 square miles.

REGIONS

Various criteria may be used in determining the division of the Soviet Union into regions. Some regions are almost self-evident autonomous divisions because of their geography, for instance, the Far East. Other regions are regarded as separate areas because of economic factors. Administratively, the government has established a number of other regions. In our breakdown, the following seven regions will be treated in some detail: European Russia, the Caucasus region, the Ural–Western-Siberian–Kazakhstan region, Soviet Central Asia, Eastern Siberia, the Soviet Far East, and the Soviet Arctic.

European Russia

This region lies west of the Volga River and north of a line from Stalingrad* to Novorossiisk and the north shore of the Black Sea. Together with the acquisitions after World War II, its territory is that of the old European Russia of the Czars. In spite of economic expansion to the east, European Russia is still the richest part of the Soviet Union and the real heart of the Soviet empire. Almost the whole of the region is occupied by the East Russian Plain, an extension of the great, flat expanse that begins at the North Sea, covers Germany and Poland, and then stretches eastward to the Urals. The average elevation of this vast plain is not quite 600 feet above sea level. It is a region of wide vistas and monotonous landscape, probably best summed up in the Russian word *prostor*, which means "spaciousness," "open expanse," "limitlessness." It is over this plain that Western invaders have come—the Teutonic knights, the Swedes under Charles XII, Napoleon, and Hitler. Although these invasions failed, they made the Russians very distrustful of the West, and the present Soviet satellite empire might be interpreted as an attempt to bolster the defense of this area.

The East Russian Plain is the Russian homeland; the rest of the Soviet Union has been gradually acquired by conquest and colonization from the sixteenth century to the present. The Grand Dukes of Muscovite Russia, a relatively small area on the Oka River with Moscow as its center, threw off the Tatar yoke at the end of the fifteenth century. By the middle of the

* Like Stalino, Stalingrad, too, was officially de-Stalinized after the Twenty-second Congress. It is now called Volgograd.

next century, Ivan the Terrible was able to take the offensive against the Tatars. The Russians quickly conquered the Volga Valley down to the Caspian and overran Siberia, reaching the Pacific early in the seventeenth century. The Ottoman Turks and their vassals, the Crimean Tatars, were not so easily dislodged from the northern coast of the Black Sea and the southwestern Ukraine, and it was not until the end of the eighteenth century, in the reign of Catherine II, that this area was wrested from the Turks.

Expansion to the west was slower and more costly. Ivan the Terrible fought a twenty-five-year war (the Livonian War) in an attempt to gain access to the Baltic Sea, and it was not until the first quarter of the eighteenth century that Peter the Great opened this "window to the West." Peter immediately built a city, St. Petersburg, on the swamps and islands at the mouth of the Neva and made it his capital. It remained the capital of Russia until 1918, when its location on the periphery of the empire became precarious. The Bolsheviks then moved the capital back to the more centrally located Moscow.

European Russia can be divided naturally into three parts: the Dvina-Pechora coniferous-forest region in the north, the forest steppe in the center, and the cultivated chernozem steppe of the south. A fourth area—encompassing the Kola Peninsula, Leningrad, and the Baltic republics—is tied together by water routes: the Lake Ladoga and White Sea canal system and the coast of the Baltic Sea.

The chief city of the Kola-Leningrad-Baltic area is Leningrad, which has long been the hub of one of Russia's main industrial complexes. At present, it is a great center of shipping, electrical equipment, machine tools, and other items whose production depends upon engineering ability and skilled labor. The Soviets have recently built a new steel plant at Cherepovets, near Leningrad, to supply that center with steel and utilize the scrap generated in its industries. The new steel plant also strengthens the ties linking Leningrad with the Kola Peninsula, which supplies iron ore to Cherepovets, and with the Pechora area, the source of coking coal for the new plant. This is probably one of the most expensive long-distance operations in the metallurgical industry.

The Dvina-Pechora region became extremely valuable during World War II, when the German conquest of the Ukrainian coal mines made the exploitation of the Vorkuta mines both necessary and profitable. A railroad was built in record time, largely by forced labor, and the discovery of oil at Ukhta further stimulated the development of the region.

In the forest-steppe region is located the political and industrial crown of the Soviet Union—Moscow. Not only is Moscow the capital and largest city, it is also the center of the country's largest industrial complex. It is the key point in a widespread network of railroads, and with the opening of the Volga-Don Canal, it has become a maritime center with access to the White, Baltic, Black, and Caspian seas by means of an intricate system of canals and rivers. As the political, economic, and cultural hub of the Soviet Union and the mecca of the Communist world, Moscow is unquestionably one of the world's most important cities.

The chernozem-steppe region has a twofold importance: Its black soil is the basis of the richest agriculture in the U.S.S.R., and its coal and iron ores provide the raw materials for a vast industrial structure. Most of this region is encompassed in the area usually referred to as the Ukraine.

The Ukraine was once called the granary of Russia, and although its proportionate share of the total production of the Soviet Union has declined since the opening of the "virgin and idle lands," it is still the richest of Russia's agricultural areas. The deep black and chestnut-colored soils abound in mineral and organic matter, chiefly as the result of centuries of low precipitation, which has prevented leaching of the soils. The light rainfall is also a drawback, as the Ukraine is never completely safe from the threat of drought. The annual precipitation in this area varies from twenty-two inches in the north to fourteen inches on the Black Sea coast. Ukrainian agriculture is diversified and, in addition to its basic output of grain, produces large commercial crops, such as sugar beets, sunflower seed, flax, and tobacco. In recent years, the government has brought pressure for a greater production of corn. The decrease in grain production is to be made up, Khrushchev hopes, from the cultivation of the new lands in Kazakhstan and Western Siberia.

In the southwest, the great coal deposits of the Donbas, the iron ore of Krivoi Rog and Kerch, the manganese of Nikopol, all contribute to the Ukraine's vast industrial complex. The huge hydroelectric installations at Zaporozhe make that city a logical center for alloy steels. Dnepropetrovsk, Stalino, Makeevka, and Zhdanov are all large metallurgical centers, and Kharkov is a machine-tool center.

All this wealth, both agricultural and industrial, is situated in the most vulnerable part of the Soviet Union. Even with the screen of satellites acquired as a result of World War II, the Soviet leaders still fear invasion. Ever since the early 1930's, there has been a continual emphasis upon shifting industry to the east, and even though returns on capital investment were less than they would have been if the same amount had been expended in European Russia, the added security was regarded as worth the price paid.

Although the European Russian area is the homeland of the Great Russians, it also has a variety of ethnic groups. The three Baltic republics, Estonia, Latvia, and Lithuania, have their own indigenous populations with well-developed languages and cultures. The other two great Slavic peoples, the Byelorussians (White Russians *) and Ukrainians (Little Russians), consider themselves distinct peoples. They have their own republics, historical traditions, and language differences. The newly acquired Moldavian Republic has a large Romanian population, and there is a Turkish population in the Crimea. North and west of Moscow, a number of Finnish peoples have kept their identity despite a long history of Russian domination.

* A nationality group here, not the opponents of the Reds in the Civil War.

The Caucasus Region

Usually, this region is divided into two sections: the area in the Russian Soviet Federated Social Republic (R.S.F.S.R.), lying north of the Caucasus Mountains; and the three republics lying south of the main range—Georgia, Azerbaidzhan, and Armenia—which combine to make up Transcaucasia.

The Caucasus Mountains are one of the world's great mountain chains—785 miles in length, 60 to 140 miles in width, and 55,000 square miles in area. The range begins at the Taman Peninsula, on the Kerch Strait, and runs in an east-southeasterly direction until it reaches the Caspian. Except for the narrow shore routes along the Caspian and Black seas and several very high passes across the mountains, the Caucasus forms a real barrier between European Russia and Transcaucasia.

The plains between the northern slopes of the Caucasus Mountains and the Manych Depression are very fertile in the west, especially the Kuban Valley with its chernozem soil. These plains gradually become less productive as they spread eastward into the valley of the Terek, and precipitation declines toward the east.

South of the Caucasus Mountains lie the Colchis lowland on the west and the long Kura Valley to the east. The Colchis is one of the few truly subtropical areas in the Soviet Union. Between the Colchis and the Kura Valley is the Suram Range, which separates the two areas and forms the watershed between the rivers flowing into the Caspian and Black seas. The Colchis and the upper end of the Kura Valley make up the republic of Georgia. The rest of the Kura Valley is in the Azerbaidzhan Republic. South of Georgia and Azerbaidzhan is the Armenian highland, most of which lies within the Armenian Republic.

With the exception of the Colchis lowland on the Black Sea, the long Kura Valley, and the Caspian lowland, the Transcaucasus area is one of the most mountainous in the world. It provides a rich source of hydroelectric power because of its swift mountain rivers, which are being rapidly utilized by means of a series of dams and reservoirs that equalize the flow. Deposits of coking coal, iron ore, manganese, and oil make the region one of the important industrial areas of the U.S.S.R.

Georgia. The Georgian Republic has a lowland area on the eastern end of the Black Sea, is adjacent to about half the main range of the Caucasus Mountains, and has a large area of highlands bordering on Azerbaidzhan and Armenia. From the military standpoint, Georgia's Black Sea ports and 150-mile common frontier with Turkey make it one of the logical points from which a Soviet attack on Turkey could issue. Three times in the nineteenth and once in the twentieth century this border was the scene of Russian-Turkish military action.

Georgia's long history as an independent cultural entity dates back to the fourth century B.C. It alternated as an independent kingdom and as a vassal of Persia, Rome, the Byzantine Empire, and the Turks until, in 1801, it became a part of the Russian empire. Although Georgia is an integral part of the Soviet Union, there is no question of assimilation because of the differences of race and language, as well as the Georgian pride in a long cultural tradition. For all that, Georgia has provided more top-level Soviet leaders than any other non-Russian group within the Soviet Union. Stalin, Beria, and Ordzhonikidze stand out in that list.

Georgia's industrial development has been rapid in the last few decades; a large steel plant at Rustavi, near Tbilisi (formerly Tiflis), provides the basic materials for the various industries and is the source of pipe for the Baku and Grozny oil fields. Tbilisi, the capital of Georgia, is now an industrial center well supplied with hydroelectric power. The manganese deposit at Chiatura is one of the largest in the world.

Azerbaidzhan. The Azerbaidzhan Republic occupies the lower Kura Valley and has a long coast on the Caspian Sea. Most of Azerbaidzhan is in a zone that becomes increasingly arid as it moves eastward across Transcaucasia. Azerbaidzhan's industrial importance is confined to one area and one product—petroleum from the great oil fields around Baku, on the Apsheron Peninsula. Although Baku now produces less than 15 per cent of Soviet petroleum because of the rapid development of new oil fields in the Volga-Ural region, it was until comparatively recently Russia's only great oil field.

The region now called Azerbaidzhan has played an important historical role for thousands of years. The narrow plain along the Caspian shore was one of the main routes for peoples and armies moving from the Middle East into the great plains of Russia and also for nomadic tribes pushing into the Middle East. Until Russia came into possession of the region, in 1828, the traditional overlord of Azerbaidzhan was usually the ruler of Persia. About three-fifths of the population of the republic are Azerbaidzhanians who speak a Turkic language and adhere to the Moslem faith. There are also many Azerbaidzhanians in that part of northern Iran that borders on the Azerbaidzhan Republic, and in 1945, the Soviet Union took a benevolent attitude toward an Azerbaidzhanian autonomous state in northern Iran. U. S.–British protests, U.N. pressure, and Iranian firmness led to the collapse of the movement. However, one possible route for invasion of the Middle East is from Azerbaidzhan, a route protected on one flank by Soviet control of the Caspian Sea.

Armenia. The Armenian Republic lies entirely in the high, dry, and very rough Armenian highland. To the south, the republic borders on Iran and, to the west, on Turkey. A country of volcanic origin with deep ravines and steep ridges, Armenia has an average altitude of about 5,000 feet. The climate is continental, with extremes of heat and cold. The average annual precipitation is between twelve and twenty-two inches. The only real body of water in Armenia is Lake Sevan, with an area of around 600 square miles.

The Armenians have one of the oldest cultures in the world, dating back to the eleventh century B.C. Their history is closely bound up with most of the great empires of antiquity, from the Medes and Persians to the Byzantine Empire. In the sixteenth century, the Armenians came under the control of the Ottoman Turks. Russia obtained control over the area of the present Armenian Republic as a result of the Russo-Turkish wars of 1827–28 and 1878. The population of the republic is 83 per cent Armenian, which is one of the highest percentages of ethnic purity in any Soviet republic.

Once predominantly agricultural and pastoral, Armenia is developing into an industrial area. Mineral resources, especially copper, together with an abundance of hydroelectric power, provide a basis for this change. In the last two decades, the Armenian chemical industry (producing calcium carbides, synthetic rubber, and plastics) has increased the importance of the republic in the over-all Soviet economy.

The Ural–Western-Siberian–Kazakhstan Region

In defining this region, there may be some question about the inclusion of Kazakhstan, since it is often treated as part of Central Asia. However, in the last two decades, close economic ties have developed between Kazakhstan and the Ural–Western Siberian region. Magnitogorsk, the steel giant of the Urals, operates mainly on coal from the Karaganda Basin, in Kazakhstan, and the vast iron-ore deposits of Kustanai, also in Kazakhstan, will soon be able to supply both the Ural and Kuznetsk Basin (Kuzbas) mills. The "virgin and idle lands" lie in both Western Siberia and northern Kazakhstan, and there are no natural boundaries separating the Kazakh from the Siberian soils.

Wedged in between the Urals, the tundra, the permafrost area of Eastern Siberia, and the deserts and mountains of Central Asia, this vast region is almost self-sustaining. It has large tracts of arable land in Western Siberia and northern Kazakhstan, good grazing lands, and ample lumber from the taiga of Western Siberia. But the real wealth of the region lies underground. The vast coal deposits of the Kuzbas and Karaganda and the smaller ones of the Urals buttress the ferrous metallurgy of the region. Iron ore, the other necessary ingredient in the iron and steel industry, is relatively plentiful in the Urals and in fair supply in the Kuzbas, but the deposits are almost unlimited in the Kustanai Oblast (Region) of northern Kazakhstan. The Urals have always been a storehouse of nonferrous metals, and since the 1930's, Kazakhstan has been credited with having the largest reserves of copper, zinc, and lead in the U.S.S.R.

This region is doubly valuable in the eyes of Soviet planners because its wealth is relatively secure from attack. In the early 1930's, Soviet planners, apprehensive about the vulnerability of the Ukraine, began to establish a second industrial complex in the Urals and Western Siberia. The key to this development was the Kuznetsk-Magnitogorsk *kombinat*: coal from the Kuzbas to smelt Magnitogorsk iron ore, and iron ore from Magnitogorsk to utilize Kuzbas coal. Later, Kazakhstan was brought into the operation when its coal fields at Karaganda were developed and a railroad built to Magnitogorsk to take advantage of the shorter haul.

The Urals. The Ural Mountains are very old and well worn, in many places offering little hindrance to east-west traffic. They have long been regarded as a boundary between Europe and Asia, but any attempt to divide the enormous land mass of Eurasia is arbitrary, particularly in view of the fact that a single power, the Soviet Union, controls the entire upper third of Asia and half of Europe. The average elevation of the Urals is 1,600 feet, and the highest peaks are only about 6,000 feet. The range is about 1,500 miles long, extending from the Arctic Ocean to the Caspian Depression. The climate of the Ural section is continental, with severe winters that last five or six months and rather hot summers. Precipitation is moderate in the central Urals, but declines in the south, where the climate is similar to that of northern Central Asia.

The central oblasts of the Urals (Molotov, Sverdlovsk, and Chelyabinsk) contain the major industries of the area—the ferrous-metallurgical plants at Magnitogorsk, Nizhni Tagil, and Sverdlovsk; the great tractor plant at Chelyabinsk; the locomotive works at Orsk; and the chemical plants at Berezniki. The central Urals are well supplied with railroads; trunk lines from Leningrad and Moscow meet at Sverdlovsk, and a number of north-to-east lines connect the various major centers. This network of railroads ends just beyond the Urals at Omsk, where the separate lines merge into the Trans-Siberian Railroad.

In recent years, oil fields have been developed in the eastern foothills of the Urals. In 1929, geologists struck oil while drilling for potash salts in the Molotov Oblast, along the Chusovaya

River. These wells have been only moderate producers, but the Ishimbay and Tuimazy oil fields in the Bashkir A.S.S.R. (Autonomous Soviet Socialist Republic) have developed prodigiously since World War II.

Western Siberia. Western Siberia is an enormous expanse lying between the Urals and the Yenisei River, which is roughly the same as the border of Eastern Siberia. This area of almost 1 million square miles is about nine-tenths level plain, with a barely perceptible gradient toward the Arctic Ocean. The Ob-Irtysh river system drains this plain, but so poorly that much of Western Siberia is swampland. This is always the case in the spring when the upper Irtysh and Ob are in flood because of thawing, and the lower course of the Ob is still frozen. In the southern portion of Western Siberia, there is a wide strip of good soil extending from the wedge-shaped Kurgan Oblast between the Urals and Kazakhstan to the Altai mountain system in the southeast. It is a good agricultural region and has a well-developed dairy industry. In the extreme southeast, Western Siberia is very mountainous. The coal, iron ore, and nonferrous metal ores of the Altai range support the heavy industry in that section.

The climate varies considerably because of the great distances involved. On the whole, however, it is continental, with an extremely severe winter, a cold spring, a short autumn, and a short, hot summer. The steppe zone in the southwest has many of the characteristics of Central Asia: low precipitation, heat, and strong winds resulting in dust storms. The Altai mountain region is more temperate, with moderate winters and cool, humid summers.

The Altai region is rich in minerals. The Kuzbas has the largest reserves of coking coal in the U.S.S.R.—estimated at over 400 billion tons. To the south, in the Ala Tau range, iron-ore deposits are within easy hauling distance of the coal, making the Kuzbas almost independent of outside iron ore and thus breaking the closely integrated Magnitogorsk-Kuznetsk *kombinat* into two independent elements. The center of the Kuzbas is Stalinsk.*

* Now called Novokuznetsk.

In the last three decades, the number of large cities in Western Siberia has greatly increased, particularly in the south. The largest city, Novosibirsk, has been called the "Chicago of Siberia." Located at the intersection of the Trans-Siberian Railroad and the Ob River, it is also the northern terminus of the Turksib (Turkistan-Siberian) Railroad. Its population has increased from slightly over 100,000 in the early 1920's to about 700,000 today. Omsk, situated at the junction of the Irtysh River and the Trans-Siberian Railroad, has likewise shown tremendous growth in the last two decades. The other large cities—Novokuznetsk (Stalinsk), Barnaul, and Kemerovo—are in the Altai industrial region.

Kazakhstan. The Kazakh Republic, second only to the R.S.F.S.R. in size, occupies 12 per cent of the territory of the Soviet Union. France, England, Spain, Portugal, Italy, Yugoslavia, Sweden, and Norway could all fit within the borders of this one republic. The distance between its extreme eastern and western points is 1,860 miles; the distance from north to south, about 1,000 miles. The position of Kazakhstan, adjacent to the Urals and the populous segment of Western Siberia, favored the development of close ties between the economies of the three regions. Most of Kazakhstan is a vast steppe area that grows more arid and desert-like toward the south.

Being far from any oceans, Kazakhstan has a continental climate that is only slightly ameliorated by the Caspian and Aral seas. There are very sharp temperature changes between summer and winter, and even between night and day. The winters are severe, especially when the arctic air masses push in from the unprotected north. Precipitation is low, and lack of water is one of Kazakhstan's most serious problems. In the last few years, the Soviets have plowed up much of the grass cover of northern Kazakhstan in an effort to expand their grain production and have thereby created a potential dust bowl. In spite of this, Kazakhstan has no equal in the Soviet Union as a grazing area.

Kazakhstan is very rich in underground wealth. It has over half the copper-ore reserves of the U.S.S.R. at Dzhezkazgan, Kounradski, and Bozshakul, over three-quarters of Soviet lead reserves, half of the zinc, and two-thirds of the silver. The Karaganda coal basin is the third largest in the U.S.S.R., and iron-ore deposits at Atasuskoe, Ayatskoe, and Kustanai promise to make Kazakhstan a great ferrous-metallurgical center. In western Kazakhstan, near the Caspian, the Ural-Emba oil fields, which produce top-grade oils, are being rapidly developed.

Kazakhstan, adjacent to both Chinese Sinkiang and Soviet Central Asia, acts as a transmission belt between those areas and the rest of the Soviet Union. Its importance is emphasized in a French appraisal:

> Consequently, it is permissible to consider that in the present state of things the Kuzbas-Karaganda-Fergana trio is complemented by Sinkiang and that this bloc is the main citadel, the donjon, or the central redoubt of the U.S.S.R. The redoubt abuts on the roof of the world, is protected naturally by the impassable mountains, is rich in its soil and subsoil and secure from intervention; a pivot upon which the vast maneuvers of the Kremlin can lean.[1]

The relation of this region to the over-all industrial picture of the U.S.S.R. can be seen in Table 1.

TABLE 1

THE SHARE OF THE URAL–WESTERN-SIBERIAN–KAZAKHSTAN REGION IN SOVIET PRODUCTION, 1932–55 *

(In Per Cents)

	1932	*1937*	*1940*	*1955*
Coal	16.8	24.1	25.0	34.1
Pig iron	24.4	28.3	28.2	43.0
Electric power	8.2	14.9	18.0	30.0

* Y. G. Saushkin, "Sorok let razvitiya proizvoditelnykh sil Sovetskoy strany" ("Forty Years of Development of the Productive Forces of the Soviet Land"), *Geografiya v Shkole, (Geography in the School),* V (September–October, 1957), 4.

Soviet Central Asia

This area is comprised of four union republics: Uzbekistan, Kirgizia, Tadzhikistan, and Turkmenistan. Soviet and non-Soviet geographers are divided as to whether to include Kazakhstan in Soviet Central Asia. Despite its geographic location, Kazakhstan is oriented toward the economic system of the Urals, and therefore is treated here as a part of that area. Soviet Central Asia is largely a belt of deserts stretching from the Caspian Sea, on the west, to the greatest mountain systems in the U.S.S.R., on the south and southeast. These enormous deserts are of all types: the classical sandy deserts, such as the Kara Kum, the Kyzyl Kum, and several smaller ones; the clay deserts, such as the Ust Urt, Krasnovodsk Plateau; and the stony deserts in the foothills of the Kopet Dagh Range and on the borders of the Fergana Valley. Much of the desert area is used for nomadic pasturage. The mountains of Soviet Central Asia are the highest in the U.S.S.R., the Stalin and Lenin peaks towering to almost 25,000 feet. On the southwest, along the Soviet border with Iran and Afghanistan, the Kopet Dagh Range stretches roughly east to west for 1,000 miles. To the southeast lie the Pamir-Alai ranges: Za-Alayskiy, Peter the First, Darvazskiy, Academy of Sciences, and others. Beyond are the very lofty highlands of the Pamirs, called the "roof of the world." Peaks of 20,000 feet are common in this area. These mountain ranges make natural barriers that protect Soviet Central Asia from outside incursions, although in the last two decades, they have served rather to protect others from the Soviets. In this area of mountains, the Soviet border runs contiguous with those of China, Afghanistan, and Iran; and a narrow strip of Afghan territory, in places not over ten miles wide, is all that separates the Soviet Union from Pakistan and India.

Soviet Central Asia, as would be assumed from the prevalence of deserts, is a very arid area. Precipitation is negligible, and the low relative humidity makes evaporation a real problem in conserving what little water is available. The largest body of water is the Aral Sea, which covers about 24,000 square miles. Two rivers, famous in antiquity under the names of Oxus and Jaxartes and now called, respectively, the Amu Darya and the Syr Darya, flow from the mountains and both empty in the Aral Sea. The mesopotamia between these rivers contains most of the fertile land in Soviet Central Asia.

Soviet Central Asia produces over three-quarters of the entire Soviet cotton crop, and in the last two decades, Soviet planners have attempted to convert the agriculture of this region into a monoculture. However, the fertile oases and river valleys still provide fruit, wine, and silk. Various nonferrous minerals are found in the region, and an industrial complex has grown up in the Fergana area. There is also a ferrous-metallurgical plant, located at Begovat.

Uzbekistan. From the standpoint of population, industry, agriculture, and location, Uzbekistan is the most important of the Soviet Central Asian republics. It occupies the central part of the region and borders on the other three republics and Kazakhstan as well. Its configuration is bewildering, but the tortuous boundaries of eastern Uzbekistan encompass the major part of the Fergana Valley, the most valuable land in Soviet Central Asia.

Uzbekistan produces four-fifths of the cotton of Soviet Central Asia, or almost half of the cotton output of the entire U.S.S.R. It also produces four-fifths of the gross industrial output of Central Asia. Two-thirds of the population of Soviet Central Asia and the majority of its large cities are in Uzbekistan, despite the fact that the western part of the republic is largely desert and the southern part very mountainous. The eastern section lies in the foothills of the Tien Shan Mountains and includes most of the Fergana Valley. Comprising only 17 per cent of the area of the republic, it nevertheless has over two-thirds of the population and the preponderance of the industry and agriculture. The loess soil of the Fergana Valley, when irrigated, is extremely fertile. Uzbekistan's industrial life, based on local coal, oil, and nonferrous metals, has burgeoned in the last two decades. The mountain rivers, running into the Fergana Valley, are being tapped as sources of hydroelectric power.

Kirgizia. The Kirgiz Republic is second to Uzbekistan in importance in Soviet Central Asia. It is located in the extreme northeast of the region, chiefly in the Tien Shan Mountains. Its eastern boundaries are contiguous with those of China, while it touches upon Kazakhstan, Uzbekistan, and Tadzhikistan in other directions.

The mountainous nature of the republic precludes large-scale agriculture, but it does permit well-developed truck gardens and vineyards and limited production of cotton, sugar beets, and tobacco. The main industries of Kirgizia are livestock-raising and mining, the latter producing principally nonferrous metals such as antimony, mercury, and lead.

Tadzhikistan. The Tadzhik Republic is the most mountainous region in the U.S.S.R. It is located in the extreme southeast of Soviet Central Asia, with its southern boundary running along the Afghanistan border for 630 miles and its eastern boundary abutting China for 270 miles. In spite of its location on the "roof of the world," Tadzhikistan has good agricultural areas, especially in its share of the Fergana Valley and in the lower southeastern section. Ranking next to Uzbekistan in the production of cotton, Tadzhikistan grows an excellent, fine-fiber cotton.

The most interesting feature of Tadzhikistan is its proximity to many Eastern nations. Stalin, in an address to some leading Tadzhik Communists, summed up Tadzhikistan's frontier position with these telling phrases: "republic of workers at the gateway to India," "the model republic for the Eastern countries," "the lighthouse for socialism in the East." China is one neighbor, and only a narrow strip of Afghan territory, nine to twelve miles in width, separates Tadzhikistan from Pakistan and India.

Turkmenistan. This is the southernmost republic of the U.S.S.R., its southern boundary being contiguous with the boundaries of Iran and Afghanistan for more than 1,000 miles. Although there is a string of oases along the Kopet Dagh Range and the Amu Darya River, a very large part of the republic is desert, either uninhabited or inhabited by nomadic herdsmen. In area, Turkmenistan stands only below the R.S.F.S.R.,

Kazakhstan, and the Ukraine, but in population it surpasses only Estonia. Turkmenistan has some oil and a small chemical industry, but otherwise it is a rather primitive region.

Eastern Siberia

This enormous region of some 2.8 million square miles is bounded on the west by the watershed between the Yenisei and the Ob-Irtysh system, on the east by the watershed along the ranges paralleling the Pacific, and on the south by Outer Mongolia and Manchuria. It extends to the Arctic Ocean in the north. The distance across Eastern Siberia from east to west is 1,900 miles; from north to south, 1,500 miles. The Central Siberian Plateau lies between the Yenisei and Lena rivers and forms the great middle portion of the whole region. To the south is the Sayan-Baikal country, a broken area containing a number of large mountain ranges, such as the Eastern and Western Sayans, the Baikals, and the Yablonoi Range. To the northeast of the plateau is the Verkhoyansk Range. The only lowlands, located west of the Yenisei, are properly part of the great Western Siberian Lowland.

The climate is extremely continental. The district around Verkhoyansk and Oimyakon is the "cold cellar" of the world. In January, 1897, a record low of —126° F. was registered at Verkhoyansk. Even lower temperatures have been unofficially reported from Oimyakon. At Yakutsk, 500 miles south of Verkhoyansk, the mean January temperature is —46° F. Snow cover is light because of the very low annual precipitation, and almost all of Eastern Siberia lies within the permafrost region. The short growing season, extreme cold, light snow cover, and permafrost combine to make agriculture virtually impossible except in the extreme south of the region. Here Lake Baikal, 400 miles long, 30 to 50 miles wide, and 2,000 to 5,000 feet deep, acts as a moderator on the extreme weather conditions of the area.

The water-power resources of Eastern Siberia are enormous; its hydroelectric potential has been estimated at 40 per cent of the total available in the U.S.S.R. In addition to the mighty

Yenisei and Lena rivers with their far-flung tributaries, the Angara, the only river flowing out of Lake Baikal, has tremendous volume. A new hydroelectric installation is being built to tap this source of power.

The region is moderately rich in minerals, especially coal, but the largest coal deposits are in areas inaccessible for economic exploitation up to the present time. However, in rare minerals such as tin, wolfram, and molybdenum, Eastern Siberia holds first place in the U.S.S.R. The Lena gold fields are the richest in the Soviet Union, and very recently diamond fields have been found in the Yakutsk area. This discovery was hailed with great enthusiasm, as industrial diamonds were previously available to the Soviets only by purchase on the world market.

Eastern Siberia is the most sparsely inhabited region in the U.S.S.R. except for the Far North. Although it is 1.5 times larger than European Russia, its population is less than that of the Moscow Oblast alone and averages less than one person per square kilometer. Non-Russian peoples are scattered over the whole region. The largest groups are the Yakuts (almost 300,000) in the Yakutsk A.S.S.R. and the Buriat-Mongols (250,000) in the Buriat-Mongolian A.S.S.R. In the even wilder areas are other non-Russian peoples such as the Evenki, Khakass, and Nentsy, all of whom have their own autonomous oblasts or national okrugs.

THE SOVIET FAR EAST

This region stretches along the shore of the Pacific from the northern border of Korea to the Bering Strait, a straight-line distance of around 2,800 miles. Mountain ranges running parallel to the Pacific cover most of the region. With the exception of the Chukotski Peninsula, which is under the influence of the arctic climate, the Soviet Far East falls in the monsoon area. In the summer, the region is warm, wet, and foggy; in the winter, it is very cold.

The Maritime Province, lying between Manchuria and the Sea of Japan, is the economic base of the region. It occupies less than one-twentieth of the Soviet Far East, but has approximately half the population. Its capital, Vladivostok (Ruler of the East), is a city of 265,000 located on a peninsula that divides the Amur and Ussuri gulfs. Vladivostok is the terminal point of the Trans-Siberian Railroad and is the largest Soviet port on the Pacific. The lowlands around Lake Khanka and along the Ussuri River produce much of the food of the entire region—rice, sorghum, and soybeans. The other agricultural area of the Soviet Far East is the Zeya-Bureya lowland, on the Amur River, which produces wheat, oats, rye, and sugar beets.

As a result of the Yalta Agreement, in 1945, the entire island of Sakhalin, just east of the Maritime Province, came under Soviet control. The crude oil from Sakhalin is transported by tanker across the Sea of Japan and up the Amur River to Khabarovsk, where it is processed.

Every effort has been made to convert the Soviet Far East into an economically viable region, since it is virtually cut off from the rest of the Soviet Union. The only communications between the two are the Trans-Siberian Railroad, air transport, and shipping via the Northern Sea Route—all rather unreliable if a conflict should break out. Some coal, iron ore, and nonferrous metals have provided a tenuous base for Far Eastern industries. Foods from the Zeya-Bureya and Lake Khanka lowlands, supplemented by fish and reindeer meat from the northern areas, go far toward making the region self-sufficient. The oil from Sakhalin lightens the load of the Trans-Siberian Railroad, especially in keeping the semiautonomous Far Eastern air force in fuel.

The Soviet Arctic

It is futile to attempt to fix a southern boundary for the Soviet Arctic. Often the Arctic Circle is arbitrarily used, but this geographic line fails to consider the fluctuating temperature and vegetation boundaries as it goes from west to east. In 1936, the Northern Sea Route Administration (Glavsevmorput) was given jurisdiction over the Arctic area, but not over most of the

European Arctic land mass. From about 60° long. to the Pacific, however, its administration encompassed everything down to 62° lat., thus giving it an enormous portion of the Siberias and the Far East. The region around Arkhangelsk and the Kola Peninsula, together with the Glavsevmorput administrative region, roughly define the boundaries of the Soviet Arctic.

The European Arctic. Most of the Soviet European Arctic is washed by the Barents Sea.* Because of the moderating influence of the Gulf Stream, which penetrates the Barents Sea, more than half the southern shore remains open throughout the year. The main port, Murmansk, on the Kola Peninsula, is one of the Soviet Union's few warm-water ports. The Barents Sea ends at the Novaya Zemlya archipelago (site of many of the Soviet nuclear tests in late 1961), and is connected with its eastern neighbor, the Kara Sea, by three straits: the Yugorski Shar, the Karskie Vorota, and the Matochkin Shar. The Kara Sea is frozen much of the year, and even when it is open to navigation, adverse winds can pile up drifting ice to the extent of blocking the straits through Novaya Zemlya.

The northern Dvina, entering the White Sea at Arkhangelsk, and the Pechora, emptying into the Barents at Naryan-Mar, are the most important rivers in the European Arctic. Two great river systems of Western Siberia empty into the Kara Sea—the Ob-Irtysh and the Yenisei.

Most of the Soviet European Arctic region is either treeless tundra, swamp, or forest (taiga). In recent years, the deposits of apatite (a phosphorus basis for fertilizers) and iron ore on the Kola Peninsula and the coal and oil of the Pechora Basin have made the European Arctic region economically very valuable.

The Asiatic Arctic. The shores of the Soviet Asiatic Arctic, from Novaya Zemlya to the Bering Strait, border upon four seas: the Kara, Laptev, East Siberian, and Chuckchee. The Kara Sea lies between Novaya Zemlya and the Severnaya Zemlya Islands.

* The conventional Western spellings of the Soviet Arctic seas are used here. Their Russian names, moving from west to east, are Barentsovo More, Karskoe More, More Laptevykh, Vostochnosibirskoe More, and Chukotskoe More.

Between the latter and the New Siberian Islands is the Laptev Sea, and along the coast of the Chukotski Peninsula lie the East Siberian and Chuckchee seas. These seas are frozen most of the year, and as one moves eastward, the pack ice of the Arctic Ocean approaches nearer and nearer the continent.

Two large rivers empty into the Laptev Sea—the Khatanga and the Lena, the latter being one of the world's largest rivers. The Indigirka and Kolyma rivers flow into the East Siberian Sea. As these rivers are frozen most of the year, they are of very limited use in penetrating the Siberias by water. Furthermore, the spring thaws begin early at the headwaters of the rivers, while their mouths are still frozen, and extensive areas are flooded each spring and early summer, especially in Western Siberia.

All the Soviet Asiatic Arctic lies within the permafrost zone, which renders the construction of buildings, rail lines, and air bases extremely difficult. The Soviets have devoted much time and effort to trying to solve the many problems associated with permafrost, and in some fields they have been very successful.

The end of World War II left only two great powers in the rapidly contracting globe, and the Arctic region is the shortest avenue of approach between them. It is probable that at least part of any Soviet attack upon the United States would go over the Pole; the Soviets are also vulnerable to Strategic Air Command retaliation along their northern border. It is understandable that under these conditions the Soviets have shown almost frantic determination to master their Arctic regions. Polar stations, airfields, and missile bases spread from the Kola Peninsula across the Arctic to the Bering Strait. Some seven drifting scientific stations (North Poles 1 to 7) are in operation to provide information that enables Soviet scientists to cope more adequately with this hostile environment.

ADMINISTRATIVE ORGANIZATION

As is implied by its name, the Union of Soviet Socialist Republics is a union of republics centrally administered by the All-Union government in Moscow. The largest of the republics is the R.S.F.S.R. (Russian Soviet Federated Socialist Republic). The use of "Federated" in the name indicates that many national groups are incorporated in the R.S.F.S.R. Fourteen other S.S.R.'s (Soviet Socialist Republics), usually called union republics, are technically free to leave the Union but in fact they have no alternative. The republics have their own legislative bodies, one-chamber Supreme Soviets, Councils of Ministers, etc., like the U.S.S.R. itself.

The next administrative layer below the union republic is the A.S.S.R. (Autonomous Soviet Socialist Republic), which also has its own Supreme Soviet and Council of Ministers but is more or less subordinate to the union republic in which it is located. An A.S.S.R. usually has a predominant nationality different from that of the parent union republic. There are also autonomous oblasts, okrugs, and national rayons to conform with the nationality groups.

The union republics and autonomous republics are subdivided into oblasts (regions) and krays (territories). The oblasts and krays, and in some cases the smaller republics, are divided into rayons (rural districts), somewhat analogous to U.S. counties. The size of the rayons varies enormously, from 150,000 square miles in the northern tundra region to less than 100 square miles in the black-earth Ukraine. The smallest local units, subordinate to the rayon, are the village and nomad soviets (see Table 2).

The urban areas have a separate regime. The largest cities are directly subordinate to the republic and are themselves broken up into rayons. Smaller cities are under the oblasts or krays, and the small towns under the rayons.

Administrative subdivisions are usually based on the demands of the current economic plan. Its rapid changes result in constant shifts in areas, boundaries, and names, and make the date of a Soviet map very important. As a small village grows in size, the ending of the name will change to accord with the gender of the noun indicating its new status. For example, a small village (*derevnya,* feminine) will have an ending in *-skaya.* If it becomes a large village (*selo,* neuter), it will take the ending *-skoye,* and if it becomes a workers' settlement (*rabochiy poselok,* masculine), it will end in *-skiy.*

Many Soviet cities are named after leading figures of the

TABLE 2
ADMINISTRATIVE-TERRITORIAL UNITS WITHIN UNION REPUBLICS, APRIL 1, 1963 *

Union Republics	*Autonomous Republics*	*Autonomous Oblasts*	*Krays and Oblasts*	*Rural Rayons*	*Industrial Rayons*	*City Rayons*	*Cities*	*Villages of City Type*	*Village Soviets*
R.S.F.S.R.	16	15 [a]	55 [b]	938	111	238	901	1,678	22,132
Ukrainian S.S.R.	—	—	25	251	2	74	355	822	8,578
Byelorussian S.S.R.	—	—	6	77	—	13	73	123	1,541
Uzbek S.S.R.	1	—	8	63	1	6	35	77	780
Kazakh S.S.R.	—	—	18 [c]	120	7	8	55	142	1,832
Georgian S.S.R.	2	1	—	37	1	7	39	51	911
Azerbaidzhan S.S.R.	1	1	—	38	—	9	45	109	823
Lithuanian S.S.R.	—	—	—	41	—	7	89	25	653
Moldavian S.S.R.	—	—	—	18	—	2	18	22	608
Latvian S.S.R.	—	—	—	21	—	5	54	34	589
Kirgiz S.S.R.	—	—	1	21	—	2	15	29	357
Tadzhik S.S.R.	—	1	—	25	—	3	15	28	214
Armenian S.S.R.	—	—	—	26	—	5	23	25	429
Turkmen S.S.R.	—	—	—	21	—	2	13	65	210
Estonian S.S.R.	—	—	—	14	—	3	33	25	241
Total	20	18	113	1,711	122	384	1,763	3,255	39,898

* *SSSR: Administrativno-Territorial'noe Delenie Soyuznykh Respublik na 1 Aprelya 1963 Goda*, p. 7.
[a] Including 10 national okrugs.
[b] Including 6 krays.
[c] Including 3 krays.

regime; if these persons fall into disfavor, the names are changed. As an example, Yenakiyevo was changed at one time to Rykovo, but with Rykov's eclipse, it was changed to Ordzhonikidze, who was then close to Stalin. With Ordzhonikidze's death and loss of prestige, the name reverted to Yenakiyevo. The most wholesale exercise in renaming came at the conclusion of the Twenty-second Congress, in October, 1961. With Stalin's denigration, his name was removed not only from the Lenin-Stalin tomb in Red Square, but from some eighty cities and towns throughout the U.S.S.R. Stalingrad, the symbol of Soviet resistance in World War II, became Volgograd. Stalino, the industrial city of the Ukraine, is now Donetsk, and Stalinabad, capital of the Tadzhik Republic, reverted to its earlier name, Dushanbe.

Some of the capitals of national areas have had their names changed to conform with the local language. This was the case in the North Ossetian A.S.S.R., where the name has undergone a fourfold change: from the Russian name Vladikavkaz (Ruler of the Caucasus), to Ordzhonikidze, to the Ossetian name Dzaudzhikau, and then back to Ordzhonikidze after his anti-Stalinism became a virtue.

2

The People

In May, 1959, the Soviets released the results of the first census since 1939; the official 1959 reading was 208.8 million. The statistical collection *Narodnoe Khozyaystvo SSSR* (*The National Economy of the U.S.S.R.*) for 1956 had listed the total population of the Soviet Union at 200.2 million, but that figure was merely an educated guess. No Western demographers had put the Soviet population so low. But Soviet losses, both direct and in expected births, were even more catastrophic during World War II than had been previously thought. In 1940, the Soviets estimated the population, including the Polish, Moldavian, Lithuanian, Latvian, and Estonian territories seized in 1939–40, at 191.7 million. In twenty years, the population increase was only 17 million. Consider the increase in the United States for the same period: from 131.7 million in 1940 to around 176 million in 1959, an increase of about 44 million. This situation is particularly critical for the Soviet Union because of the limited number of young people coming of work age in the present period. The low birth rate of 1941–46 meant that sixteen-year-old workers and soldiers were in very short supply in the Soviet Union at least as late as 1962.

The population is divided, in Soviet statistics,[1] into rural and urban groups. In 1959, the rural population was 109 million (52 per cent of the total) and the urban, 99.8 million (48 per cent). This is a marked change from 1913, when the urban population was only 17.6 per cent of the total.

The Soviet Union is made up of a large number of different nationalities speaking various languages, many of which have no affinity to each other (see Table 3). For example, the Russian

TABLE 3

MAJOR LANGUAGE GROUPS IN THE SOVIET UNION *

Major Division	*Subdivision*	*Language*	*Number of Speakers (In Thousands)*
Indo-European	Baltic	Latvian	1,400
		Lithuanian	2,326
	East Slavic	Russian	114,588
		Ukrainian	36,981
		Byelorussian	7,829
	Armenian	Armenian	2,787
	Iranian	Tadzhik	1,397
		Ossetian	410
Turkic		Uzbek	6,004
		Tatar	4,969
		Kazakh	3,581
		Azerbaidzhanian	2,929
		Chuvash	1,470
		Turkmenian	1,004
		Bashkir	983
		Kirgiz	974
		Yakut	236
		Kara-Kalpak	173
		Tuvinian	100
		Uigur	95
		Karachai	81
		Khakass	57
		Balkar	42
Mongolian		Buriat	253
		Kalmuck	106
Finno-Ugric		Mordvinian	1,285
		Estonian	969
		Udmurt (Votyak)	623
		Mari (Cheremiss)	504
		Komi (Zyrian)	431
		Karelian	167
North Caucasian		Chechen	418
		Kabardinian	204
		Avar	268
		Lezghian	223
		Darghin	158
		Ingush	106
Georgian		Georgian	2,650

* William Kleesmann Matthews, *Languages of the U.S.S.R.* (London: Cambridge University Press, 1951); Walter Kolarz, *Russia and Her Colonies* (New York: Frederick A. Praeger, 1952); *Bolshaya Sovetskaya Entsiklopediya* (*Great Soviet Encyclopedia*) (1st ed.; Moscow: Aktsionernoe Obshchestvo Sovetskaya Entsiklopediya, 1926–39); *Pravda,* February 4, 1960, pp. 1–2.

and Georgian languages have different alphabets, vocabulary, and grammar and are as far apart linguistically as English and Georgian. The 1959 census lists 108 languages in the U.S.S.R. and has, in addition, a catch-all entitled "other nationalities." The nationality problem haunted the Czarist regime from its earliest expansion, in the fifteenth and sixteenth centuries, contributed to its demise in the 1917 Revolution, and since then has been a major problem for the Communist Government.

SLAVS

The largest racial group in the U.S.S.R. is the Slavic race, which totals almost 160 million people, or three-quarters of the Soviet population. This group is a composite of the Great Russians, the Ukrainians, and the Byelorussians. The 114 million Great Russians make up over 50 per cent of the total population and are far and away the dominant group. For example, the largest single group in the present Presidium of the Party is composed of Great Russians. The official language of the U.S.S.R. is Great Russian, and anyone desiring advancement in the Soviet Union must learn Great Russian. For centuries, the colonization drive of the Great Russians has scattered them all over the U.S.S.R., and in many areas—especially the cities—they now outnumber the original inhabitants.

The Ukrainians, sometimes called the Little Russians, are the second largest group in the U.S.S.R., numbering almost 37 million. Although very heavily represented in the Ukraine, they are to be found in all parts of the U.S.S.R. as a result of the mass deportations during the collectivization of agriculture in the early 1930's and the evacuation of the civilian population before the German advance in 1941 and 1942. The Ukrainian language is similar to Great Russian but has too many differences to be considered a dialect.

The Byelorussians * are the smallest of the three Slavic groups, totaling less than 8 million. The swampy, unproductive land of

* *Byelo* means "white" in Russian; the Russian term is generally used to differentiate the nationality from the political group who opposed the Reds in the Civil War (1918–21) and were called the White Russians.

Byelorussia held back the economic and cultural development of these people. Furthermore, because the Byelorussians have been dominated by other peoples throughout their history—at first by the Poles and the Lithuanians and then by the Great Russians—they have had little opportunity to evolve a strong, independent culture and literature.

BALTS

The most recent victims of Soviet expansion were the nationalities west of the U.S.S.R. who were caught between the Nazis and the Russians. Three of these peoples are the Baltic nationalities: the Lithuanians, Latvians, and Estonians, whose combined population came to 4.7 million in 1959. Russian domination is nothing new to these peoples; they were incorporated into the Russian Empire as early as the eighteenth century and experienced freedom as separate nations only in the period between 1918 and 1939. But even before 1918, and certainly during their period of independence, they became conscious of themselves as distinct nationalities with well-developed languages, literatures, and traditions. It is doubtful if they will ever become Russianized, and the Soviet Government, acutely aware of the strategic vulnerability of the area, has deliberately colonized much of the territory with Russians.

FINNO-UGRIANS

In the enormous area lying to the east of Finland and to the north of the Urals and Western Siberia, there are a few non-Russian nationalities, mostly of Finno-Ugric stock. The Mordvinians, about 1.3 million in 1959, are the largest nationality in this group. Only about half a million live in the Mordvinian A.S.S.R., which has a total population of about 1 million. The rest are scattered about in the Urals and in the Volga region. The Udmurts (also called the Votyaks) are the next largest group, numbering around 600,000. There are also about half a million Mari people and 400,000 Komi, who belong to the Finno-Ugric group. These nationalities came under Russian influence very early, especially when the focus of Russian expansion shifted from Kiev to Moscow in the thirteenth and fourteenth centuries. In some respects, their treatment resembles that of the American Indian in the face of Western expansion. They were allowed to hold those areas for which the Russians had no particular use, and only so long as that situation continued. The discovery of coal and oil in the Pechora region illustrates the fate that overtook these peoples. The Komi constituted the majority of the population until these raw materials brought in a flood of Russians, and now the natives of the region have been swamped by the influx of settlers from other parts of the U.S.S.R.

TATARS

Russian-Tatar hostility has been endemic ever since the thirteenth century and the Mongol conquests; a large part of the Mongol forces were Tatar. The Tatars, strung out along the Volga and back to the Urals, were a block to Russian eastward expansion. In the middle of the sixteenth century, Ivan the Terrible conquered Kazan, the Tatar stronghold, and in a few decades, the Russians held the length of the Volga and were swarming over Siberia. But even under the Czarist Russification policy, the Tatars maintained considerable autonomy, and Kazan in the nineteenth century was a center for Tatar studies. Although "Tatar" is used to indicate the national groups inhabiting this area, there are really three different nationalities: Tatar, Bashkir, and Chuvash.

The Tatars have an autonomous republic, the Tatar A.S.S.R., with its capital at Kazan. But it is doubtful that the Tatars now have much influence in their own republic. The bulk of the 5 million Tatars are widely scattered today, and the 3 million people living in the Tatar A.S.S.R. include many non-Tatars drawn into the Volga-Ural area by industrial expansion.

The Bashkirs, like the Tatars, are a Moslem people and are a minority within their own republic, the Bashkir A.S.S.R. As early as 1933, the Bashkirs made up only 25 per cent of the population. Since Ufa has become not only the capital of the Bashkir A.S.S.R.

but also the capital of the "Second Baku" oil region, the ratio of Bashkirs has dropped even lower. There were 983,000 Bashkirs in the U.S.S.R. in 1959, when the population of the Bashkir A.S.S.R. was 3.3 million. Not all the Bashkirs live in their republic, but even if they did, they would make up only 29 per cent of the population.

The Chuvash are Christians, and although their language is somewhat allied to the Tatar, they have never had close cultural or national ties with their neighbors. The Chuvash consider themselves the heirs of the great Bolgarian Empire, part of whose people migrated to the present Bulgaria in the early Middle Ages. Unlike the Tatars and the Bashkirs, the Chuvash are in the majority in the Chuvash A.S.S.R. In 1939, about 700,000 of the 1.35 million Chuvash lived there. The Chuvash population totals 1.5 million today, and the Chuvash A.S.S.R. has a population of 1.1 million. The ratio of those living within their own republic to those outside it is probably about the same as in 1939.

SOVIET CENTRAL ASIANS

One of the great non-Slavic areas of the U.S.S.R. is Central Asia. According to the 1959 census, some 11.14 million non-Slavs live in this area, which has a total population of 13.7 million. (Kazakhstan is not included in Soviet Central Asia in this description, as it was similarly excluded in our geographical breakdown.) There are 2.5 million Russians and Ukrainians in the area, or a little less than 18 per cent of the total population. Most of the population of Central Asia is Turkic and speaks Turkic languages, with the exception of the Tadzhiks, who are Iranians (Persians). There are many small minority groups in Soviet Central Asia, but they play little part in the life of the region. The Uigurs, a Turkic people (numbering 95,000), are of the same stock as the Uigurs of Sinkiang (a group of around 3 million) and move back and forth across the border rather freely. The Dungans (totaling 21,000) are a very small minority of mixed Arab and Persian origin. The 7,800 Baluchis, who live in Central Asia, may prove valuable in Soviet dealings with Iran,

Pakistan, and India, each of which has a substantial Baluchi population. There is even an Arab minority of 8,000 in Uzbekistan.

Russian penetration of Central Asia began in the eighteenth century. The history of the Orenburg fort gives a capsule picture of this movement. The original fort was established in 1737 as an advance post for the eastern drive; by 1742, it was 165 miles east of its original site, having been moved twice in the direction of Central Asia. In the 1840's, a concerted push began, and the Russians reached the mouth of the Syr Darya in 1847. In 1865, Tashkent was captured, and Samarkand fell three years later. Some of the oldest cities in the world, long closed to Western travelers, now became parts of the Russian Empire. The British grew extremely disturbed about this Russian drive toward India and, upon the Russian capture of Merv, expressed their feelings with the pun "Mervousness." Much of the British-Russian mistrust in the nineteenth century is traceable to suspicion of each other's motives in Central Asia.

At the outset, the Communist regime met stiffer resistance than had even Czarist Russia in "pacifying" Central Asia. Apparently, the nationalities of the area had accepted at face value the Soviet statements on the right of autonomy. Once the opposition was silenced, the Soviet leaders proceeded to set up a Turkmen S.S.R., plus two Soviet People's Republics, Bukhara and Khorezm (now Khiva). By 1925, however, atomization of the Central Asian region appeared to be the soundest policy to achieve Sovietization and the present divisions—Kirgizia, Uzbekistan, Turkmenistan, and Tadzhikistan—had emerged.

Kirgiz

Kirgizia is one of the most valuable areas in the Soviet Union. Not only are its oil, minerals, cattle, and cotton great assets for the national economy, but its geographic position is ideal for implementing Soviet expansionist policies in Asia and the Middle East. The republics of this area border on Sinkiang, Afghanistan, India, and Iran—all targets for Soviet domination, if not incorporation.

It is not surprising that Soviet controls are very strict in the area, for the Kirgiz have been extremely restive under the Russians, both before and after 1917. The Czarist Government began to settle Russians in Kirgizia as early as the 1860's, and the process has gone on more or less steadily ever since. In 1916, the Kirgiz, along with some of their Central Asian brothers, rebelled against military conscription. They had been exempt from service until the insatiable demands of the Eastern Front forced the Czarist regime to seek new sources of manpower. It is estimated that some 150,000 Kirgiz who refused to serve were killed. Under the Soviets, non-Kirgiz colonists continued to pour in, and today only 40 per cent of the population of the republic are Kirgiz. As a result of this century-long pressure, the Russians now control Kirgizia, and its capital city, Frunze, is predominantly Russian. The 1939 census enumerated 880,000 Kirgiz in a total population of about 1.5 million; the 1959 census gave 837,000 Kirgiz in a total population of a little over 2 million.

Uzbeks

Uzbekistan is the wealthiest and most populous of the Central Asian republics (excluding Kazakhstan, as mentioned earlier). The Uzbeks, numbering just over 6 million in the entire Soviet Union, are the largest non-Slavic ethnic group in the U.S.S.R. They are an extremely proud people, as they demonstrated in the so-called Basmachi revolt against Sovietization in the early years of the Communist regime. Once the Soviet leaders gained full control, they began to pursue energetically the Czarist policy of converting Uzbekistan into a cotton-growing region. By 1950, the acreage under cotton had been increased fivefold over that sown before the Czarist conquest. The necessary cut in cereal production resulted in a dependence upon imported foodstuffs and in an intensified anti-Russian feeling. At the same time, the Soviets have done much toward industrializing Uzbekistan. The local coal, oil, and mineral resources, plus the potential water-power reserves of the Fergana Valley, made this step almost inevitable. The population of Uzbekistan in 1959 was 8.1 million, and the Uzbeks made up 5 million of that total.

Turkmenians

The Turkmenians were the last of the Central Asian peoples conquered by Czarist Russia, with the capture of Merv in 1884. They are close to the Anatolian Turks in language and consequently were favorably inclined toward all Pan-Turkic movements of the early twentieth century, especially in the wake of World War I. The 1959 census listed 1 million Turkmenians in the U.S.S.R., and 924,000 of them lived in Turkmenistan. This gave the republic an ethnic purity of 61 per cent, as the total population was 1.5 million. Since nine-tenths of Turkmenistan is sandy desert, the famous Kara Kum, it is very doubtful that it will ever become one of the prosperous Soviet republics. Oil resources discovered there in recent years have been developed considerably, and there has also been much propaganda about the irrigation of the Kara Kum, but although plans were announced in 1950 for the construction of a "main Turkmenian canal," little seems to have come of them.

Tadzhiks

The Autonomous Tadzhik Soviet Republic, established in 1925, became a union republic in 1929—a move serving Soviet foreign policy rather than administrative logic. It was self-evident that the region did not warrant such an elevation in status, but the tumbling of pro-Soviet King Amanullah from the throne of Afghanistan at that time made a Soviet countermove seem very desirable. This move and countermove in Central Asian politics express Tadzhikistan's importance in the scheme of things: It is a frontier post facing Afghanistan, India, Pakistan, and Iran, with all the implications of such a situation in the light of unceasing Soviet efforts to carry Communist gospel into Asia. For example, according to Soviet figures (obviously intended as propaganda), there are 2 million Tadzhiks, 1 million Uzbeks, and 380,000 Turkmenians in Afghanistan. Since the Tadzhiks are an Iranian people, Soviet scholars have valiantly tried to prove that the Tadzhiks are the real soul and mind of the Iranian world. The implications of this line of thought are very obvious if the Soviets should move toward either Iran or Afghanistan. There are 1.4 million Tadzhiks in the U.S.S.R., and over a million live in Tadzhikistan, which has a population of around 2 million. The republic thus has an ethnic purity of about 53 per cent.

Kazakhs

From an ethnic point of view, the Kazakhs can logically be grouped with the other Central Asian peoples. They were nomadic until recently and speak a Turkic language, as do most of the peoples of Central Asia with the exception of the Iranian Tadzhiks. Economically, Kazakhstan is closely knit into the industrial complex of the Urals and Western Siberia. The Kazakhs have fought a losing battle with the Russians since the 1890's, and by 1910, the town of Vernyi (the present capital of Kazakhstan and now called Alma-Ata) had 26,000 Russians among its 37,000 inhabitants. The whole process is reminiscent of the feud between the cattlemen and the farmers, or "nesters," in the American West at about the same period; wherever the grasslands were fertile enough for profitable agriculture, the nomadic stock-raisers were driven off.

The Kazakhs attempted a comeback right after the Revolution. They drove many Russian colonists out, and in 1927, the Communist Party of the region, controlled by the Kazakh nationalists, was able to pass a law giving Kazakhs a preference in land distribution. As a result, the Russian farmers were rapidly located on the most unproductive land. This was unacceptable to the central government, and it decided in favor of the Slav peasants. The biggest blow came when the Turksib Railroad was built across eastern Kazakhstan in 1930, encouraging further colonization. During the collectivization period, the Kazakh nomads also suffered bitterly in their fight against being confined to the collective farms. The opening up of the Karaganda coal basin, the discovery of large copper and iron-ore deposits, and the general industrial expansion added further to the decline of the traditional Kazakh way of life. In the past few years, Khrushchev's virgin-lands policy has brought in even more Slavs as settlers.

There were slightly over 3.5 million Kazakhs in the U.S.S.R. in 1959, 2.75 million of them living in Kazakhstan. However, the total population of the republic was 9.3 million, with over 50 per cent Russians and Ukrainians. Since the Kazakhs make up only 30 per cent of the population, the name Kazakhstan, which means "land of the Kazakhs," seems to be a misnomer.

NORTH CAUCASIANS

The indigenous population of the northern area of the Caucasus Range is made up of eight nationalities: Chechen, Ossetians, Kabardinians, Ingush, Karachaevs, Adighes, Balkars, and Cherkess (or Circassians). In the nineteenth century, the Russians encountered many difficulties in their conquest of the region, especially from 1840 to 1859, when most of these peoples, under the leadership of the Chechen, fought under the Moslem banner of the Imam Shamyl. It was only by cutting down whole forests, building a network of roads, and razing the native villages one by one that the Russians finally overcame the resistance.

The Communists, on coming to power, tried several approaches to these diverse peoples. In 1920, they set up the Gorskaya (Mountaineers') A.S.S.R., combining all the national groups, but they soon found that the "divide and conquer" technique would be more effective. Between 1921 and 1926, a number of separate autonomous oblasts were established, three of which became autonomous republics in 1936—Kabardino-Balkarian, Chechen-Ingush, and North Ossetian.

The German invasion of the North Caucasus in 1942 revealed the superficiality of the Soviet hold over these peoples. Four of the national groups, the Chechen, Ingush, Balkars, and Karachaevs, regarded Russia's enemy as their friend. After the Soviets had driven the Germans out of the region, they rounded up and deported to Siberia these four peoples. The Chechen-Ingush

A.S.S.R. and Karachaev Autonomous Oblast were abolished, and the Kabardino-Balkarian A.S.S.R., bereft of its Balkars, became simply the Kabardinian A.S.S.R.

By comparison with the Chechen, the Ossetians have always been pro-Russian. Although the Ossetians valiantly fought collectivization in the 1930's, they never showed the bitter animosity of the Chechen. As a reward for their pro-Soviet attitude during World War II, the Ossetians received part of the Ingush area.

In January, 1957, Khrushchev tried to rectify the harsh Stalinist measures of 1944. The Chechen-Ingush A.S.S.R. was re-established, and the Kabardinian A.S.S.R. became the Kabardino-Balkarian A.S.S.R. again. The Karachaev Autonomous Oblast was reconstituted as the Karachaev-Cherkess Autonomous Oblast.

TABLE 4

NORTH CAUCASIAN PEOPLES

Nationality	*Number in 1959*	*Administrative Area*
Chechen	418,000	Chechen-Ingush A.S.S.R.
Ossetian	410,000	North Ossetian A.S.S.R.
Kabardinian	204,000	Kabardino-Balkarian A.S.S.R.
Ingush	106,000	Chechen-Ingush A.S.S.R.
Karachaev	81,000	Karachaev-Cherkess Autonomous Oblast
Adighe	80,000	Adighe Autonomous Oblast
Balkar	42,000	Kabardino-Balkarian A.S.S.R.
Cherkess	30,000	Karachaev-Cherkess Autonomous Oblast

DAGESTANI

Dagestan is the perfect example of a polyglot area and has been aptly termed an "ethnic museum." For centuries, various peoples have moved from the Middle East and the Russian plains through the gap between the eastern end of the Caucasus Range and the shore of the Caspian Sea. Many of these travelers left small groups behind in mountainous Dagestan. The inaccessible valleys high in the mountains made it possible for these splinters of nations to survive in a relatively pure ethnic state, retaining their ancient customs and languages. As a result, Dagestan, with an area of just over 14,000 square miles, now has almost 1 million people and 32 distinct nationalities, although only 10 are listed in the 1959 Soviet census.

Russia has claimed suzerainty over Dagestan since 1813, the date of the Treaty of Gulistan with Persia, but it took nearly fifty years to "pacify" the region. Like the Chechen, the Moslem Dagestani fought vigorously under Shamyl. The glorious traditions of the Holy War forced the Communists to move very cautiously in attacking Mohammedanism in Dagestan. Even their moderate success may have been a Pyrrhic victory: It weakened the use of Arabic in the Moslem schools, and Arabic was the only lingua franca of the region. There is no predominant language in Dagestan. Even the most widespread, Avar, is spoken by only 268,000 people (27 per cent); if the Lezghian language is added, the total is a little over 50 per cent. Since 1950, the Soviets have striven to make Russian the second language of all. They have also systematically attacked Shamyl, the national hero of the Dagestani, North Caucasian, and Azerbaidzhanian peoples, but all denigration efforts seem to have been in vain.

In both the North Caucasus and Dagestan, the biggest obstacle to Sovietization has been Islam and the tenacity of the peoples in retaining their native customs and languages. Soviet propaganda has been hampered by the fact that many of the peoples cannot read the Russian language. The historical legacy of administering the North Caucasus and Dagestan from the Russian oil city of Grozny has made the job that much harder. Grozny to most of these peoples represents Russian oppression: The brutal Russian General Yermolov built the city and its name, Grozny, which means "threatening," is the same word as "terrible," in phrases such as "Ivan the Terrible."

TRANSCAUCASIANS

Strangely enough, the Russian conquest of the region south of the Caucasus Mountains, Transcaucasia, was much easier than that of the Caucasus itself. In its nineteenth-century wars with

Persia and Turkey, Russia bypassed the mountaineers and operated from the more easily controlled regions of Azerbaidzhan, Georgia, and Armenia; and these three areas were happy, on the whole, to have the Russians fighting off their traditional enemies.

At the present time, the Transcaucasian region is really a salient in the Middle East. The peoples of the area have always been an integral part of Middle Eastern history, either as opponents of the Persian and Ottoman empires, or under the control of one of them. To stir up Armenian or Georgian hatred for Turkey would be a simple task for the Soviet Union; the problem is rather to keep their enmity under control until it is needed to supplement Soviet policy.

Armenians

Armenia has a long history in Middle Eastern politics, a history that reaches back to the Greeks and the Romans. The Armenians accepted Christianity early in the fourth century, and in the fifth century, the patriarch Mesrob devised an alphabet based on Greek and Semitic letters. Armenia's position on the periphery of the Transcaucasian area encouraged one conqueror after another to sweep over the land and subject its people to vassalage. And, any small Christian island in a Moslem sea was doomed to a precarious existence in the Middle Ages. By the thirteenth century, Armenia was firmly under the heel of the Ottoman Turks, whose domination, interspersed with short intervals of Persian control, lasted until the nineteenth century.

Russia came into control of the territory roughly corresponding to the present Armenian S.S.R. as a result of the Russo-Persian Treaty of Turkmanchai in 1828. From that date until the present, Armenia has been a political pawn in the almost continuous Russo-Turkish feud, and it was brutally victimized in the early twentieth century when Turkish fears of the Russian use of the Armenian minority in Turkey led to a series of infamous massacres.

Bolshevik Russia and Kemalist Turkey temporarily made peace in the early 1920's, but unfortunately it was at the expense of the Armenians. Both powers, being opposed to the Versailles Treaty, and revolutionary, felt it in their interest to keep the Armenian question from boiling up. They cooperated closely in putting down the Dashnaks, a socialist party dating from the 1890's that was dedicated to Armenian independence. Since the 1920's, Armenia has been one of the most tractable national groups within the U.S.S.R., and has supplied many of the Soviet Union's leading figures, including Anastas Mikoyan, a perennial member of the ruling clique, his brother Artem Mikoyan, who was the codesigner of the famous MIG series of fighters, and Marshal Bagramian, the only non-Slav to become a top commander in the Red Army.

According to the 1959 census, 1.55 million Armenians live within the republic and make up almost 90 per cent of the population. This number, however, is only about 55 per cent of the total number of Armenians living in the Soviet Union. Like the Jews, the Armenians also suffered their own diaspora, and they are scattered throughout the Soviet Union and the rest of the world. Immediately after World War II, an attempt was made to gather the wandering brethren back into the Armenian S.S.R., and with the assistance of the Patriarch of the Armenian Church, some 85,000 Armenians were returned. But the word soon spread that the Soviet Utopia left much to be desired, and the great trek "home" died down to a trickle.

The Armenian S.S.R. remains a Soviet ace in the hole if expansion into Turkey should ever become more than a Kremlin aspiration. The hatred aroused by the massacres of the early twentieth century is still burning, and the Armenians would undoubtedly welcome an opportunity for retaliation.

Georgians

Like the Armenians, the Georgians have a long cultural tradition and a highly developed language and literature. And as Christians, they too suffered cruelly throughout the period of Moslem domination in the Middle East. The Georgians came to regard Christian Russia as an ally as early as the sixteenth century, when they requested the suzerainty of Ivan the Terrible. In 1801, Georgia was voluntarily incorporated into the Russian Empire and became a reliable base from which the Russians conducted campaigns against the Turks in 1828, during the Crimean War, in 1878, and during World War I.

The Russian Revolution brought the Mensheviks to power in Georgia, and they managed to stave off the Bolsheviks until 1921. At one time it even seemed possible that Georgia would become the showpiece for non-Bolshevik socialism. The Red Army, however, proved too strong. The highly cultured Armenians have provided the Soviet Union with many of its important figures, but the even more highly cultured Georgians have supplied still more. To name the Soviet leaders of Georgian birth is to call the roll of many of the Soviet great, with Stalin, Beria, Ordzhonikidze, and Yenukidze heading the list.

Again like the Armenians, the Georgians have a long-standing dislike for the Turks and would probably be particularly energetic in any war against Turkey. In 1945, two Georgian professors wrote an article in which they asserted Georgia's claim to about 170 miles of Turkey's Black Sea coastline. It is true that several hundred thousand people speaking a Georgian dialect live in that part of Turkey, but they—the Lazes—are Moslems and have lived there for centuries as Turkish citizens. *Pravda* featured the article, and the Soviet propaganda machine went into full gear. This was part of the Soviet move in 1945–47 to force Turkey to give up Kars and Ardahan and allow the Soviets to build fortified check points on the Straits. Although this attempt came to nothing, the fact remains that Georgian irredentists are always available for future use.

Georgia has a population of just over 4 million, but only 63 per cent, or 2.5 million, are Georgians. Almost a million Russians and Armenians also live in the republic, and other large groups, such as Azerbaidzhanians, Ossetians, and Jews, make Georgia a truly cosmopolitan area.

Azerbaidzhanians

The third of the Transcaucasian nations, Azerbaidzhan, does not have the long historical unity of Armenia and Georgia. In addition, the Azerbaidzhanians are Moslem in religion and Turkish in language and race. The fate of Azerbaidzhan has always been closely linked with that of its largest city, Baku. When Baku fell to the Russians, in 1806, it was clear that the rest of the nation would follow. In 1875, the Nobel brothers built the first oil refinery at Baku, and this city soon became synonymous with Russian petroleum production. The population increased from 15,000 in 1873 to 333,000 by 1913, and by 1959, the metropolitan area had expanded to include 968,000 people. Thus over a fourth of Azerbaidzhan's 3.7 million inhabitants live in Baku, while only a third of the city's population is Azerbaidzhanian.

The predominance of Baku in Azerbaidzhanian affairs played an important part in the success of the Communists. In the early days of the Revolution, both Turkish and British forces tried unsuccessfully to intervene in Azerbaidzhan, and the native Musawat (Equality) Party held power until April, 1920. But multinational Baku was the weakest link during the Musawat's brief sway and was a likely target for reconquest by the oil-hungry Communists. Another factor militating against the independence movement in Azerbaidzhan was that the Christian states of Armenia and Georgia stood between the Azerbaidzhanians and their brother Turks of Anatolia, who were deeply concerned with their own troubles at that time, having just gone down with Germany in defeat.

A clear-cut Soviet policy has governed Azerbaidzhan since 1920: Develop Baku oil, increase the acreage under cotton (as in Uzbekistan), and strive to make the republic an attractive example to the Moslems of the Middle East. On the negative side, the strategy has been to sever all cultural ties between the Azerbaidzhanians and their Moslem coreligionists in Turkey and Iran.

THE SOVIET FAR EAST

The Far East comprises the oblasts of Chita, Amur, Magadan, Kamchatka, and Sakhalin, the Khabarovsk Kray, the Primorsk Kray, also called the Maritime Region, and the Buriat-Mongolian A.S.S.R.—in short, the Pacific Coast back to the mountain ranges running parallel to it, plus the area immediately north of the Amur River as far west as Lake Baikal. Within this area of about 1.5 million square miles live some 7 million people, only a small percentage of whom are indigenous. The great majority are Slavic.

The indigenous peoples can be classified under three headings: Buriat-Mongols, Tungus, and Paleo-Asiatics. The Buriats are in the region immediately east and west of Lake Baikal. Those west of the lake around Irkutsk number about 100,000 and live in the Ust-Ordin Buriat-Mongol National Okrug. Those east of the lake form a minority within the Buriat-Mongolian A.S.S.R.; over 57 per cent of the population was Slavic as far back as 1941.

The Nentsy and the Tungus (the latter now called the Evenki), are found widely scattered throughout Eastern Siberia as well as in the Far East. The main subdivisions in the Far East are the Lamuts, or Eveni, along the coast of the Sea of Okhotsk and the Golds, or Nanais, in the Amur and Ussuri valleys. Altogether, they number no more than 70,000.

The Paleo-Asiatic peoples are divided into six main groups: about 4,000 Giliaks, or Nivkhi, along the lower Amur and on Sakhalin Island; in the north on the Chukotski Peninsula, the Chukchis—3,000 living on the coast and 9,000 tending a half million reindeer in the back country; about 6,000 Koryaks, or Nymylani, in northern Kamchatka, also subdivided into coastal and reindeer-breeding types; some 1,100 Kamchadals, or Itelmeni, on the Kamchatka Peninsula below the Koryaks; and finally, about 1,600 Eskimos on the Bering Sea coast and about 500 Aleuts on the Komandorskie Islands. Except for the Chukchis and Koryaks, who raise reindeer and can thus keep to themselves, most of these indigenous peoples are being rapidly assimilated.

The Soviet Far East also contains some nonindigenous minorities, including 25,000 Chinese, 300,000 Koreans, and a few Japanese. In the Jewish Autonomous Oblast, in the Khabarovsk Kray, there were 108,000 Jews in 1939. But all these minorities, indigenous and nonindigenous, are overwhelmingly outnumbered by the Slavs. Strictly speaking, there is no nationality problem in the Soviet Far East in the same sense as in Soviet Central Asia and the Caucasian area.

NATIONALITY POLICIES—PAST AND PRESENT

When the Communists came to power, in 1917, they inherited the nationality problem, and it was indeed a chaotic problem complicated by Czarist mishandling. By the 1880's, a policy of Russification had been initiated as part of the "autocracy, orthodoxy, and nationalism" concept of governing adopted by Alexander III. Both the Marxist radicals and the liberals referred to Imperial Russia as the "prison house of nations." In the cultural sphere, Russification consisted in liquidating or minimizing local schools and in imposing the Russian language and the Orthodox Church upon the various nationalities. The Russification policy was furthered by playing one nationality against another, as was the case in the Transcaucasian region. But the most bitterly resented practice was that of sending Russian colonists into a nationalistic area, as in Central Asia, where they took over the best land, gained a monopoly in local business, and gradually drove the natives to penury.

These policies reacted against the Czarist regime in the revolutionary situation that prevailed from 1905 to 1917. During that time, in most nationalities, there was a native intelligentsia who gave their allegiance primarily to the liberal and radical anti-Czarist organizations. And the Communists made every effort to appeal to these dissident nationality groups.

Marx was an internationalist with no interest in such concepts as "nation" and "nationality." In the *Communist Manifesto*, he summarily dismissed the problem:

> The working men have no country. We cannot take from them what they have not got. Since the proletariat must first of all acquire political supremacy, must rise to be the leading class of the nation, must constitute itself *the* nation, it is, so far, itself national, though not in the bourgeois sense of the word.[2]

But Lenin and his companions could not take such a cavalier attitude toward the nationality problem. They were planning a revolution in a huge ethnic conglomerate, Imperial Russia, and needed the support, or at least the neutrality, of the nationalities making up half the population. Lenin urged his "wonderful Georgian," Stalin, to tackle the problem, and in 1913, Stalin brought forth his essay *Marxism and the National Question,* written in Vienna under Lenin's close supervision. According to Stalin, the main fallacy of the "nation" concept was its unification of the employers and workers, who, according to Marxist dogma, were natural enemies. However, Stalin could not allow the bourgeoisie sole proprietorship of the appeal of nationalism, and he admitted that autonomy, federation, and separation were permissible under certain "concrete historical conditions." The Communist doctrine contradicted itself on the nationality question: It maintained the right of each nationality to self-determination, including the right of independence, but at the same time it maintained the international solidarity of the working class with the obligation to prefer the working class of a neighboring country to its own bourgeoisie.

So much for the theory. In actuality, after the Communist seizure of power, the problem of the independence or inclusion of the various nationalities within the Soviet Union was decided, not on theoretical principles, but upon the geographic position of the countries and by the military might of the Soviet state. The Poles, Finns, Lithuanians, Latvians, and Estonians became independent of Russia because they were occupied by Germans at the beginning of the Revolution and were later able to call upon the Allies for help, which was available because the Allied fleet dominated the Baltic. Georgia, Azerbaidzhan, and Armenia kept a semblance of independence for a few years with assistance from first Germany and then Britain, but when Turkey and the Soviet Union found it expedient to subjugate them, the Red Army quickly moved in.

By 1921, the nationalities still within the Soviet Union were almost completely controlled by Moscow. But the control was not firm enough to warrant arousing any unnecessary antagonism. From 1921 to 1928, the Bolsheviks walked and talked softly in the spheres of economics and nationality: This was the era of the New Economic Policy (NEP) and the *korenizatsia* policy in the nationality problem. The term *korenizatsia* comes from the Russian word *koren,* meaning "root," and refers to the rooted population or indigenous people. The slogan for this period was "Culture—National in Form, Socialist in Content." To illustrate concretely, although newspapers in Georgia were printed in the Georgian language, in content they differed not at all from *Pravda.* Attempts were made to give an alphabet to those nationalities having no written language and to simplify existing alphabets and make them more phonetic. For example, the Latin alphabet was substituted for the Arabic, partly because it was thought to be a more efficient alphabet and partly in an effort to break the hold of the Islamic clergy over the cultural life of the people. The emphasis, however, upon the history, culture, and language of the various national groups began to boomerang; the native intelligentsia, although Communist, tended to side with their fellow nationals against undue Russian influence.

The *korenizatsia* policy came to an end with the introduction of forced industrialization and collectivized agriculture. The merciless centralization necessary to a wholly planned economy was at cross purposes with self-rule in the nationality groups. Stalin carried out his plans ruthlessly, however, and the "national in form" slogan became merely a camouflage for total Russian domination. The Great Purges of the 1930's finished the job; among the first large-scale casualties were the intelligentsia of the national groups. All national cultures were now instructed to stress in their literature, art, and music certain general themes more compatible with Russian domination: the backwardness of the older culture, the cleansing power of the Revolution, the advantages of the classless society, and the progressiveness of Russian culture—before and after 1917. This formula was a reversal of the themes that had been stressed under the *korenizatsia* policy: the glory of the past ages, the folk heroes, and the valiant struggle against the Czarist conquest. Although the majority of ministers in the union republics remained non-Russian, the deputy ministers were usually Russians, and there was little doubt as to which of the two held the reins. It soon became evident to ambitious native bureaucrats that only those who became proficient in Russian were allowed to rise in the officialdom.

Even the army was affected by the changes in the nationality policy. In the 1930's, the national divisions were abolished, and the non-Russian troops were placed in ethnically mixed units, with Russian as the language of instruction and command. (In 1942, when the Soviet leaders had to generate a spirit of resistance against the German invaders, they reverted to ethnic grouping in the armed forces.)

This period also saw religious persecution at its worst; like the kulaks, priests and church officials were tortured and exiled. Most of the churches, Orthodox, Moslem, Jewish, or Buddhist, were either destroyed or turned into antireligious museums, libraries, or schools. The main objective of this antireligious crusade was to gain control of the minds of the younger generation, and in the urban areas, it seems to have been largely successful.

Finally, on March 13, 1938, the Soviet Government ordered the obligatory teaching of Russian in all non-Russian schools. In many cases, this meant that the students had to learn two alphabets: either that of their native tongue or the relatively new Latin alphabet, and the Russian Cyrillic. As an answer to this problem, the Soviet Government began its second alphabetic revolution by replacing the Latin alphabet with the Russian Cyrillic. Although this made books printed before the switch to the Cyrillic alphabet useless, it was a giant step toward making Russian the dominant language even in the national areas. Since there are over 100 different languages in the

U.S.S.R., the magnitude of the problem is such that even with the most radical steps, total conversion to Russian will take many years.

Victory in World War II produced not only a resurgence of Russian nationalism in the official propaganda, but also an identification of patriotism with the Stalinist version of the totalitarian state. Opponents of the regime were now regarded as traitors to the *Rodina,* the motherland. Whole nationalities that had been tolerant of German occupation or were suspected as potential traitors were wiped out. The Volga Germans, Crimean Tatars, Chechen-Ingush, Karachaevs, Balkars, and Kalmucks—all these fell victim to deliberate, systematic extermination.

The Great Russian people became synonymous with Soviet patriotism. Stalin gave his support to the new Great Russian chauvinism when he made this famous toast, on May 24, 1945:

> I want to drink a toast to the health of our Soviet people, and, first of all, to the Russian people.
>
> I drink, first of all, to the health of the Russian people because it is the most advanced of all our nations in the Soviet Union.
>
> I drink to the Russian people because it served in this war as the leading force of the Soviet Union among all the peoples of our country.
>
> I drink a toast to the health of the Russian people, not only because it is the leading people, but also because it has a clear mind and a sturdy, enduring character.[3]

The Soviet Union had become one of the two great world powers after 1945, a world power with an empire of its own. This new phase of Soviet imperialism led to fresh assaults upon the national traditions of the non-Great Russian peoples of the Soviet Union. Accordingly, the national heroic poetry of the Moslem peoples was condemned, and the histories of the various peoples were rewritten to stress the benefits not only of Soviet domination but of even the Czarist conquests. Russian culture was valuable, regardless of how it had been imposed. Part and parcel of this theme was the campaign against "cosmopolitanism."

The Tadzhiks were called upon to forget their common culture with the Persians and to emphasize the gains from their contact with Russian culture. The Germanic influences in the Baltic area were now automatically regarded as bad influences. The Jews suffered especially, they were naturally "cosmopolitan," and the establishment of the Israeli nation poured oil on the already burning anti-Semitism. Even Ivan the Terrible was refurbished as a great Czar who had been libeled by bourgeois historians.

RESULTS OF THE NATIONALITY POLICIES

Without a doubt, the nationality groups, like all other groups in the Soviet Union not created by the Communist regime, have been atomized and are now tightly controlled by the state. But how much of this can be attributed to Russification? In the Georgian and Armenian republics, there is little if any Russification. These are nations with long histories, well-developed languages, and strong cultural traditions; they are governed chiefly by their own citizens. The Ukraine is largely governed by Ukrainians today, but the strong Russian elements are much more influential than their numbers would suggest. In Azerbaidzhan, the large Russian population in Baku offsets to some extent full Azerbaidzhanian control of the republic.

For strategic reasons, there have been mass deportations of local populations and mass colonization by Russians in such areas as the Western Ukraine, the Baltic countries, Bessarabia, and Sakhalin Island. This same type of Russian-Ukrainian colonization has also appeared in the new industrial centers of Central Asia, the "Second Baku" region, and the Buriat-Mongolian capital of Ulan Ude. The genocide of much of the Kazakh population during the collectivization left a vacuum to be filled with Russian colonists, and Khrushchev's new agricultural policy of tilling the virgin and idle lands bodes further trouble for the Kazakhs. The Crimea has also been completely Russified since the extermination of the Tatar population.

Many factors, then, have contributed to the Russification of the various nationalities that make up the Soviet Union. One of the most important, of course, is the required use of the Russian language in the secondary schools and universities in the national areas. Another is the use of the Cyrillic alphabet with the Asiatic languages and the gradual accretion of Russian words to the vocabularies of these languages. And usually upon the extermination of dissident groups, colonization by Russians was the next step. All nationalities are constantly reminded of the "beneficial results" of their contacts with progressive Russian culture throughout history.

Is this Russification the result of a deliberate Kremlin policy along the lines laid down by Alexander III and Nicholas II? Here the evidence is contradictory and the authorities differ widely. According to Hugh Seton-Watson,[4] the Soviet Government is not primarily interested in Russifying the non-Great Russians. He states that the conflict exists, not between the Russians and the little nationalities, but between these little nationalities and the centralized totalitarian regime. The regime persecutes all groups not created by it; in the case of the little nations, it uses Russians as its instrument, flattering their national pride in order to get them to carry out its policies. But the aim of the regime is absolute power, and to attain this, the Soviet Government systematically atomizes society. The two groups that are most deeply rooted in the past and are thus independent of Communism for spiritual nourishment are the religious groups and the nationalities. As long as a Moslem looks first to the Koran and the Islamic law, the Sharia, for guidance, or an Uzbek feels more closely allied to other Uzbeks than to his Communist leaders, the Party cannot be certain of his unswerving allegiance.

The Uzbek, watching his church become the object of Russian derision, his literature suddenly appear in Cyrillic, and his heroic poetry take queer and unfamiliar turns in the hands of Soviet scholars, cannot but feel menaced. The fact that he sees all evil emanating from a Kremlin full of Great Russians makes him equate Russification with all that is foreign and frightening. But the exiled Russian kulaks and the Orthodox clergy are Russians persecuted by Russians, and their hatred of the Kremlin leaders is just as intense as the Uzbek's.

THE NATIONALITY PROBLEM TODAY

A new intelligentsia has arisen among the nationalities. Among the Ukrainians, Byelorussians, Tatars, Georgians, Uzbeks, and others, there are hundreds of thousands of students, teachers, engineers, and bureaucrats. These people owe their careers to the Soviet Government. Are they grateful and have they become stanch supporters of the regime? A possible answer by analogy can be found in the tens of thousands of intelligentsia in the Middle East, Asia, and North Africa who were trained in the schools and universities operated by France, Britain, and the United States. Are these natives grateful for their education and are they deeply attached to the Western powers? On the contrary, they have become the leaders of their peoples in the struggle against those same powers. A similar process may be going on within the intelligentsia of the Soviet nationality groups, especially among the Asiatic segments. The recurrent Soviet campaigns against "bourgeois nationalism" are indirect evidence of this.

On the other hand, it would be unwise to count this as a serious weakness within the Soviet Union. Planned economy within the U.S.S.R. is making it increasingly difficult for local regions to be self-sufficient. For example, the economy of the Ukraine and Russia complement each other very closely; Central Asia has practically converted to monoculture (of cotton) in the last thirty years, and many of the smaller nationalities have been so firmly welded into the over-all industrial structure and planned agriculture as to be incapable of survival outside of it. The predominance of Russians in the large urban centers and their control of the skilled and technical positions in the economy make unlikely any effective movement toward autonomy on the part of the national groups.

George Fischer, a keen observer of the Soviet scene, states that the very process of industrialization, with its sociological effects, is gradually eliminating the nationality problem. Industrialization demands an urbanization of population. The mixed composition of these populations tends to weaken the homogeneity of the nationalities. Industrialization and urbanization in themselves produce a standardized existence—a mass culture, mass education, and mass press—and these are easily controlled by the central government.[5]

3

A Brief History

Throughout the period of modern history, the Russian people have occupied the great plain between nomadic Central Asia and Europe. When nomadic peoples in Central Asia migrated, they usually passed through the Caspian-Ural gap on their way to Europe, for there were no natural barriers between these points. With each migration, the Slavs were overrun. Later, when the Germans and Swedes expanded, the great plains of Poland and Russia offered little natural protection to the Russians. This continuous pressure from the east, west, north, and—with the advent of the Ottoman Empire—the south, accounts partly for the structure the Russian state developed.

RUSSIAN AUTOCRACY—A LOGICAL DEVELOPMENT

If national survival was to be achieved, Russia had to become an armed camp. And as is the case with any effectively organized armed group, systems of leadership and discipline were logical outgrowths. Thus up to 1917, first from necessity and later from custom, Russia was an autocratic state operating under the slogan of "Autocracy, Orthodoxy, and Nationalism." Until the establishment of the State Duma, as a result of the 1905 Revolution, the Czar's right to absolute rule was questioned only by a small segment of the population.

The problem of maintaining the autocracy did not become serious until after the national catastrophes of defeat in the Crimean War (1854–56) and in the Japanese War (1904–5).

On the whole, the Czars were able to maintain their position, up to 1917, with aid of a relatively small police force and a rather indifferent censorship. The Czarist charism sufficed for the landowning aristocracy and the peasantry; a strong middle class was nonexistent; and the troublesome intelligentsia could find no popular base from which to launch an attack.

Despite great unrest, there were only sporadic eruptions, usually in the form of peasant uprisings against specific grievances or assassination attempts by revolutionary extremists. A familiar statement was that the government of Russia was Czarist absolutism tempered by the fear of assassination.

EXPANSION OF THE RUSSIAN EMPIRE

By the nineteenth century, the Russian Empire included enormous areas inhabited by non-Russian peoples. In an effort to consolidate these peoples into an organic Russian state, the autocracy encouraged a Russification program. The main result was the birth of counternationalistic movements that tended to weaken the state.

The Russian Empire had reached gargantuan proportions by the end of the Napoleonic Wars and throughout the nineteenth century had striven to consolidate areas such as the Caucasus and Central Asia. The further expansion of the empire fluctuated with pendulum-like regularity, alternating between the Near East and the Far East. There was also a constant jockeying with Great Britain in Central Asia. These territorial drives met with little success. In the Balkans, the Russians ran athwart the Austrian drive in the same direction; in the Far East, they clashed with Japanese expansion; and on the northern borders of India and Persia, they had to find a *modus vivendi* with Great Britain. The most consistent Russian expansion in this period was in the Near East and the Balkans, largely at the expense of the decaying Ottoman Empire.

Any analogy between the expansionist aims of Imperial Russia and the Soviet Union is dubious. The geographic position is the same, of course, and this encourages the drawing of pseudo analogies. Pan-Slavism in the Balkans and Eastern Europe and pro-Christian propaganda in the Ottoman Empire had some similarity to the present Communist methods, but on the whole, the expansionist methods of Imperial Russia were very similar to those of the other great powers in the nineteenth century.

THE PEASANT PROBLEM

One of the constant difficulties of the Czarist regime—the peasant problem—continues to harass the present regime. In 1860, Alexander II, stating frankly that revolution from above was preferable to revolution from below, emancipated the serfs. Although this action temporarily relieved the pressure, the problem remained without an adequate solution. The peasant allotments were too small, the indemnity payments too large, and the retention of the communal methods of administering and farming the land too backward. Most of the agricultural surplus used to feed the urban population and to pay for imports had come from the better-managed estates, now largely eliminated. Industrialization proceeded too slowly in Russia to siphon off the excess population, and, consequently, the agricultural areas were overpopulated.

The last half-century of the old regime was a period of constant peasant discontent, and revolutionary groups tried to capitalize on this situation. In light of the Marxist philosophy of the Bolsheviks, it is paradoxical that the backbone of their staying power from 1918 to 1921 was their manipulation of this agrarian discontent.

In the economic sphere, Russia was always the retarded child of the European family of nations. When the industrial revolution finally did accelerate in Russia, it took a peculiar course of development. E. H. Carr has summarized this situation:

> First of all, large-scale Russian industry almost from the moment of its birth was geared to the production of "war potential," including railway construction, rather than to the needs of the consumer market. It was "planned" in the sense that it depended primarily on government orders, not on spontaneous market demand; it was financed by loans accorded for political reasons rather than for

the traditional "capitalist" motive of earning commercial profits. In these respects it anticipated much that was to happen in Russia under the Five Year Plans 30 years later.

Secondly, the tardy arrival of industrialization in Russia meant that it skipped over many of the earlier stages through which the much slower growth of industrialization had passed in Western Europe—the gradual transformation from the single-handed craftsman to the small workshop, and the first primitive factory to the giant agglomeration employing hundreds and thousands of workers.

When modern Russian industry was born at the end of the Nineteenth Century, it immediately assumed the characteristic modern shape of the large scale factory. Already before 1914, one quarter of all Russian industrial workers worked in factories employing more than one thousand persons each. . . .[1]

DEVELOPMENT OF THE INTELLIGENTSIA

Because of the highly centralized, autocratic nature of the Russian Government, the middle class, the intellectuals, and the professional classes found themselves without influence in the operation of the state. An unusual development occurred: the formation of the group known as the intelligentsia. This term almost defies definition. It cut across class lines, and it was more nearly a statement of faith than anything else—and that faith was a belief in some kind of an evolution or revolution that would bring on a limitation or elimination of the Czarist autocracy. Most of the intelligentsia were intellectuals, but not all intellectuals were in sympathy with the intelligentsia. The badge of the intelligentsia was not only learning but also an antiregime attitude. Among the intellectuals, an antiregime group had been developing for at least a hundred years before 1917. From the time of the strictly aristocratic revolt of the Decembrists, in 1825, the Russian autocracy was constantly beset with conspiratorial-revolutionary plotters. These were generally ineffectual; nevertheless, they established a conspiratorial tradition later capitalized on by the Bolsheviks. Some of these groups advocated terrorism as a weapon, and the assassination of Alexander II was their work.

Behind this persistent agitation lay two factors: One was the importation of Western ideas and the attempts of the Czarist regime to stifle them; the second was the lack of a strong middle class to act as a buffer between the extremist ideas of the revolutionaries and the autocratic absolutism of the regime. Finally, this agitation undermined the confidence of the nobility, already economically ruined by the breakup of the estates following the emancipation of the serfs.

THE REVOLUTION

By 1917, the stage was set for the collapse of the Czarist regime; Russia's ineptness and failure in World War I sealed its fate. The establishment of the State Duma following the 1905 Revolution had only whetted the appetite of the intelligentsia for an active parliamentary government. The peasants wanted peace and land. The non-Russian national groups were restive under the Russification program, and the economic structure collapsed under the pressures of war. A combination of these factors was too much for the creaking machinery of the Czarist Government, especially one headed by such an ineffectual and irresolute monarch as Nicholas II. A bread riot in St. Petersburg in March, 1917, was enough to topple the whole precarious structure.

The striking feature of the Revolution of March, 1917, was its spontaneity; it occurred with a suddenness that left a power vacuum at the top of the huge, sprawling empire engaged in a major war. From March until November, 1917, all efforts to curb the Revolution failed. If any law can be applied to revolutions, it is the principle that they always move to the Left in their initial stages. The population of Russia, from the war-weary peasants to the power-hungry intelligentsia, wanted some kind of definite program to seize upon, and the leaders, prior to the advent of Lenin on the Russian scene, offered little.

In April, 1917, the German High Command, with malice aforethought, allowed Lenin to cross Germany on his way from Switzerland to Russia. Their purpose was to inject the virus of subversion into the already staggering Russian Army. The rise of Lenin to power and the resulting Treaty of Brest Litovsk bore out the expectations of the German military leaders. Once in Russia, Lenin offered a program that brought together three of the major trends in Russian revolutionary thought: Western ideas in the form of Marxian socialism, a conspiratorial party (the Bolsheviks), and an appeal to the discontented peasants with the slogan of "Bread, Peace, and Freedom."

Always aware of the realities of power, Lenin saw that it would be necessary to destroy the Russian Army as the bulwark of the regime, and in April, 1917, the Bolsheviks set up a centralized agency, the Military Organization, to propagandize the simple but effective slogan of "Bread, Peace, and Freedom" among the soldiers. But even while engaged in destroying the old army, Lenin was also trying to establish a military force of his own. This was the Red Guard, a factory militia with its roots in the 1905 Revolution.

By November, 1917, Lenin and Trotsky felt that the revolutionary situation was ripe. The Provisional Government had failed to achieve peace, to solve the land problem, or to show the people a definite program. Desertion in the army had become wholesale; as Lenin put it, "The army voted for peace with its legs." The Bolsheviks, with a maximum of planning and a minimum of force, were able to oust the Provisional Government in two days, November 5–7,* 1917.

THE BOLSHEVIKS IN POWER

The power gained so easily proved to be much harder to retain. The new government was faced with a number of crucial problems, among them: how to establish the peace they had glibly promised; how to handle the legally elected Constituent Assembly, which had a non-Bolshevik majority; how to force the peasants to release enough grain to feed the urban population; how to cope with the anti-Bolshevik elements; how to halt

* October 23–25 according to the Julian calendar, then in use in Russia; hence the designation "October Revolution."

the disintegration of the empire, already advanced in Poland, Finland, the Ukraine, and other areas. The techniques used by the new Bolshevik Government in solving these problems have endured throughout the forty-five years of Bolshevik rule.

To Lenin, the peace problem was simple: Sign an armistice with the Central Powers and take whatever terms they would give. With world revolution just around the corner, any temporary retreats could be compensated for later; in fact, in a world controlled by the proletariat, international boundaries would be of little consequence. However, the bulk of the Party refused to jettison their national consciousness, and a sharp struggle developed. Trotsky, the chief negotiator at Brest Litovsk, thought that he had the solution in the novel attitude of "No peace, no war." But the Germans reminded him that although it may take two to make a war, it takes only one to claim the fruits of war. The German advance forced the Party to submit to Lenin, and the Treaty of Brest Litovsk followed.

The problem of the Constituent Assembly was easier of solution. When the Reds found that the electorate had given them only a small minority of the delegates, they simply dissolved the Assembly by means of the Red Guard. Under the muzzles of their rifles, any hope that democracy had come to Russia disappeared.

Armed detachments were likewise sent to the rural areas to confiscate the grain from peasants unwilling to relinquish their crops to a government that had nothing to offer in payment.

The anti-Bolshevik elements became more and more troublesome as time went on. The expression of opposition did not accord with Lenin's ideas of a monolithic Party in complete control of the situation. Finally, in December, 1917, the Cheka (Extraordinary Commission for Combating Counterrevolutionaries, Saboteurs, and Speculators) was established. This was an out-and-out terroristic secret police and the progenitor of an infamous brood: OGPU, NKVD, MVD, MGB, and KGB.

Faced with the centrifugal forces that were tearing away national groups on the periphery of the empire, the Bolsheviks were in a quandary. One of their slogans, proclaimed loudly at Brest Litovsk, was the right of self-determination of peoples.

Now these peoples were deciding to assert this right. Again the Bolsheviks resorted to force, and the Red Army was used in the reincorporation of the Ukraine, the Caucasian republics, and the Central Asian territories.

In four out of five of these solutions, the Bolsheviks relied on military coercion. The probable explanation is that the Bolsheviks were a tiny minority among the teeming millions in Russia, but they controlled the only organized force that could act effectively. And being a minority, they had to use other than democratic means to accomplish their ends. Thus, the pattern was set at that time.

The years from the Bolshevik coup of 1917 until 1921 are usually known as the period of War Communism, during which the Bolsheviks faced civil war within Russia and foreign intervention from without. It was also the era of radical Communism, involving almost complete nationalization of industry, transportation, banking, trade, and food distribution. The Bolsheviks believed world revolution to be imminent, and their diplomacy reflected that expectation.

Overriding all other considerations in the period of War Communism was the armed threat of the anti-Bolshevik elements, both Russian and foreign. The Germans, in spite of the Treaty of Brest Litovsk, pushed into the Ukraine and the Caucasus. On November 7, 1917, the very day the Bolsheviks took power, General Kaledin assumed leadership of the anti-Bolshevik forces in the Don region; similar so-called White armies sprang up on the periphery of the empire, and were soon pushing in from all sides. On March 7, 1918, four days after the signing of the Treaty of Brest Litovsk, the British landed troops at Murmansk, and foreign intervention was under way. Toward the end of May, 1918, the Czech troops, who were in the process of being moved to the Western Front via Vladivostok, seized and held the Trans-Siberian Railroad from Kazan to the Pacific.

ESTABLISHMENT OF THE RED ARMY

To meet these numerous threats, the Red Guard proved inadequate. In January, 1918, the Bolsheviks started organizing a more effective force and, on February 23, announced the establishment of the Red Army. Lenin set a goal of 3 million men by the spring of 1919, and by fervent exhortation and ruthless application of the draft, this goal was attained by the end of 1919. The Red Army proved capable of protecting the Bolshevik regime from the badly organized Whites and the halfhearted foreign intervention, and by 1921, the Civil War and intervention had come to an end. The Reds had several advantages in this conflict. First, they had internal lines of communications and were able to coordinate their activities. Second, they had inherited the military equipment of the Czarist regime. Third, they were able to appeal to the patriotic sentiments of the population because of the foreign intervention and aid to the Whites. And, fourth, they managed to win over a large percentage of the peasants, who feared a restoration of land to the former owners if the Whites should win.

Despite victory on the field of battle, the Bolsheviks faced chaos in their newly proclaimed workers' paradise. The little vitality remaining in Russian industry at the time of the Bolshevik triumph had been effectively strangled by the new nationalization decrees of 1918. The peasants seized all available land in line with the Bolshevik invitation, but even the government's most ruthless troops were finding it hard to extract grain from the rural population, which was planting only enough for its needs and was skillful in hiding that. The vision of world revolution was fading by 1921, even among the members of the newly established Comintern. But since the Soviet Government was so obviously backing subversive movements abroad, foreign nations tightened their diplomatic boycott of the new state. Even within the Soviet Union, the Kronstadt revolt, in March, 1921, had shocked the Bolshevik faithful. It was clear to the realistic Lenin that something drastic must be done, and he undertook an amazing shift in policy by launching the New Economic Policy (NEP).

LENIN'S NEW ECONOMIC POLICY

The NEP meant retreat on all fronts—economic, diplomatic, and even ideological—or so it seemed to some of the old-line Bolsheviks. Lenin, however, believed the retreat would not jeopardize the Revolution as long as the state held the "commanding heights" on the economic front—in the fields of banking, international trade, transportation, and key heavy industries. Internal trade and small manufacturing plants were left to private enterprise; a definite tax in kind supplanted grain requisitions. Inasmuch as the tax in kind left the peasant with a grain surplus, some free trade had to be legalized. In short, the heavy hand of the state was relaxed and Russians were encouraged to "enrich themselves," in Bukharin's words.

Lenin had been forced into the retreat. The Kronstadt revolt accurately reflected widespread popular discontent with War Communism, especially on the part of the peasants. If the great mass of peasants, the main ally of the small proletariat, deserted the regime at this stage, it was doubtful that it could survive. Lenin knew that a tactical retreat had to be made to keep the peasants aligned with the regime or at least prevent them from attacking it.

The first three years of the NEP were difficult ones, and it was a touch-and-go proposition on the economic front. In September, 1922, Trotsky described the situation as the "scissors crisis": Prices of industrial goods were rising steadily, and those of agricultural products falling. Trotsky urged the government to force down industrial prices before the gap widened more disastrously. By 1924, the worst seemed over, and a degree of stability ensued.

THE RISE OF STALIN

In 1922, Lenin suffered a stroke and was forced into partial retirement. Stalin, who had become the General Secretary of the Party, immediately began to fill Party and government positions with his own men. Even at this early date, Stalin saw the value of controlling the organizational structure of the Party. Lenin, becoming aware of Stalin's objectives, wrote a "testament" toward the end of 1922, in which he advised the Party to appoint another General Secretary, for the reason that Stalin was too "rude" in his management of Party affairs. Stalin, however, had little to fear from the ailing Lenin; his great opponent was Trotsky, the organizer of the Red Army and Lenin's closest collaborator in the strategy of the October Revolution. Many leading Bolsheviks expected Trotsky, rather than the almost unknown Stalin, to become the man on horseback. Stalin, therefore, had little trouble in persuading Zinoviev and Kamenev to ally with him in the famous "troika." * Trotsky, away from Moscow when Lenin died, on January 21, failed to attend his funeral. Trotsky contended that Stalin had deliberately misinformed him about the date of the funeral. Certainly, the Stalinist group made political capital of the error. Trotsky's influence with the Red Army was undermined when the troika appointed his rival, Mikhail Frunze, as his chief assistant and removed his most trusted subordinates to distant or nonmilitary posts. Stalin also diluted the old Bolshevik element by a wholesale enrollment of new members in the Party and clinched his control by appointing loyal Stalinists to all important Party positions. Thus, when the Thirteenth Party Congress met, in 1924, Stalin had absolute control. In the meanwhile, Zinoviev had eliminated the Trotsky element in the Comintern, both at home and abroad. Trotsky tried to retaliate in a book entitled *1917*, in which he pointed out Zinoviev's and Kamenev's refusal to go along with

* Literally, in Russian, a vehicle drawn by three horses. Its figurative sense here—and in the recent discussion of the office of the U.N. Secretary General—is equivalent to "triumvirate."

Lenin in the Bolshevik Revolution of November, 1917. But the day of the monolithic Party had dawned, and Trotsky was accused of trying to splinter the Party, from then on the most heinous crime in the Bolshevik lexicon.

In 1925, there was a complete reversal: Zinoviev and Kamenev deserted Stalin to join hands with Trotsky. Stalin quickly turned to the Right wing of the Politburo for help. The seven-man Politburo now consisted of Trotsky, Zinoviev, and Kamenev on the Left; Rykov, Bukharin, and Tomski on the Right; and Stalin in the Center, the most maneuverable position. While a stalemate continued for two years on the top level, Stalin relentlessly transformed the Party organization into a pro-Stalinist instrument. On the tenth anniversary of the Bolshevik Revolution, November 7, 1927, when the Trotsky faction tried to set off an anti-Stalin demonstration, it failed completely. Trotsky was expelled from the Party a week later, and in January, 1928, he was exiled to Alma-Ata, in Kazakhstan.

INDUSTRIALIZATION

Having disposed of Trotsky and his Leftist bloc, Stalin immediately turned on his allies on the Right. He announced the First Five-Year Plan for the industrialization of the Soviet Union under forced draft, and the Sixteenth Party Congress backed him. The Rightist bloc, Rykov, Bukharin, and Tomski, opposed this *volte-face,* but the Stalin machine was now a smoothly functioning instrument of power, and the Right Opposition lasted less than six months. By the end of 1929, Stalin was firmly established as an absolute dictator.

The idea of a planned and forced industrialization of the Soviet Union was not new with Stalin; it had been formulated by the Leftist bloc that Stalin defeated in alliance with the Rightists. It had also been fully discussed by Mikhail Frunze in his essay "The Front and Rear," and Lenin had laid the groundwork for this type of planning in his Goelro plan for the electrification of the Soviet Union. But Stalin began to drive toward his goals with a ruthless tenacity that would very likely have been beyond the capacity of Lenin, Frunze, or Trotsky.

October, 1928, became the most important date in Soviet history—except for November 7, 1917—with the inauguration of the first of the Five-Year Plans. It marked the beginning of the "Second Revolution," the conscious attempt to speed up the productive basis for equipping and maintaining a modern military force. The new Soviet industrialization reversed the capitalist sequence: development of consumer demand, leading to an expansion of consumer-goods production, and that in turn stimulating industrial production. Under the Five-Year Plan, the goal was heavy industry, and the consideration of consumer-goods industries was secondary. The prime targets were steel, coal, oil, machinery, and armaments. For example, steel production did not regain its prewar level of 4.5 million tons until 1928, but by 1938, it had risen to over 18 million tons.

Shortly after the first Plan got under way, it was decided to establish a large part of heavy industry in the East. The Ural-Kuznetsk *kombinat* was one of the outgrowths of this decision, and it would seem to have been at least partly motivated by military considerations. The same amount of investment capital poured into the ferrous-metallurgical industry of the Ukraine would have produced far more steel but would have placed plants in the extremely vulnerable plain area.

COLLECTIVIZATION OF AGRICULTURE

Along with the industrialization of the Five-Year Plans went the collectivization of agriculture. The peasant problem had many facets. Some 25 million individual peasant households striving to "enrich themselves" were just that many bourgeois units; this was not at all compatible with the new socialist offensive. Stalin saw that collectivization would solve many of the problems involved in the industrialization program. First, consolidating the peasant holdings and using agricultural machinery would produce a surplus rural population that could help supply the insatiable demands of the new industry. Second, collectivization would ease the problem of getting grain from the peasants to feed the urban population by reducing the number of collection points to watch. Third, collectivization would create a rural proletariat; the farmer would lose the psychology of independence that came with tilling his own land. And, fourth, the industrial program had to be financed largely from the output of the peasant. Collectivization was thought to be ideal for keeping peasant consumption on a low level, which would leave a surplus for export and for feeding the factory workers.

The Party began its campaign for collectivization by attacking the kulaks,* or richer peasants, as early as the fall of 1928. The program was accelerated in 1929–30, and the term kulak came to mean any peasant who opposed the collectivization policy. So rapid was the tempo that by March, 1930, some 55 per cent of all peasant households had been forced into collectives. At this point, Stalin intervened and in his letter "Dizzy with Success" called for a slowdown and leniency. But it must be remembered that the whole program was his to begin with, and it was he who insisted on the speed with which it had been implemented. The peasant's antagonism to the collective farm immediately became manifest; some 9 million out of the 14 million households dropped out of the collective farms in the first two months of the new policy. The carrot was now given more prominence than the stick, and by assuring the peasants of private ownership of their homes, garden plots, livestock, and small tools; by giving them preferential treatment in taxes; and by setting up machine-tractor stations for the distribution of agricultural machinery, the government succeeded in enticing peasant households into the collective farms. By the end of 1932, some 14 million households were collectivized.

The cost of collectivization had been enormous. Livestock was down by almost 50 per cent; 1931 and 1932 had seen man-made famine in the Ukraine and the Northern Caucasus that cost millions of lives; and untold numbers of kulaks had been torn from their homes and shipped to Siberia and the plains of Kazakhstan.

* "Kulak" means "fist" in Russian, and it has long been used to describe a rich peasant who "squeezed" his poorer neighbors.

CONSTITUTIONS

Although the Soviet Union has had three constitutions in its brief history, it is the Party, not the constitutional government, that runs the state. In July, 1918, the Fifth Congress of Soviets promulgated the first Constitution for the Russian Socialist Federated Soviet Republic (R.S.F.S.R.), then the official name of what is today the entire U.S.S.R. Under this Constitution, the supreme power was vested in the All-Russian Congress of Soviets, and between Congresses, the authority went to a Central Executive Committee (VTsIK) of about 200 members. The Executive Committee, in turn, designated the Council of People's Commissars (Sovnarkom). In addition to establishing the figurehead government, the Constitution had the usual provisions for free speech, free press, and freedom of religious worship—provisions that were almost entirely ignored.

In 1924, under the aegis of Stalin, a new Constitution was adopted for the U.S.S.R. (the official name of the new state since December, 1922). The new Constitution made a few changes in the governmental structure. The Central Executive Committee was divided into a Council of the Union, with representatives from the Union as a whole, and a Council of Nationalities with various quotas of representatives from union republics, autonomous republics, and autonomous regions. Its main importance was in listing changes in the nomenclature of the various governmental organs.

The "Stalin Constitution" of 1936 was even more at variance with Soviet practice than its two predecessors. In June, 1936, a draft form was published, and the newspapers were filled with discussions on various aspects of the new document. Stalin presented the Constitution in its final form to the Eighth Congress of the Soviets for ratification in November. On the surface, this document is almost a model of good democratic government, even to extending the suffrage to all over the age of eighteen and providing for the secret ballot. It established a Supreme Soviet of two houses, the Soviet of the Union and the Soviet of Nationalities, as the supreme authority in the state. Between meetings of the Supreme Soviet, all authority is held by the Presidium. Responsible to the Supreme Soviet, or its surrogate, the Presidium, is the Council of People's Commissars (renamed the Council of Ministers in 1946).

Like its predecessors, the Stalin Constitution enumerated many "rights" belonging to the citizens, including the rights to work, to leisure, and to social security; the usual list of freedoms, such as speech, press, religious assembly, petition, and demonstration, was given. The nature of these "rights" was amply demonstrated by the purges then being carried out on a wholesale scale. All the elaborate provisions for the judicial system of the U.S.S.R., spelled out at length in the Constitution, meant little to the millions tried and convicted by secret police tribunals—if they were tried at all.

Unlike the two previous Constitutions, the 1936 version did at least mention the Communist Party and pointed out in Article 126 that it represents the vanguard of the workers. But this only hinted at the fact that the real power lies in the Party. All candidates for election to government office have to be approved by the Party before the electorate has a chance to vote; therefore, the voter is restricted to the right of approval or disappoval of the picked list of candidates.* All the People's Commissars (now the Ministers) are selected by the Politburo of the Party, and their elevation is merely ratified by the "legislative organs."

The ostensible reason for the promulgation of the new Constitution was to mark the completion of the building of socialism in the U.S.S.R. The real reason was to persuade both the Soviet citizens and the world outside that the U.S.S.R. was moving toward Western democracy. This was the era of the United Front, the period when Communists everywhere were urged to stand shoulder to shoulder with "other" democrats against the rise of fascism. There can be little doubt that the Stalin Constitution did impress many in the West, but it is doubtful if many in the U.S.S.R. were equally impressed.

* The emptiness of the right to vote was also demonstrated by the fact that there were no elections to the Supreme Soviet from 1937 to 1946.

THE GREAT PURGE

Ironically, this new Constitution was promulgated on the eve of the most deadly reign of terror in Russian history, the *Yezhovshchina.* (Nikolai Ivanovich Yezhov was the head of the NKVD—People's Commissariat of Internal Affairs—at the height of the Purge, and his name came to designate this epoch of Russian history.) In December, 1934, a leading Soviet figure, Sergei Kirov, was assassinated in Leningrad. Apparently, Stalin considered this a manifestation of a powerful opposition, although one school of thought—to which Khrushchev belongs—believes that Stalin was behind the assassination. At any rate, a purge began that gradually grew until, by 1938, it reached staggering proportions. Accurate statistics are lacking, but it is certain that millions of Soviet citizens were arrested, interrogated, and sentenced without trial. Most of the old Bolsheviks, including such famous ones as Bukharin, Zinoviev, Radek, and Pyatakov, were shot. Even the officer corps of the Red Army was radically purged and most of its high-ranking officers executed. In 1938, the Purge had grown so extensive that industry was in danger of collapse. At this point, Stalin stepped in, removed Yezhov, and put Beria in charge of the NKVD. What lay behind the Purge? Dozens of theories have been advanced, and none offers a complete answer. Stalin apparently sensed a widespread opposition to the rigors of the forced industrialization and collectivization, plus a growing demand for more democracy. The Purge was his way of eliminating this opposition, especially among the old Bolsheviks. In 1934, four out of every five delegates to the Party Congress had joined the Party before 1920; in the 1939 Congress, the figures had been reversed—only one out of five could date his membership to 1920 or earlier. Since the Purge changed composition and leadership of the Party, it became more amenable to Stalin's control. The delegates were now Stalin trained and obedient to the line laid down by him. Once the Party and the police were solidly in his grasp, the only other element in the Soviet Union capable of opposing

Stalin would have been the Red Army, but this threat had been removed by the military Purge in 1937 and 1938. In summary, the two main results of the Purge were a Party directed by Stalin alone and an extension of police controls to the point where government without a secret police became inconceivable in the Soviet Union.

GERMANY VERSUS THE SOVIET UNION

Stalin's interest in collective security began to wane after the Munich settlement and the rape of Czechoslovakia, and he embarked on a *rapprochement* with Hitler. On August 23, 1939, the Soviet-German Pact was announced to the unsuspecting world, and almost immediately the Nazi forces triggered off World War II by their invasion of Poland. Stalin, who had expected a long and bitter war between Hitler and the Allies, must have been amazed at the speed with which his partner gobbled up country after country. The Polish and French armies provided little more than good training for the Nazi forces. Stalin tried to buttress his own security by absorbing the Baltic countries, Bessarabia, and a sizable chunk of Poland and driving the Finns out of the area nearest to Leningrad, but he remained faithful to the provisions of the pact on the assumption that Hitler would keep his attention riveted on the West.

On June 22, 1941, the *Wehrmacht* crossed the Soviet borders and the newest German *Drang nach Osten* was under way. Hitler, placed between an undefeated England in the west and a voracious, unscrupulous Russia in the east, decided to knock out Russia first and then use the food and raw materials of a defeated Soviet Union to finish off the war with Great Britain.

The opening of the German offensive in Russia, three weeks late because of the invasion of Yugoslavia, was an impressive operation in terms of planning, manpower, and strategy. The estimated 180 German divisions included about 25 divisions of Finns and Romanians and 20 armored divisions with approximately 8,000 tanks. In addition, the *Luftwaffe* had committed three air fleets with a first-line strength of 3,000 aircraft.

Numerically, the Red Army capability was about the same as the German—some 160 divisions, 54 tank brigades (around 10,000 tanks), and an air strength of 6,000 planes. However, in training, battle experience, and strategic know-how, the Germans held a distinct advantage.

The German plan of attack called for three army groups, each to penetrate deeply into Russia in order to encircle, break up, and destroy the Soviet armies before they could stabilize their fronts. The northern army group, under Field Marshal von Leeb, was to proceed against Leningrad, taking the Baltic states as it went. The central army group, under Field Marshal von Bock, was to move in the general direction of Moscow. The southern army group, commanded by Field Marshal von Rundstedt, was to move into the Ukraine. In the far north, an army of Finns and Germans under General von Falkenhorst was to operate against the Kola Peninsula with the objective of either cutting off or capturing Murmansk. In the far south, under Von Rundstedt's control, there was a Romanian army. With a front around 1,800 miles long, the logistics problems were colossal.

The Soviets gave the commands in the south and north to the old heroes of the Civil War, Budenny and Voroshilov. Timoshenko was put in command of the center.

For the first month, the Germans seemed all-powerful, and the Russians were engaged in retreating or in fighting their way out of traps. Von Leeb moved rapidly toward the north and, on September 4, began his assault on Leningrad. Von Bock's group, paced by his panzers, advanced hundreds of miles in a few weeks. Finally, he forced the Russians to fight at Smolensk, and their resistance was formidable enough to hold him up for three weeks, July 20 to August 9. In the meanwhile, Von Rundstedt was slowly proceeding from southern Poland into the Ukraine. At Zhitomir, a tank battle lasted an entire month, but part of the German force reached Kiev by July 21. At this point, German strategy was changed, and part of Von Bock's forces, Guderian's panzers in particular, were sent to help surround Kiev. On September 26, Kiev fell, and the Germans rounded up some 675,000 prisoners. The whole of the Ukraine now lay open to the invaders.

But the diversion of part of Von Bock's force to Von Rundstedt had delayed the advance on Moscow. From October 1 until December 5, the Germans tried both frontal attacks and pincer movements in an attempt to seize Moscow. The combination of overextended German lines and an early winter gave the Soviets an advantage. On December 6, Zhukov threw his carefully hoarded reserves against the Germans, and the Nazi drive was not only stopped but thrown back.

The Soviets had experienced a bad six months in 1941. The old Civil War heroes, Budenny and Voroshilov, had failed miserably, and both were sent to the rear to train reserves. Even Timoshenko, the hero of the Finnish War, had a series of reversals and was removed from the Moscow front to the south. The real hero of 1941 was Zhukov, the defender of Moscow. But with a fairly profitable winter offensive in the Moscow area and Timoshenko recapturing Rostov in the south, the Russians were confident of their ability to withstand the coming German offensives.

Early in 1942, however, the Germans delivered several severe blows. In the spring, Manstein had taken all the Crimea except for Sevastopol, and by July 2, he had taken that strong point. Timoshenko, trying to forestall a Nazi offensive, attacked south of Kharkov but was badly beaten. Meanwhile, the Germans had decided to strike southward at the Caucasus, the lower Volga, and eventually at the Baku oil fields. The main objective in this drive was the city of Stalingrad, which straggles for twenty miles along the west bank of the Volga at the great bend. For more than two months, from September 14 to November 19, the Germans battled to take Stalingrad, but their superiority in mechanization, air power, and maneuverability was dissipated in this type of positional warfare. When Zhukov was able to collect his reserves, he staged a counteroffensive, which resulted in the encirclement of Paulus and his Sixth Army. Paulus surrendered in February, 1943. The Germans lost 330,000 men killed and 200,000 captured, 60,000 trucks, 6,700 guns, and 1,500 tanks. It was the worst defeat ever suffered by a German field army. It was also the turning point of the war on the Eastern Front; from now on, the Russians were on the offensive.

The fiasco at Stalingrad made the German positions in the Caucasus and the middle Don untenable, especially since the Russians had mounted offensives in these areas simultaneously with the Stalingrad counteroffensive. By the end of February, 1943, the Soviets had retaken all the territory the Germans had overrun in 1942. In the north, Zhukov led an offensive that wiped out the Rzhev salient and alleviated that danger to Moscow.

There was no relaxation for the Germans; the new Soviet offensive was unrelenting and was now supported by superiority in manpower and matériel. By the end of the summer of 1943, the Germans had been pushed back along the whole front, and were attempting to set up a defensive line on the Dnieper. Even winter did not stop the Russian offensive. By December, 1943, the Germans had lost Kiev, they were in a shaky position on the Dnieper bend, and they were isolated in the Crimea.

Russian industry had been steadily increasing its output throughout 1942 and 1943, and Allied aid had poured in continuously; by January, 1944, the totals, for only a few items, amounted to 7,800 aircraft, 4,700 tanks and tank destroyers, and 170,000 trucks. The Soviets now had air superiority for the first time, and their 320 divisions gave them a comfortable margin over the 250 Axis divisions. With this mass of men and equipment, the Russians cleared the Dnieper bend, raised the siege of Leningrad, encircled ten German divisions at Korsun, and recovered the Crimea. In the center, the Germans had been pushed back to the Pripet Marshes. By the end of the winter offensive of 1944, the Red Army was in complete control of the Soviet Union.

In the summer and fall of 1944, the Russian offensive gathered new momentum. It began by knocking Finland out of the war. With their superiority in men and matériel, the Soviets were able to shift the attack to the weakest spots on the German front. They cut off thirty German divisions in the Baltic states and then proceeded to deal with the trapped Germans piecemeal. Another Russian front drove into East Prussia, while a third front hammered away at Poland. Romania collapsed at the end of August, and Bulgaria followed shortly. On December 30, a Provisional Hungarian Government declared war on the Reich. Germany was now without allies.

During 1945, until the German surrender on May 8, the Russians drove relentlessly across Poland and Prussia and reached Berlin by April 22. Four days later, they had contacted patrols of the U.S. Ninth Army at Torgau, and Berlin surrendered on May 2.

THE APOTHEOSIS OF STALIN

As the Soviet armed forces gave way before the Nazi onslaught during the dark days of 1941, the men in the Kremlin saw that their best hope lay in patriotic appeals. It was difficult to rouse the populace to fight for the tenets of a Marxist-Leninist-Stalinist philosophy, but they would struggle mightily for "Mother Russia," *Rodina*. Every effort was made to stress Russia's glorious history: Military heroes of the past were restored from oblivion; decorations and awards were showered upon the military heroes; and even the Guard Regiments were reinstated. With a slightly eased censorship—still absolute by Western standards—enough information leaked through about Allied aid to destroy the carefully built myth of "encirclement." The climax was reached when the Church was induced into an alliance with the atheistic Kremlin.

At the end of the war, Stalin and his associates found themselves faced with the problem of nullifying this propaganda, which had outlived its purpose. Even during the war, the Soviet press had been untiring in its praise of the leadership of Stalin. It was relatively simple to turn the "great leader" into the "architect of victory." In this way, the military heroes, such as Zhukov, were thrown into the shadow. The next step was to remove the popular heroes from Moscow to obscure and distant posts. Soon the Soviet victory was hailed as the triumph of Stalin, and the Party under his wise leadership.

The deification of Stalin was not restricted to Stalin the military strategist. Day after day, from 1945 to 1952, the Soviet propaganda organs glorified the "Great Stalin"; his achievements were expanded to include the fields of science, literature, and linguistics. Every congress of scientific or literary workers, every political gathering, devoted a large part of its agenda to praising the accomplishments of the leader (*vozhd*). In short, there was no room in Soviet communications for any other hero.

Even before hostilities ended the Soviet press had begun drying up the reservoir of good will toward the West. The terms "imperialist warmongers," "Fascist bandits," and "lackeys of Wall Street" came to be synonymous with the United States and Britain. Anyone who shrank from using these epithets was labeled a "rootless cosmopolitan," and this term soon became equivalent to an accusation of treason.

The actual apparatus for controlling the nation remained much the same in the postwar period, at least until the Nineteenth Party Congress, in October, 1952. On March 15, 1946, all commissariats were rechristened ministries by a constitutional change, but their functions were left intact. A gradual reduction in the number of ministries, especially those concerned with economic affairs, began in 1948. From fifty-nine in 1947, the total dropped to forty-eight in 1949. But the major reduction in ministries came after Stalin's death. In March, 1953, Malenkov reduced them to twenty-five, and Khrushchev abolished all but a few in 1958. In October, 1965, twenty-eight new ministries were created, and thus the cycle continues.

THE COLLECTIVE LEADERSHIP

Soviet historians have a penchant for viewing events in terms of periods, and there is no better dividing line in postwar Soviet history than the death of Stalin. The domestic scene had been essentially stagnant after the war, with the membership of the Politburo remaining relatively stable.* In 1946, Kalinin died, and Voznesenski replaced him; Bulganin and A. N. Kosygin became members in 1948. There was a shake-up in 1948, when

* From 1939 to 1946, the Politburo included the following: Stalin, Molotov, Voroshilov, Kalinin, Kaganovich, Andreyev, Mikoyan, Zhdanov, and Khrushchev. Malenkov and Beria were candidate members from 1939 until 1946, when they became full members.

Andrei A. Zhdanov died (or was executed), thereby triggering off the mysterious "Leningrad Affair." Apparently, Zhdanov, Secretary of the Leningrad Party, had vigorously advocated the use of force to solve the Berlin situation and to depose Tito. Malenkov led the opposition to this policy and, after Zhdanov's death, wiped out many of his followers in Leningrad, including Voznesenski. Kosygin, however, escaped the general purging of Zhdanovites and has come to the fore recently. While in power, Khrushchev continued to harp on the "Leningrad Affair" in his diatribes against the "anti-Party group" of Malenkov, Molotov, and Kaganovich.

In October, 1952, Stalin convoked the Nineteenth Party Congress, the first since 1939. At the Congress, he changed the name of the Politburo to the Presidium and enlarged its membership from eleven to twenty-five. The name "Bolshevik" also disappeared from the full title of the Party, henceforth to be known simply as the Communist Party of the Soviet Union. The title of the chief theoretical journal of the Party was also changed from *Bolshevik* to *Kommunist*. Presumably, Stalin had decided that "Bolshevik" had connotations of bomb-throwing revolutionists, and the old *vozhd* was not very revolutionary minded by 1952.

The outstanding feature of the Nineteenth Party Congress was the radical change in the upper echelon of the Party, the diluting of the old eleven-man Politburo by the appointment of a twenty-five-member Presidium. It looked as though Stalin meant to weaken the position of his old comrades, although a Bureau of the Presidium was formed that had the same functions and personnel as the old Politburo.

Rumors began that Stalin was preparing a new purge on the 1936–38 *Yezhovshchina* scale, with the addition of a strain of anti-Semitism. In January, 1953, *Pravda* published the story of the indictment of nine doctors, six of them Jews, who were accused of having "medically murdered" Zhdanov and others and who were said to be planning more of these murders of highly placed people. Beria was accused, by implication, of being insufficiently alert in the protection of high Kremlin figures. As fear of the new purge mounted, Stalin died. Just how, with or without help, is a mystery, but few leading figures in the Soviet Government die without suspicion that their rivals are implicated. For all that, the timing of Stalin's death seemed almost too convenient to have occurred naturally.

For years, speculation had been rampant in the West about the effects that Stalin's death would have on the course of Soviet history. There is no method of legitimate succession in the Soviet system. Actual power, as opposed to the "legal" elective system, is obtained by intrigue and force. Once the old *vozhd* was gone, what was to keep such powerful figures as Malenkov, Molotov, and Beria from war to the death to seize the fallen mantle? Ever since the Nineteenth Party Congress, Malenkov had been the heir apparent, but how could he consolidate his power if the rest of the inner group of the Presidium were opposed to him?

Immediately upon the death of Stalin, the inner group called on the people to avoid "confusion and panic" and promised a solid collective leadership of the Leninist type. The twenty-five-member Presidium was abolished, and the inner group of the old Politburo resumed its powerful position.* Real power seemed to lie in the hands of Malenkov, Beria, and Molotov, with Kaganovich and Mikoyan able to shift allegiance enough to keep the collective leadership going. Malenkov became the Chairman of the Council of Ministers and Beria the head of the newly consolidated police. (The MGB—Ministry of State Security—was merged with the MVD—Ministry of Internal Affairs—into a single ministry.) Apparently the other collective leaders feared Malenkov's control of both state and Party and, within two weeks, forced him to relinquish control of the Party to Khrushchev. Malenkov must have believed that the state apparatus had grown more powerful than that of the Party, although Stalin's rise to power through his control of the Secretariat of the Central Committee was relatively recent history.

The nonviolent period of collective leadership lasted less than four months; on July 10 came the announcement of Beria's arrest. Several charges, including treason dating back to the

* The new ten-member Presidium was made up of the "old hands"—Malenkov, Beria, Molotov, Bulganin, Kaganovich, Voroshilov, Mikoyan, and Khrushchev—and two relatively new figures, Saburov and Pervukhin.

1920's, were leveled at him. It is impossible to make sense out of most of the charges; fear of Beria's police empire was probably the underlying cause of his demise. This was followed by a mass purge of Beria men in the police and among the Party organizations in the union republics, especially in Georgia.

In an attempt to please his managerial elite and the population in general, Malenkov encouraged expansion in consumer production and a higher standard of living. He was willing to slacken the pace of heavy industrial development and to reduce the military budget to accomplish this goal. Khrushchev, who had been building up power through his manipulation of Party appointments, hit out at Malenkov's policies late in 1954. An unusual situation arose in December, 1954, and January, 1955: *Izvestia*, the state organ, and *Pravda*, the Party newspaper, supported two different leaders, Malenkov and Khrushchev, respectively. The gauntlet had been thrown down, and in February, 1955, Malenkov resigned as Chairman of the Council of Ministers. Khrushchev immediately nominated his own man, Bulganin, for the job. Khrushchev's power was becoming evident to all.

THE END OF THE COLLECTIVE LEADERSHIP

The Bulganin-Khrushchev team made a pilgrimage to Belgrade in May, 1955, to woo Tito—first by blaming past misdeeds on the dead Beria and then by promising no interference in the future. In the summer of 1955, the pair went to the Summit in Geneva, and although nothing was accomplished there, they exuded good will and the spirt of tolerance. In that same summer, Shepilov, a former editor of *Pravda* and the new favorite of the Bulganin-Khrushchev team, was in Egypt negotiating an arms deal with Nasser that would destroy the "spirit of Geneva" in 1956.

In February, 1956, the Twentieth Party Congress met as scheduled and was dominated by Khrushchev from start to finish. The Congress approved the Sixth Five-Year Plan (1956–60), which emphasized a continuation of heavy industrial development; it conceded that Tito had the right to take a different road to socialism; and it heard Khrushchev explode the myth of the "Great Stalin." Even Stalin's opponents in exile or his foreign enemies could not have done a better job of blackening his reputation than Khrushchev did in his "Secret Speech" to the Twentieth Party Congress.

Khrushchev's control of the Presidium remained weak, and his only victory was the addition of several of his people as candidate members of the highest body. He did, however, strengthen the power of the Secretariat by adding Ekaterina A. Furtseva and Leonid I. Brezhnev, then, respectively, the First Secretary of the Moscow Party and the First Secretary of the Party in Kazakhstan. These were dynamic, younger people with strong Party connections. Marshal Zhukov and Nuritdin A. Mukhitdinov, First Secretary of the Party in Uzbekistan, were made candidate members of the Presidium.

The denigration of Stalin and a general loosening of controls in the satellites led to appalling results from the Soviet standpoint. In June, 1956, an uprising of workers in Poznań plunged the Polish Communist Party into chaos; Gomulka, imprisoned in 1948 for Titoism, was elected First Secretary of the Party in October. This brought Khrushchev rushing into Warsaw, but Gomulka faced him down. A few days later, the students in Budapest revolted, and the sad, yet heartening, events of the Hungarian Revolution followed. The only source of satisfaction for Khrushchev during this period was the incredibly botched Israeli-British-French attempt at an armed solution of the Suez situation, and the ambivalent stand of the United States. By accusing the British and French of being "imperialist bandits," the Soviets managed to divest themselves of some of the onus for their own imperialism in Hungary. But it was a besmirched Soviet Communist Party that emerged from the October events of 1956.

In early 1957, Khrushchev managed to remove Malenkov's last source of power and at the same time achieve the benefits of "decentralizing" the economy. He divided the U.S.S.R. into over 100 economic regions and set up an economic council to control industry in each of these regions. The economic regions coincided with the political divisions of the country, either oblasts or union republics, and the Party leaders in each region dominated the local economic council. This increase in the role of the Party in the nation's economy, plus the abolition of the powerful ministries in Moscow, weakened Malenkov's position both in the government (he was then Minister of Electric Power Stations) and in the Party. Malenkov's chance of making a comeback became very dubious.

Khrushchev had built well in the lower and middle echelons of the Party structure since March, 1953, and it stood him in good stead in June, 1957. The anti-Khrushchev bloc in the Presidium outvoted him, which was presumed to be tantamount to ending his power. But Khrushchev was not to be overthrown that easily, and he took his case to a special meeting of the Central Committee of the Party, where his adherents were more numerous. Just what happened there is still a mystery, but after several days of wrangling, the majority stood by Khrushchev, and the nucleus of the "anti-Party group"—Malenkov, Molotov, Kaganovich, and Shepilov—was dismissed from the Presidium and the Central Committee. It has been speculated that Marshal Zhukov put the army behind Khrushchev and that this tipped the scales in his favor. If this is true, Zhukov acted with more than usual stupidity, for the only way the army could continue to have a voice in the leadership of the Soviet Union was to see to it that no one man obtained all the power. Khrushchev, now the supreme boss, repaid Zhukov in October, 1957, by returning him to the obscurity he had known under Stalin after World War II. The Party had again attained unquestionable dominance, and Khrushchev controlled the Party after June, 1957. The final act occurred in September, 1958, when Bulganin was deposed and Khrushchev became Chairman of the Council of Ministers. He now held the top job in both the state and Party hierarchies.

The new Khrushchev Presidium and Secretariat, after the defeat of the "anti-Party group," in June, 1957, emphasized career Party men. By December, 1959, the fourteen-member Presidium and the ten-member Secretariat were composed mostly of First Secretaries of union republics or big city Party organizations. Representatives of the so-called "managerial elite" were scarce in both these top organs; their membership included, rather, the new breed that had come into the Party through technological schools and industry. They were really capable of wearing both hats, but their first allegiance was to the Party.

The Twenty-second Party Congress convened in October, 1961, primarily to launch the last stage in the march toward the hitherto elusive "state of Communism"—the era of plenty for all. But domestic issues were pushed into the background by the developments in foreign relations. Khrushchev insisted upon the exclusion of Albania from the Communist bloc and bitterly assailed the leader of the Albanian Communists, Enver Hoxha, because he had carried out a purge of Moscow-oriented Albanian Communists. Chou En-lai, the head of the Chinese Communist delegation to the Congress, walked out after objecting to this public airing of differences within the bloc. He was effusively greeted by Mao and the top Chinese leaders on his return to Peking, an obvious demonstration of approval of his actions in Moscow.

The trouble that came to a head at the Twenty-second Congress had been brewing for some time. The Chinese and Russian leadership have held opposite views on the efficacy of Khrushchev's "coexistence" policy ever since its inauguration, at the Twentieth Party Congress in 1956, and although they seemed to have patched up their differences at the Moscow meeting of the eighty-one Communist Parties in November–December, 1960, there remained a fundamental divergence of views. During this infighting between Mao and Khrushchev over foreign policy, Albania placed herself squarely on the side of the Chinese, and Peking was furious at Khrushchev's public castigation of its only European ally. Furthermore, Mao knew that every attack on Hoxha was really directed at him.

Khrushchev again attacked the "anti-Party group" and was especially vitriolic in his remarks against Molotov. Inasmuch as Molotov's views on Communist policy toward the West coincided with those of Mao, Khrushchev was probably aiming his barbs at the latter. In addition, there is reason to believe that the "anti-Party group" represents the views of a segment of the Soviet Party membership. Khrushchev, therefore, was not flailing a dead horse. Incidentally, Voroshilov was included in the "anti-Party group" in this second attack.

Finally, the denigration of Stalin was continued at the Twenty-second Congress; This time, however, unlike the 1956 attack *in camera,* his sins were revealed openly. Practically every top Party leader who spoke at the Congress disclosed some detail of the late *vozhd's* iniquitous behavior. The climax came with the removal of Stalin's mummy from the Lenin-Stalin mausoleum and its burial near the Kremlin wall. He was judged unfit to lie by the side of Lenin.

During 1962, Khrushchev seemed to lose his touch and he began to flounder about in the making of domestic, as well as foreign, policies. The Sino-Soviet quarrel grew in intensity, and Mao and Khrushchev were now berating each other directly, without the subterfuge of using Tito and Hoxha as whipping boys. When Khrushchev came a cropper in the Cuban missile fracas, the Chinese brethren rose to new heights of vitriolic commentary, this time on his "adventurism in putting the missiles in Cuba" and his "cowardice in taking them out." It is evident since Khrushchev's ouster that the Chinese estimate of his awkwardness in this crisis was shared by some of his Soviet colleagues.

It had become clear by 1962 that all was not well on the economic front. Brezhnev, the successor to Khrushchev's Party job, in a speech to a plenary session of the Central Committee in March, 1965, pointed out that although Khrushchev had promised to increase agricultural output by 70 per cent during the Seven-Year Plan (1959–65), actually it had been increased by only 10 per cent during the first six years of the Plan, or by less than 2 per cent a year. Thus it scarcely kept up with the population increase. The same gloomy picture was also true of animal husbandry: the number of hogs, sheep, and poultry had declined during the first six years of the Plan.[2]

The turning point in Khrushchev's career was the catastrophic grain-crop failure of 1963, when the Soviet Union had to purchase 12 million tons of wheat from the "imperialist" countries. He barnstormed the countryside in a desperate effort to raise agricultural production, but to little avail. By this time even the dullest Soviet citizen was aware that Khrushchev's boasts about the Soviet Union overtaking and surpassing the United States in the per capita production of meat, butter, and milk in the early 1960's were pipe dreams.

Although the standard of living was certainly better in 1964 than in 1953, Khrushchev had merely whetted the Soviet citizen's appetite. Furthermore, he had promised the consumer more, much more, than he could deliver. Housing was going up much more slowly than promised, clothing was still expensive and shoddy, and unbelievably poor distribution made it difficult for the shopper to buy even those things that were being produced. All in all, Khrushchev's image was becoming rather tarnished.

In October, 1964, while Khrushchev was vacationing on the Black Sea, the Presidium of the Central Committee decided to oust its leader. The plan must have been carefully laid, since it was necessary to bring the army and the police into the plot as allies or at least as neutrals. The members of the Presidium also took the lesson of June, 1957, to heart and coordinated their plans with enough members of the Central Committee to insure the backing of that body. They knew that Khrushchev would appeal to it. Although the sources are vague and conflicting about just what happened when Khrushchev appeared before the Presidium and later before the Central Committee, the net result seems to to have been an overwhelming rejection of him. He lost his job as First Secretary of the Party to Leonid I. Brezhnev, his former protégé, and his job as Chairman of the Council of Ministers to Aleksei N. Kosygin, his deputy in that body.

The new leaders, Brezhnev and Kosygin, are competent men, but hardly popular leaders imbued with that vague quality called charisma that enables a leader to influence large numbers of people. As a matter of fact, once the decision was made to dump Khrushchev, Brezhnev and Kosygin were the residual legatees in the absence of any really outstanding personalities on the top level. How long this double-headed government can control the system that Stalin so ingeniously tailored to fit a dictator is a moot point that haunts Kremlinologists.

The new leadership almost immediately did away with Khrushchev's two-track Party hierarchy (agricultural and industrial Party organizations) and reverted to the pre-1962 setup. They eased the restrictions that Khrushchev had imposed on the peasant's private plot, and even encouraged the peasant by authorizing the State Bank to lend him money to buy cows and heifers. In March, 1965, Brezhnev, at a plenary session of the Central Committee, outlined a new strategy for increasing agricultural output. He stated bluntly that an upsurge in agriculture was vitally necessary for the economic health of the nation and that farming must be given a firm economic foundation. After promising a number of badly needed changes, he stated that the government was going to invest 71 billion rubles ($1.10 to the ruble at the time) during the next Five-Year Plan (1966–70). If Brezhnev and Kosygin can keep the other sectors of the economy going, fight off the leaders of heavy industry and the military, and actually fulfill the program outlined at the March, 1965, plenum, they should be able at least to ameliorate the agricultural situation in the next six years. But there are a considerable number of "ifs" in the preceding sentence.

4

Communist Ideology

The struggle that splits the world today—the clash between totalitarianism, as exemplified in the Communist bloc, and the nontotalitarian way of life of the free world—is fundamentally an ideological struggle. In the course of the Cold War, both sides have simplified their ideologies in order to gain wider appeal, but there is nothing new about this. No matter how complex the base from which it started, an ideology, by the time it has been widely adopted, usually consists of a rather short list of easily comprehended terms, symbols, and slogans. The Communists have reduced the complicated arguments of Marx and Lenin to such terms as the "dictatorship of the proletariat," "democratic centralism," "capitalist encirclement," the "Communist stage of development" with its promise of "from each according to his ability, to each according to his need," and other clichés that evoke powerful emotional responses from their conditioned audiences. But to dismiss this ideology as a collection of *ad hoc* rules conjured up by a small group of bandits is to fly in the face of history. On the eve of the February Revolution of 1917 in Russia, the total number of Bolsheviks was about 23,600. The ideological heirs of that small band now rule some 900 million people, 40 per cent of the world's population. To underestimate the force of the Communist ideology is to play ostrich.

MARXISM

The present Communist ideology might be described, somewhat simplistically, as Marxism Russianized by Lenin and Stalin, and Marxism itself as an amalgam of several ideological currents of Western Europe in the early nineteenth century (see Figure I). Lenin wrote that Marx continued and brought to fruition the three main ideological currents of the nineteenth century: classical German philosophy, classical English political economy, and French socialism.[1] Although it may be doubtful that these were the main ideological currents, or that Marx brought them to fruition, the statement at least summarizes the sources from which Marx derived his basic ideas.

Figure I. The Ideological Roots of Communism

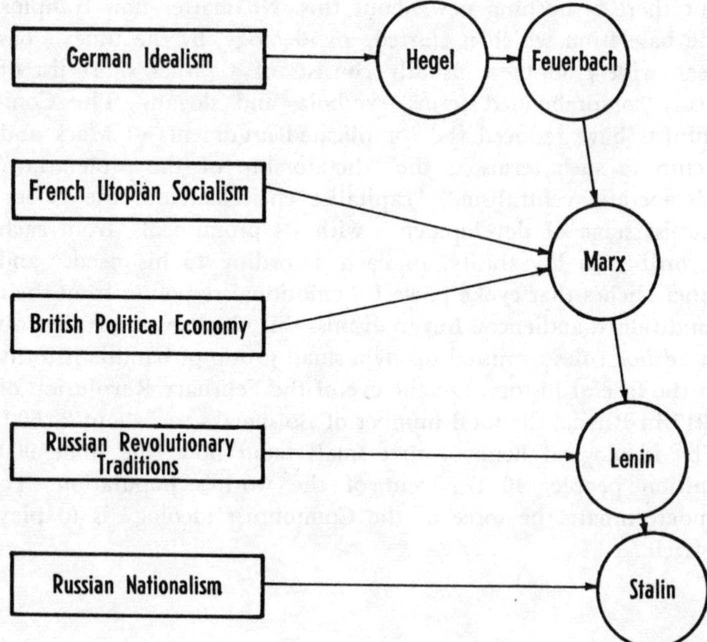

Of all the makers of socialist systems in a century that spawned them so prodigally, Karl Marx stood head and shoulders above the rest. Whether one reveres, is indifferent to, or even hates Marx and Marxism, the immense importance of the man and his work is unquestionable. Neither Mohammed nor Luther has had more influence on the course of history than Marx. Even non-Marxist scholars, consciously or unconsciously, find the heavy imprint of Marxism on history, economics, sociology, and other disciplines. In the ideological struggle now engulfing the entire planet, one side traces its basic tenets back to Marx, and it thus behooves us to take more than a cursory glance at his teachings.

Marx the Man

Karl Marx was born in Treves in the Rhineland in 1818. His father, a moderately prosperous lawyer, had abandoned the ancestral faith of Judaism, but the long line of rabbis on both sides of the family seems to have passed on to Karl a disposition toward religious fervor and moral indignation, which has led more than one writer to call him the last of the great Old Testament prophets.

Marx first studied in the University of Bonn, where he went through the typical experiences of a German student in the 1830's, even to fighting his duel and gaining the coveted scar. He soon moved on to the University of Berlin, at that time the intellectual center of the Germanies, and decided to give up his legal studies in order to become a philosopher. Hegel was then at the height of his popularity, and it was almost axiomatic that any apprentice philosopher would be a Hegelian. But Marx, the born rebel, became disenchanted with Hegel very soon in his philosophical career and came under the influence of a pair of Neo-Hegelians, Bruno Bauer and Ludwig Feuerbach, who objected to the extreme idealism of the Hegelian *Weltgeist* (world spirit).

Failing to obtain a university post upon the completion of his studies, Marx became the editor of a newspaper, the *Rheinische Zeitung,* in 1842, but his forthright antigovernment stands on several sensitive issues led to the suppression of the sheet in 1843.

Marx then went to Paris, where he influenced and was influenced by the French socialist Pierre-Joseph Proudhon and formed a literary partnership with Friedrich Engels. This association endured throughout Marx's lifetime and even beyond it, for Engels was responsible for editing and seeing through to publication the second and third volumes of Marx's magnum opus, *Capital,* long after his friend's death. Soon after they met, Engels supplied Marx with facts and figures on the English industrial revolution, about which he had firsthand information as the manager of his family's textile plant in Manchester. Engels' information brought Marx's studies in abstract German philosophy and French socialistic thought down to earth.

In the period from 1844 to 1847, the two men devoted themselves to a series of studies largely aimed at ridiculing the profundities of the German philosophers of that age. Marx also made a ferocious attack upon his former friend Proudhon, apparently as much for personal reasons as for philosophical ones. Proudhon was not capable of the fanaticism of a Marx, and in answer to Marx's invitation to contribute to an organized correspondence among the Communists in various countries, Proudhon wrote that he was willing but added, "for God's sake, after we have demolished all the dogmatisms a priori, let us not of all things attempt in our turn to instill another kind of doctrine into the people. . . ." This showed Proudhon's prescience, but trying to prevent Marx from promulgating dogma was an utterly futile undertaking.

Marx and Engels became public figures when they published their *Communist Manifesto,* early in 1848. Few documents in history have been so solidly packed with explosive ideas as was this little pamphlet of some forty pages. In terse prose, very different from Marx's usual style, it enunciated a general philosophy of history, analyzed European society, and sounded a clarion call for revolution. From its opening sentence, "A specter is haunting Europe—the specter of Communism," to its concluding exhortation, "Working men of all countries, unite!" the *Communist Manifesto* is a document supercharged with emotional appeal. Probably no better summary is possible than the following extract from Engels' preface to a reissue of the pamphlet in 1888:

> The "Manifesto" being our joint production, I consider myself bound to state that the fundamental proposition which forms its nucleus belongs to Marx. That proposition is: that in every historical epoch, the prevailing mode of economic production and exchange, and the social organization necessarily following from it, form the basis upon which is built up, and from which alone can be explained, the political and intellectual history of that epoch; that consequently the whole history of mankind (since the dissolution of primitive tribal society, holding land in common ownership) has been a history of class struggles, contests between exploiting and exploited, ruling and oppressed classes; that the history of these class struggles forms a series of evolution in which, nowadays, a stage has been reached where the exploited and oppressed class (the proletariat) cannot attain its emancipation from the sway of the exploiting and ruling class (the bourgeoisie) without, at the same time, and once and for all, emancipating society at large from all exploitation, oppression, class distinction, and class-struggles.

Marx attempted to play an active role in the revolutions of 1848 in both Germany and France, and on the failure of these movements, he became *persona non grata* in both countries. From 1849 until his death, in 1883, Marx lived in England. Life was extremely hard for Marx in London, and his only income during this period was a pittance he received as European correspondent for the *New York Tribune* and gifts from Engels. After ten years of this hand-to-mouth existence, Marx was granted an allowance of £350 a year from Engels. During this decade of poverty, however, Marx did his hardest work. He went daily to the British Museum and worked from opening to closing time on *Capital*.

From 1864 to its demise, in 1874, Marx played a major role in the First International. But Marx never worked well with others, except Engels, and his decade in the First International was one long series of feuds with its other leaders, Giuseppe Mazzini, Proudhon, and, finally, Mikhail Bakunin and his anarchists, whom Marx hated violently. In fact, it was this bitter Marx-Bakunin feud that killed the First International.

At long last, in 1867, the first volume of *Capital* was published.

The book sold few copies in the first years after publication, but within a decade, translations into French and Russian and a second edition in German gave the work a wide circulation. By the late 1870's, it was becoming the fundamental authority for socialists all over the world. As R. N. Carew Hunt points out, the Bible of the Communist religion is *Capital* and its Creed is the *Communist Manifesto*.[2]

The last fifteen years after the publication of the first volume of *Capital* saw the hitherto dynamic Marx gradually running down, largely because of his shattered health, probably badly undermined during his years of poverty and overwork. He died in 1883, still trying, in a desultory way, to finish *Capital*. Engels brought out the second volume in 1885 and the third in 1894.

The Marxist System

If the pristine, theoretical Marxism * herein described seems much at variance with what it has become in the modern Communist world, this should occasion no surprise. Marxism has become a religion, and religions have often developed along lines that would startle their founders. Fundamentally, the goal of Marxism was anarchistic—the state was supposed to wither away—yet it has spawned the most monolithic states the world has ever seen. Marxism was antireligious, but it has become one of the world's largest religions. Its economics was based on a "scientific" approach, but today only an act of faith enables its adherents to swallow its outdated and fallacious assumptions.

This is not to disparage the appeal of Marxism, for it is not the "scientific" sociology of Marxism that has attracted millions to its banner but the vague promise of the higher stage of socialism, Communism, with its slogan of "from each according to his ability, to each according to his need." Georges Sorel,

* In the following description of Marxism, we shall refer to Marxian writings as though Marx alone expounded the doctrine that bears his name today. Much of this doctrine, in fact, was contributed by Engels; but since Engels was a modest man and admitted to being the junior partner, their joint product is usually called Marxism. The reader may substitute in his mind "Marxism-Engelsism" for "Marxism" if he wishes.

a leader of the revolutionary syndicalists, put his finger on the appeal when he stated that a movement designed to capture the masses should have a "myth" that excites their imagination and inspires them to action. It was not Marx the scientist but Marx the prophet who created just such a "myth."

Marxism as a Philosophy

Marxism is a materialistic philosophy; that is, it makes the basic assumptions that the world around us exists independently of our senses, everything can be reduced to matter, ideas are derived from material processes. In this respect, Marx differed from Hegel, who taught that the substance of history was spiritual and that all history was the progressive unfolding of the *Weltgeist,* culminating finally in the orderly operations of the Prussian monarchy of the early nineteenth century. Marx, influenced by Bauer and Feuerbach, could not accept the premise of the *Weltgeist.* He contended that he found Hegel standing on his head, and he set him right side up by discovering that history is not an unfolding of ideas but the development of ideas from material processes. From this it is possible to infer that Marxism makes man the slave of his material environment; in other words, that Marxism is a deterministic philosophy. Marx, however, never pushed it that far. He presumed man and his environment had a functional relationship: They reacted upon each other. Nevertheless, the pressure of environment in tailoring man's actions is certainly greater in Marxism than in most philosophical systems. As Marx himself put it, men do not make their own history under circumstances of their own choosing, but under circumstances then existing, which have been transmitted from the past.

Although Marx claimed to have stood Hegel on his feet in attributing the development of ideas to material processes, he took over the Hegelian engine that drove history forward—the "dialectic." The fundamental idea in the dialectic is that there is a connection between opposites, called "the law of the unity of opposites" in the esoteric jargon of the Marxists. Each unity contains an opposite within itself; for example, the positive and negative poles of an electron. To give another example, the bourgeoisie and the proletariat are opposites and in a state of conflict but are also a unity in that they are both classes in a single social system, capitalism. The dialectic operates in a triangular manner: The "thesis" affirms a proposition, but because of its internal contradictions, it gives rise to an "antithesis" (the negation of the thesis, in Marxian terms), which tries to overcome the contradictions within the thesis. The contest results in a "synthesis," which includes the valid elements of both the thesis and antithesis but on a higher level than either. The new synthesis, in turn, becomes a thesis that develops its antithesis, and the cycle goes on and on. Returning to our example, according to the Marxists, the contradiction between the bourgeoisie and the proletariat will be solved by the revolution, which will lead to a synthesis, socialism.

In Marxism, the transition from one stage to the next does not proceed in an evolutionary manner, but by "jumps" or, as the Marxists say, by "the transformation of quantity into quality." Change takes place by imperceptible steps until these quantitative steps become qualitative. The traditional example is the change in water as the amount of heat varies. When the water reaches 212° F., it turns to steam, and when it reaches 32° F., it turns to ice, although it still looks like ordinary water until it reaches either of these critical temperatures. In human history, these "jumps" are revolutions, and when enough quantitative mutations have taken place in capitalism, a "jump" to socialism will inevitably occur.

Marx, in his attempt to diagnose the entire social structure, present and past, needed some conceptual scheme to use as a framework. He found this in what is usually referred to as "historical materialism," which is simply dialectical materialism applied to social relationships. The common end all men pursue is, first, to wrest a livelihood from their natural environment and, next, to exchange the things they produce. The shape a society takes is largely determined by the way in which its production is organized—its division of labor. When the technological level rises, the division of labor broadens into a class structure. It is the class structure that is the key feature of any society, and Marxism asserts that class relationships are necessarily exploitative; one class lives off the labors of another. The ruling class maintains this state of things by its control of the means of production.

These productive relationships, which constitute the economic structure of a society, are the real basis of the society and determine the religion, legal system, ethics, art, and other elements or, in Marxian language, determine the "superstructure" of the state or society. Marxists admit that the superstructure can influence the basic economic structure somewhat; but on the whole, the economic basis of society determines the shape of the superstructure.

The fundamental force that moves world history is the class struggle, not the clash of nations. According to Marx, a close analysis of the wars between nations will show them to be in reality wars between classes. In a society with classes, when the contradictions between the productive forces and the productive relationships maintained by the ruling class become pronounced, revolutions occur. These revolutions, in Marx's words, are "the locomotives of history," by which history moves forward to a new and higher synthesis, namely socialism. But the socialist synthesis will not develop any antithesis in its turn, for it will be a classless society, in which, by definition, the class struggle is excluded. History will grind to a halt, Nirvana will have been attained, and the cruel round of the dialectic will be over.

Marxism as a System of Economics

Modern economists, or at least the majority of economists outside the Communist bloc, would hardly give serious attention to Marx's economic system as blueprinted in *Capital*. Marx had devoted his life and his considerable learning to the study of economic theory, but what was a keen economic analysis in the middle of the nineteenth century is no longer necessarily valid. The reputations of most great economic theorists have been based on their thinking in their own time. Because the Marxists have elevated *Capital* to a scriptural eminence, they must defend the entire body of Marx's economic theories.

Marx was an ardent student of Adam Smith, Ricardo, and Malthus, and to a large degree, his theory is based upon their findings. His view of the unending misery of the working class and the inevitable increase in the affluence of the owners of industry was not much different from the doctrine of his classical predecessors. The main difference was that Marx refused to be reconciled to such a state of things. He applied historical materialism to the course of economic development and concluded that capitalism was doomed by its own contradictions.

Marx accepted the Ricardian thesis that the worker must inevitably remain at the margin of bare subsistence, but he attributed this less to the workers' tendency to have larger families when their wages are increased than to their weak positions vis-à-vis their employer. The large number of workers competing for jobs—what Marx called the "industrial reserve army"—makes it futile for the worker to argue for a higher wage. If he is dissatisfied with what he is getting, there are plenty who are ready to replace him. Even if there is a shortage of labor in a boom period, and the competition for labor forces wages up, the costs of production also rise and bring the boom to an end. If the worker gets a bigger slice of the profits of industry, he does not benefit in the long run.

Marx's chief contribution to economic theory, at least in his own period, was his theory of "surplus value." The idea of labor as the source of value of a commodity in exchange dated back to Locke and it was accepted by Ricardo. Marx developed this theory as the cornerstone of his economic analysis. He maintained that all value in a commodity was the result of the labor involved in its production. Since labor is the only value-producing agency, the price of a commodity in exchange is dependent upon the amount of labor it took to produce it. But all the value added to a commodity does not go back to labor. Rather, it consists of two parts: one received by the worker and the other retained by the employer. This idea was not original with Marx; Adam Smith had pointed out that the value the workers add to their materials was what paid their wages and gave their employer his profit. What was merely a descriptive assessment on the part of Adam Smith became a moral crusade for Marx. The second part, the employer's share, was labeled "surplus value" by Marx—a term that was redolent with fraudulence and intentionally so. If the worker toiled ten hours and it took only five hours of his labor to pay his wages (the amount necessary to maintain him at a subsistence level), then the additional five hours were spent enriching his employer. This, Marx believed, was outright exploitation.

Having established the theory of surplus value, Marx went on to expand the theory on this basis. The wages paid to labor, which alone produces value, Marx called "variable capital." Machinery, which is something labor has already produced, is called "congealed labor" or "constant capital." Inasmuch as profits can come only from surplus value, the rate of profit depends upon the proportion of variable capital to constant capital, that is, of the cost of labor to the cost of machinery. As the technological level advances, the employer will use more machinery and less labor, and his rate of profit will constantly decline. This cannot be avoided, says Marx, and bitter competition will reduce the number of successful capitalists, leading inevitably to the formation of monopolies. The capitalists will become fewer and richer, the workers more numerous and poorer. This is the famous "law of increasing misery," which Marx described vividly in *Capital:*

> Along with the constantly diminishing number of the magnates of capital, who usurp and monopolize all advantages of this process of transformation [the destruction of the individual producer and his transformation into a laborer, the growth of large industry, etc.], grows the mass of misery, oppression, slavery, degradation, exploitation; but with this too grows the revolt of the working class, a class always increasing in numbers, and disciplined, united, organized by the very mechanism of the process of capitalist production itself. The monopoly of capital becomes a fetter upon the mode of production, which has sprung up and flourished along with

> and under it. Centralization of the means of production and socialization of labor at last reach a point where they become incompatible with their capitalist integument. This integument is burst asunder. The knell of capitalist private property sounds. The expropriators are expropriated.[3]

One of the really puzzling elements in this neat Marxian thesis is this: Why should the capitalists, who have been successfully extracting the lion's share of the wealth from the economic structure, blunder stupidly into their own destruction, while the exploited and pauperized workers suddenly become energized and are the only ones capable of directing the industrial machine intelligently? The answer is in Marx's image of the proletariat. As capitalist exploitation is intensified, the worker becomes more and more a specialized adjunct to his machine. He becomes a simple commodity to be bought and sold in the market place. The very viciousness of the worker's treatment under capitalism leads him to understand it clearly, and his reduction to bare subsistence under the law of increasing misery has left him with nothing to lose if he revolts. From the individual system itself, he has learned how to work in an organization with discipline and cooperation. Later, even Marxists, including Lenin, found this explanation unconvincing.

Marx was on solid ground in pointing out that labor was not getting a fair share under the *laissez faire* system of his period, but in the next hundred years, the capitalists turned out to be less stupid than anticipated. They have, often under duress, allowed labor to get a larger share of the profits of industry, and the phenomenal growth in productivity during this same century has reversed the law of increasing misery.

Marxism as a Political Program

In comparison with Marx's amorphous political program, his philosophy and economics seem extremely lucid. The reason is that Marx never analyzed the period that lay beyond the "inevitable" revolution. In this sphere his successors, especially Lenin and Stalin, have had to find their own way.

Marx admitted that the class struggle in the middle of the nineteenth century was not a clear-cut bourgeoisie-proletariat contest, because the bourgeoisie were still combating the survivals of feudalism. The revolution, therefore, would have to come in two phases. In the first phase, the proletariat would have to side with the bourgeoisie so that capitalism could come into its own and develop those things necessary for a successful socialist state. Then the proletariat could, in the second stage, make its own revolution. This alliance was, of course, only a tactical one, and the fundamental antagonism remained. It was this two-stage revolution that led to the many bitter debates among Marx's heirs.

Once the proletariat has risen and taken over, its first duty would be to smash the existing bourgeois state machinery. Between the destruction of the bourgeois state and the establishment of the Communist stateless society, there would be an interim rule, the dictatorship of the proletariat. Marx is vague on what this dictatorship of the proletariat will be like and how long the interim rule will last. But only after the bourgeois elements have been thoroughly eliminated can society enter upon its Communist stage. Inasmuch as the state is a product of the class struggle, an instrument by which the ruling class maintains its control of the means of production and thereby also control of the exploited classes, the advent of the classless society makes the state redundant, and it simply "withers away."

This theory of the withering away of the state has proved perpetually embarrassing to the rulers of the Soviet Union. Fundamentally, the end product of Marx's political program was anarchistic, an end incompatible with the demands of a complex industrial society in which nationwide planning has reached new dimensions. Marx's political program posed more problems than it answered and left his successors with a set of means that are at variance with the end proposed. Stalin finally advanced the theory that as long as the socialist state is surrounded by capitalist nations, there can be no diminution in the absolute controls that accrue to the state as the agent for the "dictatorship of the proletariat."

The Decline of Marxism

The course of Marxism after the death of its founder was anything but smooth. The canon of Marxian writings covered too much too vaguely to lend itself to clear-cut doctrine. As the nineteenth century drew to a close, it became more and more evident that Marx's inexorable laws concerning the imminent doom of capitalism were not operating; the institution had never looked healthier. The law of increasing misery, which vividly portrayed a proletariat reduced to dire straits, also seemed to have gone awry. Industry burgeoned as never before, and the workers were getting an ever larger share of the benefits. In Germany, the locale Marx had picked for the coming revolution, capitalism was progressing. The Marxist German Social Democratic Party had become a mass party by the 1890's, a party replete with a bureaucracy and a tendency to appeal to liberal voters—thus making revolution undesirable. The old Marxian slogans were still mouthed by the faithful at all party conventions, but there was little fire in their enunciation. The party had become essentially reformist.

At this point, a section of the party, with Eduard Bernstein as its main spokesman, began to bring the theory nearer to the actual reformist tactics. Bernstein attacked the Marxist economic fallacies by showing that small producers were multiplying in spite of the rise of large industry and that the workers were not getting poorer and poorer. He used irrefutable statistics to undermine Marxian theory. Bernstein also rejected the Marxian blueprint of the road to socialism. Socialism, he asserted, was desirable, and all means should be utilized to achieve it, but its advent was not determined by historical laws. This being the case, socialism did not have to come through bloody revolution but could be arrived at through union activities and parliamentary pressures for social legislation. In short, Bernstein advocated a gradualist approach in place of the revolutionary one. Although Bernstein denied it, his association with the English Fabians, dyed-in-the-wool gradualists, seems to have influenced his thinking.

LENINISM

Lenin's contributions to Marxism were three: He Russianized the revolutionary heart of Marx's doctrine by tying it to the tightly organized revolutionary group; he put new vitality into Marxism by explaining the reasons for the delay in the collapse of capitalism; and he broadened the base of the revolution to include the peasants. When he was done, there was little of the original Marxism that had not been changed. Marx had been a theorist studying the past and the present in order to elicit laws that would determine the future. He advocated unity of theory and practice, but his laws were inexorable: Capitalism had within it the seeds of its own destruction, and the only possible heir was the proletariat. Lenin, however, was an activist. Theory was the tool to be used to bolster the line of action that circumstances made possible. Power was the goal, and if the tools had to be changed now and then to attain that goal, he had no scruples against changing them.

The Revolutionary Tradition in Russia

The factors that were making the Social Democrats in Germany and the Fabians in England less revolutionary—factors such as the growth of labor unions, social legislation, and higher wages—did not exist in Russia. The reluctance of the Czarist regime to relinquish an iota of its absolute power drove even moderate reformers into underground activity. On his advent to the throne, Nicholas I had been greeted by the Decembrist revolt, carried out by a conspiratorial group of noble army officers, and he spent the next thirty years trying to wipe out all opposition to Czarist autocracy. His successor, Alexander II, was wise enough to abolish serfdom and initiate a series of reforms in government, education, the army, and the legal system—but they were too little and too late.

Many of the revolutionary intelligentsia held the view that Russia was unique in its possession of a peasant landholding system based on the *mir* or *obshchina,* a system under which the land was periodically divided among the villagers according to the size of the family. To many revolutionists, this institution seemed to provide a solid basis for socialism, one that would enable Russia to go from feudalism to socialism without the intervention of a long period of capitalist development. All the intelligentsia had to do was arouse the innate revolutionary fervor of the peasants. Taking Aleksandr Herzen's slogan of *V Narod* (To the People), these so-called Narodniks flocked to the countryside to live with the peasants, to lead them along the path to revolution. The movement was a fiasco. The gulf between the intelligentsia—many of them nobles—and the peasantry was too deep to bridge so easily.

Some of the intelligentsia, disillusioned about the innate revolutionary fervor of the peasant, turned to direct action—terrorism—to overthrow the government. This group, the Narodnaya Volya (The People's Will), stressed the organization and demanded a complete subordination of the individual to the discipline of the group. The climax came in March, 1881, when the Executive Committee of the Narodnaya Volya succeeded in assassinating Alexander II with a bomb. This act, instead of causing the people to rise in revolutionary wrath, horrified them. Popular enthusiasm for the terrorists disappeared. The Narodnaya Volya movement, however, had furthered the tradition of a tightly knit clandestine organization of the revolutionary elite, that had existed as early as 1825.

The Rise of Marxism in Russia

The reaction in Russia evoked by the terroristic activity of the Narodnaya Volya had driven many revolutionists abroad, and one group, under the leadership of Georgi Plekhanov, made its headquarters in Zurich. Plekhanov and his followers shifted their emphasis from the Narodnik concept of revolution by the peasantry to the Marxist doctrine of revolution by the urban proletariat. In the next two decades, Georgi Plekhanov won the revolutionary youth of Russia to Marxism.

Russia was undergoing an intense industrial development

in the last two decades of the nineteenth century, and the attention of everyone, including the revolutionists, was diverted from the country to the city. The burgeoning industrial labor force, interested in unions, dissatisfied with their low wages and poor working conditions, and literate on the whole, seemed made to order for revolution. In contrast, the illiterate peasantry was still a dark and mysterious force, and the revolutionists were still rankled by the rejection of the Narodniks.

The "scientific" aspect of Marxism was another attraction to a generation that worshipped science. In Turgenev's novel *Fathers and Sons,* the character Bazarov personifies this adulation of science and contempt for traditional values. Marxism assured the revolutionists that they were riding the wave of the future, that history had to pass through capitalism to socialism.

Even the police made the path of Marxism easier, for they had developed a theory that the Marxist approach to revolution was "scholarly" and therefore much more tolerable than the terrorism of the Narodnaya Volya type of revolutionist. The Marxist approach also channeled the dislike of the workers against their employers and the capitalists, instead of against the Czar. The publication of Marxist literature, especially in thick, pedantic tomes, would, the Czarist police hoped, have the effect of diverting young people with a revolutionary bent away from the clandestine plotting of violence and draw them into the more open activity of hairsplitting Marxist debates.

The combination of these currents turned the majority of Russia's revolutionists in the direction of the new "scientific" socialism of Marx. The mecca of those who managed a trip abroad was Plekhanov's group in Switzerland, and if there was an authoritative voice among the revolutionists within Russia, that voice was Plekhanov's.

Lenin the Man

Despite Marxism's deflation of the hero in history and its emphasis upon the mode of economic production as the determining factor, in no historical movement have the leaders played a greater role. In the fifty years of Bolshevik history from 1903 to 1953, three personalities determined the course of events. Lenin and Trotsky were towering figures in bringing about the Bolshevik Revolution of 1917 and in establishing the new regime on a firm foundation. Stalin, in turn, by the sheer force of his personality and control of the smoothly running Party machine, directed the course of the Revolution for three decades after Lenin's death and created a state that in many ways mirrored his personal view of the world. To ignore the biographical factors in outlining the growth of Communism in Russia is impossible.

Vladimir Ilyich Ulyanov, better known as Lenin, was born April 22, 1870, in Simbirsk, a small provincial center on the Volga now called Ulyanovsk in honor of its most famous son. His father, a hard-working inspector of schools for the district, rose to the class of hereditary nobility by his ability. His mother came from a petty bourgeois family of German origin. In Lenin's childhood, no discernible conflicts existed. He admired his father and was devoted to his mother, especially after his father's premature death, in 1886. His record as a student was brilliant.

The first event that stands out in Lenin's generally uneventful early life is the execution of his older brother, Aleksandr, for complicity in a plot to assassinate Czar Alexander III in 1887. Lenin's brother was a gifted student who, out of perverted idealism, had joined a conspiratorial group and had become a bomb expert. Just what effect the death of his brother had on young Vladimir is one of the questions that have intrigued his biographers. As a scientific socialist of the Marxist faith, he was bound to decry the inefficiency of trying to swerve the course of history by assassination, but as the brother of one of the conspirators in the long tradition of Russian revolutionary activity, he must have been sympathetic with the revolutionists. Perhaps his brother's death gave Lenin the first impetus for amalgamating Marxism with revolutionary doctrine.

The immediate effect of Aleksandr's execution was to make it almost impossible for Lenin to follow the conventional university career. He did enter the University of Kazan, and by one of the ironies of history, he owed this largely to the recommendation of his headmaster in Simbirsk, who was the father of Aleksandr Kerenski (his future antagonist and head of the Provisional Government in 1917). But within a few months, Lenin was expelled from the university for attending a meeting of a revolutionary character. In reality, with the name Ulyanov, he was a marked man, and only an absolute divorcement from politics could have kept him out of the hands of the police. With the help of his mother, who besieged her dead husband's influential friends in the educational hierarchy, Lenin got permission to study law on his own and take the state examinations. He passed them with honors, but as a young lawyer in the small town of Samara, on the Volga, he was far from successful and soon devoted himself more and more to the study of Marxism and economics.

Lenin's experiences in rural Simbirsk and provincial Samara left him with little enthusiasm for relying on the peasant as the main lever of the coming revolution. His study of Plekhanov and Marx confirmed this conclusion. In the autumn of 1893, Lenin went to St. Petersburg and gravitated almost immediately into an underground Social Democratic group. He soon became one of the leading Marxist revolutionaries in the capital and, in 1895, spent a few months abroad, where he met Plekhanov, the acknowledged fount of Marxist lore for Russians. This re-entry into revolutionary activities brought his arrest by the Czarist police at the end of 1895.

In spite of the notoriety that history has given the Czarist police and Siberian exile, a political prisoner under the imperial regime was almost pampered, in comparison with the treatment later meted out to political prisoners by the Communists. Lenin spent a year in prison in St. Petersburg and three years in Siberia, at Shushenskoe, a small town on the upper Yenisei River near Tannu Tuva, an area that Lenin referred to as "the Siberian Italy." While in prison in St. Petersburg, he managed to obtain a steady flow of books and periodicals, to smuggle out tracts inciting strikes, and to begin his largest work, *The Development of Capitalism in Russia.* In Siberia, Lenin was allowed to complete his book, to marry, and to translate several works, for which he received payment—all this under the "horrors" of the Czarist police system. In reality, the four years that Lenin spent in prison and in Siberia were quiet years of study and writing, and he emerged, in 1900, with his ideas clarified and his revolutionary philosophy almost crystallized.

Iskra and the Tightening of Party Organization

Shortly after his release from Siberia, Lenin went abroad and joined Plekhanov and his group. While in Siberia, Lenin had worked out two programs that he was eager to put into operation: The Social Democrats should have a newspaper, published abroad and smuggled into Russia, which would direct and unify Marxist political action throughout the country; and the revolutionary organization of the group should be greatly improved. The two programs would supplement each other. The secret distributing agents of the paper would at the same time be links in the party organization. Lenin even had a name for the paper, *Iskra* (*The Spark*), derived from Pushkin's line "Out of the spark shall spring the flame." *Iskra* began publication in December, 1900, in Leipzig. To facilitate handling in the underground, it was printed in small type on sheets of onionskin paper. *Iskra* became what Lenin had advocated, the doctrinal fountainhead of the Russian Marxist movement. The loosely organized Social Democratic Party in Russia was given a voice, a source of direction, and a central doctrinal authority.

Lenin still thought that the party organization was much too loose and the members amateurish. He reiterated constantly that a revolutionary movement had no place for dilettantes. Just as he had decided early in his career that the peasant was really a petty bourgeois at heart, he now maintained that trade unionism by itself would become only "petty and inevitably bourgeois." What was needed was a vanguard for the proletariat, which would be drawn largely from the intelligentsia and would consist of professional revolutionaries who would "devote to the revolution not only their spare evenings, but the whole of their lives." [4] This vanguard would rule in the name of the proletariat until the latter was able to undertake the dictatorship for itself. Many of the Marxists, however, advocated a wider conception of party membership, and a series of bitter disputes arose within the editorial board of *Iskra*.

Lenin's fanatical insistence on organization was no spur-of-the-moment tactical move; it was a vital part of his whole strategy. Unlike Marx and Engels, Lenin had little faith that the proletariat would ever realize that the time was ripe for revolution and then automatically respond to that realization. Lenin saw the worker becoming more and more interested in trade unionism and willing to settle for some crumbs from the capitalist table—shorter working days, more wages, and better working conditions. In Lenin's view, only a relatively few workers had the necessary "revolutionary consciousness" to enable them to resist the palliatives offered by trade unionism. This small group would have to be tightly organized in order to act as a vanguard for the proletariat and push the mass along the main road of inevitable historical development.

The dispute within the *Iskra* editorial board came into the open at the Party Congress in 1903. This Congress opened in Brussels, but police pressure forced its removal to London. Lenin took an uncompromising stand on the issue of tight party organization, and with temporary support from Plekhanov, he managed to get a majority of the delegates to support his stand. The opposing minority would not yield, and the Social Democratic Party was split into two wings: Lenin's majority, the Bolsheviks (from the Russian *bol'shinstvo,* "majority"), and the defeated elements, the Mensheviks (from the Russian *menshinstvo,* "minority").

The Communist Party of the Soviet Union, which dates its birth from an obscure meeting in 1898, ought instead to celebrate Lenin's triumph in 1903. Although Lenin's Bolshevik wing became a minority almost immediately after the Congress of 1903, he did attain his goal of building up a tightly organized party of professional revolutionists. During the years of bitter, arid debate and hairsplitting that characterized Russian *émigré* politics from 1903 to 1917, Lenin never allowed this central element of his doctrine to be tampered with, no matter how small the Bolshevik wing became at times. He even resigned from the editorial board of his beloved *Iskra* rather than see his doctrine diluted in a compromise with the Mensheviks, and he fought *Iskra* by founding a new newspaper, *Vyperyod (Forward),* in 1904.

The arguments that the opposing delegates bitterly hurled at each other in London in 1903 were fraught with future significance. Lenin's opponents were justifiably worried about the absolute control his organizational scheme would give to a small nucleus at the center of the party. From this concept of Lenin's developed modern Soviet democratic centralism, which is the flow of all authority from the top down, with the authority at the top being concentrated in as small a group as possible and ultimately residing in one man. After the Congress of 1903, Trotsky, with prophetic insight, summed up the danger inherent in Lenin's doctrine: "The organization of the Party takes the place of the Party itself; the Central Committee takes the place of the organization; and finally the dictator takes the place of the Central Committee."

In the 1920's, even before Lenin's death, Stalin began to take advantage of the theoretical base so conveniently erected, and by the 1930's, he had pushed the theory to its logical conclusion and had become dictator. In their attempts, from 1953 to 1955, to restore the "collective" authority supposedly encompassed in the theory, Stalin's successors foundered miserably. The system is inherently too favorable to dictatorship to be easily diverted.

Lenin's Contributions to Marxism

There was a strong tendency at the end of the nineteenth century to make Marxism more evolutionary and less revolutionary. Bernstein and the revisionists in Germany traveled far along this road, and a similar movement went on among the Russian Marxists in the same period. There was no large labor party in Russia and little expectation of getting social benefits from the Czarist regime, but it was a period of rapidly developing industrialization, and the Russian Marxists were agreed that capitalism would have to bloom luxuriantly in Russia before a proletarian revolution could take place. Temporarily, there was a similarity of interests between the bourgeoisie and the workers; both would gain by the further development of capitalism in Russia.

It was during this period, in 1894, that Peter Struve was able to publish a pro-Marxist, anti-Narodnik work, *Critical Notes on the Problem of the Economic Development of Russia.* This did not mean that all censorship was dead, however, and generally those desiring to publish had to tone down their revolutionary views. The "Legal Marxists" began to expound almost exclusively on the economic struggle, to emphasize the value of trade unions, and to appeal to the liberals. This new "Economism" splintered any unity that had existed in the Russian Marxist movement.

Lenin attacked the "revisionist" group, but eventually realized that organization was not enough. He could not disregard Bernstein's statistically buttressed arguments that pointed out the fallaciousness of Marx's predictions about the course of capitalism's fall. So, boldly rifling the ideas of Hobson, Hilferding, Rosa Luxemburg, and Bukharin, Lenin, in August, 1917, came up with a pamphlet entitled *State and Revolution,* in which he portrayed the contemporary world as in a period of imperialism and monopolistic finance capital. He claimed that this was the highest and last stage of the old capitalistic system; it was also the answer to what had gone wrong with Marx's law of increasing misery for the proletariat.

Production in the advanced capitalist countries had been concentrated in the hands of relatively few industrial giants. The industrial giants had entered into mutual associations and agreements to form monopolies that completely controlled the various branches of industry. Furthermore, there had developed an interlocking of banking and industry that produced finance capital, and a small group of finance capitalists was able to control the economic and political policies of the capitalist countries.

The rise of monopolistic finance capital, on the other hand, led to keen competition for profits, and in this race for profits, capital was exported to underdeveloped areas where cheap raw materials, low wages, and inexpensive land resulted in incredibly high profits. Through the exploitation of peoples of the underdeveloped areas, the pauperization of the proletariat of the advanced capitalist countries was postponed. In other words, the workers of the advanced capitalist countries were temporarily saved because they were living off the proletariat of the underdeveloped countries—a proletariat's proletariat. And in addition, a favored class of highly skilled workers arose, a labor aristocracy, who sold their souls to the bourgeoisie.

Because of the race for profits in the backward areas, all available exploitable regions were staked out by the advanced capitalist states, and by the end of the nineteenth century, the late-comers found nothing available. The desire of the "haves" to hold onto their possessions, and the desire of the "have-nots" to get a redistribution of the exploitable areas, led to armed conflicts that would get rapidly more severe as the twentieth century progressed. The toiling masses of the exploited areas would rise against their exploiters in national-liberation movements and exacerbate the situation. In this way, an era of armed conflicts of ever-mounting severity was bound to bring capitalism to ruin.

Lenin thereby accounted for the apparent vitality of capitalism; he explained away the failure of Marx's law of increasing misery for the worker; and he showed that although capitalism had temporarily evaded destruction, it was inevitably doomed.

Lenin and the Peasant Question

At first, Lenin followed the lead of Plekhanov in his contempt for the role of the peasantry in the coming revolution. This attitude had several bases: Marx had assigned the task of carrying out the revolution to the proletariat and had been wont to refer to the peasantry as immersed in their "rural idiocy"; Plekhanov's experience with the Narodniks in Russia had done nothing to bolster his faith in the revolutionary potentialities of the peasantry; and Lenin himself had seen the ineffectiveness of the Narodnik leaders.

Marx and Plekhanov, however, were "theorists" who relied on history and their observations of contemporary events to derive the laws that would determine the future. Marx called for action, but he also held that the inexorable process of history had doomed capitalism; the seeds of its own destruction were within it. Lenin, on the other hand, was an "activist"; to him, theory was valuable chiefly as a tool to be used to bolster the line of action that circumstances dictated or, even, made possible. This probably explains why Lenin advocated an elite party of professional revolutionaries under centralized direction that could act quickly. It would also account for his flexibility on the peasant problem.

The radical activities of the Russian peasantry in the 1905 Revolution and its aftermath were a revelation to Lenin. As a result, in 1906, at the "Unity" Congress in Stockholm, he called for the nationalization of all land and its distribution to the individual peasants through local peasant committees. It was becoming obvious to Lenin that a successful revolution in Russia would be impossible without the help of the peasantry. Eventually, he began to speak of the revolutionary democratic dictatorship of the proletariat *and the peasantry*. By the middle of 1917, Lenin had moved to the point where he was willing to hold out any bribe to the peasants, and he came up with the famous slogan of "Land to the Peasants," with no governmental restrictions.

Marxism-Leninism in Power

The Bolshevik seizure of power in November, 1917, was in itself a demonstration of Lenin's doctrinal flexibility. According to the traditional Marxian doctrine, the dictatorship of the proletariat would follow the full development of capitalism, and backward Russia was far from being a fully developed capitalist country. Many of Lenin's own followers felt that the Russian Revolution would have to go through its bourgeois development before the dictatorship of the proletariat could ensue. But Trotsky had pointed out some time before, in his thesis of the "permanent revolution," that if the Russian bourgeoisie established itself firmly, it would be able to solve the peasant problem and thereby deprive the small proletariat of its main ally. The solution to the dilemma was to "telescope" the two revolutions and for all intents and purposes skip the bourgeois stage, or at least nip it in the bud before it could establish itself. Initially, Lenin rejected the Trotsky thesis, but by 1917, he had come much closer to Trotsky's idea. After the first revolution, in March, 1917, Lenin saw two revolutions occurring at the same time: one in which the Provisional Government represented the bourgeoisie, and another in which the Soviets represented the masses. The Bolshevik tactic was to get control of the Soviets, concentrate all power in the Soviets, and act as the revolutionary vanguard in carrying out the socialist revolution. Lenin even had the audacity to state that the bourgeois revolution had already run its course. This might be a departure from traditional Marxian doctrine, but it was good strategy for seizing power.

The power so easily won proved harder to maintain, and to maintain it within the confines of Marxian doctrine was even harder. By skipping the bourgeois stage, Lenin had taken a Russia that had little of the plenty that Marx had predicated as necessary for socialism; even the proletariat was only a tiny segment in contrast with the mass of Russian peasantry. Lenin had reversed Marx's process by engineering the political revolution before the completion of the economic revolution; now he had to establish the economic conditions that would make the political revolution viable. During the Civil War, everything had been subordinated to sheer survival, and the so-called War Communism of the period used terrorism as one of its main weapons. By the early part of 1921, it became evident to Lenin that new tactics were needed to solve the ever-worsening economic crisis. With characteristic doctrinal flexibility, Lenin decreed the New Economic Policy, which was referred to as a "strategic retreat." The NEP was a tacit admission that the bourgeois revolution had been far from completed in mid-1917, and that a great deal of economic development was needed before the socialist revolution could be carried to completion. The NEP was, to use a contemporary phrase, the coexistence of petty capitalism for the peasant and the trader with the "commanding heights" of the national economy held by the state. The evidence seems conclusive that Lenin intended this pattern to last for a considerable length of time.

STALINISM

Lenin suffered a stroke at the end of May, 1922, and his tight control of the Party relaxed steadily until his death, in January, 1924. Who was to inherit the mantle of the leader was the great question during the middle 1920's, and the choice narrowed down to Stalin or Trotsky. Stalin finally emerged victorious in 1927 largely because of his ability to manipulate the Party organization as a weapon against Trotsky, for as General Secretary of the Party, Stalin was able to put his men into, and ease Trotsky's adherents out of, the key positions. The Leninist concept of the tightly organized party obedient to direction from the top reached its apogee under Stalin, and Trotsky's prophecy of 1903 that this would lead to a dictator was amply fulfilled.

In his struggle with Trotsky, Stalin could not rely entirely on the organizational weapon; he had to have some ideological arguments around which his followers could rally. The first step was to show that Trotsky was not a true Leninist, and his thesis of the "permanent revolution" provided material for this purpose. Although Lenin had adopted much of Trotsky's thesis in 1917, there were enough Lenin diatribes against it before 1917 to supply Stalin with quotations to buttress his attacks.

As the ideological battle became more intense, Stalin employed the idea of "socialism in one country" as a counter to Trotsky's thesis.

Socialism in One Country

In his *Foundations of Leninism,* published early in 1924, Stalin had asserted that the organization of socialist production in a single country, especially in one as backward as Russia, was impossible. But in his *Problems of Leninism*, published later the same year, he reversed his stand. He now maintained that a complete socialist economy could be established in Russia alone and could be based entirely on Russian resources. This was far from Leninism. Lenin had fought hard in the early years of the Revolution to maintain Bolshevik control in Russia, always, however, with the thought in mind that a Bolshevik-controlled Russia would be a spark to ignite revolutions in the advanced capitalist countries. It was inconceivable to Lenin that an economy of scarcity such as prevailed in Russia could become the basis of a viable socialism without outside help.

Stalin had discovered a winning slogan. By 1924, hope was fading that revolutions in the advanced countries of Europe were just around the corner. European capitalism looked very stable, and a series of unsuccessful revolutionary attempts in Germany had dispirited the Party faithful in Russia. Stalin struck a patriotic chord with his clarion call to forge socialism within Russia and stop counting on uncertain help from abroad. The simplicity of Stalin's thesis was appealing: Industrialize Russia, make it into a going socialist state, and the example alone would help bring on revolutions abroad. A man could be a good Marxist and a patriot at the same time. In contrast, Trotsky's message looked more and more like that of a "rootless cosmopolitan," although that term had not yet been invented.

Stalin, who had been a constant critic of those urging a speeding up of industrialization—he called them "superindustrializers"—made a sudden switch late in 1928, and advocated industrialization as rapidly as possible. Although the NEP had enabled the economy to get on its feet again, Stalin could see little chance of achieving "socialism in one country" on the basis of such a semibourgeois system. And if the new state was to survive in the midst of the capitalist world, it would have to have the means to defend itself, that is, a capacity to produce the heavy goods needed to build a modern army.

The decision to embark upon industrialization at top speed, to lift Russia to the level of the advanced countries, and do this without outside help, made a drastic increase in the authoritarian character of the regime inevitable. There were definite limits to the amount of labor obtainable by appeals to national pride; the vision of a Promised Land for future generations also has its limitations as an incentive. As the opposition grew, or as Stalin thought it was growing, the controls became stricter. After a small-scale purge in 1933, aimed chiefly at technicians, Stalin began to lash out at the opposition in a progressively more ruthless and sweeping manner. Purge followed purge with ever greater severity, reaching unbridled proportions in 1936–38.

Simultaneous with the step-up in industrialization came the collectivization of agriculture. By 1928, it had become evident to Stalin that an agriculture based on 20 million individual peasant households could not support the march to socialism. Lenin's tactic in 1917 of allowing the peasants to break up the large estates had brought many peasants to the Bolshevik side when the Bolsheviks needed help badly, but it was no long-range solution of the agricultural problem. Most of the peasants were barely able to raise enough for their own needs on their small farms, farms that they tilled with crude implements in the same manner as their ancestors. The surplus necessary to feed the urban population was provided mostly by the larger farms of the kulaks. With the acceleration of industrialization, the urban population expanded, bringing a corresponding increase in the food required for the cities. The collectivization of agriculture was Stalin's answer.

The program began modestly enough. It called for the collectivization of about 12 per cent of the crop area and was aimed largely at expropriating the kulaks. For one thing, machinery was not available to collectivize at any higher rate, and in addition, concentrating the attack on the kulaks won over the poor peasants and neutralized the middle ones. Toward the end of 1929, however, the tempo of the campaign was increased drastically, and it was extended to include the large mass of middle peasants. Soon the overwhelming majority of peasants were resisting collectivization, and as their resistance grew, Stalin became more ruthless; open warfare broke out between the peasants and the government. By March, 1930, even Stalin realized that the brutal methods being used to incorporate the peasants into the collective farms were creating such antagonism that the whole program was being negated. For instance, the peasants had been slaughtering animals rather than surrender them to the collectives, and a severe deficiency in draft animals had already been felt. At this point, Stalin published an article entitled "Dizzy with Success," in which he blamed overenthusiastic subordinates for the failures, and he switched from outright brutality to more subtle methods of persuasion. Under these, more than 96 per cent of the peasant households were collectivized by 1940. But the program had been enormously costly. Millions of peasants had been sent to labor camps in Siberia and Kazakhstan, millions had starved to death in man-made famines, and the rest endured their new way of life with sullenness at best.

Brutal and inhuman as collectivization had been, it had succeeded in fitting agriculture into the new industrialization scheme. The change from 25 million individual farms to a relatively small number of collective farms facilitated the collection of grain to feed the growing urban population, and also made it easier to keep down peasant consumption so that a surplus would be available. It also enabled the government to siphon off rural overpopulation and thus man the new industries. At the same time, it removed the threat offered by 20 million little bourgeois units in opposition to socialism and brought the peasant nearer the status of a rural proletariat.

Stalin, in essence, was standing Marxism on its head: He was creating the highly industrialized state after the Revolution; he was creating an ex post facto proletariat. By the late 1930's, Stalin could claim that the foundations for socialism had been laid in the Soviet Union, and in the late 1940's, he could assert that socialism had arrived.

"Sharpening of the Class Struggle"

To Marx's prediction that the state would wither away when the socialist stage was reached, Stalin's answer was simple and probably effective so far as the faithful were concerned. The Soviet Union was a socialist fortress in a capitalist world, and as long as the capitalist encirclement lasted, just so long would the apparatus of the centralized state have to exist. To abolish the state while the Soviet Union was encircled by ravening capitalist powers would be to invite disaster.

The Great Purge of 1936–38 reached such monumental proportions that Stalin sought to explain to the people why, after more than twenty years of living in the environment of the Soviet state, so many were still tainted with the remnants of capitalist philosophy. According to Stalin, the class struggle grew sharper as socialism grew nearer. The enemy, both inside and outside the Soviet Union, grew more desperate. More and more vigilance was necessary.

After World War II, Stalin moved quickly to quash the Soviet population's expectations of more political and cultural liberty. The alliance with the great democracies during the war had weakened the fear of capitalist encirclement. The all-out appeal to patriotism and for self-sacrifice had led the people to anticipate a better life after the war as a reward for their efforts. Instead, Stalin loosed his cultural hatchet man, Zhdanov, and literature, the theater, the cinema, and even science were whipped into conformity with Stalin's interpretation of "socialist realism," a shorthand term for state control of thought. Even the field of linguistics was invaded by Stalin, the "greatest genius of all time," and the scholars had to comply with his dicta on this abstruse subject. Trotsky's Cassandra-like prophecy of 1903 had come to pass completely: The dictator had taken the place of the proletariat, the Party, and the Central Committee. Marxism-Leninism had become what the dictator said it was; his interpretation of doctrine was infallible. In the rare instances when Communist scholars were unable to dredge up texts from the Marxian-Leninist scriptures to support a new policy, Stalin simply created new doctrine.

The "collective leadership" after Stalin's death, and Khrushchev after 1955, discarded much of the Stalinist doctrine. The ideology is at present in a state of flux. Khrushchev was not able to assume Stalin's stature as the high priest of the Communist faith to the degree that the latter had attained in the late 1940's. Khrushchev, in fact, treated doctrinal matters in a rather cavalier fashion. But Mao Tse-tung's stature as an authority in ideological matters, and Tito's constant appeals to the Marxist-Leninist scriptures to justify his deviations, forced Khrushchev to pay more attention to doctrinal matters.

Khrushchev's attack on Stalinism in 1956 gave an added impetus to the growing "nationalism" in the various countries of the Communist bloc. The tendency to look to national interests first, which Tito had started in 1948, became stronger and stronger after 1956. The chief opponent of Khrushchev's anti-Stalin line was Mao Tse-tung—he was in the midst of his "Stalinist period" and here was Khrushchev condemning the policy. In addition, Mao was opposed to Khrushchev's "coexistence" policy. The Chinese Communists wanted Moscow to take a more aggressive line against "foreign imperialism," i.e., the United States. In Mao's opinion, Khrushchev's talk about the necessity of avoiding war weakened the chances of expanding the Communist faith. On the other side, Khrushchev was very dubious about the Chinese experiment with communes, especially when it was hinted in Peking that this was a short-cut to the stage of Communism, and a way of avoiding the Russian path through socialism to Communism.

In June, 1960, at the Romanian Party Congress in Bucharest, the Russians and Chinese compromised their doctrinal differences, at least on the surface. They agreed that a major war was not inevitable, but also stated that there should be no let up in agitation and subversion in the underdeveloped areas of the world. But it was a compromise of expediency, a flimsy bridge across the doctrinal gulf that separated Peking and Moscow.

The doctrinal issue came up again at the meeting of eighty-one Communist Parties, in Moscow, in November–December, 1960, and the declaration that resulted again supported Khrushchev's position. The Chinese were dissatisfied, however, and made their dissatisfaction very evident at the Twenty-second Party Congress, in Moscow, in October, 1961.

The Sino-Soviet split grew wider and wider between 1960 and 1965. The opponents began to accuse each other of deviationism, of heresy. Mao maintained that Khrushchev was as bad as Tito, that they were both "revisionists," that they were no longer Marxist-Leninist revolutionaries. Khrushchev, on the other hand, accused Mao of refusing to move with the times, of being unable to use Leninism as a guide.

When Khrushchev was ousted, the Chinese Communists at first boasted of their role in bringing about his fall. But they were soon disillusioned—the new leaders seemed no more willing to follow the Peking line than Khrushchev had been, and the polemics soon became as bitter as ever.

On September 3, 1965, Lin Piao, Minister of Defense of the People's Republic of China, published a long article in which he summarized Peking's foreign policy—Mao's strategy for the "countryside surrounding the cities" on a global scale—and in which he condemned the Moscow line in no uncertain terms.[5] He accused the "Khrushchev revisionists" of coming to the rescue of U.S. imperialism "just when it was most panic-stricken and helpless in its efforts to cope with the people's war." He accused Moscow of working hand in glove with the United States. The Khrushchev revisionists, he stated, are opposed to the people's war because they: (1) have no faith in the masses; (2) are afraid of the U.S. nuclear blackmail; and (3) are afraid that a people's war may escalate into a world war with nuclear exchanges.

The Sino-Soviet split is a part of the phenomenon of "polycentrism" now plaguing the Communist world. Soon after the Communist "religion" becomes incarnate in a national state, the leaders of the new Communist nation begin to resent the overbearing attitude of either a Moscow or a Peking. Although still Communists, they are also nationalists. Thus, a Romanian leader tends to look with Romanian eyes, but through Marxist spectacles, at the events going on around him. Even the "nonruling" Communist parties—those parties existing in non-Communist countries—have been afflicted by polycentrism. Whatever may be the fate of world Communism in the next few decades, it will never have the monolithic unity it once had under the iron discipline of Stalin.

5

The Government

The government of the U.S.S.R. is a composite of the symbols of democracy and the actual apparatus of a police state. On the symbolic side stands the Constitution, a very liberal document that describes the system of courts, the legislature, and the individual rights of the Soviet citizens. But behind this façade are the real levers of power: the all-powerful Party and the secret police. Through these two instruments of power, absolute control of the U.S.S.R. is concentrated in the hands of a small ruling clique and, ultimately, in the hands of the dictator.

The entire system operates under a formula called "democratic centralism." In theory, this formula provides for the transmission of protests and suggestions from the grass roots—the Party cells in the plants, collective farms, and army units—upward through the Party hierarchy to the top organs. At these heights, the protests and suggestions are supposedly carefully considered and their implications reflected in the decrees and decisions filtered back through the chain of command. Once a decision is made, however, debate is no longer permissible, and the single subject the lower organs may discuss is how best to implement the decision.

In practice, only one route exists in the system, and that is downward. If any discussion is allowed on the lower levels, it is for propaganda purposes. Otherwise, only the "centralism" part of the formula is operative. Decisions are made at the very top—by Stalin alone for many years and probably by Khrushchev alone

Figure II. Structure of the Government of the Soviet Union

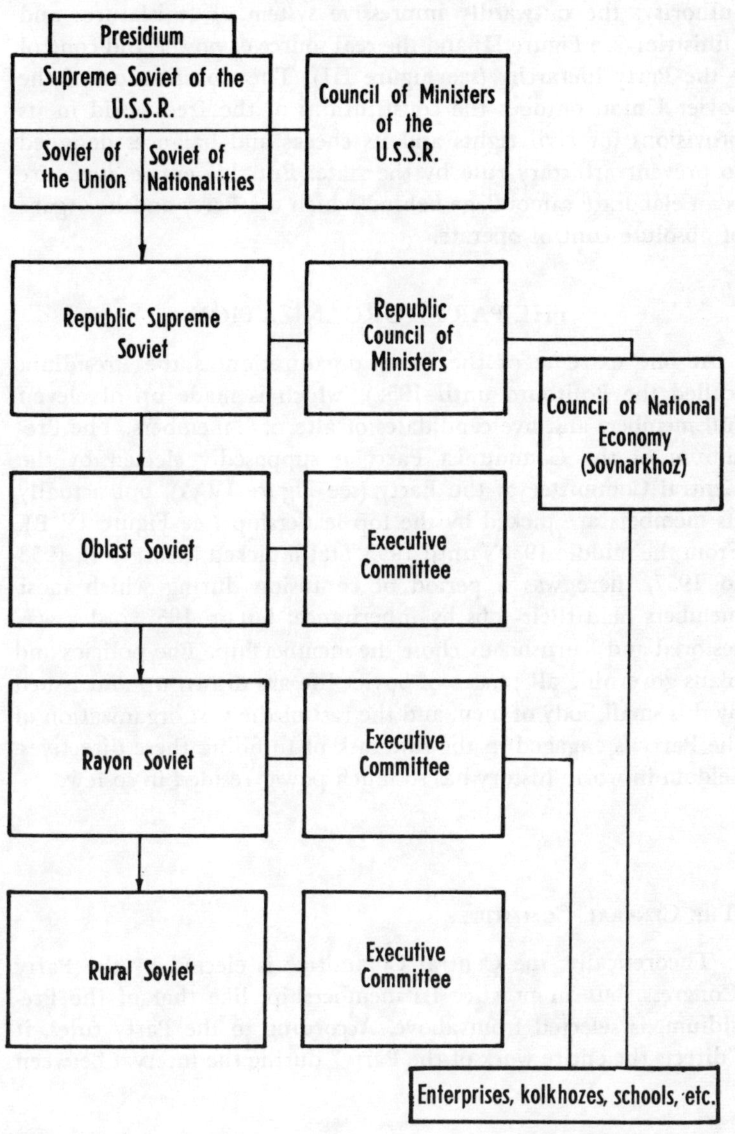

between 1957 and 1964. Who makes the decisions today is a debatable question. These decisions determine the Party line; hence, they are expected to be carried out without question.

The Soviet Government is composed of two separate lines of authority: the outwardly impressive system of legislatures and ministries (see Figure II) and the real source of power and control —the Party hierarchy (see Figure III). The Constitution of the Soviet Union outdoes the constitutions of the free world in its provisions for civil rights and its checks and balances designed to prevent arbitrary rule by the state. But this entire structure is an elaborate camouflage behind which the Party and its organs of absolute control operate.

THE PARTY ORGANIZATION

At one extreme of the Party organization is the Presidium (called the Politburo until 1952), which is made up of eleven full members and five candidates or alternate members. The Presidium of the Communist Party is supposedly elected by the Central Committee of the Party (see Figure IV A), but actually its members are picked by the top leadership (see Figure IV B). From the middle 1930's until 1953, Stalin picked them; from 1953 to 1957, there was a period of confusion during which most members held their jobs by inheritance; but in 1957, order was restored and Khrushchev chose the membership. The policies and plans governing all phases of Soviet life are drawn up and issued by this small body of men, and the rest of the vast organization of the Party is engaged in the sole task of fulfilling these directives. Seldom in world history has so much power resided in so few.

The Central Committee

Theoretically, the Central Committee is elected by the Party Congress, but in practice its membership, like that of the Presidium, is selected from above. According to the Party rules, it "directs the entire work of the Party" during the interval between

Figure III. Organization of the Communist Party of the Soviet Union

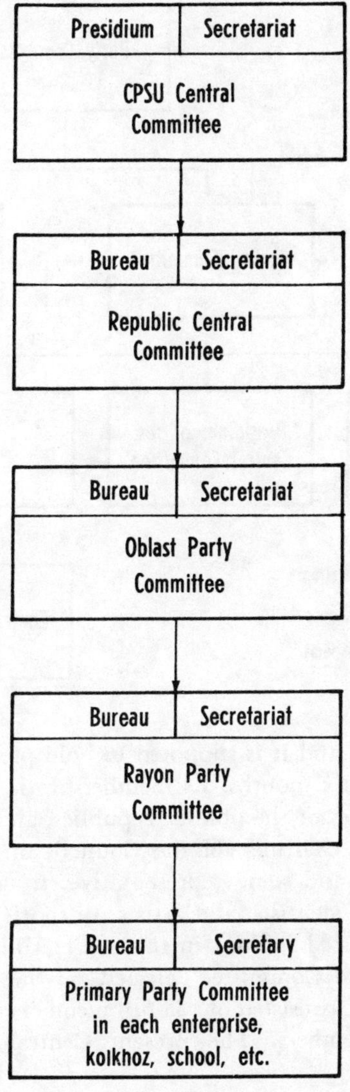

Figure IV A. Theoretical Flow of Authority in Communist Party

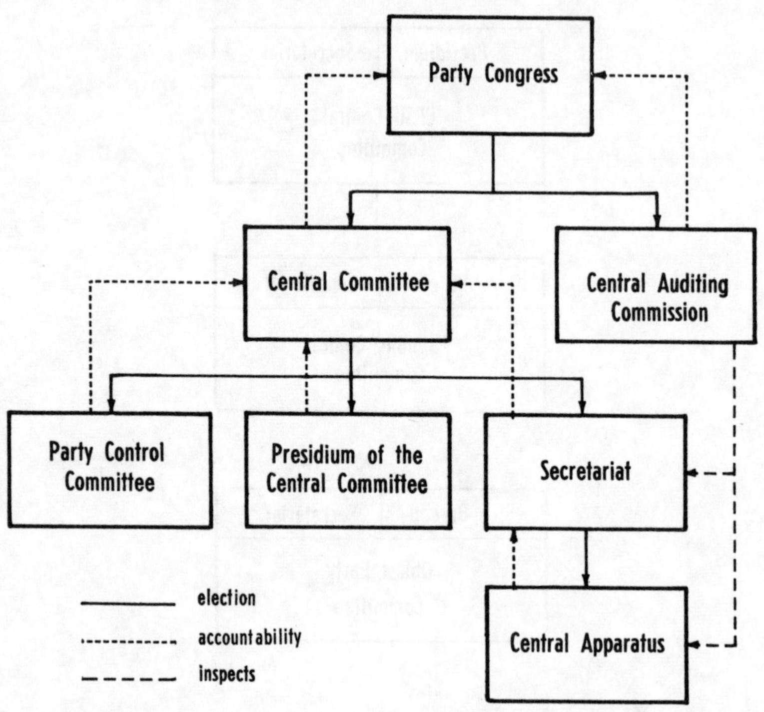

Party Congresses, and it is supposed to hold plenary meetings at least once every six months. Its membership is made up largely of Party secretaries of the oblasts, republics, and regions, a number of ministers, chairmen of the Councils of Ministers of the union republics, and some representatives from among the top military leaders, scientists, and artists. In short, it represents the groups with a vested interest in the Soviet Union in its present state. The Central Committee "elected" at the Twentieth Party Congress, in 1956, consisted of 133 full members and 122 alternate or candidate members. The present Central Committee, an-

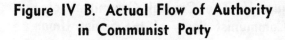

Figure IV B. Actual Flow of Authority in Communist Party

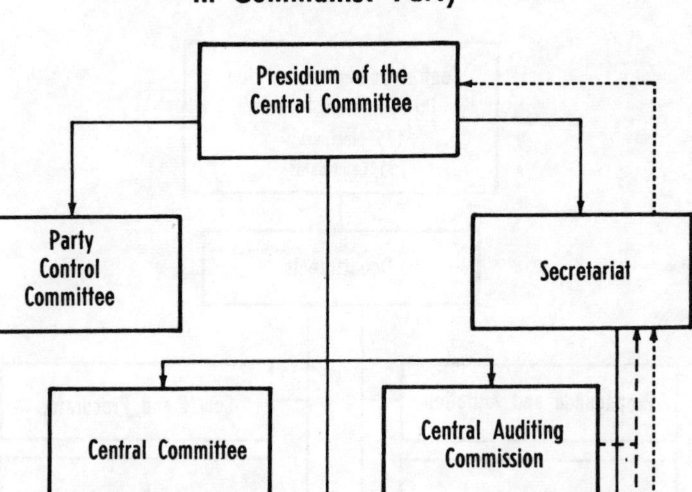

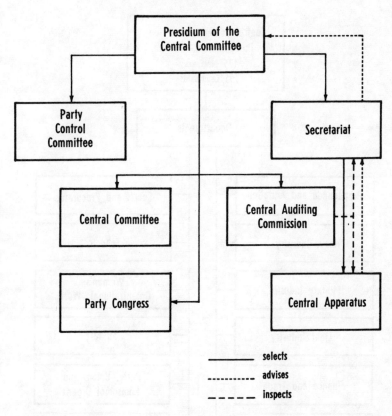

nounced at the Twenty-second Congress, in 1961, is the largest in Soviet history: 175 full members and 155 alternates (see Figure V).

The meetings, activities, and authority of the Central Committee were long shrouded in mystery and unreported in the press. It seemed to be a body concerned solely with casting an aura of legality about the actions of the boss and his friends in the Presidium. But in June, 1957, Khrushchev called in the Central

Figure V. The Central Committee of the Communist Party of the Soviet Union

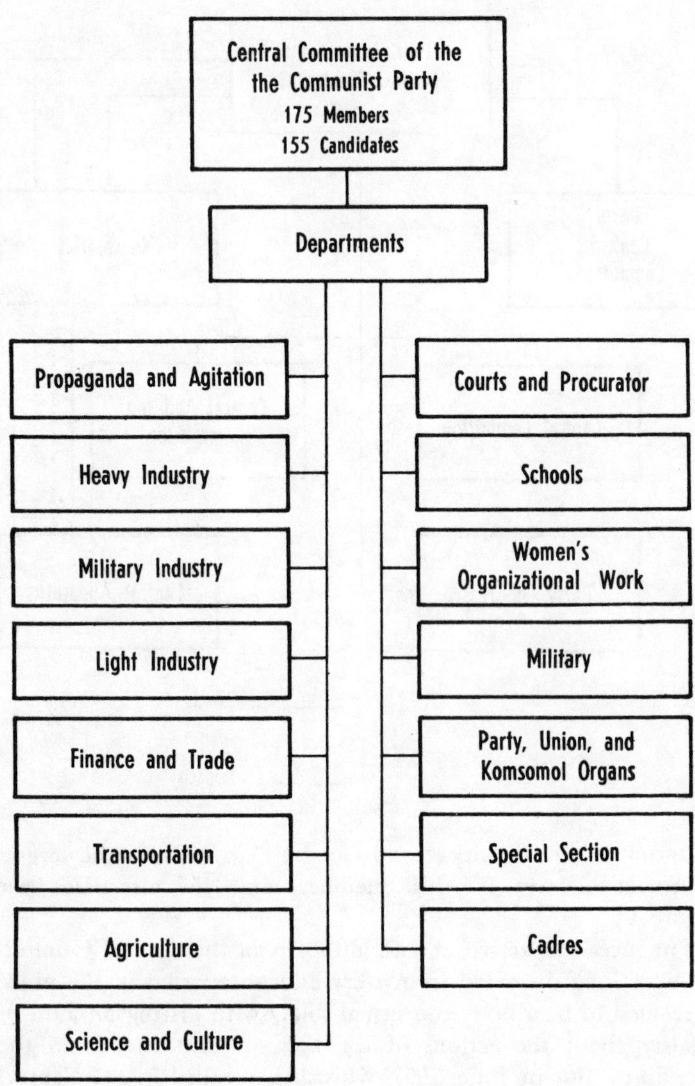

Committee to override a decision against him in the Presidium. The maneuver worked—probably with the backing of Zhukov and the army—and as a result, Malenkov, Kaganovich, Molotov, and Shepilov were cast out.

Khrushchev, it would seem, strengthened the power of the Central Committee too much while he was eliminating the power of the army, the secret police, and the bureaucracy. When the Party leaders decided to dispense with his leadership in 1964, he had no other pillar of power to depend on. The Party had become his only source of power; with the source cut off, he was out.

During the Khrushchev era, plenums of the Central Committee were convened much more often than the twice a year specified by Party rules. They were convened to oust Khrushchev's political opponents, to legitimize Khrushchev's numerous organizational changes, to abolish the MTS, to approve speeding up the development of the chemical industry, and to attend to other Khrushchevian "harebrained" schemes too numerous to mention. In many of these plenums, Khrushchev brought in hordes of outside specialists to overawe the members of the Central Committee, a practice that influenced many of the members in their repudiation of his leadership in October, 1964.

The Party Secretariat, theoretically subordinate to the Central Committee, is composed of the First Secretary of the Party, now Brezhnev, and a varying number of Secretaies. Stalin derived much of his power from his position as General Secretary of the Party, and Khrushchev gained his ascendancy as First Secretary of the Party. Brezhnev, too, seems to be basing his power primarily on his position as First Secretary. The Secretariat directs the day-to-day activities of the Party machine and plays a large role in the selection of personnel in lower-echelon Party jobs.

Prior to 1962, the Central Committee used a subordinate organ, the Party Control Committee, to act as its eyes and ears in matters of discipline throughout the lower echelons of the Party. The Control Committee had representatives in the local Party organs in the republics, oblasts, and regions. These agents were independent of the local bodies and responsible only to headquarters. However, a plenum of the Central Committee, in November, 1962, merged the Party Control Committee with the State Control Committee to form a new organ, the Party-State Control Committee. The new body was intended to cope with the growing problem of embezzlement, corruption, and waste. It was to have representatives in the republics, oblasts, and regions, just as the former Party Control Committee had, but its investigatory powers were to embrace government as well as Party matters. The Party-State Control Committee was headed by Alexander N. Shelepin, at one time chief of the KGB, but on December 9, 1965, it was announced that Shelepin would henceforth concentrate on his activities within the Central Committee of the Party and that the Party-State Control Committee would be renamed the People's Control Committee.

The Party Congress

In Soviet mythology, all the powers of the Presidium, the Central Committee, and the Secretariat flow from the Party Congress. Originally it was scheduled to meet every three years, but as Stalin consolidated his power, the intervals between meetings grew longer. The Sixteenth Congress met in 1930, the Seventeenth in 1934, the Eighteenth in 1939, and the Nineteenth in 1952. The new rules drawn up at the Nineteenth Congress made it mandatory that Party Congresses convene at least every four years, and the Twentieth Congress met on schedule, in 1956. In January, 1959, the Twenty-first Party Congress was assembled to give its approval to Khrushchev's new Seven-Year Plan. The Twenty-second Congress, which was held in October, 1961, elected a new Central Committee, approved Khrushchev's program for the Communist Party's future course, and witnessed a bitter dispute between Khrushchev and the Chinese Communists.

At the Twenty-first Congress, there was one voting delegate for every 6,000 Party members, and one nonvoting delegate for every 6,000 candidate members of the Party. The number of delegates elected to the Twenty-second Party Congress (4,408 voting delegates and 405 nonvoting delegates) was more than three times the number elected to the Twenty-first Congress. There was one voting delegate for every 2,000 Party members and one nonvoting delegate for every 2,000 candidate members. Since the delegates are carefully chosen by the top echelon of the Party for their reliability, there is little danger of any undirected initiative being generated by them. In reality, the Party Congress is a large chorus periodically gathered to chant a loud *da* to any and all changes, policies, and plans put before it by the Presidium of the Party.

Figure VI. Organs of Authority in the Oblasts

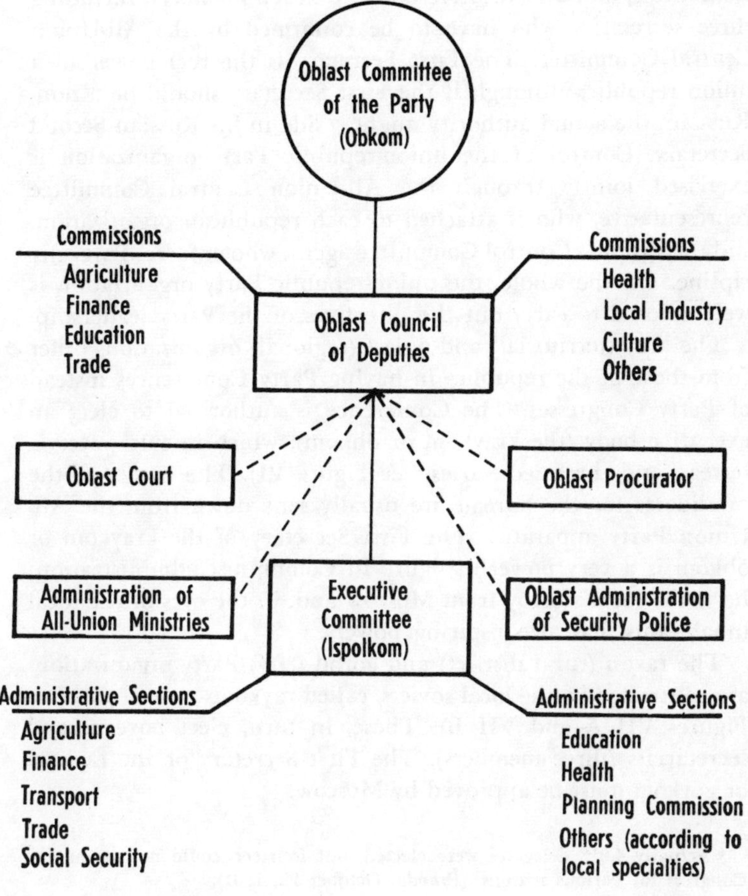

To the 4,799 delegates who assembled in October, 1961, at the Twenty-second Congress,* the chief attraction was a free trip to Moscow and an opportunity to attend the rites and ceremonies associated with the convocation of this body.

The Lower Party Organs

The Party organization of the union republics closely resembles the All-Soviet organization. Each has its Party Congress, Central Committee, and an executive body of eleven members, including three secretaries who have to be confirmed by the All-Union Central Committee. The First Secretary is the real power in a union republic, although if the First Secretary should be a non-Russian, the actual authority might reside in his Russian Second Secretary. Control of the union-republic Party organization is exercised jointly through the All-Union Central Committee representative, who is attached to each republican organization, and the People's Control Committee agent, who enforces Party discipline. On the whole, the union-republic Party organization is well tailored to carry out the directives of the Party leadership.

The kray (territorial) and oblast (regional) organizations differ from those of the republics in having Party Conferences instead of Party Congresses. The Conference is authorized to elect an executive body (the kraykom or obkom), which in turn elects a bureau and three secretaries (see Figure VI). The names of the candidates for the bureau are usually sent down from the All-Union Party apparatus. The First Secretary of the kraykom or obkom is a very powerful figure in Communist administration; he is the local viceroy from Moscow and, in the eyes of the local inhabitants, has awe-inspiring powers.

The rayon (rural district) and gorod (city) Party organizations are controlled by the local soviets, called raykoms or gorkoms (see Figures VII A and VII B). These, in turn, elect bureaus and secretariats (three members). The First Secretary of the raykom or gorkom must be approved by Moscow.

* Actually 4,813 delegates were elected, but fourteen could not attend the Congress for various reasons (*Pravda,* October 22, 1961).

Figure VII A. Organs of District (Rayon) Authority

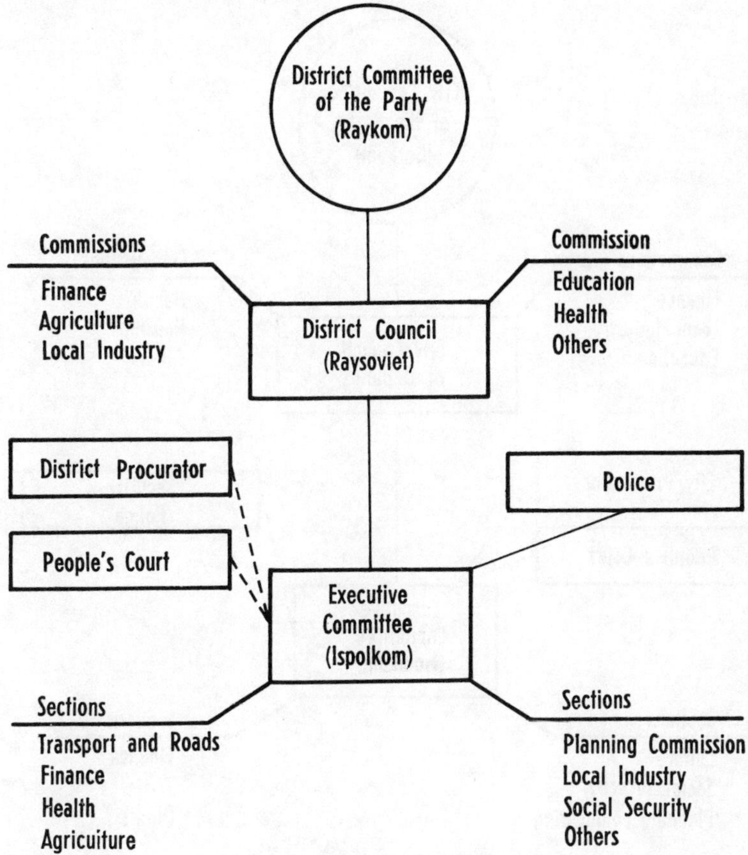

Below the level of the city and district Party organizations are approximately 300,000 Party units, or cells. These are primary units, and any enterprise or institution having at least three Party members can organize a cell. Even the first Soviet polar drifting station, North Pole 1, had a Party cell and conducted meetings during its drift about the Arctic Basin. If there are no

Figure VII B. Organs of City (Gorod) Authority

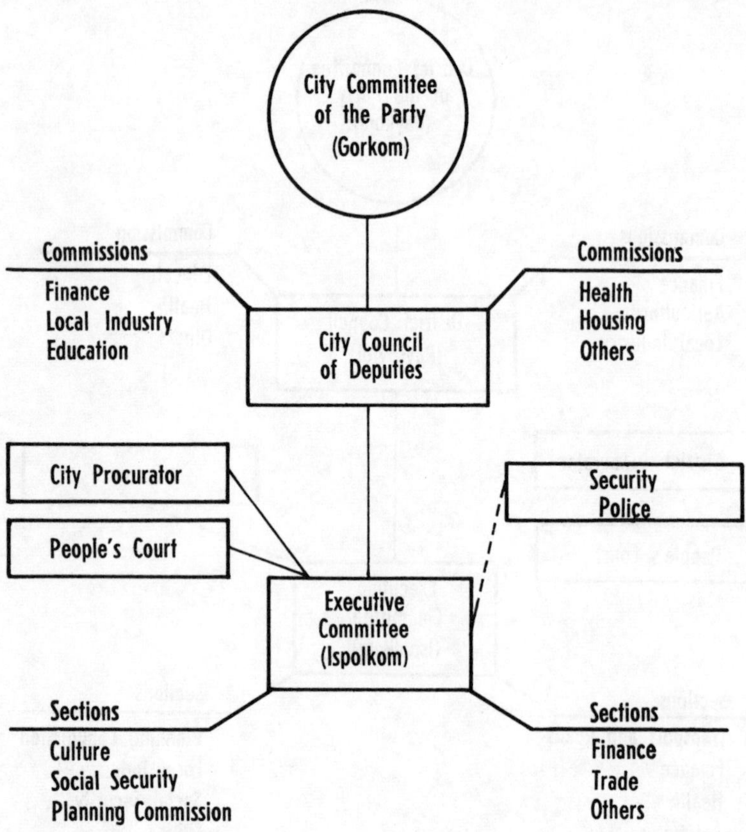

more than 100 members, the bureau and secretary are not exempt from their regular jobs and must serve without pay. If there are over 100 members, the Party secretary is a full-time, paid Party official. The job of the Party cell is to conduct Party education, recruit new members, and create enthusiasm for the Party objectives—usually more and better production.

THE NON-PARTY STRUCTURE OF THE SOVIET UNION

The "official" government of the Soviet Union consists of a complex hierarchy of legislatures, ministries, and courts. The prerogatives and duties of these governmental organs are spelled out in detail in the Constitution of the U.S.S.R. To anyone who might be unaware that it is merely a façade behind which the Party manipulates the state, the structure would be impressive. Although the titular head of the Soviet state is the Chairman of the Presidium of the Supreme Soviet, this office has usually been held by a relatively powerless member of the Politburo, such as Kalinin, Shvernik, or Voroshilov. In the last few years, however, first Brezhnev and then Mikoyan held this job, and nobody would describe either of them as being relatively powerless. The present incumbent is Nikolai V. Podgorny, former First Secretary of the Ukrainian Communist Party, who replaced Mikoyan on December 9, 1965.

The Supreme Soviet

Article 30 of the Constitution of the U.S.S.R. states that the Supreme Soviet is the "highest organ of state power in the U.S.S.R." This is pure fiction, of course. Although the Party Congresses uncritically endorse the motions put before them, they do at least represent local power. But the delegates to the Supreme Soviet have very little power locally and even less to say about the bills that they ratify. The Supreme Soviet is merely window dressing behind which the Party operates.

The Supreme Soviet is made up of two houses: the Soviet of the Union, with one deputy for each 300,000 inhabitants; and the Soviet of Nationalities, with twenty-five deputies from each union republic, eleven from each autonomous republic, five from each autonomous region, and one from each national district (see Figure VIII). The deputies are elected for four years and are scheduled to assemble twice a year. If the houses disagree, the Presidium of the Supreme Soviet can dissolve them and order new elections. To date, they have never disagreed, nor are they ever likely to.

Figure VIII. Soviet of Nationalities

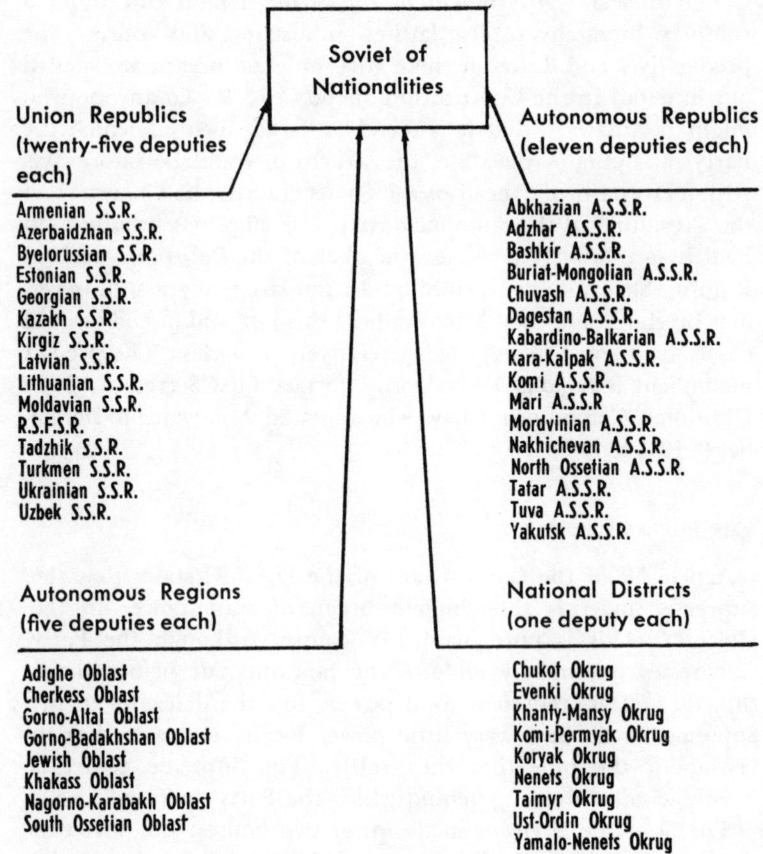

The elections of deputies to the Supreme Soviet is a major attempt of the Party to portray the Soviet Government as democratic and popular. Everybody eligible to vote is dragooned to the polls, including the halt and the blind. But, usually, there is only one candidate to vote for, and over three-quarters of the candidates selected are Party members. Needless to say, the non-Party members who are allowed to run for office are very reliable from the Party's point of view.

The Supreme Soviet, according to the Constitution, "exercises all rights vested in the Union of Soviet Socialist Republics in accordance with Article 14 of the Constitution," which lists twenty-four rights extending from questions of war and peace to issuing acts of amnesty.

Presidium of the Supreme Soviet

Between sessions of the Supreme Soviet, its powers are vested in the Presidium of the Supreme Soviet. This body is elected at a joint meeting of both houses and is made up of thirty-four members: a Chairman, a Secretary, fifteen Deputy Chairmen, and seventeen members. The term of office is four years. The Constitution states that the Presidium of the Supreme Soviet has the power to convene and dissolve the Supreme Soviet, appoint and discharge ministers on the recommendation of the Council of Ministers, interpret the laws of the U.S.S.R., ratify treaties, proclaim martial law, mobilize the armed forces, and declare war when the Supreme Soviet is not in session.

Of course, most of these powers and duties exist only in the realm of theory. The streamlined operation of this totalitarian state would be thrown out of kilter if the Supreme Soviet ever tried to exercise its constitutional rights. In the equally unlikely event that the Presidium of the Supreme Soviet should be authorized to govern, the unwieldy body, unused as it is to authority, would have great difficulty in acting effectively.

The Presidium of the Supreme Soviet confines itself to issuing state awards to outstanding workers, prolific mothers, and deserving civil servants; it announces changes in the top personnel of the government, and its ukases on these topics help fill the front page of *Pravda*.

THE COUNCIL OF MINISTERS

Article 64 of the Constitution states that the Council of Ministers is "the highest executive and administrative body of the State power in the U.S.S.R." In Article 65, it is described as accountable to the Supreme Soviet or to the Presidium of the Supreme Soviet. The Council of Ministers resigns *in toto* when a new Supreme Soviet convenes; however, its members are all re-elected immediately unless the powers that be decide to drop some of them. Under the Constitution, the Council of Ministers has the authority to supervise the operations of the ministries, to direct the national economic planning, to conduct foreign affairs, and to control the armed forces.

The Council is made up of a Chairman (at present, Kosygin), First Deputy Chairmen, Deputy Chairmen, ministers, heads of committees, and other important officials. There are more than sixty members in the Council. Authority in the Council of Ministers lies in its Presidium, which is composed of the Chairman, the First Deputy Chairmen, the Deputy Chairmen, and a few top-ranking ministers.

There is little doubt that major policies emanate from the Presidium of the Central Committee and that the Presidium of the Council of Ministers merely carries them out. But there is probably a good deal of give and take between the two organs in the process of arriving at new policies. The fact that Kosygin is a leading member of both bodies must help smooth out the transmission of policies from one to the other. The new policies and governmental directives are issued as decrees (*postanovleniya*) of the Council of Ministers and are signed by Kosygin, as Chairman, or by one of the First Deputies, acting for him. Decrees of the Council of Ministers are binding as law on all in the Soviet Union.

Below the policy-making level, the Council of Ministers plays a very important role in the operation of the Soviet Government. It functions through sixteen ministries, numerous state committees, and several agencies. These ministries, committees, commissions, and administrations enable the Presidium of the Council to coordinate and direct the economic, cultural, and political life of the nation.

There are two types of ministries: the all union, which directly administers its subordinate plants and activities regardless of where they are located in the Soviet Union, and the union republic, which operates through counterpart ministries in the republics. For example, the Ministry of Transport Construction is all union and has direct control over construction of all transportation facilities throughout the U.S.S.R., but the Ministry of Agriculture, a union-republic ministry, works mainly through the agricultural ministries of the various republics. The Minister is assisted by a First Deputy Minister and several Deputy Ministers, and they together form a presidium, or collegium. Below them are the directorates and departments in charge of the different activities of the ministry.

The State Committees are usually coordinating bodies that supervise the work of other agencies engaged in some broad field of activity. Among these committees, the State Planning Committee (Gosplan) stands out in authority and importance. The Committee for State Security (KGB) is the main police force of the Soviet Union.

In addition, the Council of Ministers has under it such agencies as the Central Statistical Administration and the State Scientific-Economic Council, which coordinates research on technical matters, especially as it applies to the fulfillment of the economic plans.

LOWER GOVERNMENT ORGANS

The union republics have a one-chamber Supreme Soviet, a Presidium, and a Council of Ministers. The main task of these organs is not to look out primarily for the welfare of their republics, but to see to it that the over-all policies of the Soviet Union are properly executed.

The autonomous republics have very similar organizations, but on a much smaller scale. Most autonomous republics have little in the way of heavy industry and, therefore, do not need large Councils of Ministers.

The oblasts, krays, rayons, and cities have Soviets elected for two years and Executive Committees (*ispolkoms*), which are theoretically responsible to them. The *ispolkom*, however, is very likely to be the real power, and the Soviet only a legal screen.

CONTROLS

The complexity of organization in the U.S.S.R. has made relatively efficient operation difficult. This problem is aggravated by the tendency of "selfish" local interest to pursue their own ends, to the detriment of the over-all government plans. Over the forty years of Soviet experience, a system of controls has emerged that acts as the eyes and ears of the top Soviet hierarchy. These agencies operate in both the economic and political spheres of Soviet life—spheres which are much more closely welded together than in the capitalist countries. Where the political begins and the economic ends is difficult to determine when dealing with the Soviet Union, which approaches a closely supervised industrial enterprise on a national scale.

In an arbitrary breakdown, the Soviet controls can be considered in the following categories: (1) the Party, (2) the secret police, (3) financial controls (Gosplan and Ministry of Finance), (4) the People's Control Committee, and (5) legal controls.

THE PARTY

The Communist Party of the Soviet Union makes no pretense of being other than a very elite group * whose mission is to propagate any line decided upon by the latest Kremlin interpretation of the gospel of Marx and Lenin. As a member of the elite group, the Party member gains certain privileges, but he also takes on heavy obligations. He must pay Party dues, attend lectures and study courses, act as an agitator and ward heeler, and constantly spur on non-Party workers to fulfill the Party's economic, social, and political programs. As far back as 1903, Lenin described the role of the Bolshevik as a tightly controlled, obedient, twenty-four-hour-a-day worker in the cause of Marxism and revolution. Of course, all Bolsheviks do not live up to these

* In 1961 there were 8,872,516 Party members and 843,489 candidates—9,716,005 in all. On January 1, 1965, the official figures for the Party membership were 10,811,443 members and 946,726 candidate members, or a total of 11,758,169. *Partiynaya Zhizn* (*Party Life*), No. 10 (May, 1965), p. 8. Inasmuch as the official figure for the population of the U.S.S.R. on January 1, 1965, was 229,100,000, this meant that over 5 per cent belonged to the Party, demonstrating a widening of the Party base in recent years.

demands, but the dedicated members give the Party an effective instrument for carrying out the government's policies.

The close-knit Party hierarchy, from the Presidium of the Central Committee down to the smallest cell, makes an ideal channel for transmitting orders from the top to the bottom throughout the length and breadth of the U.S.S.R.—and abroad as well. Every plant, collective farm, and army unit has its Party group, which keeps alert for signs of deviation and which strives to spur the fulfillment of current Party goals.

The Secret Police

Scouting out deviation, however, is not left entirely in the unspecialized hands of the average Party member. Behind the façade of monolithic Party unity, there has always been a tendency for heresies to arise, for cliques to form, and for dissident groups to develop. To deal with this problem, a vast secret-police system soon came into being.

The police not only ferret out and destroy any heresy in Party membership, but they are indispensable in keeping the nose of the Soviet people to the grindstone and in extracting universal obedience to the state. Immediately upon coming into power, the Bolsheviks found that as a minority group they needed terror to keep their subjects in line. The Cheka deliberately used terror tactics to immobilize or eliminate all opposition to the regime. In 1922, this organization was given a new name, the GPU (State Political Administration), but its functions did not differ an iota from that of its bloody predecessor. Since then, the secret police have had several names, but always the same function—uncovering real or imaginary opposition to the regime. Designated in the 1930's as NKVD (People's Commissariat of Internal Affairs), it gained world-wide infamy as the agency in charge of the Great Purges.

The secret police has been the bludgeon with which the Soviet regime has cowed and beaten its subjects into conformity with its plans. It has always lurked in the immediate background ready to pounce upon anyone suspected of deviationism, wrecking, or sabotage. These terms have special meanings in Soviet jargon. "Deviationism" is any straying from the Party line, and if the line changes, those who do not change fast enough are guilty of deviationism. The Soviet subject cannot stand still and remain safe. "Wrecking" and "sabotage" usually refer to sins in the economic sphere. Managers who are inefficient, who make mistakes in judgment, who are assigned quotas beyond the capacities of their enterprise, or who fail to receive necessary materials are often charged with wrecking and sabotage. Another task of the secret police has been to supply the large pools of forced labor needed in those areas shunned by free labor.

After World War II, two secret police forces replaced the NKVD. The MVD (Ministry of Internal Affairs) devoted itself largely to the supplying and managing of forced labor, while the MGB (Ministry of State Security) concerned itself with the traditional security tasks of ferreting out heresy, breaches in army security, and espionage, and guarding the frontiers of the Soviet Union—primarily to keep the population inside. After Stalin's death, in 1953, the MGB assumed a new name, the KGB (Committee for State Security). A slight lowering of prestige accompanied its reduction from the status of a ministry.

Since the downfall of Beria, and Khrushchev's bloodcurdling revelations concerning the Great Purge, the secret police has lost much of its prestige, but it remains an essential part of the totalitarian state and acts as a bulwark against the formation of either overt or covert opposition.

Financial Controls

The top elite of the Soviet Communist Party is, in the words of Milovan Djilas, former vice president of Yugoslavia under the Tito regime, a "new class." This "new class obtains its power, privileges, ideology, and its customs from one specific form of ownership—collective ownership—which the class administers and distributes in the name of the nation and society." [1] Although this is an oversimplification, nevertheless, following this analogy, the owners of Soviet business—the Communist elite—have every incentive to increase the worth of their holdings. The terror engendered by the secret police and the evangelical exhortations of the Party faithful are not enough to keep Soviet business operating in the black. Reporting to the Eleventh Party

Congress, in 1922, Lenin stated in unequivocal terms that the Communists must learn to trade, must learn from the "ordinary salesmen [who] have had ten years' warehouse experience and know the business. . . ." From 1922 to 1928, the NEP period, the Communist elite literally went to school to learn their new profession, namely, how to run a huge nation as one national business.

Once the Five-Year Plans had begun, from 1928 on, one of the big problems facing the Soviet leaders was just what branches of industry should be developed, where investment capital should be placed. There was no question of choice between consumers' goods and heavy industry; the latter was regarded as a *sine qua non*. As Lenin put it as early as November, 1922: "Unless we save heavy industry, unless we restore it, we shall not be able to build up any industry; and without heavy industry we shall be doomed as an independent country. . . ." Stalin wanted heavy industry both for the reason given by Lenin and because it alone could make the Soviet Union a potent military power. But within heavy industry itself, there were alternatives.

Gosplan

To solve these difficulties, the Soviet leaders established an intricate planning mechanism based on five-year periods and a system of control groups to set up feasible goals, to offer guidance toward the accomplishment of those goals, to reward managers overfulfilling their quotas, and to penalize the laggards. The main organ within the control structure was Gosplan (State Planning Commission), the rudiments of which had been laid down as early as February 22, 1921, when it was assigned the task of "working out a single general State economic plan as well as the means and order for its fulfillment." Its functions were further defined by a statute in August, 1923, and in 1938, it became a permanent, eleven-member commission under the Council of Ministers (called the Council of People's Commissars at that time). Gosplan developed into a powerful instrument with which the Soviet leaders could manipulate the economy. Its duties were to plan the long-term, yearly, and quarterly goals of the entire economy, to keep track of progress, and to reward or punish, depending upon achievement. In 1948, Gosplan was raised from commission to committee rank, becoming the State Planning Committee. It would be hard to overestimate the importance of Gosplan in both the planning and supervision of the national economy. Its power has grown steadily since 1921, and Khrushchev's moves toward the decentralization of the economy, strangely enough, gave Gosplan an even larger role in the Soviet economy.

Ministry of Finance

The unified budget of the U.S.S.R. includes all the local and central budgets; it is approved by the Supreme Soviet and the Council of Ministers and then turned over to the control of the Ministry of Finance. This ministry is in charge of the banking system that grants all long- and short-term loans to enterprises for current operations and expansion. Such loans are based on the balance sheets of the enterprises, and the Ministry of Finance assigns its own inspectors to check on the validity of the records.

People's Control Committee

Since the earliest days of the Soviet regime, there have been agencies whose task is to check on how efficiently the Party and government officials carry out their assignments. At times there have been two agencies, one for the Party and one for the government; at other times the agencies have been merged into a unified organ. Stalin, with his penchant for playing one group against another, kept them divided, and they remained so until the November, 1962, plenum of the Central Committee unified them into the Party-State Control Committee.

At this plenum, Khrushchev told the Central Committee that the pilfering and embezzlement of state property had become intolerable. The new organization, working closely with the local Party authorities, the Komsomol, and the trade unions, was to stamp out the prevalent corruption and theft.

Alexander N. Shelepin, former chief of the KGB, was appointed to head the Party-State Control Committee and was made a member of the Secretariat of the U.S.S.R. Central Committee. At the time, some observers thought that Shelepin was Khrushchev's personal agent and that his new job gave him tremendous power, for his agency could collect complaints against any state or Party official. Shelepin, however, apparently deserted his patron in the October, 1964, crisis and opted for the Brezhnev-Kosygin team. He was rewarded by an appointment to the Presidium. However, the fact that he was in the Presidium probably meant that the Party-State Control Committee had come under the firm control of the Presidium as a whole. The agency was too powerful to leave in the hands of one man without adequate supervision by the top echelon of the Party.

Early in December, 1965, Shelepin was removed from his position as head of the Party-State Control Committee and the name of the organization was changed to People's Control Committee. Apparently, the committee will confine its activities to governmental matters and no longer act as a watchdog over Party affairs.

Legal Controls

Like any other complex society, the Soviet Union has a legal system, laws, and enforcement agencies. Because of the fierce tempo of industrial development and the tight control of consumption, the laws of the Soviet Union are more complex, more closely interwoven—politically, socially, and economically—and more rigidly enforced than are laws in most capitalist states.

The hierarchy of courts ranges from the Supreme Court of the U.S.S.R. and the Supreme Courts of the union republics, elected by the Supreme Soviets of the U.S.S.R. and the union republics, down to the People's Courts, elected by the citizens of the rayons. The whole elaborate procedure is described in Articles 102 through 112 in the Constitution of the U.S.S.R. Article 112, which states that "judges are independent and subject only to the law," must have been grimly humorous to the millions of Soviet citizens condemned in the secret-police tribunals in the last four decades.

More to the point in controlling various ministries is the system headed by the Procurator-General of the U.S.S.R. Appointed by the Supreme Soviet for a seven-year term, he has "supreme supervisory power to ensure the strict observance of the law by all ministries and institutions subordinate to them." He in turn appoints procurators for the republics, krays, and oblasts, and approves the procurators selected by rayons and cities. The procurators supervise the courts, prevent state organizations from exceeding their powers, and serve as public prosecutors. They carry out their functions independent of any local organs and are subordinate only to the Procurator-General of the U.S.S.R. Until recently, however, they have had little control over the secret police, although the office of Procurator was founded in 1933 partly to supervise the legality of the activities of the GPU.

6

The Leadership

There has always been support for the belief that a small, tightly organized group is more effective than a large, amorphous body. From its very inception, the Bolshevik Party has followed this policy, and Lenin's adamant stand at the Second Congress of the All-Russian Social Democratic Labor Party, in 1903, was precisely on the issue of a small, elite party versus one with a broader, looser organization. From 1903 until the present, the Leninist concept of the Party as a minority group guiding the overwhelming majority has prevailed wherever Communism has gained a foothold. Even within the select Party, there is a hierarchical structure that pyramids ever smaller echelons of administrators up to the center of authority—the *vozhd*, or dictator.

Throughout the history of the Bolshevik Party, the criteria for the selection of the ruling elite have changed with the fortunes of the Party. The idealistic revolutionists of the October victory, internationalist in outlook and training, gave way to the more conservative operators of the NEP period. Stalin made the organization an end in itself by the late 1920's and transformed it into his own image by the 1930's. The era of planned economy and socialism in one country called for, not only administrators versed in the intricacies of industrial management, but also Party men, obedient to the every whim of the *vozhd*. Fertile and independent minds of the Trotsky stamp were anomalies in this bustling, cruel, and regimented milieu, and in the Great Purge of 1936–38, the Old Bolshevik type was eliminated.

Paradoxes existed even in the Stalinist world, however. The

efficient professional needed to build and operate industrial plants and the professional soldier indispensable to an effective army were often in conflict with the Party's insistence on absolute obedience. The Party would first urge one-man control, *yedinonachalie,* in industry, and then crush those who went so far as to put industrial efficiency ahead of obedience to the ever-shifting Party line.

In the post-Stalin era, the criteria of leadership have also been ambivalent. Some Sovietologists have described the role of the emerging "managerial elite"—the professional in science, in the armed forces, in industry, and even in the arts—and have seen the gradual triumph of this group over the ossified Party leaders who no longer have any contribution to make to the progress of the Soviet Union. The Twenty-second Congress gave evidence of this trend. But the Party leaders of today are not glorified ward heelers who have worked up through the ranks merely by toadying to the whims of their superiors; most of them have been technologically trained, have experience in industrial management, and have proved their abilities as administrators. Unlike the professional manager, however, their instinctive reaction is toward Party supremacy, not industrial efficiency.

In tracing the shifting criteria that determined the selection of the Soviet elite over the last half century, the ideal method would probably be a series of biographies of leaders typical of each period. Unfortunately, biographical details about Soviet leaders have become scarcer as the years have gone by, and we know far more about some of Lenin's relatively unimportant companions than we do about many of the most important figures in the Khrushchev regime. Our approach to this problem will be to describe the Leninist concept of the elite Party and its organization and then show how the elites have been selected as conditions have changed in the Soviet Union.

THE LENINIST CONCEPT OF THE ELITE PARTY

In spite of the varied attempts to paint Lenin as fundamentally a democrat who used totalitarian methods merely because of the force of circumstances—a picture usually drawn to load the iniquities of the Soviet dictatorship on Stalin's back—the truth remains that Stalin built upon foundations well established by Lenin: The Bolshevik Party had been created in the image of Lenin. By the late 1890's, he had clearly in mind the type of organization he wanted, and as early as 1902, he had described the main outlines of his future Party; it was to be an elite Party, a tightly organized band of full-time revolutionists.

Early in 1902, Lenin published *Chto Delat? (What Is to Be Done?)*, a small book bearing a title previously used by the famous nineteenth-century radical Chernyshevski. Most of the book is devoted to bitter diatribes against practically all the other revolutionary, radical, or liberal movements in the Europe and Russia of that time, but the meat of the book is an exposition of the Leninist concept of the role of the revolutionary party. At first, Lenin had no confidence in the labor movement as such, no faith that labor unions would evolve a revolutionary doctrine if left to themselves, and the history of the labor movement since Marx's time confirmed Lenin's doubts. He stated bluntly that the labor unions would become engrossed only in getting the additional kopeck to go with the ruble and, in this manner, end up under the domination of the bourgeoisie.

To become an effective part of the revolutionary movement, the proletariat had to be led by a vanguard, which practiced the true revolutionary theory. As Lenin pointed out: "Without a revolutionary theory there can be no revolutionary movement." [1] The vanguard must be trained in the theory, and proper training was a full-time job. Not all the elite would come from the intelligentsia; talented and promising workers could be coopted into the vanguard. But these outstanding workers, according to Lenin, "*must not be left* to work eleven hours a day in a factory." [2] They must go underground and be maintained by the Party.

Since the main army of the coming revolution would be the proletariat, the more widespread their unions, the better. The more organization the proletariat had, the more its feeling of solidarity. And the unions were to carry the load of fighting for economic and social benefits, not a very important task in the eyes of Lenin. The Party's job was to penetrate the unions, to organize secret cells of hard-core Party members, and to preach the revolutionary theory to the workers so that they would not settle for the nonessentials such as wage increases and shorter hours. The political objectives established by the Party must be the enduring aims of the proletariat, aims that would be kept alive and vigorous only under the guidance of the Party faithful. In short, as early as 1902, Lenin was describing the Communist strategy of using "front groups."

For Lenin, the key to building and maintaining an effective elite Party lay in its ideology. Nor was it enough that the vanguard have an unshakable devotion to the ideology; it was also necessary to get the ideology to the workers, the mass army of the revolution. The Leninist view envisaged only two possible ideologies: the socialist and the bourgeois. If the workers were not indoctrinated in the socialist ideology, then they would fall victims to the bourgeois variety. Lenin hammered this point home repeatedly, and summed it up as follows: ". . . the *spontaneous* development of the labor movement leads to its becoming subordinated to bourgeois ideology. . . ."[3]

Given the need for a Party of devoted revolutionists to spread the "true" Marxism and to lead the proletariat, Lenin proceeded to lay definite steps for organizing it. It must be a disciplined, conspiratorial band with its tentacles everywhere, but with a central command that could ensure doctrinal purity and coordinate all Party activities. The newspaper, *Iskra,* was to be the means of building up the organization. The paper was printed abroad, thus assuring a safe headquarters, and it was distributed throughout Russia by agents who acted as the Party's lines of communication between the headquarters and the local outposts. As the voice of the keepers of doctrinal purity, *Iskra* would establish the Party line for all Russia; it would coordinate the activities of local groups and help eliminate deviations from the over-all goals of the Party.

The conspiratorial party was not a Russian invention, but the Russians had developed it to a very high degree of efficiency during the nineteenth century, largely because the Czarist regime blocked even the mildest attempts at open criticism. Lenin had a sincere admiration for the Zemlya i Volya (Land and Freedom) groups, probably the most highly organized of the nineteenth-century revolutionary movements. He found nothing inconsistent in the marriage of Marxism to the conspiratorial party; he openly advocated such a union. "And only a gross failure to understand Marxism," said Lenin, "could prompt the opinion that the rise of a mass, spontaneous labor movement *relieves* us of the duty of creating as good an organization of revolutionaries as Zemlya i Volya had in its time, and an even incomparably better one." [4]

When Lenin split the Russian Social Democratic Labor Party in 1903 and emerged as the leader of the Bolshevik wing, he did it deliberately with the program of what he wanted clearly thought out beforehand. He had outlined the model a year previously, when he stated: "The only serious organizational principle the active workers of our movement can accept is strict secrecy, strict selection of members, and the training of professional revolutionaries." [5] His devotion to this organizational program was so fanatical that he broke with comrade after comrade, often close friends or revered teachers. He spent the years from 1903 to 1917 heading a tiny party, refusing to join hands with the Mensheviks at the price of modifying his stand on an elitist party. He had the true understanding of Marxism, his interpretation was the only possible one, and any deviation from it was heresy. Stalin may have been cruder, but his invective against those who deviated from the doctrine was no more fervent than Lenin's. The present Communist intolerance of all opposing views is the legitimate offspring of the Leninist doctrine.

EARLY SOVIET LEADERSHIP

Theoretically, the Leninist concept of the leadership of the Communist Party was a collective one. The interpretation of Marxist doctrine and Party strategy were to be decided upon in the Central Committee, or by its surrogates—a selected few. The theory even encompassed discussion at the lower echelons—

that is, until a decision had been made, when absolute obedience then became mandatory. To some extent, decisions were made by majority vote among the top leaders in the early years of the Soviet regime. A vivid example is Lenin's struggle to get a majority of the Central Committee to accept the terms of the Treaty of Brest Litovsk. For the Bolsheviks—a small minority trying to control an enormous country internally and to beat off military onslaughts externally—to have purged all opposition within the Party during the years of the Civil War would have weakened them to the point of abdication of power. But the weapons forged in the struggle with non-Bolsheviks in those years were ready at hand when the situation became stabilized enough for their use within the Party.

During the October Revolution and the Civil War, Lenin tolerated considerable antagonism on the part of many leading Bolsheviks toward his highhanded methods against the Mensheviks, Social Revolutionaries, and liberals. He used argument and persuasion to lead these erring brethren back into the fold. But opposition outside the Party got a short shrift. Nowhere was his cynical attitude toward democratic processes better demonstrated than in the dissolution of the legally elected Constituent Assembly, probably the first and last elected body in Russia representing the political views of the total population. Since the Bolsheviks could not dominate this group, they dispersed it with bayonets. All opponents of the Bolsheviks lost any chance of a forum for their views when a strict censorship was imposed, while underground activities were gradually liquidated by the newly organized secret police, the Cheka. It may be asserted that these moves were necessitated by the exigencies of war, but victory over the external enemy and the internal opposition brought no diminution in the use of censorship or the Cheka.

The Bolshevik leaders during the pre-Revolutionary period and the early years of the Soviet regime were an elite selected according to the Leninist formula. They were devoted revolutionists, trained in the Leninist version of Marxism, and many were wholly convinced that they were building a new, more perfect society. They were obedient to the Party line, once it had been established, but not slavishly so, and many argued their right to disagree. There were numerous cases in which Bukharin, Zinoviev, Rykov, and others publicly disagreed with the majority decision, and not over mere quiddities, but on essential points of policy. The usual procedure was, however, to voice one's arguments before a majority decision, and then capitulate to the adopted line. The term "majority" applied only to the ruling elite.

The leaders of this period, for the most part, were an entirely different breed from those later brought to the fore by Stalin. Trotsky, a latecomer to the Bolshevik Party, was a brilliant writer and orator, a born organizer—as his leadership of the Red Army demonstrated—and as an internationalist, he was incapable of believing that backward Russia could be a prosperous Communist state in the midst of a hostile capitalist world. Bukharin was a brilliant theorist, a Marxist scholar, and also above the parochial view that later came to characterize Russian leaders. Lunacharski was emotional, a dabbler in things aesthetic. Radek, Kamenev, Mme. Kollontai, and others were ideal revolution-makers but poor stuff for administering the totalitarian state that developed from Lenin's principles under the guidance of Stalin. Unable to discard their ideals completely, they instinctively resented the cold reality of the police state that had emerged in place of the workers' paradise of their dreams. Zinoviev, the first President of the Executive Committee of the Comintern, was typical of the kind of leader who flourished in this early period. He was ideally suited to evolve vague plans for the world revolution that were the stock in trade of the early Comintern leaders; he was an excellent ham actor, a fiery orator, and could charm the foreign comrades. But when he tried to outdo Stalin in political chicanery, he displayed an utter lack of ability in that exacting game.

Stalin and Molotov, the archetypes of the later breed of Communist leaders, seemed almost inarticulate in the midst of the verbose, cosmopolitan Leninist clique. While their colleagues debated theory and scanned the world horizon for signs of the collapse of capitalism, Stalin and Molotov tended the Party organization, appointed the lesser Party bosses, and got rid of the "unreliable" comrades. Trotsky frightened his colleagues because he had the attributes of the man on horseback who had ended so many previous revolutions, but Stalin looked like a harmless drudge immersed in the Party files. Although Lenin had invented the organizational juggernaut, even he seems not to have realized the power that could accrue to the man who controlled the selection of personnel. Not until he was mortally ill did Lenin realize that Stalin, as General Secretary of the Party, was a threat to the collective leadership. By then, Stalin, flanked by his faithful subordinates Molotov and Kuybyshev, was in an impregnable position. To a myriad of followers strategically located throughout the Soviet Union, he was the voice of the Party.

The Communist Party, the elite body that was supposed to fulfill the role of the "dictatorship of the proletariat," was an extremely small group on the eve of the October Revolution, hardly more than 20,000 members. During the Civil War, the membership increased rapidly until by 1921, it totaled around 575,000, which was still only about one Party member for every 250 Soviet citizens. And this ratio was made lower by the purge of 1921, in which some 175,000 Party members lost their cards. Every effort was made to increase the proletarian purity of the Party, to mold it closer to the Marxist ideal of the "dictatorship of the proletariat." Nevertheless, the workers made up only slightly over 40 per cent of the membership. On the other hand, even this could be regarded as outrageous over-representation in a country whose population was well over 80 per cent peasant. The Party was in the awkward position of having to rely on peasant support, and at the same time fearing a large peasant membership in the Party.

THE EVOLUTION OF SOVIET LEADERSHIP UNDER STALIN

The NEP period was a dull, drab era compared to the supercharged atmosphere that prevailed during the Revolution and the Civil War. Russian economy was teetering on the brink of a complete collapse, and some branches had gone over the edge. War Communism, with its complete control of the economy and its forcible collection of grain, had just not worked. Lenin the ideologist capitulated to Lenin the politician, and he put on the best face possible in what was obviously a retreat. Grain procurement was regularized by a tax in kind, small industry was returned to private ownership, and small traders were encouraged to come out of the black-market underground.

To many of the Old Bolshevik leaders, the NEP was a betrayal of the ideals they had fought for in the Civil War, and they felt somewhat out of place in this climate. The Party organization, however, flourished. This was the ideal milieu for the Party bureaucrats to carry on their task of making organization a thing in itself. The road to power now lay within the Party bureaucracy, the movement from the lower echelon to the higher one; fiery orators and war heroes were expendable in this system. This was Stalin's natural environment. The political machine Stalin had carefully nurtured during the period when most of the Bolshevik leaders were engaged in other tasks now became his special weapon. On the strategic level, Stalin split his potential opposition. First, he combined with Zinoviev and Kamenev against Trotsky, letting his fellow triumvirs fling mud at Trotsky and get besmirched in turn. Then Stalin abandoned his allies and shifted to an alliance with the Right wing of the Politburo—Rykov, Bukharin, and Tomski. Trotsky was again the main target. By 1927, Trotsky, Zinoviev, and Kamenev were politically dead, and two years later, Stalin completed the destruction of his erstwhile Right-wing allies.

Throughout the bitter contest for power, Stalin's control of the Party machinery proved to be his decisive advantage. As early as 1924, he had succeeded in getting most of Trotsky's friends either out of the country on diplomatic missions or in obscure posts far from Moscow. The rapid growth of the number of full-time, paid Party officials, most of whom owed their jobs to Stalin, gave them a vested interest in the bureaucracy. Any attack on Stalin was interpreted as an attack on the system. Because Stalin controlled the majority in the Central Committee, he could accuse the opposition of "factionalism," of breaking the monolithic unity of the Party. He claimed that his opponents were not criticizing Stalin's policy but sabotaging the Party line. As the battle raged on through the 1920's, the Party line became equated with the Stalinist line, and to his henchmen, who dominated the Central Committee, opposition to that line was treason. Where Lenin had used arguments and sometimes invective to beat down his opponents, the Stalinist machine resorted to noisy heckling and even strong-arm squads to silence the opposition.

The new Soviet elite was made up of successful *apparatchiki,* Party officials who followed the Stalinist line without argument. Their job was to implement policy, not question it. Their chief characteristics were absolute obedience to their superiors and ruthless imposition of their authority on those below. Lenin's concept of the monolithic Party had come into actuality, although it is doubtful that he would have admitted the paternity of this ugly offspring. Most of Stalin's companions in the Politburo in the early 1930's were men who had worked up through the Party apparatus, men who had no pretensions to culture or education superior to Stalin's own limited abilities in that respect. Seven of the Politburo (Molotov, Kaganovich, Kirov, Kossior, Kuybyshev, Ordzhonikidze, and Rudzutak) were perfect *apparatchiki.* Voroshilov had scaled the heights on his military reputation and luckily had been on Stalin's side in the latter's bitter controversies with Trotsky during the Civil War. Kalinin was the regime's professional peasant; he looked like a muzhik, right down to the long beard. The contrast between this group of bureaucrats and the cosmopolitan leaders of the Leninist period could not have been sharper.

But life in the rarified atmosphere of the Politburo was a risky thing. Kirov was assassinated (possibly on Stalin's orders) in

1934. Kuybyshev and Ordzhonikidze died shortly after, and the "naturalness" of both deaths has long been questioned. (Khrushchev, at the Twenty-second Congress, said that Ordzhonikidze had committed suicide.) Rudzutak and Kossior perished in the great Purge. There was no safe niche during the Stalin regime; no member was too low or too high to avoid the unpredictable anger of the *vozhd*. The men who replaced the fallen were model specimens of the *apparatchiki*—Mikoyan, Andreyev, Zhdanov and Khrushchev—but apparently a little quicker on their feet; three of them outlasted Stalin.

During the 1930's, the Soviet Union was engaged in a feverish struggle to build a heavy industry and a modern army in record time. The demand for engineers, plant managers, scientists, and skilled technicians was insatiable. These were the jobs that were beyond the training and abilities of the *apparatchiki*, and Stalin had to take the pressure off the "old specialists" and even hire foreigners. He could not depend upon such unreliable sources forever, and a crash program for educating a Soviet intelligentsia got under way. The "progressive education" of the 1920's was discarded, and there was a reversion to the pre-Soviet type of schooling—strict discipline and stress on basic subjects. Rote memorization and competitive examinations were reinstituted, and the emphasis on mathematics and sciences was especially heavy. To encourage the best students to undergo the rigors of this "tough" education, the regime offered tempting rewards; the successful became part of a new technological and managerial elite. Although no one was really safe in the Great Purge, the Yezhov machine tended to strike down the older managers and technicians, and the younger professionals found that the way up was wide open. The Party made every effort to recruit its membership from among the new intelligentsia, and for a very good reason: One-man control in the industrial plant reduced the authority of the Party representative, but if the manager was a Party man, the danger of his straying from the official line was minimized. Stalin's experience with the intelligentsia was typical of his paradoxical situation in general. He needed skilled and creative ability to accomplish his industrial goals, but he feared the growth of any entrenched stratum in Soviet society.

THE *YEZHOVSHCHINA* AND THE SOVIET ELITE

The purge was an integral part of the Bolshevik organizational philosophy from the very beginning. Lenin, in his *What Is to Be Done?* of 1902, used a quotation from a letter Lassalle wrote to Marx in 1852 to adorn the title page, a quotation in which Lassalle pointed out that party struggles gave a party strength, and a party became stronger by purging itself at intervals. Lenin's inflexibility from 1903 to the October Revolution acted as an automatic purge in weeding out all but the most stalwart comrades, but once in power, the Bolsheviks found their Party being inundated by opportunists. In an effort to rid itself of those whom Lenin referred to as "rascals" and "bureaucrats," the Party carried out a purge of its ranks in 1921.

The purge technique soon became the standard method of ridding the Party of deadwood. For a matter of fact, there was no other way in which Party efficiency could be maintained under the Communist system. The privileges and power that accrued to Party members tended to attract large numbers of people who were merely searching for a sinecure. Unless the Party were to become so large that its elitist philosophy would be endangered, these parasites had to be cleaned out periodically—thus the *chistka,* the Russian word for "purge" or "combing out." With all authority concentrated at the top, the bureaucrats on the lower levels could protect each other, thus rendering the transmission of Party authority ineffectual at the important area where it came into contact with the masses. The periodic purge was directed at eliminating these idle cogs in the Party machinery, and the fear of the purge kept potentially slothful comrades on their toes.

By 1934, however, Stalin was using the purge for another purpose; he was utilizing it to protect his monopoly of power. The purge now became not just a personnel shake-up to get rid of the deadwood, but a system of terror to prevent the formation of any opposition to Stalin's supreme power, or even *potential* opposition. Between 1936 and 1938, the *Yezhovshchina* period, the bloodletting reached its nightmarish climax—the Great

Purge. The Old Bolsheviks, with a few exceptions, disappeared; the leadership of most national areas was eliminated; the top hierarchy of the Red Army was liquidated; the Party organization itself suffered catastrophic losses; and, finally, even the agents of the Purge, the NKVD, were purged. The *chistka* was no longer restricted to the Party; all Soviet citizens fell in its path.

By 1938, the terror had reached such hysterical proportions that even the industrial life of the nation was endangered. At this point, Stalin relaxed the pressure, removed Yezhov, and installed Beria as head of the NKVD. But his objective had been achieved: Any clique or group that might have served as a point of departure for an opposition movement against Stalin's absolute power had been dispersed. The remnants of the pre-Stalinist Party had been smashed, and only those slavishly committed to the Stalinist program remained. The terror had been so far reaching that among ordinary Soviet citizens hardly anyone trusted his neighbor.

The Soviet elite that emerged from the Great Purge was vastly different from that of the late 1920's and early 1930's. At the Eighteenth Party Congress, in 1939, Malenkov reported that only about 8 per cent of the members had joined the Party before 1920, while 70 per cent had joined the Party since 1929. Half the delegates to the Congress were under thirty-five, and 97 per cent under fifty.[6] Because most of the new recruits were technologically trained men, the educational level of the Party members was much higher in 1939 than ever before. The criteria for the selection of the elite had changed drastically since Lenin's time. The idealistic Old Bolshevik who believed the Marxist-Leninist message about the egalitarian society just over the horizon had been replaced by the technician-manager who was chiefly interested in maintaining his status in the burgeoning industrial society. However much it may have longed for some security, the new elite was above all obedient to Stalin.

To gain the allegiance of the masses and the elite, Stalin turned to nationalism early in the 1930's. Having no illusions about the imminence of the world revolution, he had staked his career on the successful industrialization of the Soviet Union, on carrying out socialism in one country. The history of Czarist

Russia was no longer an unrelieved tale of iniquities, no longer the black story of the downtrodden masses and a bestial autocracy. It was now peopled with glorious heroes: Alexander Nevski, Peter the Great, Suvorov, Kutuzov, and even Ivan the Terrible. The Czarist conquests of the Caucasian and Central Asian peoples were now hailed as a part of Russia's civilizing mission, the Russian version of the White Man's Burden. The Great Russian Communist proconsul in Uzbekistan was carrying on the work of his ancestors. But above all, to question Stalin's authority was now treason; he personified Russia in the same way that Ivan the Terrible had, and to be anti-Stalinist was to be anti-Russian.

THE GLORIFICATION OF STALIN

The series of catastrophes that followed the Nazi invasion of 1941 and early 1942 demanded some relaxation of domestic controls in the Soviet Union. Party regulars were adequate for a peacetime officer corps and a managerial elite, but they lacked the creativity, the ingenuity, needed to stop the German onslaught, to build up the Soviet defense production. It was the golden opportunity for the professional officer and industrial manager to show initiative and skill. Even the artist, the journalist, and the teacher were allowed more freedom in order to use their talents in whipping up patriotism. A naïve faith arose that once the Nazis were defeated, a better world would emerge, a world in which the individual would be safe from the whims of the dictatorship. After all, this was a crusade of the Democracies against Fascism.

The Nazis had hardly been pushed back over the Soviet borders before Stalin brought these ingenuous hopes crashing to the ground. Asserting an almost God-like omnipotence, he intervened in the arts, and through his cultural errand boy, Zhdanov, molded the writers, musicians, and painters into conformity with his version of *socialist realism*, which, freely translated, meant the glorification of Stalin and the Party, in that order. Even linguistics and science received his personal guidance, and the field of genetics was handed over to the charlatan Lysenko.

On the other hand, no effort was spared in developing a technical intelligentsia. Engineers and scientists were trained in great numbers. The Fourth Five-Year Plan, for the reconstruction of the war damage, was pushed at a breakneck pace, all emphasis being put on heavy industry. The living standards of the mass of the population, reduced to a low level during the war, rose very slowly during the Fourth Five-Year Plan, with little or no assistance going to the staggering agricultural sector of the economy.

Stalin had to use all the force and persuasion available to him in order to keep the Soviet population at work, despite their lack of clothing, decent food, and adequate housing. The old bugaboo of capitalist encirclement was revived; only a rapid rebuilding of the Soviet economy and the production of the latest in armaments could ensure the safety of the Soviet Union. The all-powerful Party, backed by the ubiquitous police, guaranteed the fulfillment of the government's directives. And rewards to the elite captured their allegiance to the regime; the well-heeled had a vested interest in the maintenance of the system.

THE STALIN ELITE

In retrospect, it is obvious that Stalin had a firm grip on the Party machinery by the time of the Fourteenth Party Congress, in 1925, and the Party Congresses from then on were convened largely to ratify changes that guaranteed Stalin stronger domination of the apparatus. As his personal power increased, the lapse of time between Party Congresses grew longer. Instead of meeting every three years, as originally scheduled, the Congresses met every four or five years, until thirteen years passed between the Eighteenth and Nineteenth Congresses. It became increasingly difficult to sustain the theory that the Central Committee was merely the executive agent of the Party Congress between its sessions, as well as the concomitant thesis that the Politburo and Secretariat were elected by, and responsible to, the Central Committee.

The Central Committee had been a vital institution in Lenin's time, and was used even by Stalin, along with the Secretariat and the Party Control Commission, to offset his minority position in the Politburo until his victory in 1925. In 1924, at the Thirteenth Party Congress, Stalin buttressed his strength by having the Central Committee enlarged to fifty-three members and thirty-four candidates, most of the newly appointed members being Stalin-oriented *apparatchiki*. At the Fourteenth Congress, in 1925, the Central Committee was further enlarged to sixty-three members and forty-three candidates. From that point on, it was so largely a creature of Stalin that its role as a vital Party organ became negligible.

Stalin's real control of the Party lay in the Secretariat and the Party Control Commission. The Secretariat had the responsibility of removing, transferring, and appointing Party personnel; this enabled Stalin to put his own followers in key positions and to remove the adherents of his opponents. The Party Control Commission, originally established to hear the complaints of local officials against the iniquities of the central bureaucracy, soon became a Stalinist instrument to shut off such complaints and punish those making them. Furthermore, it enabled the bureaucrats at the center to force conformity upon the local officials. The beauty of the Stalin machine was its ability, through the Secretariat and the Party Control Commission, to appoint and control the Party secretaries on the republic and oblast level—the same group from which the members of the Central Committee were recruited later on. The apparatus could get right down to the grass roots and woe to the secretaries on the lower levels who failed to heed a change in the Stalin line.

The role of the Secretariat became even greater after the inauguration of the Five-Year Plans; it became charged with the selection of technical-managerial personnel as well as of Party functionaries. The Organizational Assignment Section, which had worked well enough from 1924 to 1930, broke down under the new burden, and in that year, the Assignment Section was subdivided into eight sections, each handling a separate branch of the economy. The industrialization of the Soviet Union necessitated a vast enlargement of the role of the Party apparatus, and the selection of an efficient managerial elite became as important as the assignment of reliable local Party secretaries. The Party and the government were now openly merged.

In 1937, Stalin himself spelled out the composition of his elite in a speech to a plenum of the Central Committee.

> In our Party, if we have in mind its leading strata, there are about 3,000 to 4,000 first rank leaders whom I would call our Party's corps of generals.
>
> Then there are about 30,000 to 40,000 middle rank leaders who are our Party corps of officers.
>
> Then there are about 100,000 to 150,000 of the lower rank Party command staff who are, so to speak, our Party's non-commissioned officers.[7]

The "corps of generals" probably referred to the top echelons of the Party, the men in the Politburo, Secretariat, and Party Control Commission, as well as the Party secretaries in the republics and oblasts, and the key figures in industry and the armed services. The "corps of officers" included Party officials on the intermediate and lower levels, the more important plant managers and industrial ministers, high-ranking military officers, top diplomats, and police gauleiters. The "non-commissioned officers" included the horde of small Party functionaries, bureaucrats in the industrial structure, and political officers in the armed forces. The total of some 150,000 to 200,000 made up the elite in the prewar Stalin regime. Stalin failed to mention, however, the great gulf that lay between the dictator and his generals, corps of officers, and noncommissioned officers.

The military terminology in Stalin's description of the Soviet elite was appropriate; the Party functioned through a military-like network of command channels, with all authority flowing from the top to the lower echelons and absolute obedience the watchword. But unlike its military counterpart, the top brass of the Party was not allowed to fob off its responsibilities on its staff and pass the buck to lower commands. Stalin needled the top leaders into feuds with each other to prevent their forming consolidated opposition groups, and he made a practice of favoring new men to offset the older leaders. Thus Zhdanov and Malenkov, while still only candidate members of the Politburo, were favored over Molotov, Kaganovich, and other old companions. Stalin probably fanned the feud between Zhdanov and Malenkov, as well.

Stalin apparently became worried about his corps of generals in the last years of his life, and as Khrushchev pointed out in his "Secret Speech," at the Twentieth Party Congress, even such a close friend as Kliment Voroshilov was in danger. In 1952, the Nineteenth Party Congress was convened, the first in thirteen years. The old Politburo, made up of Stalin and eight "old-timers" (Voroshilov, Molotov, Kaganovich, Mikoyan, Malenkov, Beria, Bulganin, and Khrushchev), was transformed into a Presidium with twenty-five members. It looked as if the *vozhd* was deliberately diluting the authority of his henchmen and giving new men training for positions about to become vacant. To the initiated, who had weathered previous purges, all the signs pointed to a large-scale *chistka* in the near future. It was also evident that the main targets were to be those who had stood closest to Stalin over the years. The purge never materialized, for Stalin died in March, 1953.

THE POST-STALIN LEADERSHIP

Immediately upon Stalin's death, the enlarged Presidium was dissolved and the members of the old pre-Nineteenth Party Congress Politburo assumed power, although the group kept the name Presidium. Two newcomers were added, Saburov and Pervukhin. In March of 1953, Stalin's heirs were fearful about how the Soviet people would react to the death of the hated *vozhd*. The transfer of power from the dead dictator to a new regime was something new in Soviet experience. Stalin had spent almost thirty years building a system of government that was tailored to his desire for absolute rule, and it required a new strong man, a ruthless dictator. His epigones lacked his stature, and they did not trust each other enough to designate a successor. They had played politics in Stalin's Byzantine court long enough to know that any new dictator might well send his potential rivals to the gallows.

Under an uneasy truce, a period of "collective leadership" was proclaimed as the true Communist way of life, in keeping with the spirit of Lenin. Although Stalin's real denigration did not start until Khrushchev's speech in 1956, hints about the iniquity of the "cult of personality" were made in justification of the new regime. The only way the "collective leadership" could work was to divide the power among several leaders: Beria had the police already and he retained his control; Malenkov was assumed to be Stalin's heir, but early in the new regime, he was forced to choose either the Secretariat or the Chairmanship of the Council of Ministers, and he opted for the latter; Khrushchev took over the Secretariat, the lever that Stalin had used with great effectiveness. Now, of the four pillars of power in the Soviet Union—the Party, the managerial elite, the police, and the army—only the last was a relatively free agent. This system of rule by a collegium was a shaky arrangement at best and contrary to the centralization set in motion by that very Lenin whose spirit was invoked to bless it.

Any chance of a harmonious balance among the leaders ended abruptly in July, 1953, when his fellow Presidium members turned on Beria. He was arrested, "tried" *in camera,* and executed. His police empire was partly dismantled, and one pillar of power was gone. Apparently the rest of the leaders were frightened by Beria's attempt to enlist popular support in a program of more legality and better treatment for the nationalities in the U.S.S.R. With the backing of the people, plus the powerful MVD, Beria would have been supreme.

Malenkov, having decided to base his power on the industrial-managerial elite, came out for more consumer goods, a slackening in the hectic drive for more heavy industry, and a reduction in the military budget based on a "retaliatory force." This may have pleased the managerial elite and the populace in general, but it alienated the army leaders and alarmed the other Presidium members. In February, 1955, Malenkov lost his

Chairmanship of the Council of Ministers, and Khrushchev's man, Bulganin, supplanted him. As in the earlier power struggle when Trotsky allied himself with Zinoviev and Kamenev too late to stop Stalin, Malenkov was joined by Molotov and Kaganovich too late to stop Khrushchev. In June, 1957, Khrushchev was outvoted by the "anti-Party group" in the Presidium, but like Stalin, he used the Central Committee, well packed with his own *apparatchiki,* to maintain his position. Malenkov's fall removed another pillar of power from the contest, the managerial elite; now only the Party and the army had strong power positions.

A comparison of the composition of the Presidium between 1953 and 1957 summarizes the maneuvers executed by the top leaders of the Soviet Union in this period (see Table 5).

TABLE 5

THE POLITBURO-PRESIDIUM, 1939–65

POLITBURO (1939–46)

J. V. Stalin	M. I. Kalinin (died in 1946)
A. A. Andreyev	A. I. Mikoyan
K. Y. Voroshilov	V. M. Molotov
A. A. Zhdanov (died in 1946)	N. S. Khrushchev
L. M. Kaganovich	

L. P. Beria and G. M. Malenkov added in 1946
N. A. Voznesenski added in 1947; dropped and executed in July, 1949
N. A. Bulganin added in 1948; A. N. Kosygin added in 1949

PRESIDIUM (October, 1952) a

Old members retained	*New members added*	
J. V. Stalin	V. M. Andrianov	N. A. Mikhailov
L. P. Beria	A. B. Aristov	M. G. Pervukhin
N. A. Bulganin	S. D. Ignatiev	P. K. Ponomarenko
K. Y. Voroshilov	D. S. Korotchenko	M. Z. Saburov
L. M. Kaganovich	V. V. Kuznetsov	M. A. Suslov
G. M. Malenkov	O. V. Kuusinen	D. I. Chesnokov
A. I. Mikoyan	V. A. Malyshev	N. M. Shvernik
V. M. Molotov	L. G. Melnikov	M. F. Shkiriatov
N. S. Khrushchev		

Presidium (March 6, 1953) [b]

L. P. Beria (executed in July, 1953)
N. A. Bulganin
K. Y. Voroshilov
L. M. Kaganovich
G. M. Malenkov
A. I. Mikoyan
V. M. Molotov
M. G. Pervukhin
M. Z. Saburov
N. S. Khrushchev

Presidium (July, 1957) [c]

N. S. Khrushchev
A. B. Aristov
N. I. Belyayev
L. I. Brezhnev
N. A. Bulganin
K. Y. Voroshilov
E. A. Furtseva
G. K. Zhukov
N. G. Ignatov
A. I. Kirichenko
F. R. Kozlov
O. V. Kuusinen
A. I. Mikoyan
M. A. Suslov
N. M. Shvernik

Presidium (May 4, 1960) [d]

N. S. Khrushchev
A. B. Aristov
L. I. Brezhnev
K. Y. Voroshilov
E. A. Furtseva
N. G. Ignatov
F. R. Kozlov
A. N. Kosygin
O. V. Kuusinen
A. I. Mikoyan
N. A. Mukhitdinov
N. V. Podgorny
D. S. Polyansky
M. A. Suslov
N. M. Shvernik

Presidium (October 31, 1961) [e]

N. S. Khrushchev
F. R. Kozlov
L. I. Brezhnev
G. I. Voronev
A. N. Kosygin
A. I. Mikoyan
N. V. Podgorny
D. S. Polyansky
M. A. Suslov
N. M. Shvernik
O. V. Kuusinen

Presidium (October, 1965)

L. I. Brezhnev
A. P. Kirilenko
A. N. Kosygin
K. T. Masurov
A. I. Mikoyan
N. V. Podgorny
D. S. Polyansky
A. N. Shelepin
P. E. Shelest
M. A. Suslov
G. I. Voronov

---

[a] Stalin greatly enlarged the Politburo and changed its name to Presidium at the time of the Nineteenth Party Congress.

[b] The enlarged Presidium was reduced after Stalin's death, during the period of "collective leadership."

[c] The membership was altered following the Khrushchev–"anti-Party-group" conflict in June and July, 1957.

[d] Khrushchev drastically reshuffled the Presidium personnel in May, 1960.

[e] The Twenty-second Party Congress reduced the membership to eleven.

When Khrushchev obtained power for himself, he faced very different problems from those that confronted Stalin in the late 1920's—largely because of the successful industrialization of the U.S.S.R. The pressure of an educated industrial group upon the regime could not be so blithely ignored as in Stalin's time. Khrushchev's adoption of the very aims for which Malenkov had been condemned—an increase in living standards—is proof of this. Stalin himself, in calling in 1931 for an accelerated training program to obtain a Soviet intelligentsia to meet the needs of the planned economy, created a potential rival to the Party elite. Nothing could stop the new managerial and technical intelligentsia from occupying positions of power in the new Soviet society, that is, nothing short of abandoning the industrialization of the country.

Stalin tried to incorporate the new intelligentsia into the Party and keep it enthusiastically devoted to the Party ideology, even to the point of presenting it with a new scripture at the Nineteenth Party Congress—his own last will and testament entitled *Economic Problems of Socialism in the U.S.S.R.* His success in raising the educational level of the Party was demonstrated at the Nineteenth Party Congress, in 1952. Of the 1200 delegates, 85.2 per cent either had completed their secondary education or had received at least some higher education, as contrasted to only 22.9 per cent at the Sixteenth Party Congress, in 1930. Furthermore, 709 delegates, or 59.5 per cent of those present, had completed their higher education.[8] The Party now had its share of the intelligentsia.

Khrushchev may well have doubted whether the 282 graduate engineers who were delegates at the Nineteenth Party Congress were primarily Party men or had a tendency to lean toward the managerial-technical intelligentsia, for at the Twentieth Party Congress, four years later, the over-all educational level of the delegates had dropped. Only 76.9 per cent had completed their secondary education or had some higher education, a decline of 8.3 per cent from 1952.[9] It would seem doubtful that such a reversal could become serious and still leave the Party intellectually capable of competing with the managerial elite.

The delegates to Party Congresses, of course, are not necessarily a fair selection of the best-educated Party members. Most of the top leaders in all fields of endeavor in the Soviet Union are Party members, whether they are army officers, scientists, managers, educators, or artists. Although Party membership is almost a necessary passport to the top levels, it may very well signify no more than lip service to the Party ideology. The reluctance of the professional to put up with Party propaganda was well illustrated in the armed forces in recent years. The professional officers resented the time "wasted" by their *zampolits* (political officers) in the ideological training of the troops, let alone their own enforced attendance at Party meetings and study circles. One of the charges against Zhukov in October, 1957, was his attempt to reduce the role of the political officer in the armed forces, but Zhukov's fall does not mean that his fellow officers have changed their opinions on this subject. Whether the Soviet managerial elite, professional miltary officers, technicians, and professional people regard the Party as a bit obsolete in the new industrial world they have created is a mystery, but the fact remains that the structure has been built and *could* operate without the Party; the burden is on the Party to prove that it is still useful.

TABLE 6

EDUCATION OF PARTY MEMBERS *

	January 1, 1962		*January 1, 1965*	
	Party Members	Per Cent of Total	Party Members	Per Cent of Total
Total	9,891,068	100.0	11,758,169	100.0
Higher education	1,349,535	13.7	1,763,262	15.0
Incomplete higher education	282,061	2.9	301,255	2.6
Secondary education	2,693,457	27.2	3,542,005	30.1
Incomplete secondary education	2,811,708	28.4	3,277,024	27.9
Primary-school education	2,754,307	27.8	2,874,623	24.4

* *Partiynaya Zhizn* (*Party Life*), No. 10 (May, 1965), p. 11.

The ouster of Khrushchev in October, 1964, has not changed the type of tough *apparatchik* whose duty it is to implement the changes the new leadership may want to institute. Today, 85 per cent of the Party members have a secondary education or less, and about 25 per cent of them an elementary education or less. It would seem a fair assumption that a large percentage of the *apparatchiki* are extremely limited in education, were trained under Stalin (57 per cent have been in the Party over ten years and some over thirty), and are suspicious of new ideas. Yevgeny Yevtushenko had this type in mind when he wrote, in his poem "Stalin's Heirs," that Stalin, from his coffin, was still in touch with his "heirs." They were, that is, still Stalinist at heart.

Paul Wohl has pointed out another weakness in the Party organization today—it has become a mass party. He sums up the problem as follows:

> On January 1 the party had 11,758,000 members and candidate members. Of these, 9,407,000 were men more than 26 years old. Up to that age Soviet citizens are supposed to belong to the Komsomol, the Communist youth organization.
>
> The Soviet statistical yearbook lists the total number of men between 25 and 69 as 41,775,000. This means that 10 out of 44 men of that age group are party members.
>
> This is an average for the Soviet Union as a whole. In major cities, where there are proportionately more party members, the relation between members and nonmembers probably is one to three.
>
> In other words, the party has become part of the people, sharing its doubts and its day-to-day aspirations. It has ceased to be the iron phalanx of an inexorable revolution.[10]

The Soviet Union is again under collective leadership, always a mark of a period of confusion and stagnation. Brezhnev seems to be in control of the Party *apparat* through his positions as First Secretary of the Party, a member of the Presidium of the Supreme Soviet, and as head of the R.S.F.S.R. Bureau. Kosygin, the other half of the collective leadership, is Chairman of the Council of Ministers, as well as a member of the Presidium of the Central Committee. He appears to be the economic expert of the duumvirate. But trouble may arise, for the *apparat* and the managerial-technical bureaucracy are at loggerheads on many issues. That which may be good for the Soviet Union in the opinion of the economic experts is too often regarded by the *apparat* chieftains as detrimental to the Party. This is a problem that must be harassing the Brezhnev-Kosygin team, and it will probably remain a serious problem long after a single leader supplants the present duumvirate.

7

Agriculture

There can be little doubt that the weakest link in the Soviet economy is agriculture. Even in Czarist Russia, the source of much trouble was the problem of the ownership of land, and starting in the sixteenth century or perhaps even earlier, the agricultural population was chained to the land to support a class that provided administrators and military leaders. By the end of the eighteenth century, this class, the nobility, had shunted off most of its responsibilities and kept all its privileges. There was a growing resentment on the part of the small middle class and the peasantry, who realized that they were paying heavily in return for very little. When the huge and expensive army proved inept in the Crimean War, the pressure came to a head. Almost immediately after the war, in 1861, the serfs were emancipated. But since the emancipation decree had given the peasant too little and charged him too much, the problem of land ownership still haunted the central government. Bad as the system was, in the early years of the twentieth century, individual ownershp was increasing rapidly, and a responsible, vigorous farming class was beginning to dominate the agriculture of Russia.

Immediately after coming to power, in November, 1917, the Bolsheviks wrecked the agricultural system by urging the peasants to seize all the land and tools in sight and regard them as their own. The larger, more profitable estates and farms were atomized, and the 20 million individual peasant holdings that resulted were good for little except subsistence farming, especially in an economy powerless to offer either goods to encourage an increase in production or the machinery and fertilizer to make such an increase possible. In spite of, or perhaps because of, prodigious efforts on the part of the Communist regime to force agriculture into higher production, the darkest sector of the Soviet economy is still agriculture.

AGRICULTURAL RESOURCES

A chief stumbling block for Russian agriculture over the centuries has been the poor resources in soil and climate upon which it is based. The chernozem and chestnut soils occupy only a small part of the 8.4 million square miles that make up the U.S.S.R., and the podsolic soils of the forest-steppe regions are too far north to have an adequate growing season for most crops. In addition, Russia has always been short of the fertilizers necessary to make the podsolic soils productive. A recurrent in the announced goals for each Five-Year Plan is an increase in the production of mineral fertilizers, but the goals are low and attainment very dubious. In March, 1958, Khrushchev announced that one of the reasons for increasing livestock production was to get more animal fertilizer for agriculture—but that would not go far toward satisfying the demand.

Most of the agricultural land of the Soviet Union lies north of the latitude of Minneapolis—45° N. Lat.—and 43 per cent of the U.S.S.R. is in the permafrost area. It is further handicapped by a continental climate and an insufficiency of moisture. The four republics of Central Asia are almost entirely dependent upon irrigation, and this arid belt reaches far into Kazakhstan and much of the region just above the Caspian Sea, the Caucasus, and the Black Sea. The Southern black-soil belt of the Ukraine gets only sixteen to twenty inches of precipitation a year. There is enough moisture in the forest-steppe area above this belt, but this advantage is offset by poor soils and a short growing season.

As a result of the relative scarcity of good soils (in comparison with the total area of the U.S.S.R. and its large population), the northern latitudes in which the country is located, and the almost marginal precipitation in most of the agricultural areas, the untapped agricultural resources of the U.S.S.R. are extremely limited. Strenuous attempts have been made to push agriculture to the north, but with poor results. In the last few years, marginal acreage—the "virgin and idle lands"—has been put under cultivation in southern Siberia, Kazakhstan, and the northern Caucasus, but the results have varied enormously from year to year. There is little doubt that the tearing off of the grass cover of these marginal areas has resulted in soil erosion on a large scale. The whole Kazakhstan virgin-land region could become a gigantic dust bowl in the relatively near future.

In analyzing Soviet agriculture, the combination of inadequate statistics with the government's reluctance to disclose actual figures on the lagging side of the economy makes the use of informed guesses mandatory. To add to the confusion, available Soviet statistics continually shift their bases, including variously the area of Russia in 1913, the area of the Soviet Union before 1939, and the present area of the country.

According to the official Soviet figures, the total agriculturally useful land in Russia in 1913 (in the area comparable to U.S.S.R. boundaries before 1939) was 875 million acres. In 1957 (using the same area), it had risen to 1.26 billion acres.[1] The new land brought into use was almost sufficient to keep up with the increase in population—70 per cent more land and 75 per cent more people. The increase in sown area—from 282 million acres in 1928 to 545 million acres in 1963, or less than 50 per cent—is probably a more meaningful figure. However, "may be" is the operational part of the sentence, for Russian agriculture is still extensive, not intensive, and "sown area" has come to include some very marginal land. Even if the highest Soviet figures are accepted, the increase in land under cultivation has not much more than kept up with the increase in population and is not capable of indefinite expansion in the future (see Tables 7*a* and 7*b*).

COLLECTIVIZATION

Imbued with the Marxist doctrine that only large-scale industry would be effective in the socialist state, the Communist leaders transferred this concept to agriculture and began, in the early

TABLE 7*a*

DISTRIBUTION OF AGRICULTURAL LAND IN THE U.S.S.R. ON NOVEMBER 1, 1958 *

(In Millions of Acres)

	General Agricultural Area	*Total Agriculturally Useful Land* [a]	*Plow Land* [b]	*Plow Land in Cultivation*
Kolkhoz land				
Land in general use, including long-term lease from the State Land Fund and State Forest Fund	1,869.6	778.9	387.7	368.2
Personal plots of collective farmers	15.8	15.0	13.6	13.6
Total	1,885.4	793.9	401.3	381.8
Land of the sovkhozes and other state agricultural enterprises	660.5	437.8	163.6	154.0
Land for personal use				
Land of workers and employees	4.2	3.7	3.0	2.7
Other groups	0.2	0.1	0.1	2.8
Total	4.4	3.8	3.1	2.8
Grand Total	2,550.3	1,235.5	567.9	538.6
State Land Fund area not under lease to kolkhozes and sovkhozes	646.0	197.0	3.2	1.2
State Forest Fund area not under lease to kolkhozes and sovkhozes	2,192.5	30.0	2.0	1.0
Other land in use	129.5	42.0	4.6	3.5
Total	2,968.1	269.0	9.8	5.7
Total Lands	5,518.4	1,504.5	577.7	544.2

* *Narodnoe Khozyaystvo SSSR v 1958 Godu,* p. 383. Sum of subtotals may not equal totals because of rounding.

[a] Includes plow land, gardens, vineyards, virgin soil, hayfields, and pastures.

[b] Includes fallow land.

TABLE 7*b*

THE SOWN AREA IN THE U.S.S.R.*
(In Millions of Acres)

	1928	*1940*	*1950*	*1960*	*1962*	*1963*
Total sown area	282.00	375.00	365.00	508.00	540.00	545.00
Total area in grain	230.00	275.00	255.00	288.00	320.00	325.00
Winter grains	75.00	95.00	90.00	73.00	87.00	83.00
Winter rye	60.00	56.00	58.00	41.00	42.00	41.00
Winter wheat	15.00	36.00	31.00	31.00	45.00	42.00
Spring grains	152.00	180.00	164.00	215.00	230.00	242.00
Spring wheat	52.00	65.00	65.00	121.00	123.00	120.50
Maize	11.00	9.00	12.00	12.00	17.00	17.50
Spring barley	17.00	26.00	20.00	28.00	35.00	46.00
Oats	42.00	50.00	40.00	32.00	17.00	14.00
Millet	14.00	15.00	10.00	9.50	11.00	10.00
Buckwheat	7.00	5.00	8.00	6.00	5.70	4.50
Rice	0.50	0.50	0.25	0.25	0.25	0.25
Legumes	2.50	8.70	8.70	8.00	18.00	27.00
Technical crops	21.00	29.00	30.00	32.00	35.00	37.00
Cotton	2.40	5.00	5.70	5.50	6.00	6.00
Sugar beets	2.00	3.00	3.20	7.50	7.80	9.00
Flax	3.40	5.20	4.70	4.00	4.20	3.60
Hemp	2.10	1.50	1.40	0.90	0.75	0.75
Oil seed	9.60	8.60	9.00	13.00	15.00	15.50
Vegetables	19.00	24.00	26.00	28.00	27.00	26.00
Potatoes	14.00	19.00	21.50	23.00	22.00	21.00
Garden produce	2.00	3.70	3.20	3.70	3.70	3.60
Fodder and grasses	9.60	45.00	51.70	158.00	155.00	158.00

* *Narodnoe Khozyaystvo SSSR v 1958 Godu,* pp. 386–89; *Narodnoe Khozyaystvo SSSR v 1963 Godu,* pp. 242–43. The sums of the components do not equal the totals in the originals, and these figures reflect slight additional inaccuracies due to conversion from hectares to acres.

1920's, to convert the 20 million independent farms into larger units. During the NEP period (1921–28), they tried to lure the farmer into the larger collectives, the kolkhozes,* by giving every advantage to these units. But the effort was very unrewarding. By 1927, according to Soviet figures, only .008 per cent of the farmers had joined the kolkhozes. At this point, the "second"

* In Russian, *kollektivnoe khozyaystvo* (collective economic unit), which is abbreviated to *kolkhoz.*

Figure IX. Animal Husbandry in the Soviet Union (1916-55)

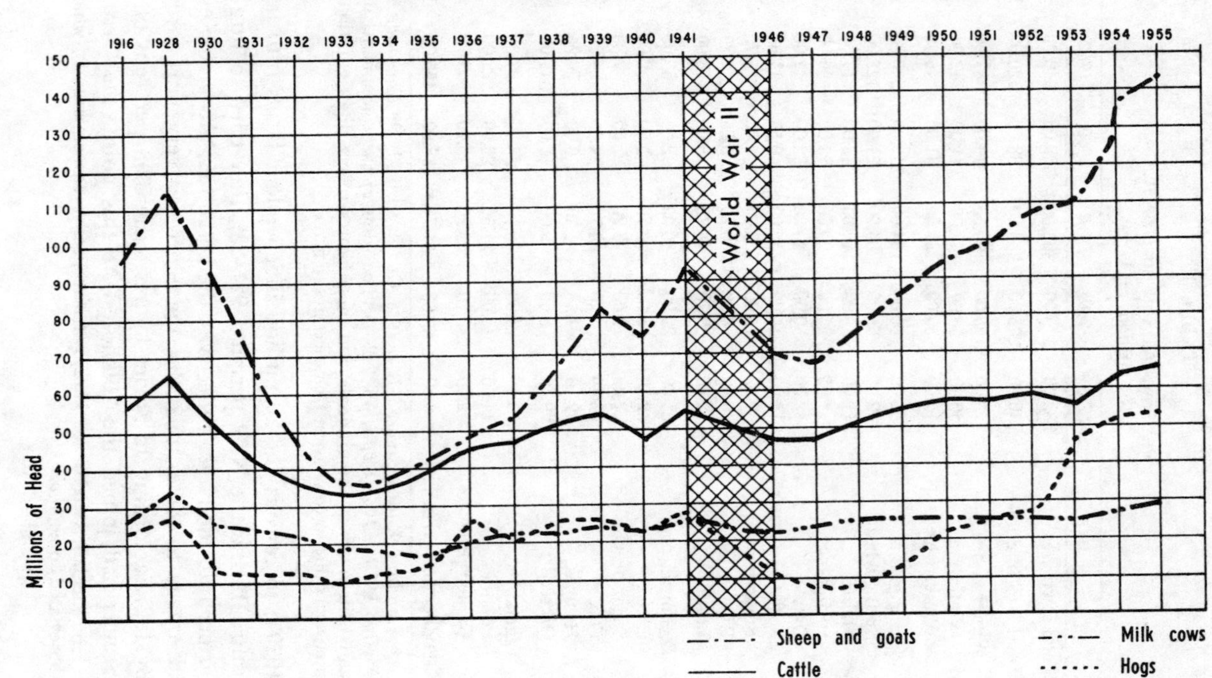

revolution took place—the forced industrialization under the Five-Year Plans—and Stalin felt that the time had come to exert overt pressure for collectivization. Four years later, by 1931, some 52.7 per cent of the farmers were in the kolkhozes, and by 1940, some 97 per cent, along with 99.9 per cent of the cultivated land of the U.S.S.R.

A small price had to be paid for the victory, however. The government was forced to allow the peasant to retain his own house, some tools, a few animals, and a small plot of land. These remnants of private enterprise soon became the focal point of the peasant's real affections. He devoted an inordinate amount of time to his own animals and small plot of land, and that much less to his assigned work on the kolkhoz. Much of his cash income in the last thirty years has come from the sale in the free market of the products of his own plot—one of the few examples of really intensive agriculture in the Soviet Union.

The human suffering caused by the forced collectivization, especially in the 1929–33 period, is beyond statistical calculation. Millions of kulaks were exiled to Siberian forced-labor camps or left to starve, because even their seed grain had been confiscated. The peasants fought back at first, and the figures for livestock show the catastrophic effects of collectivization. Rather than turn over their livestock to the kolkhozes, the peasants slaughtered them, either to sell the meat or eat it themselves. In 1928, there were 66.8 million head of cattle, 27.7 million hogs, and 114.6 million sheep and goats. By 1933, the totals had dropped to 33.5 million cattle, 9.9 million hogs, and 37.3 million sheep and goats, a decrease of about half in cattle and two-thirds in other livestock. Not until 1955 was the 1928 cattle level restored (see Figure IX). Probably an even more severe blow was the sharp decrease in the number of horses, which the peasants also slaughtered for food. Plans had been made for the kolkhozes to be mechanized, and they eventually were, but the disappearance of half the horses in the 1928–32 period left the farmers extremely short of draft power for plowing and harvesting.

In addition to the kolkhozes, the Soviet leaders began to

establish model farms, sovkhozes,* immediately after the Revolution. These were to be examples of progressive agriculture for the kolkhozes to emulate. By 1928, the government had set up 1,407 of these state farms, but they were poor exhibits on the whole and did little to entice the peasants into joining larger agricultural units. By 1940, the number of sovkhozes had risen to 4,159.

In order to utilize the scarce farm machinery to the greatest extent possible, as well as to act as agencies for the collection of the kolkhoz crops at artificially low government prices, machine-tractor stations (MTS) † were established during the period of forced collectivization. In 1928, there were only six MTS, but by 1940, the number had increased to 7,069. These stations dispatched both machinery and operators to the various kolkhozes and sovkhozes the stations were assigned to service; they also kept track of the crop yields so that the government's share would not be eaten by the collective farmers. The MTS had an additional role, that of watchdog for the Party, because the rural areas were weakest in the number of Party enthusiasts.

The kolkhozes, sovkhozes, and MTS combined, although at a terrible cost in human suffering, to carry out the mission of the government. They served as controls upon the peasant's consumption of his own produce. To finance the enormous costs of the forced industrialization of the Soviet Union, a profit had to be derived from the peasant. Inasmuch as the new industry was operating primarily to produce heavy capital goods, there were few consumer goods to exchange for food. It was only by confiscating a large part of the agricultural production that the state was able to feed the growing urban population and pay for the needed tools and machinery from abroad. In the early 1930's, while millions of peasants starved to death, the Soviet Union shipped grain abroad to pay for imported equipment and the services of foreign technical experts. To watch 20 million individual farms was an impossibility, but with the aid of the MTS, it was possible to maintain surveillance over a quarter of a million kolkhozes.

* *Sovkhoz* is the abbreviation for the Russian words *sovetskoe khozyaystvo*, literally "Soviet economy," but usually translated as "state farm."

† MTS is an abbreviation of the Russian *mashino-traktornaya stantsiya* (machine-tractor station).

In keeping with the Marxist contention that large-scale units are the most efficient and profitable form of organization, the government began in the late 1930's to consolidate the kolkhozes into larger units. By 1940, the number of kolkhozes had dropped from a high of 243,500 to 236,900. In World War II, the Germans plunged across the richest agricultural area of the U.S.S.R., destroying some 98,000 kolkhozes. After the war, the Soviet regime took advantage of the disorganization and reconstituted the kolkhozes into units of a much larger size. By 1955, the number had been whittled down to 87,500 and in 1958 still further, to around 78,000. In 1963, there were 39,500 kolkhozes. The average size was 15,000 acres, 7,000 acres of which were sown, and each kolkhoz employed about 400 workers.[2] Only 2 per cent of American farms are over 500 acres. Gigantism seems to be one of the major ills of Soviet agriculture.

Khrushchev was an ardent advocate of bigger farms, both kolkhozes and sovkhozes, and as early as the last years of the Stalin regime he backed the idea of *agrogorods* (agricultural cities), but failed in his attempts to obtain acceptance of the concepts. During his period of power, he looked more and more favorably upon the sovkhoz as the hope of the future. By 1963, there were 9,176 sovkhozes. The average sovkhoz consisted of 70,000 acres, with 25,000 acres sown, and employed 775 workers.[3] The sovkhozes are much more Marxian than the kolkhozes. Here is the factory farm with wage earners, i.e., a rural proletariat. The ulcerous problem of the peasant's private plot and the privately owned cow is more easily resolved on the sovkhoz than on the kolkhoz.

With the increasing size of the agricultural units and the growing demand for food to maintain a rapidly expanding urban population (rising from 17.6 per cent of the total population in 1913 to 53 per cent in 1964), Soviet agriculture has developed a voracious appetite for machinery. The production of tractors in the U.S.S.R. began in 1923 with the construction of two machines; by 1928, when collectivization was under serious consideration, the output was 1,300. By 1963, the output had increased to 325,000 units, and the Soviets claimed to have a park of 1,442,000 tractors. The total number of available grain-harvesting combines rose from 182,000 in 1941 to 517,000 in 1963.[4] These are startling increases, but the large farming units are still clamoring for more machinery. As the number of horses and oxen available for draft power has declined seriously since 1928, and little effort has been made to revive the breeding of horses, it is not surprising that the need for machinery has become critical.

THE LIVESTOCK AND DAIRY PROBLEM

"We must overtake and surpass the United States in per capita production of meat, milk, and butter" was a favorite slogan under Khrushchev. It appeared in the press frequently and it was emblazoned on banners hung in the Park of Culture and Rest. Fulfillment of the slogan was regarded as the first installment in the transition from the relative scarcity of socialism to the opulence of the stage of Communism. Khrushchev made completion of the first installment his personal responsibility. In the opinion of some foreign observers, he became somewhat hysterical in his search for short cuts to the promised land of meat, milk, and butter. But the prevalence of poor breeding stock, the indifference of the peasant to the collective's animals, and the lack of adequate animal feed conspired to defeat Khrushchev.

Statistically, the Soviet totals compare unfavorably with those of the United States. In 1964, the United States had 106.5 million head of cattle to the Soviet Union's 85.5 million, while the number of cows was 48.6 million in the United States and 38.3 million in the Soviet Union. The United States had 58.1 million hogs to the Soviet Union's 40.9 million, but this was a radical change from the previous year. In 1963, the Russians had 70 million hogs, but because of the serious grain shortage of that year, they were forced to slaughter about half of them. Thus the Soviet population received a temporary bonanza in meat. In sheep, however, the Soviet Union outnumbers the United States, some 133 million to 28 million.[5] Even with the temporary rise in meat production induced by the feed shortage, in 1964 the U.S.S.R. produced only about 70 per cent of the U.S. production, and the Russians have 30 million more mouths to feed.

Numbers are not the entire story. The quality of the animals is even more important. The weight of the beef cattle, the total milk output of the dairy cow, the butterfat content of the milk—

in all these factors, the Soviet animal falls well below American standards. Improvement of the characteristics of Soviet livestock is bound to be a long and arduous task. The long reign of Lysenko as the absolute dictator of the field of genetics reduced the science to quackery, and in hopes of speedy improvements, Khrushchev for a long time supported his quest for accelerated mutations.

Furthermore, the peasant's cow has been one of the conflicts that has soured the relationship between the government and the collective farmer. The peasant finds the kolkhoz tolerable only so long as he has his own little plot and his own cow. But it is going to be hard to improve the cattle as long as almost 50 per cent of all cattle and over half the milk cows belong to the individual collective farmer or even to the nonagricultural worker (see Table 8). Under Khrushchev's urging, many kolkhozes built so-called "cow palaces" as part of the drive to put more capital investment into the improvement of the collective's herd. The writer visited one of these "cow palaces" on a kolkhoz in Samarkand. It was a well-built structure with cement floors, good stanchions, and elaborate milking apparatus, but the inefficient use of manpower was appalling. The manure was gathered, the straw removed by hand, and then it was molded into cakes and set out on boards to dry. But at least the building and the

TABLE 8

Ownership of Cattle in the U.S.S.R. on January 1, 1964 *

	Number of Head (In Millions)	*Per Cent of Total*
Total, all cattle	85,448	
Sovkhozes and other state enterprises	24,069	28
Kolkhozes	37,297	43
Privately owned	24,082	28
Total, milk cows	38,348	
Sovkhozes and other state enterprises	8,576	22
Kolkhozes	13,770	36
Privately owned	16,002	42

* *Narodnoe Khozyaystvo SSSR v 1963 Godu*, p. 312.

equipment were there; the rationalization of labor may be worked out in time.

Agriculture has long been the poor orphan in the Soviet economy. Since Stalin's death, however, it has been getting a larger slice of the total capital investment; for example, the Soviets claim that total investment in agriculture increased from 2.2 billion rubles in 1953 to 8 billion in 1962.[6] The production of mineral fertilizer, long a crying need in Soviet agriculture, was increased from 5.5 million metric tons in 1950 to 19.9 million in 1963.[7]

KHRUSHCHEV'S AGRICULTURAL POLICIES

One U.S. idea that Khrushchev eagerly sought to emulate was that of the corn-hog production cycle. Delegations of Soviet agronomists and other experts toured the Corn Belt looking into the American methods in this field, and Khrushchev himself spent some time on his American tour in 1959 getting a firsthand view of the fabulous productive capacity of Kansas and Iowa in corn and hogs. As a result, much of the rich grain land of the Ukraine was converted to corn to increase the supply of animal feeds. *Kukuruza*, the Russian word for "corn," appeared constantly in Soviet writings on agriculture and in the daily press. Because of the low precipitation and rather short growing season in most parts of the Soviet Union, this essay into corn growing has so far been less than a complete success. Some idea of the importance of the crop during the Khrushchev regime can be gained from the fact that an entire building at the permanent exhibition in Moscow was devoted to *kukuruza*. But the statistics speak for themselves: The area sown to corn went from 9 million acres in 1940 to 85 million acres in 1963. Since the ouster of Khrushchev, the *kukuruza* mania has subsided considerably.

Although the population has been constantly increasing, the total grain area of the U.S.S.R. as late as 1953 was somewhat less than it had been before the war. This is a very serious matter in a country that is dependent upon bread for its main staple. The attempt to raise the productivity per hectare (2.471 acres) failed, so in 1954, the attack on the grain problem was shifted to increasing the acreage. In the 1954–56 period, more

TABLE 9

The Main "Virgin and Idle Lands" Developed in 1954–60 *

(In Millions of Acres)

Kazakh S.S.R.	63,000
Volga region (Saratov and Stalingrad oblasts)	3,500
Ural region (Kurgan, Orenburg, Sverdlovsk, Chelyabinsk oblasts and Bashkir A.S.S.R.)	9,800
Western Siberia (Kemerovo, Novosibirsk, Omsk, Tomsk, Tyumen oblasts and Altai kray)	17,200
Eastern Siberia (Irkutsk and Chita oblasts, Krasnoyarsk kray, Buriat A.S.S.R., and Tuva autonomous oblast)	8,300
U.S.S.R. Total	101,300

* *Narodnoe Khozyaystvo SSSR v 1958 Godu,* p. 433; Khrushchev's speeches in Sverdlovsk (*Pravda,* March 7, 1961, pp. 1–3), in Novosibirsk (*Pravda,* March 12, 1961, pp. 1–3), and in the Virgin-Land kray (*Pravda,* March 19, 1961, pp. 1–4).

than 100 million acres were plowed up in the "virgin and idle lands" (see Table 9). Most of these lands, which lie in Western Siberia and Kazakhstan, had been "virgin and idle" up to 1954 for a very sound reason: Almost all the acreage concerned lies in areas with low precipitation that had been used largely for grazing, if used at all (see Figure X). The land is so marginal that three good crops out of five is a normal expectation, but even this would mean a vast increase in the grain supply of the Soviet Union. The number of bushels produced per acre (1954, 13.5; 1955, 4.3; 1956, 15:8; 1957, 6.8; 1958, 13.4; 1959, 12.6; 1960, 12.5; 1961, 9.6; 1962, 9.5; 1963, 5.3) shows an interesting alternation of good and bad years, but an over-all drop during the last decade.

Every appeal and all types of pressures were used to persuade young people to settle the virgin lands. Men being discharged from the armed forces were urged to become pioneers in the great project. By the end of 1956, the virgin lands in Kazakhstan alone had absorbed some 600,000 "pioneers." But the living conditions are appalling, even by Russian standards, and the turnover in personnel has remained a serious problem.

The evidence is building up that the great Kazakhstan virgin-

Figure X. The Main Region of "Virgin and Idle Lands" in the Soviet Union

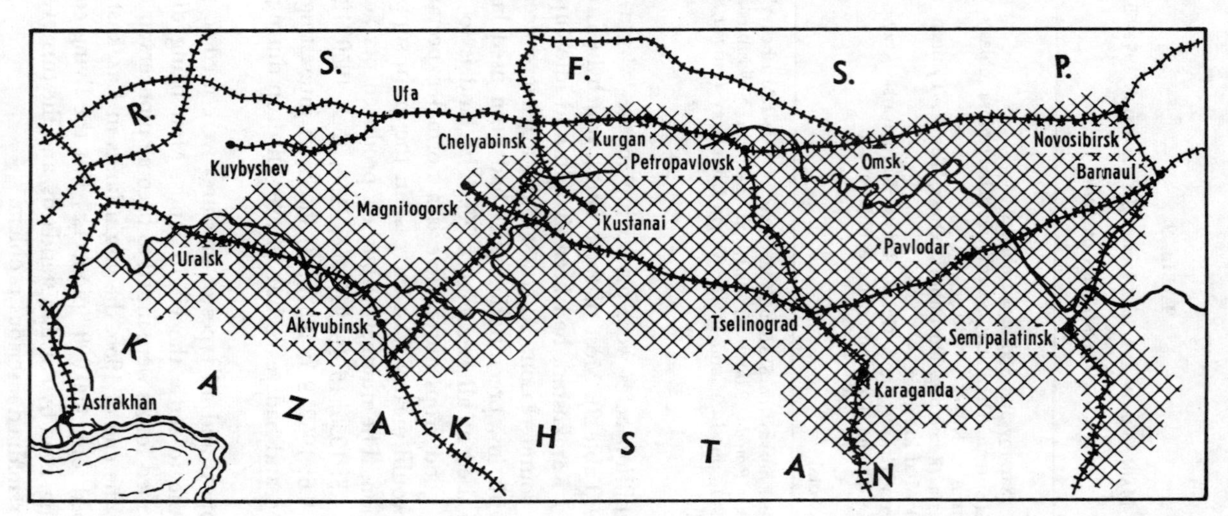

land region is becoming a dust bowl. The hot, dry winds sweeping out of the adjacent deserts have wrought havoc with the light soil so recently denuded of its sparse grass cover. Soviet observers have noted serious wind erosion over some 15 to 20 million acres—areas subject to "black storms" as the soil is blown about by the hot winds. Lack of moisture and very poor dry-farming techniques are at the root of the present trouble.

Khrushchev, however, did not rely entirely on the establishment of enormous sovkhozes in the arid virgin lands, nor on emulation of the Iowa hog-corn cycle, to solve the agricultural problem. He also attempted to encourage the collective farmers by rationalizing the state procurement system, and by raising prices, thus making it worth while to produce more, especially on the less prosperous collectives.

Previous to the reforms of 1958, the state procurement of agricultural products was a complex system of compulsion and ineffective incentives. The government set up quotas for the amounts of grain, potatoes, meat, and other products that the collective must produce per hectare. These were compulsory deliveries and were paid for at a confiscatory rate. Collectives raising industrial crops such as hemp, cotton, or sugar beets were paid according to a graduated scale in order to spur the production of badly needed products. State purchases above the quota received a considerably higher price and the prosperity of a kolkhoz was dependent upon its extra-quota sales. The services of the MTS were paid for in kind.

After Stalin's death, in 1953, some of the worst features of the state procurement system were gradually eliminated. More emphasis was put on paying extra-quota prices, and compulsory deliveries were reduced drastically. As a result, the cash income of the collectives went from 42.8 billion rubles in 1952 to 130 billion in 1958. Cash distributions to the individual peasants on the collectives could then be made—totaling 12.4 billion rubles in 1952 and rising to 42.2 billion rubles by 1956.[8] Furthermore, since January 1, 1958, the collective farmers and state farm workers have been freed from compulsory deliveries of farm products and livestock from their private plots. The sale of these products in the free markets in the cities enables the peasant to increase his cash income appreciably.

In June, 1958, state procurement was rationalized. Compulsory deliveries were abolished, but the government retained its power to set quotas for production per hectare. The state agreed to pay uniform prices for commodities in the various rayons, and also to review the prices annually. The annual price adjustments seek to ensure some stability in farm income, although this policy involves some compromise with the capitalist law of supply and demand. Premium prices were abolished, and with the demise of the MTS, so were payments in kind. The new system favors the less prosperous collectives; those growing industrial crops had been hit hard by the abolition of premium payments. But Khrushchev, in a speech to the plenum of the Central Committee of the Party, charged that many collectives raising industrial crops were being overpaid per unit of a commodity in comparison with the smaller collectives.[9] In addition, the new decree promised the establishment of uniform prices for farm machinery, petroleum, and fertilizer for all types of farms.[10]

The abolition of the MTS in itself was a radical departure from the lines Stalin had developed. Khrushchev, however, stated that it was time to get rid of "two bosses on the land." Several factors made this drastic move feasible: the increase in the size of the farms, the strengthened Party apparatus in the rural areas, and finally, a desire to avoid inflation by giving the collective something in which to invest its cash. By mid-1959, most of the collectives owned their own machinery.

A bumper crop in 1958 (the Soviets claimed a total grain harvest of 141.2 million metric tons) seemed to make Khrushchev overoptimistic about the future growth of agriculture and he began to make reckless promises. He talked about catching up with the United States by 1960 or 1961 in the per capita production of meat, milk, and butter. This meant the production of 70 million tons of milk and 20 million tons of meat. The euphoria of the 1957–58 period waned and finally turned to bitterness as agricultural production leveled off during the next five years and then failed catastrophically in 1963, when grain production fell to 107 million metric tons.

Khrushchev sought to get agriculture out of the doldrums, but his remedies were mostly organizational. He reorganized the Ministry of Agriculture in an attempt to make it actually carry the latest in scientific techniques to the grass-roots level. He set up a new State Procurement Committee to handle purchases more efficiently and also to supervise agriculture at the farm level. To replace the gap left by the abolition of the MTS, a new organization —the All-Union Farm Machinery Association (Soyuzselkoztekhnika)—was set up. This outfit acted as a liaison between the farm and the agricultural-machinery manufacturers and also took over the farm-machinery repair centers.

Reorganization after reorganization seemed to do little good. Again Khrushchev went in for extending the acreage under crops, this time at the expense of fallow lands and those planted in grasses. For example, fallow land decreased from 40 million acres in 1961 to 15.7 million acres in 1963. In June, 1962, the government announced an increase of 30 per cent in the price of meat and 25 per cent for butter, an attempt to inspire the collective farmers to raise more livestock (money was actually being lost on every pound of meat produced on collectives prior to the price increases). But public dismay was widespread, and there were even riots and bloodshed in many areas.

Finally, in November, 1962, Khrushchev resorted to the truly desperate remedy of splitting the Party into industrial and agricultural branches. He reasoned that since the Party leaders on the local, rayon, and oblast levels had to divide their time between industrial and agricultural matters, they were not proficient in either field. Under the new arrangement, they could specialize in one field or the other.

By the autumn of 1964, Khrushchev's colleagues in the Presidium had taken all they could of his *ad hoc* solutions in agriculture, industry, and foreign affairs, and they ousted him. In November, 1964, the new leadership canceled Khrushchev's division of the Party into agricultural and industrial branches and encouraged the collective farmers to expand their private plots and increase their livestock holdings, forms of ownership that Khrushchev had frowned upon.

Khrushchev's attempts to increase agricultural output drastically were probably doomed from the start. He realized that the Soviet population was increasing at a rate that made increased farm output a necessity. Furthermore, the urban population was clamoring for a more varied diet, especially for more meat, dairy products, eggs, vegetables, and fruit. His attempts to solve the dilemma through the expansion of the area under cultivation and the growth of more corn as animal feed proved futile by the beginning of the 1960's. When he tried to move his colleagues to agree to a drastic increase in the chemical industry in order to get more fertilizer, and tried to persuade them to put more investment capital into the farm-machinery industry, he trod on the toes of too many vested interests. Such outlays of capital would have meant a curtailment of funds for heavy industry and the military, and his colleagues were reluctant to accept it.

Perhaps, however, the fundamental reason for Khrushchev's failure was the fact that all his moves to increase agricultural output had to be made within the framework of collectivized agriculture. The large kolkhozes and sovkhozes are not efficient agricultural units; they are too overburdened with bureaucrats and provide insufficient incentives for the man at the bottom, who does the work. The fact that the Soviet production of meat, milk, butter, eggs, vegetables, and fruit comes to such a large extent from the private plots of the individual farmers points up where their hearts are, and where they expend their best efforts. Khrushchev's measures, which did remove some of the worst aspects of collectivized agriculture, were, after all, but home nostrums administered to a patient in need of major surgery.

On March 24/25, 1965, a plenary session of the CPSU Central Committee was held in Moscow to deal with the agricultural problem. Brezhnev delivered the main address, and in it he issued some drastic directives aimed at curing the major headache of the Soviet economy.[11] He began by damning the Khrushchev program, pointing out that the Seven-Year Plan (1959–65), designed to increase the gross agricultural output by 70 per cent, had, in fact, increased agricultural production by only 10 per cent in the first six years of operation. Grain production was the sorriest of the failures, although animal husbandry was also far behind the plan figures (the number of pigs, sheep, and poultry had actually declined). According to Brezhnev, one cause of these troubles was the improper handling of procurements. Prices had not always covered the costs of production, and grain-procurement plans had been fulfilled a mere three times in the last ten years (1956, 1958, and 1964).

Brezhnev then described a new strategy for boosting agricultural production. First, grain-procurement plans were to be set for the next six years (1965–70), and the prices to be paid were to be increased substantially. Grain purchases made by the state above the procurement plans would receive a price 50 per cent higher than the grain procured under the plan. Some of the grains that are known to the Russians as "groats"—such as rice, buckwheat, and millet—were to receive much higher prices in the future, in order to encourage their wider planting. Second, livestock-procurement plans were also to be fixed for the next six years, and prices raised from 30 to 70 per cent according to the type of meat and the geographical location of the farm. Third, the Seventh Five-Year Plan (1966–70), which envisaged a 71-billion-ruble investment of state resources and collective-farm funds in agriculture, was to increase farm construction and the production of farm machinery, as well as to allow for other investments aimed at upping production. The tractor-production goal for 1970 was set at 625,000 units, and 1,790,000 tractors were thus to be delivered to the farms during the Seventh Five-Year Plan. Grain combines were to be increased from the current 84,000 a year to 125,000 annually by 1970. Finally, during the new Five-Year Plan some 7.5 million acres of land were to be irrigated and 15 million acres of soggy soil drained.

Of course, grandiose goals are nothing new in Soviet agricultural planning, and whether Brezhnev's rosy picture of how agriculture will fare in investment allocations over the next six years is realistic, only time will tell. When it comes to actually making the allocations between 1965 and 1970, he may find it hard to fob off the other sectors of the economy year after year.

Notable in Brezhnev's speech was the near absence of any mention of a boost in the chemical industry for the production of fertilizer, insecticides, herbicides, and defoliants. This was Khrushchev's favorite subject in the final years of his reign.

If, however, Brezhnev and his planners can come up with the funds to implement the agricultural sector of the new Five-Year Plan, the additional machinery and the higher price schedules show at least an effort to put Soviet agriculture on a more solid footing.

8

Industry

Several observations are fundamental to any discussion of the Soviet industrial structure. First, the entire industrial economy of the Soviet Union is owned and operated by the state, and the state is synonomous with the top rung of the Communist Party. Second, the Soviet economy has been a totally planned economy since 1929. Finally, production goals are established by a small group at the top of the Party hierarchy and are directed toward bolstering the Party's power, increasing the military effectiveness of the Soviet armed forces, and promoting the expansion of the Soviet Union and the world-wide domination of Communism.

DEVELOPMENT OF THE PLANNED ECONOMY

These considerations have led the Party leadership, logically enough, to emphasize heavy industry and relegate the consumer-goods industries to a secondary role in all plans. The Soviet planners have subsidized heavy industry at the expense of the consumer through the turnover tax and, in some cases, at the expense of other segments of the economy—for example, the railroads.

The emphasis upon industries that contribute to military strength began in the early years of the Soviet state. In 1920, the first industrial plan was launched—the Goelro plan, which established the State Commission for the Electrification of the Soviet Union. Soviet historians now term this the first step toward over-all planning of the economy and credit Lenin with its conception.* However, Lenin actually opposed any all-encompassing economic scheme for some time. A more fitting candidate for the role of prophet of the planned era was Mikhail Frunze, a leading military commander and military theorist who replaced Trotsky as Commissar of War in 1925. Frunze stated that the military forces of a nation reflect the nation itself, that war in the future would be total, and that the rear was as important as the front in total war. The immediate task was to raise the industrial production of the Soviet Union to match that of her probable opponents in Western Europe.

This idea of the coordination of all aspects of the nation's life in preparing its total military machine is nothing new. Several Communist leaders observed Germany's efforts toward coordination in World War I, during which one of Russia's chief weaknesses was its inability to coordinate, but Frunze spelled out the idea in detail. We find him telling the Red Academy in 1924 that the tasks of defense could not be shouldered alone by the Commissariat of War; they were the responsibility of the whole people. In the future, the entire governmental apparatus and the entire people must prepare for war long before war begins. At the conclusion of this speech, he summed up the program in these words:

> Future work must be concentrated on working out plans for mobilizing the economy of the country, the carrying out of suitable economic enterprises; *it must militarize all our Soviet work from economy to education* [italics added].[1]

In 1928, when Stalin had consolidated his power, he began to convert the Soviet Union into a totality of force ready at all times to meet the problems, internal and external, accompanying the over-all Communist strategy. The inauguration of the First Five-Year Plan, in October, 1928, set in motion the "Second Revolu-

* Lenin made this proposal to the Eighth Congress of the Soviets, in 1920, and it is usually associated with his oft-repeated dictum: "Communism is Soviet power plus the electrification of the whole country."

tion"; it marked the conscious attempt to speed up the productive base at the expense of all other considerations. Without attempting a full-scale analysis of the first three Five-Year Plans, put into operation before World War II, one can gauge the tempo of industrialization by analyzing the production of steel, the basic element in heavy industry and armaments. In 1919–20, the output of pig iron dropped to the unbelievably low figure of 115,000 tons a year—4 per cent of the 1913 level of 4.5 million tons. It was not until 1929 that the 1913 level was again reached. In 1930, the decision was made to build the Ural-Kuznetsk *kombinat*. This was a decision based to some extent on military considerations. The amount of capital poured into the Ural-Kuznetsk *kombinat* would have produced far more steel if invested in the Ukraine, but the new location was not so vulnerable as the Ukraine. By the middle of the 1930's, the steel bottleneck had been largely overcome; production ran in the vicinity of 20 million tons. Gradually, Soviet dependence upon imports lessened. In 1931, the U.S.S.R. imported about 1.2 million tons of metal, or 22 per cent of its needs; by 1940, the import figure had dropped to 97,300 tons, then 0.7 per cent of Soviet consumption. A simultaneous attack had been made upon coal output, electric power, and other essential components of a heavy industry.

The Soviet effort to solve the problem of economic backwardness by emphasizing heavy industry has led to an extremely lopsided economic development. While the Urals and the Ukraine bristle with gigantic blast furnaces and oil-cracking plants, and the mightiest Russian rivers are being harnessed to produce electric power, poor Ivan Ivanov still finds it difficult, often impossible, to get shoes, meat, and adequate housing. From 1940 to 1955, the output of expensive metal-cutting machine tools rose from 58,000 to 117,000. During the same period, the output of cotton fabrics increased from 4 to 6 million yards, and the production of domestic washing machines rose from zero to 87,000—to supply a population of more than 200 million. These are Soviet figures, and doctored or not, they still look bad. This imbalance was not accidental; such accidents do not happen in the U.S.S.R. In order to have the capital to reinvest constantly in expanding heavy industry, it was necessary to keep consumer goods at a very low level. If the Soviet economy had produced 10 million washing machines in 1955, when steel production was 50 million tons, it would have meant diverting steel, labor, and machinery from the production of steel-making equipment, machine tools, and tanks.

FORMAL STRUCTURE OF SOVIET INDUSTRY

Until the reorganization of 1957, Soviet industry was organized along "branch" lines; a large number of ministries was created, each to control one sector of the economy throughout the U.S.S.R. Theoretically, each minister had complete charge of his ministry, but in reality, Party and police controls continually infringed his authority. Below the ministry were the Chief Administrations, or *Glavki* (singular, *Glavk*), subministries in charge of plants producng similar products in a single geographical area. Originally below the *Glavk* were trusts, but in many cases the trusts were indistinguishable from the *Glavk,* and gradually the trusts disappeared. Below the *Glavk* was the *kombinat*—a large plant, or a group of plants, producing a variety of products and by-products based on a single raw material. The Magnitogorsk *kombinat,* based on the rich iron ore of Mount Magnitnaya, is a good example. This *kombinat* has its own blast furnaces, open-hearth furnaces, coke ovens, and rolling mills. In the case of large enterprises,* there was often a direct line of control between it and its ministry, bypassing any intermediate *Glavk.*

Until May, 1957, Soviet ministries were predominantly all union, that is, directly controlled from Moscow. These were essentially heavy-industrial ministries dealing with the means of production and defense items, often referred to by the Russians

* The word "enterprise" is a literal translation of the Russian word *predpriyatie.* It can mean a plant, a group of factories, a railroad, etc. A Soviet authority, A. Arakalian, defines an enterprise as the "basic and decisive link in the system for administering socialist industry."

as Group A. The light and food industries producing consumer goods, Group B, were often union-republic ministries, although they received considerable guidance from Moscow. Small industries, concerned chiefly with satisfying local needs, came under the jurisdiction of local councils, which, however, often received unsolicited advice from the union-republic ministries.

This system of "branch" ministries was very complex. Thirty to forty ministries extended their tentacles throughout the entire U.S.S.R. And each ministry had a tendency to build its own empire, as is the wont of bureaucractic institutions. Oleg Hoeffding points out that the Ministry of Machine-Tool Production controlled only fifty-five of the 171 plants making machine tools; nineteen other ministries had insinuated themselves into control of the balance.[2]

The supreme body in the organization and management of Soviet economic life is the Council of Ministers. This institution was organized as early as 1918, and since then has grown steadily in power and complexity. It was called the Council of People's Commissars until 1946, when it became the Council of Ministers. But the change in title in no way affected its functions. In the early years of Bolshevik power, the Council, with its Commissars for Defense, Foreign Affairs, and other necessary departments, was similar to the cabinets of most Western powers. It included an additional section called the Supreme Economic Council, which was designed to coordinate industry and solve economic problems. In 1932, the Supreme Economic Council was abolished and replaced by a number of industrial commissariats, each in direct control of one segment of the economy. There was a steady trend toward the creation of more and more commissariats, especially in the field of economic control. For instance, in 1939, the Commissariat of Heavy Industry was broken down into nine commissariats: three in machine tools, and one each for coal, oil, iron and steel, nonferrous metals, chemicals, and electric power. During World War II, the "specialization" in commissariats increased even faster because of the defense industries, for example, the Commissariat for Tank Production. By 1947, under the revised Constitution, there were sixty all-union ministries, thirty-seven of which were economic ministries or outgrowths of the old Supreme Economic Council. Since then, the number of ministries has varied—now a big reduction, now a sudden burgeoning.

On May 7, 1957, Khrushchev addressed the Supreme Soviet on the subject of an over-all reorganization of Soviet economic management and announced some very drastic changes. It is too soon to evaluate the effects of this reorganization, and several theories have been advanced on the underlying motives for the changes. Officially, it was alleged that the Soviet economy was too highly centralized, and that a move toward more autonomy on the lower levels was long overdue. In announcing the new program, Khrushchev stated:

> The tasks of further advancing the national economy at the present stage of its development, as has already been said, make it necessary to shift the center of gravity of operational guidance of industry and construction closer to enterprises and construction projects. However, this can be done only by a transition from the management of the national economy through the industrial ministries and agencies to management based on territorial principles. The Party Central Committee and the U.S.S.R. Council of Ministers hold that the economic administrative regions should become the organizational form of such management.[3]

Whether this was the primary motive is another matter. Some students of the Soviet scene think that Khrushchev's main objective was to strengthen the position of the Party leaders at all levels and to curb the growing independence of the technological-managerial class. Whatever the reasons, the shake-up had in it the seeds of a far-reaching reorientation of the methods of operating the Soviet economy.

Under the new system, economic planning and administration in the U.S.S.R. still began at the very top, in the Central Committee Presidium and Secretariat. Their decisions were transmitted to the Council of Ministers, which, in turn, used Gosplan and the State Committees to break the broad directives down into detailed plans and administer them. These steps took place at the all-union level. The responsibilities then devolved on the organs

Figure XI. U.S.S.R. Industrial Organization

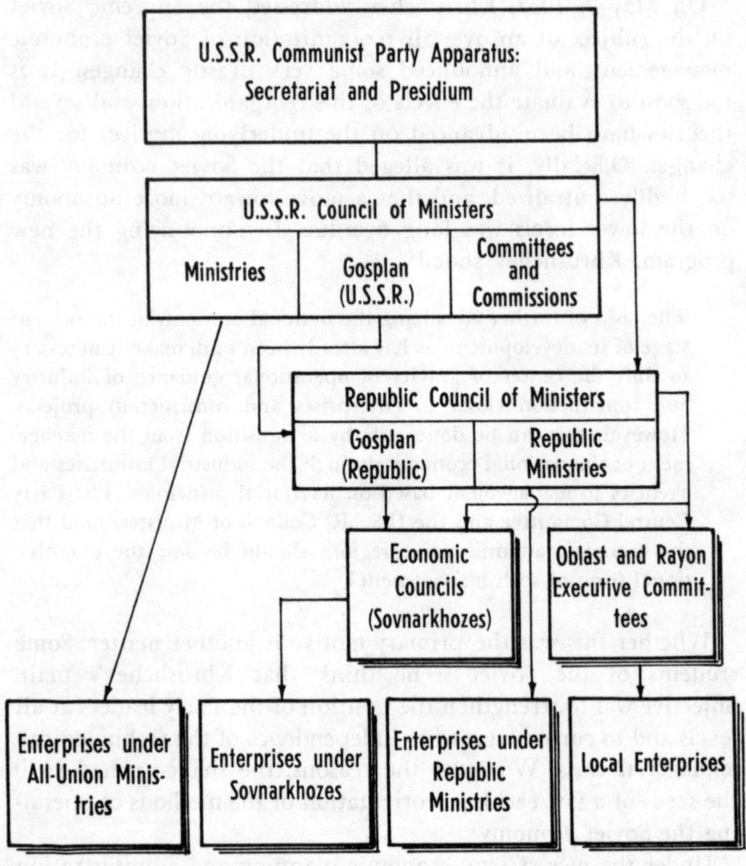

at the republic level: the Republic Councils of Ministers and Gosplans, which, in turn, sent the directives to the economic administrative regions and their economic councils (sovnarkhozes). The sovnarkhozes then supervised the operations of the enterprises, kolkhozes, and other basic units of production (see Figure XI).

The economic administrative region with its economic council was the basic administrative unit in the new system. Khrushchev envisaged ninety-two economic councils for the whole of the U.S.S.R.: sixty-eight in the R.S.F.S.R., eleven in the Ukrainian S.S.R., and one in each of the other union republics. The number was subsequently increased; many republics felt that they needed more than one economic administrative region. This was in keeping with Khrushchev's statement that "it will be expedient to entrust the union-republic governments with the solution of questions connected with the formation of economic administrative regions and their economic councils, with subsequent approval by the U.S.S.R. Council of Ministers."

In connection with the reorganization, the composition of the U.S.S.R. Council of Ministers underwent drastic changes. Only

Figure XII. Council of Ministers

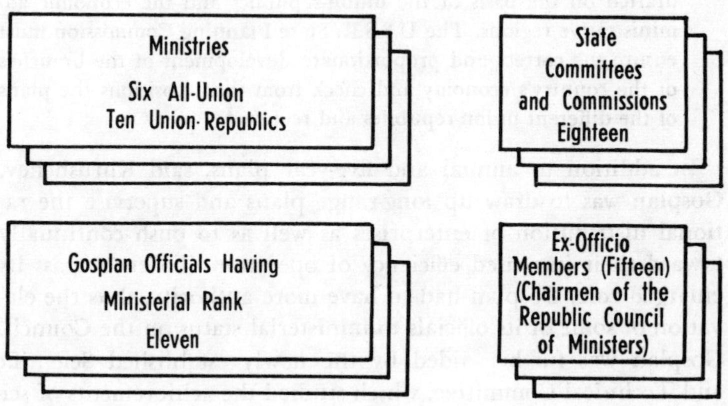

six all-union ministries—those directing Construction of Electric Power Stations, Foreign Trade, Medium-Machine Building, Railways, Sea Fleet, and Transport Construction—and ten union-republic ministries were retained. This was a drastic reduction from the sixty ministries in 1957. The Council of Ministers also includes a Presidium of around ten, the fifteen chairmen of the Republic Councils of Ministers, eighteen chairmen of State Committees and Commissions, and eleven high officials of Gosplan who have been raised to ministerial rank. So the U.S.S.R. Council of Ministers still has more than sixty members (see Figure XII).

Under the new system, the importance of the U.S.S.R. State Planning Commission, or Gosplan, was augmented considerably. Khrushchev summed up the role of Gosplan in his speech of May 7, 1957:

> The U.S.S.R. State Planning Commission [Gosplan U.S.S.R.] must become the scientific-economic planning agency of the country. It is called upon to submit the requirements of the national economy to profound and comprehensive study, to take into consideration the achievements of science and technology, and on this basis, to draw up proposals for the development of all branches of the national economy, taking the potentialities for the integrated development of the economy most carefully into account, and to utilize resources rationally in the general interests of the state. Under the new conditions, the national economic plans will be drafted on the basis of the union-republics and the economic administrative regions. The U.S.S.R. State Planning Commission must ensure the correct and proportionate development of the branches of the country's economy and check from these positions the plans of the different union-republics and regions.[4]

In addition to annual and five-year plans, said Khrushchev, Gosplan was to draw up long-range plans and supervise the rational distribution of enterprises as well as to push continually toward their increased efficiency of operation. To encompass its enlarged role, Gosplan had to have more authority, thus the elevation of some of its officials to ministerial status on the Council. Gosplan was further aided by the newly established Scientific and Technical Committee, which studied the achievements of science and technology in the U.S.S.R. and abroad, and published information about them.

The increased importance of Gosplan, however, belied the official assertions that the reorganization was aimed primarily at "decentralizing" Soviet industry. The old process of sending the plan figures through channels from Gosplan to the lower echelons, getting their comments on the feasibility of fulfilling the goals, reviewing these objections, and then resubmitting definitive plans backed by the force of law still obtained in the Soviet Union. The only change was in the channels. The old route from Gosplan to ministry to *Glavk* to enterprise was changed to travel from Gosplan to Republic Councils of Ministers and their Gosplans to sovnarkhozes to enterprise. The lower echelons were still severely limited in local autonomy, and the over-all national objectives had first priority. Furthermore, since there were no rational economic criteria applied in the creation of the economic administrative regions—the regions were made to coincide with existing political administrative machinery—it would seem that political considerations were at least as important as economic criteria in the reorganization.

One of the recurring features of Soviet economic life has been the dispute over the amount of autonomy to be given to the manager of an enterprise. On the whole, the tendency has been toward one-man control, or *yedinonachalie*. Until the early 1930's, the enterprises were usually managed by a group; the director was concerned primarily with coordinating the independent supply, production, planning, and financial branches of his enterprise. In 1930, in his report to the Sixteenth Party Congress, Stalin made the following comment on this topic:

> We cannot any longer put up with our factories being transformed from productive organizations into parliaments. Our Party and trade union organizations must at length understand that without ensuring one-man management and strict responsibility for work done, we cannot solve the problems of reconstructing industry.[5]

Gradually the director has come to control all divisions of his enterprise and also to assume all responsibility. He issues orders to the chief engineer, and the latter transmits them through channels—the shop chiefs, foremen, and brigade leaders. The director is the final authority within the enterprise and is solely responsible if the quotas are not attained, although he can exercise authority and show initiative only within the limits delegated to him by the sovnarkhoz. The director also has to keep an eye on the Party organization, which is more powerful than he.

In spite of all these restrictions, the plant director is often a dynamic individual who adheres to the *yedinonachalie* concept, even to the point of using illegal methods to boost his production. Undoubtedly, the Soviet Government often condones this as long as it produces results. On the other hand, the Party periodically makes efforts to control industrial management when it tends to follow its own laws of development. The danger that the "owners" of industry may lose control of "management" is just as real in the Soviet Union as in the United States.

Another way of controlling the fulfillment of production plans and checking on the responsibility of management is the so-called cost-accounting, or *khozrachet,* system. Under this method, each enterprise has its own budget, which is a means of compelling the enterprise to explore all possibilities of economy in production and to show a profit. Since Soviet economic literature censures high production costs and praises enterprises that show a profit, the *khozrachet* system appears to be a return to capitalism. On the other hand, the higher echelons control raw materials, set production quotas, and establish the prices of the finished product—all of which limits drastically the functioning of anything comparable to a capitalistic profit system.

INCENTIVES.

In the absence of an ordinary profit system, what stimulants motivate management to fulfill the plans assigned to it? It must be assumed that, over a forty-year period, something above and beyond Party propaganda has provided the necessary drive to the managers and workers of Soviet industry. The Soviet method of stimulating and controlling management is twofold: premium payments and negative sanctions—the familiar carrot-and-stick technique.

The payment of substantial monetary rewards for the fulfillment and overfulfillment of production targets is the Soviet equivalent of the profit motive in a capitalistic society; it is the main incentive for keeping Soviet management on its toes. The apparent frequency with which premium payments are dispensed may be accounted for by two factors: the realistic, or attainable, targets set by the planners, and the ability of management to arrange for assigned plans to be well within maximum plant capacity.

Negative sanctions are designed to discourage too many short cuts in the fulfillment of plans. Joseph S. Berliner, an authority on the informal aspects of Soviet industrial management, lists the following offenses that are liable to sanctions:

> . . . overpayment of wages, technological breakdown, illegal procurement, failure to meet planned assortment, breach of financial discipline, falsification of reports, political deviation, subquality production, plan underfulfillment, financial overexpenditures, failure to produce spare parts. The following are the negative sanctions linked with these actions: being brought to trial, charge of wrecking, imprisonment, reprimand, fine, dismissal from job, and shooting.[6]

The Soviet manager must be able to evaluate and choose among possible sanctions. If faced with the alternatives of subquality production or failure to fulfill the plan, he will usually choose the former as it entails a less serious sanction. But if the output is military goods, where the quality factor is sacrosanct, the manager will choose underfulfillment in preference to subquality production.

INFORMAL METHODS OF SOVIET MANAGEMENT

An expression used by Soviet defectors in describing their life in the Soviet Union is *zhit spokoyno* (to live peacefully). But "to live peacefully" in the Soviet industrial complex usually involves unlawful, or at least questionable, actions. To keep production up to the planned targets, the manager must resort to wheedling reasonable plans from his superiors, filling out false work orders to keep his subordinates satisfied, and using illegal methods of procuring materials to keep production running. The necessity of committing illegal acts in order to live peacefully is one of the dubious aspects of the Soviet scene. It must be just as ulcer-producing among Soviet managers as is competition among American executives. The desire to obtain premiums, to avoid negative sanctions, and to live peacefully results in a definite pattern of behavior on the part of Soviet management. Berliner has reduced the pattern to three principles of behavior: *strakhova,* the safety factor; *ochkovtiratelstvo,* simulation; and *blat,* a combination of bribery and simple reciprocity.

One safety factor consists in having the output target set below the enterprise's abilty to produce. The manager is aware that success is judged not by an absolute volume of output, but by the ratio of actual output to planned output. Hoarding materials is another safety factor, since lack of materials is the chief bottleneck of Soviet production. Management may also try to undertake new production for which time, labor, and other cost factors are unknown. By concentrating on items that are easy to produce and utilizing machinery supposedly laid up for repair, management can distort the planned production schedule. The manager must constantly and feverishly maneuver for enough slack so that shortages of materials and breakdowns of machinery will not disrupt his planned production to the extent of underfulfillment.

Simulation, the second principle of Soviet unorthodox economic behavior, chiefly demands shifty bookkeeping and an ability to get away with stratagems in meeting plan figures. Literally, the Russian word *ochkovtiratelstvo* means "to throw dust in one's eyes, rub one's spectacles," or in our idiom, "pull the wool over someone's eyes." Because large machine units count for more in judging plan fulfillment than does the production of spare parts, managers in the Soviet Union avoid that section of the plan if possible, and spare parts are perennially in short supply. Some managers find ways of crediting the output of one period to another period or concealing overproduction as a safety factor to ensure fulfillment of the next plan. Reduction in quality is also a common device.

The third principle of informal behavior is *blat,* the real lubricant of the ponderous economic machine. However, *blat* occurs in all phases of Soviet life. If you do an official a favor, and he finds you an apartment to which you are not strictly entitled, that is *blat. Blat* is most prevalent in the procurement and supply areas of the Soviet industrial structure. Even an allocation order with high priority may not enable a manager to get the materials necessary to keep his production lines in full operation. In many cases, when the materials are vital to plan fulfillment, the manager resorts to a *tolkach,* a "pusher" or expediter. The *tolkach* has an extralegal position in the Soviet economy, but since his services help to smooth the flow of supplies, the regime "looks through its fingers" at this nonplanned activity. The successful *tolkach* gets to know the people having supplies, knows how to approach them, and even knows who is open to influence. If a coal enterprise needs lumber badly, the *tolkach* will haunt lumber camps until he finds an executive who is willing to exchange coal for the required amount of timber. Usually good relations are established over a period of time by a series of gifts, perhaps a bottle of vodka now and then to a responsible worker who can speed up the loading and shipping. *Blat* is often used to influence the drafting of a plan that can be fulfilled, or in getting the difficult and unprofitable kinds of production shifted to another plant.

These informal aspects of Soviet industry keep the ponderous planned machine operating. So it is not surprising to find the ministry willingly deceived by managers who indulge in extralegal maneuvering *as long as they are successful in fulfilling their plans.*

RECENTRALIZATION

The reorganization of 1957 seemed to cause more problems than it solved, and Khrushchev busied himself for the next seven years in trying to make his system work efficiently. In April, 1960, Gosplan U.S.S.R. was restricted to the annual plan, and a new organ—the State Scientific-Economic Council (Gosekonomsovet)—took over long-range planning (twenty years) and medium-range planning (five to seven years). But Gosplan's authority in guiding the separate branches of industry was actually increased—it took on many of the functions of the former ministries. The republic Gosplans were also revamped to fit in with the changes in Gosplan U.S.S.R. Gosplan gained more and more control of interrepublican deliveries, i.e., it came to control the supplies going to the various enterprises in different republics. This dependence upon a highly centralized supply system led many of the enterprises to engage the services of *tolkachi* to expedite deliveries of vitally needed inputs.

The Councils of Ministers in the multi-sovnarkhoz republics found themselves overburdened with detail in their attempts to settle disputes among their sovnarkhozes. The R.S.F.S.R., for example, had sixty-seven sovnarkhozes to cope with. In July, 1960, all-republic sovnarkhozes were set up in the R.S.F.S.R., the Ukraine, and Kazakhstan to deal with sovnarkhoz problems within their jurisdiction.

In May, 1961, the Soviet leadership came up with a plan to establish seventeen large economic regions (ten in the R.S.F.S.R., three in the Ukraine, one in Kazakhstan, one for the three Baltic republics, one for the Transcaucasian republics, and one for the four Central Asian republics). The creation of these large economic regions was an attempt to coordinate the production of the various sovnarkhozes more along the lines desired by the central planners. But nothing, it seemed, could solve the problem of "localism." New protective "family circles"—composed of the top officials in the sovnarkhoz, the enterprise, and even in the republican Gosplan—were constantly emerging, and severe penalties apparently did little to stop the tendency. These officials, whenever they thought they might go undetected, put their local welfare first and the national plan second. To be independent of the vagaries of outside sources of supply, the sovnarkhoz sometimes tried to make itself self-sufficient, even though local inputs cost more to produce. In other words, they, on a local level, were guilty of the same sin that the former ministries had been accused of. Finally, in November, 1962, Khrushchev drastically reduced the number of sovnarkhozes; in the R.S.F.S.R. the number dropped from sixty-seven to twenty-four, and the four sovnarkhozes in Central Asia were combined into the Central Asian Interrepublic Sovnarkhoz.

By November, 1962, Khrushchev had apparently gone overboard on the matter of reorganization as a tool for stimulating the economy. All construction was taken out of the hands of the sovnarkhozes and given to the U.S.S.R. State Committee for Construction (Gosstroi). Gosekonomsovet was abolished, its long-range planning functions given to Gosplan, and a new organization—the All-Union Economic Council—took over short-term planning. Only four months later, in March, 1963, a new organ—the Supreme Council of the National Economy—was imposed on the bureaucratic crazy quilt in an attempt to coordinate the activities of Gosstroi, the All-Union Economic Council, and Gosplan. With the establishment of the Supreme Council of the National Economy, the decentralization of 1957 had been largely liquidated and the Soviet economy was again centralized.

A year after the ousting of Khrushchev, the new leadership brought the organization of the Soviet economy completely back to the pre-1957 system of ministries. Mazurov, in a speech to the Supreme Soviet on October 1, 1965, announced the formation of twenty-eight new ministries to replace many of the committees and commissions in the Council of Ministers and to carry out the responsibilities of those sovnarkhozes that had been abolished.[7] Eleven of the new ministries are all union and seventeen are union republic. The eight-year period between Khrushchev's drastic reorganization of the economy (1957) and the complete liquidation of that reorganization (1965) has been a hectic one indeed.

Recently, some Soviet economists have been discussing economic reforms that seem somewhat un-Marxian and that may, if seriously implemented, have far greater repercussions in the

Soviet Union than any of Khrushchev's shifting of the bureaucratic structure. Soviet economists are now writing about the need for a more rational *price system,* the desirability of being able to impose *charges on fixed capital* (interest, in the bourgeois world), and the use of *profitability* as a basis for bonus payments to managers. This last concept, *profitability,* is being tried out today on a limited scale.

Professor Yevsei Liberman, of the Kharkov Engineering and Economics Institute, is the central figure in this debate. The Liberman Plan is a scheme to cure the evils at the plant level without eliminating over-all central planning. Under the plan, the government would retain the job of planning the volume of output, the assortment of goods, and the delivery schedules. But at the plant level, profits would constitute the only index for bonus payments to the plant manager. Inducements to the manager to reveal his full productive capacity would be made in the following manner: (1) The bonus payments would be based on the rate of profit on the total rubles invested. In other words, the concealment of capital goods would lower the base upon which the manager's bonus is paid. (2) The norms of profitability for a branch of industry would be kept stable over an extended period of time. Thus a productive and efficient manager would not be penalized. (3) Full bonuses would be paid for plan fulfillment, but only half as much for overfulfillment. This would encourage the manager to plan up to his full capacity. It would also help keep the system more stable, for overfulfillment can upset economic planning as much as underfulfillment. (4) No bonuses would be paid on the production of goods that were not sold. Thus producing the "wrong" assortment (e.g., nothing but one-pound bolts) or shoddy goods that never get out of the warehouse would be discouraged.

Liberman's proposals have received serious consideration at the highest levels of academic circles, have been published in *Pravda,* and were even mentioned favorably by Khrushchev. But the more conservative economists and Party members view Liberman's plan and its progress as the camel of capitalism getting his nose into the tent of Marxian economics.

SOME BASIC FACTORS IN SOVIET INDUSTRIAL CAPACITY

A relatively sound picture of Soviet industrial capacity can be obtained by looking at some of the factors essential to heavy industry: the production of coal, steel, petroleum, electric power, and metal-cutting machine tools (see Table 10).

TABLE 10

SOVIET PRODUCTION OF BASIC INDUSTRIAL GOODS *

	1913	*1940*	*1955*	*1960*	*1961*	*1962*	*1963*	*1964*
Coal (millions of tons)	32	182	430	564	561	569	589	609
Steel (millions of tons)	5	20	50	72	78	84	88	93
Oil (millions of tons)	11	34	78	162	182	205	226	244
Metal-cutting machine tools (thousands of units)	2	58	117	155	165	177	182	184
Electric power (billions of K.W.H.)	2	48	170	292	327	369	412	459

* *Narodnoe Khozyaystvo SSSR v 1963 Godu,* pp. 145, 151, 154, 157, 163, 168; *Pravda,* January 30, 1965.

COAL

In the early 1950's, coal accounted for nearly three-quarters of all fuels consumed by the Soviet economy. But in 1957 a fifteen-year plan was devised that called for all emphasis to be placed on oil and natural gas. Coal was to account for only 30 per cent of total fuel production by 1972. A good guess would be that coal accounted for 40 to 45 per cent of fuel consumption in 1965,[8] and is therefore still the most important source of energy in the Soviet Union.

The most important coal-mining areas in the Soviet Union are the Donets Basin (Donbas), the Kuznetsk Basin (Kuzbas), the Karaganda Basin, and the Pechora Basin. These four basins contain an estimated 100 billion metric tons of coal.

The Donbas, located on the Donets River, a tributary of the Don, is the fuel base for the huge Ukrainian industrial complex. This 10,000-square-mile basin yields the coking coal, chemical raw materials, and fuel for the Central and Volga industrial areas as well. Although the output of coal in the Donbas in absolute figures rose from 25.4 million tons in 1913 to 258 million tons in 1965, it dropped from 78 per cent to 40 per cent in the total Soviet output—a clear indication of the shift in industry from west to east.

The second most important coal basin is the Kuzbas, which lies along the upper Tom River, an affluent of the Ob. In area, the Kuzbas is about the same as the Donbas, and its reserve is slightly smaller than that of the Donbas. Kuzbas coal is of first-class quality, comes in thick seams, and is easy to mine because the seams are close to the surface. In the 1930's, the Kuzbas was the eastern end of the Ural-Kuznetsk *kombinat;* coal was hauled to Magnitogorsk and iron ore back to Kuznetsk. Since World War II, local iron ore at Kuznetsk has supplanted that of Magnitogorsk, and the ferrous-metallurgical cycle in the Kuzbas is almost autonomous. In 1913, only 750,000 tons of coal were mined in all Western Siberia. By 1940, the Kuzbas was producing more than 20 million tons, and by 1965 it was producing 118 million tons.

In the late 1930's, coking coal was shipped for the first time from Karaganda to Magnitogorsk—a shorter haul than from the Kuzbas. Also, the discovery of iron ore in Kazakhstan, especially at Kustanai, has resulted in a growing ferrous metallurgy within that republic. Karaganda is a newcomer, raising its production of coal from 100,000 tons in 1913, to 7 million tons in 1940, to an impressive 57 million tons in 1965.

The Pechora deposit was developed under forced draft during World War II to ease the shortage caused by the German offensive in the Ukraine. A railroad was built in record time, largely by forced labor. The excellent coking coal of Pechora answers the fuel needs of the Leningrad area, and a steel plant has been opened recently at Cherepovets to supply the machine-tool industry of that area. In 1965, almost 22 million tons of coal were mined in the Pechora Basin.

There are other coal deposits scattered about the Soviet Union, and grandiose plans are being made to set up new industrial complexes based upon them. But on the whole, the main use of these deposits is to reduce the long-distance hauling of fuels and to supply the railroads. According to Soviet figures, a total of 609 million tons of coal was mined in 1964.

Steel

The backbone of industry, especially heavy industry, is steel, and it is probably the best barometer of the increase in Soviet industrial capacity. The manufacture of steel is dependent upon two main ingredients, coking coal and iron ore, as well as upon some of lesser importance, such as limestone for flux, various clays for the firebrick lining of furnaces, and manganese. On the whole, the Soviet Union is well supplied with all these materials, although they vary in quality from area to area.

The area of the Urals, lower Western Siberia, and northern Kazakhstan is now supplying more than half of Soviet steel production, and at its present rate of growth will become far and away the greatest Soviet steel center of the future. As we have seen, in the early 1930's, this center was based on the iron ore of Magnitogorsk and the coking coal of the Kuzbas. Since then, the Magnitogorsk plant has turned to Karaganda for its coal, and some of its iron ore comes from the Kazakhstan deposits and scattered Ural mines. The Kuznetsk region has developed its own iron-ore supply from the Kondoma and Gorno Sharskaya groups of deposits, all of which are within easy hauling distance of the Kuznetsk steel plants. According to Soviet accounts, the Kustanai iron-ore deposit in northwest Kazakhstan should be enough to supply the entire area for years to come. Reports are that this deposit is 463 square miles in area and that the ore can be mined cheaply by open-pit methods.

The Ukraine was the traditional steel center of the U.S.S.R., at least up to World War II. Its importance was based on the iron ore of Krivoi Rog and the coking coal of the Donbas. These two great concentrations of raw materials are about equidistant from the Dnieper River, and the total distance from Krivoi Rog to Donetsk (formerly Stalino), in the Donbas, is only 300 miles.

These twin blessings make possible tremendous shipments of ore and coal within the Donbas area. As late as 1940, the Ukraine was the source of half of the Soviet steel production; by 1958, its output was down to 39 per cent, although its actual production had risen from around 9.8 million to around 23 million tons. Of course, the wartime destruction of Ukrainian ferrous metallurgy and the necessary relocation of much of its skilled personnel and equipment to the east help explain the present differential.

Although the overwhelming percentage of Soviet steel production comes from the Ukraine and the Ural-Kuznetsk area, smaller quantities also come from the Moscow region, Cherepovets, and the Rustavi plant near Tbilisi, in Georgia. Total Soviet steel output in 1964 was about 93 million tons.

Petroleum

Until a very few years ago, it was generally accepted that the Soviet war potential was seriously limited by a lack of petroleum. As late as 1940, more than 74 per cent of Soviet oil came from the Baku fields, which made an extremely vulnerable air target. Today the situation is entirely different, with about 10 per cent of Soviet petroleum coming from Baku and most of it coming from the Volga-Ural oil fields, a relatively dispersed and distant target. Total Soviet petroleum production increased from 34 million tons in 1940 to 244 million tons in 1964, and the rate of increase has gone up sharply in the last few years. Today Soviet military requirements in petroleum are being met more than adequately.

Soviet estimates of their petroleum reserves verge on the fantastic—some 8 billion tons, or more than half the world's estimated total. Most non-Soviet authorities would agree that the U.S.S.R. has a large proportion of the world's petroleum reserves, but probably very much less than the Soviets claim. Today the big Soviet problems are procurement, processing, and economical distribution.

The Caucasian oil deposits at Baku, on the Apsheron Peninsula, and at Grozny and Maykop, in the Caucasian foothills, were known and worked in the late nineteenth century. In 1913, almost 90 per cent of Russia's oil came from this region, and as late as 1940, the percentage was still very high. Hitler's desire to control this lush area of black gold had much to do with the overextension of the German logistics in their mad dash to the Volga and Caucasus in 1942–43. Today the Baku wells extend out into the Caspian Sea, but in spite of all efforts, in 1963, Baku produced only about 22 million tons, about 10 per cent of the total Soviet output. Grozny, which yielded 15 per cent of the U.S.S.R.'s oil in 1940, now produces only a small percentage of the total.

The major source of Soviet oil is the so-called "Second Baku," an immense oil field located between the middle Volga and the Urals, from 52° to 60° N. Lat. (the Kuybyshev and Molotov oblasts and the A.S.S.R.'s of the Bashkirs and Tatars). The output of this region jumped from 6 per cent of Soviet production in 1940 to about three-quarters by 1958. The "Second Baku" has the further advantage of being nearer to the growing industrial areas of the Volga, Urals, and Western Siberia than are the Caucasian oil fields.

The Emba oil field, whose reserves have been estimated at a billion tons, lies just northwest of the Caspian Sea. It produced just over 1.5 million tons in 1958. In the Pechora Basin, near the new city of Ukhta, there are petroleum fields with a fairly respectable yield of over 1 million tons a year. The oil deposits on Sakhalin Island in the Pacific Ocean, although producing only 1 million tons a year, are very valuable because they help to supply the Far East region and thus take some of the load off the limited capability of the Trans-Siberian Railroad. Oil has been discovered in Uzbekistan and Turkmenistan in recent years, and in 1958, these two republics produced around 6 million tons.

It is only in recent years that the Soviets have gone into the extraction of natural gas on a large scale. As late as 1928, only 304 million cubic meters of gas were utilized in the U.S.S.R. But the value of natural gas as a fuel is now being realized, and in 1963, the total production had risen to around 90 billion cubic meters. The lack of adequate piping caused a delay in utilizing gas in the last few years, but there is a definite drive on to expand gas production.

Electric Power

Although steel is the backbone of an industrial structure, the Soviets have given far more publicity to the development of electric power. One reason may be Lenin's dictum: "Communism is Soviet power plus the electrification of the whole country." Also, the first industrialization plan for the Soviet Union was Lenin's Goelro plan, in 1920, and today, since Stalin's denigration, the great prophet is Lenin. Another factor may help to explain the Soviet fascination with electric power: It gives the publicists a chance to think on a grandiose scale, to discuss the harnessing of rivers and the building of man-made seas and mighty dams.

Although not equal to the impression one gains from the Soviet journalists, the total output of electric power in the Soviet Union has increased at a rapid tempo. In 1929, the beginning of the First Five-Year Plan, Soviet capacity was 5 billion kilowatt-hours; in 1964, it had risen steeply, to 459 billion kilowatt-hours.

In 1963, some 20 per cent of this power was hydroelectric; the rest came from thermal power stations operating on coal, oil, and peat. But the hydroelectric plants are the ones that catch the imagination. A Soviet economist gives this glowing description of the Soviet hydroelectric accomplishments and potentialities:

> The Soviet land has the richest water-power reserves in the world. The potential capacity of the hydroelectric power resources of the U.S.S.R. comes to 340 million kilowatts with a possible output of around 3,000 billion kilowatts, four times that of the U.S.A. Devotion to the development of hydroelectric stations is a red thread that runs from the Goelro plan through all the Five-Year Plans. The relative share of the GES's [hydroelectric stations] in the output of electricity in 1913 was negligible. At the end of the First Five-Year Plan it was about 6 per cent; in 1940, 10.6 per cent; and in 1956, 15 per cent.

Many of the GES's already built, and those now under construction, are important landmarks in the development of the electrical power of the country: These are the Volkhovskaya, Dneprovskaya, Svirskaya, Shcherbakovskaya, Mingechaurskaya, and Kuybyshevskaya [GES's already built]; under construction, the Stalingradskaya, Bratskaya, and Krasnoyarskaya GES's.

The growth in the capacity of the GES's (from the first Soviet hydroelectric station, the Volkhovskaya GES, up to the Krasnoyarskaya and Bratskaya stations now under construction) is described in the following figures (in thousands of kilowatts): Volkhovskaya, 66; Dneprovskaya, 650; Kuybyshevskaya, 2,100; Stalingradskaya, 2,300; Bratskaya, 3,300; Krasnoyarskaya, 3,200.[7]

However, in August, 1958, Khrushchev, while presiding at the opening of the world's largest hydroelectric plant, at Kuybyshev, argued the case for more investment in thermal power stations. Apparently, a more careful look was, and still is, being taken at the merits of enormous hydroelectric stations versus the smaller thermal ones.

Metal-Cutting Machine Tools

Metal-cutting machine tools have been selected from the total Soviet machine production, because they are closely associated with an increased capacity in heavy industry, especially in the production of military equipment. They might well become a very valuable constituent in the economic struggle in the underdeveloped parts of the world. This branch of industry produces milling, gear-cutting, shaping, and grinding machines, and all kinds of drilling equipment. The increase in the production of these items has been almost phenomenal in the last thirty years—from slightly under 2,000 in 1928 to 130,000 in 1957, of which 35,641 were turning, turret, and automatic lathes. The total output in 1964 was 184,000 units.

The two great centers of machine-tool production are the Moscow area and Leningrad. But this type of manufacturing is found in many other areas, including the Georgian Republic, the Fergana Valley in Central Asia, and many cities in the Ukraine and the Urals, in the industrial region of Western

Siberia, and even in the Far East. Wherever high-grade steel can be shipped and a power line brought in, the manufacture of machine tools can be set up. The Soviet educational system, with its extreme emphasis on technological training, has made the skilled manpower available.

In actual, and even in per capita, production of machine tools, the Soviet Union has outstripped the United States. Apparently assembly-line techniques and mass production have paid off in this field.

9

Transportation

Soviet planners, up to and including Khrushchev, have had to cope with two hard facts: enormous distances and inadequate transportation. In addition to the physical vastness of the Soviet Union, occupying almost one-sixth of the world's land area, there is also the problem of the extremely northern location and the related problem of permafrost, which seriously complicates the building of railroads and motor highways.

The Soviet need for transportation is especially acute because resources are widely scattered. The two largest centers of industrial fabrication are Moscow and Leningrad, neither of which is near the great coal- and steel-producing areas. Steel from the Ukraine, the Urals, and Western Siberia has to be hauled to the fabricating centers. Cotton for the textile plants, largely concentrated in the Moscow region, has to be brought from Central Asia and Azerbaidzhan. Since the fabricating and heavy industrial centers are not self-supporting in foodstuffs, transport must also be assigned to this task. Even oil is moved principally by rail or water, but the present major expansion in pipelines should rectify this situation in the near future. The very rapid rise in oil production (244 million tons in 1964) and a more plentiful steel supply (93 million tons in the same year) make a sharp increase in oil-pipeline mileage very probable in the near future. Furthermore, there is a definite state policy toward increasing conversion to oil as a fuel in industry.

Soviet planners have tried to offset the increased load on the available rail-transportation system by promoting greater efficiency in its operation. Efforts, apparently successful, have been made to cut down on the number of idle cars by speeding up turnaround time. Despite attempts to encourage the use of other forms of transportation, railroads are still hauling four-fifths of the freight. A broad picture of the load carried by each type of Soviet transportation is given in Tables 11 and 12.

TABLE 11

FREIGHT TURNOVER OF ALL TYPES OF SOVIET TRANSPORTATION *
(In Billions of Ton-Kilometers)

Year	*All Types*	*Railroad*	*Maritime*	*River*	*Truck*	*Oil Pipelines*	*Air*
1913	126.0	76.4	20.3	28.9	0.1	0.3	—
1928	119.5	65.7	19.9	28.5	0.1	0.3	—
1940	487.4	415.0	23.8	35.9	8.9	3.8	0.02
1950	713.1	602.3	39.7	45.9	20.1	4.9	0.14
1955	1,164.7	970.9	68.9	67.4	42.5	14.7	0.25
1960	1,885.7	1,504.3	131.5	99.6	98.5	51.2	0.56
1961	1,998.2	1,566.6	159.1	106.0	105.7	60.0	0.80
1962	2,116.9	1,646.3	173.4	109.9	111.9	74.5	0.89
1963	2,301.7	1,749.4	226.3	114.5	119.7	90.9	0.91
1964	—	1,850.0	—	124.4	—	113.1	—

* *Narodnoe Khozyaystvo SSSR v 1963 Godu*, p. 373; *Pravda*, January 30, 1965.

RAILROADS

Although freight may be transported by railroad much more cheaply than by truck or air, and much more speedily than by water, a very small segment of the total investment capital of the Soviet Union has gone, and is going, into the railroad system. It has been the general practice of other countries in developing their economies to build more than adequate transportation facilities in advance of the need, but the Soviets have not developed their transportation until the need has arisen. According to official Soviet figures, the general economy expanded its output over 2,700 per cent between 1913 and 1955, while the length of railroad mileage increased less than 70 per cent during the same period.[1] The growing burden on the railroads can be seen from the following figures: In 1913, Russian railroads carried 76.4 billion ton-kilometers; in 1964, the total was 1,850 billion ton-kilometers—an increase of over 24 times. The period in question included the Civil War (1918–21), the dislocations associated with the introduction of the Five-Year Plans and the collectivization of agriculture, and World War II, all of which militated against efficiency of operation.

One of the more widespread theories before World War II was that the Soviet railroad system would go into a tailspin if any unusual strains were put on it. In the middle of the 1930's, there was a railroad crisis severe enough to bring in the old trouble shooter Kaganovich to straighten it out. But the railroad system did not collapse, then or in World War II. There are several reasons for its continuing vitality. The Soviets have improved to an extraordinary degree the operating efficiency of the rail network inherited from the Czarist regime. Between 1928 and 1940, the average turnaround time per freight car decreased from 10.5 days to a little over 7 days, and the average speed of freight trains increased from about 9 miles an hour to more than 12 miles an hour. By 1956, the turnaround time was down to 6.3 days and the speed up to 15.4 miles an hour, with stops included.[2] These figures indicate a rise in efficiency of about 60 per cent. Much of this increase can be credited to better locomotives, especially in the last few years. The steam locomotives have become heavier and more efficient, and there has been an increased use of electric and diesel engines, which are faster, can haul larger loads, and operate much better on long and steep grades. At present, a little less than 20 per cent of Soviet locomotives are diesel or electric, but it is planned to have over 60 per cent diesels or electrics by 1965. One Soviet writer even expects the steam locomotive to be eliminated by 1970.

The wider use of heavy four-axle freight cars and improved automatic signaling systems has also helped boost the capability of the Soviet railroad system to bear up under the ever-increasing demands being made upon it. The traffic density over Soviet rail lines is astonishingly high.

Another factor accounting for Soviet railroad efficiency is the rapid loading and unloading of freight; little time is lost by having cars held up in the yards. Unlike the American user, the Soviet user has to fit his requirements into the freight schedule, and it is his responsibilty to see to it that cars are quickly unloaded. With the railroads in the dominant position, the movement of freight can be planned well in advance and the alternation of high and low density of traffic avoided.

The distribution of railroad mileage in the Soviet Union is extremely uneven. Most of the routes are concentrated in former European Russia (see Figure XIII), while the north, both Siberias, and Central Asia have practically no tracks (see Figure XIV). The railroad lines in the west (the Baltic, northern, central, Ukraine, Caucasus, and Volga regions) carried about 65 per cent of Soviet freight in 1949; the lines in the east (the Urals, Central Asia, both Siberias, and the Far East) carried only 35 per cent in the same year. Looking at the problem from another angle, the density of railroad mileage in the Moscow area and the Ukraine is over 5 miles per 100 square miles; in the Far East it is only 0.2 miles.

The constant emphasis upon heavy industry, especially steel, has put a burden on Soviet railroads. In the 1930's, the building of the Magnitogorsk-Kuznetsk *kombinat* led very nearly to a collapse of the railroad system. Today, the railroad lines between Magnitogorsk and Kuznetsk, Magnitogorsk and Karaganda, and Krivoi Rog and the Donbas are bearing the brunt of the iron-ore and coal hauling that keeps steel production steadily climbing. Because of the expansion of Soviet industrialization to the east, the railroads crossing the Volga at Saratov, Kuybyshev, Ulyanovsk, Kazan, Gorky, and Yaroslavl have become vital lifelines in the Soviet economic system.

The new railroads built during the Soviet period have been aimed primarily at increasing the industrial productivity of the country. The Czarist regime usually planned a new railroad line in the light of military strategy—the transport of troops and supplies to the frontiers. But what was good military strategy in the late nineteenth and nearly twentieth centuries became outmoded by the time the Soviet regime was ready to consider building railroads. Soviet planners soon realized that heavy industry, the backbone of military might, was the real strategic necessity of agrarian Russia. To follow a policy at variance with the great European powers, the Soviet Union could not depend upon them for the technical instruments of war. In pursuance of this policy, the Soviet regime built the Turkistan-Siberian (the Turksib) and the South Siberian (Yousib) railroads, both of which have contributed much toward the economic development of Central Asia and the industrial south of Western Siberia. During World War II, with the Germans in control of the industrial complex of the Ukraine, these regions proved the validity of such strategic thinking. During the war, the Soviets built a new railroad (732 miles long) to the Pechora coal basin, to make up to some degree for the loss of the coking coal of the Donbas. Since the war, the line has been double-tracked, and spurs pushed on to the sea at Amderma and Kara. Another spur went to the estuary of the Ob at Salekhard and recently was extended to Igarka, 620 miles away.

But construction of new railroads accounts for only a comparatively small portion of the increased Soviet freight turnover, some 20 per cent, according to the Soviets themselves. The greatest part (80 to 85 per cent) of capital investment going into railroads has been put into the networks inherited from the previous regime. Electrification of mountain routes, double-tracking, expanded switching yards, automatic signaling, more powerful locomotives, and heavier cars have been regarded by the Soviet planners as more productive than an extension of mileage.

The share of capital investment allotted to transportation shows a steady decline, according to Soviet statistics. The only figures available to this writer combined transportation with communications, but they indicate the magnitude of the decrease: In the First Five-Year Plan, transportation and communications received 18.6 per cent of the total; in the Fourth Five-Year Plan, they slipped to 14.2 per cent; and in 1958, they were given 8.9 per cent.[3] In the Seven-Year Plan (1959–65), they were allotted only 6 per cent of the total capital investment. One reason for the decrease has been the recent policy of making the users pay the cost of shipping plus a profit. For years, the railroads were really subsidizing the growth of industry. The rapidly falling costs of operation have put the railroads in the black in the last few years.

The vulnerability of the Soviet railroad system in any future

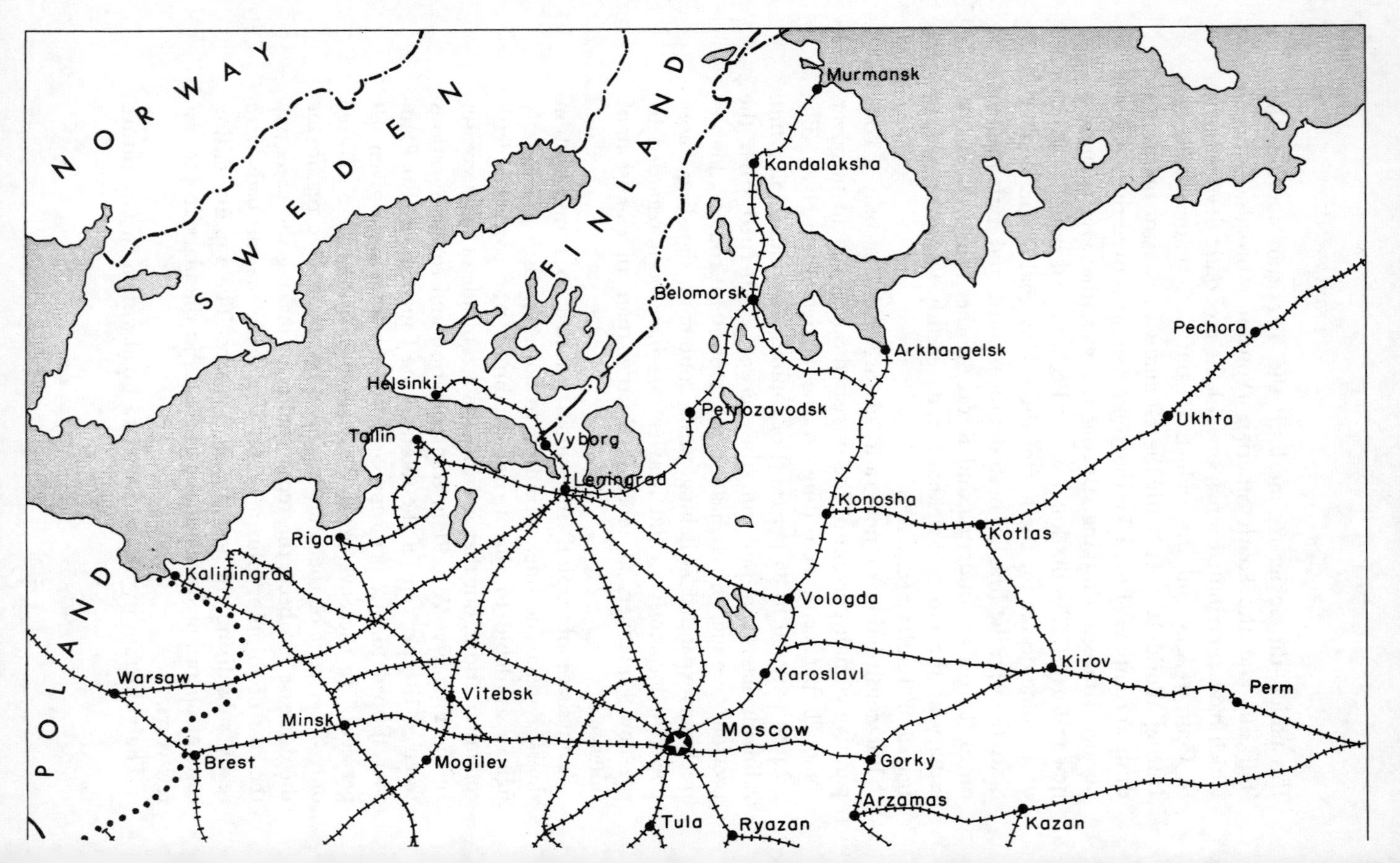
NORWAY
SWEDEN
FINLAND
POLAND
Murmansk
Kandalaksha
Belomorsk
Arkhangelsk
Pechora
Ukhta
Helsinki
Petrozavodsk
Tallin
Vyborg
Leningrad
Konosha
Kotlas
Riga
Kaliningrad
Vologda
Kirov
Yaroslavl
Perm
Warsaw
Vitebsk
Minsk
Moscow
Brest
Mogilev
Gorky
Arzamas
Kazan
Tula
Ryazan

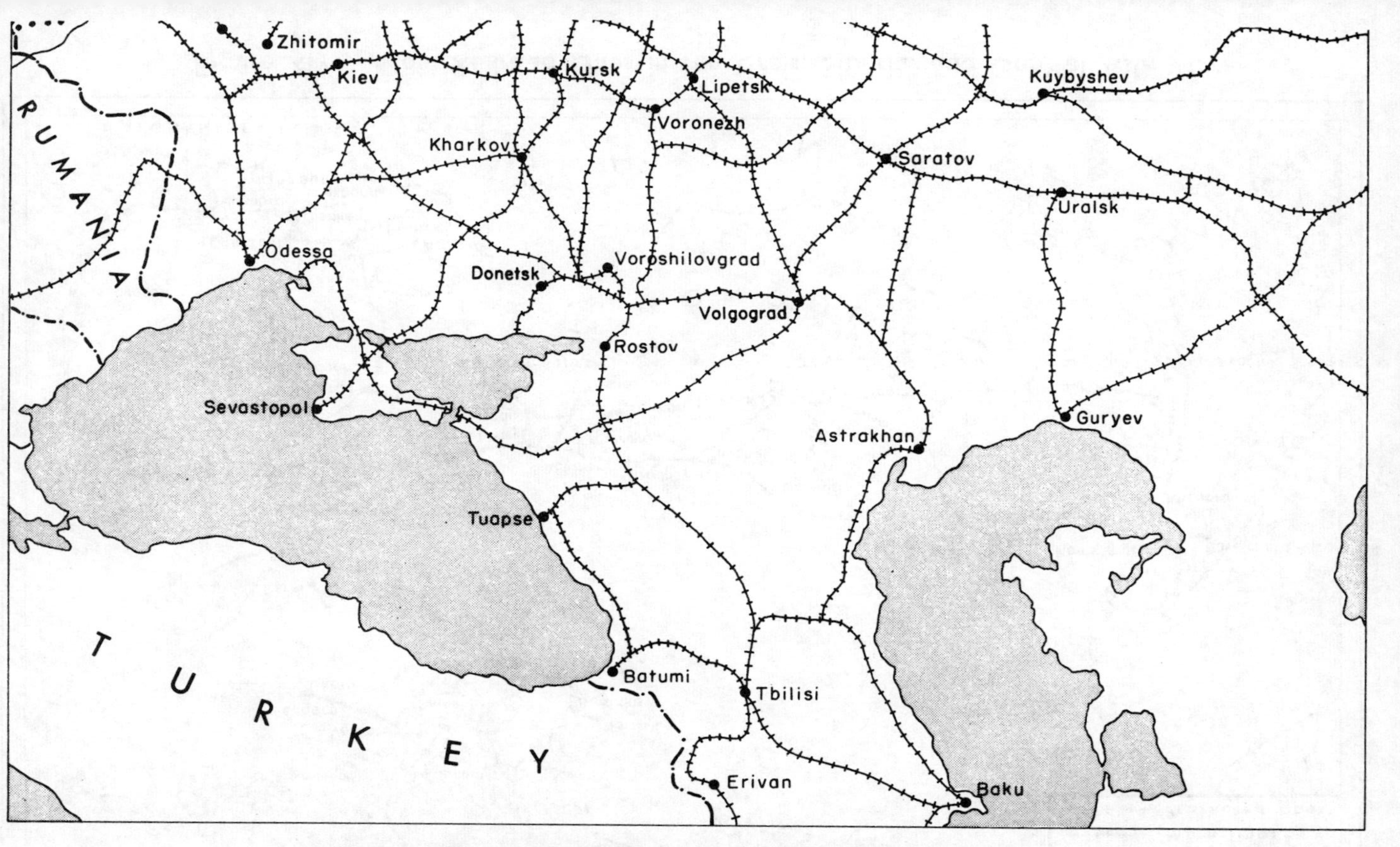

Figure XIII. Main Railroad Lines in European Russia

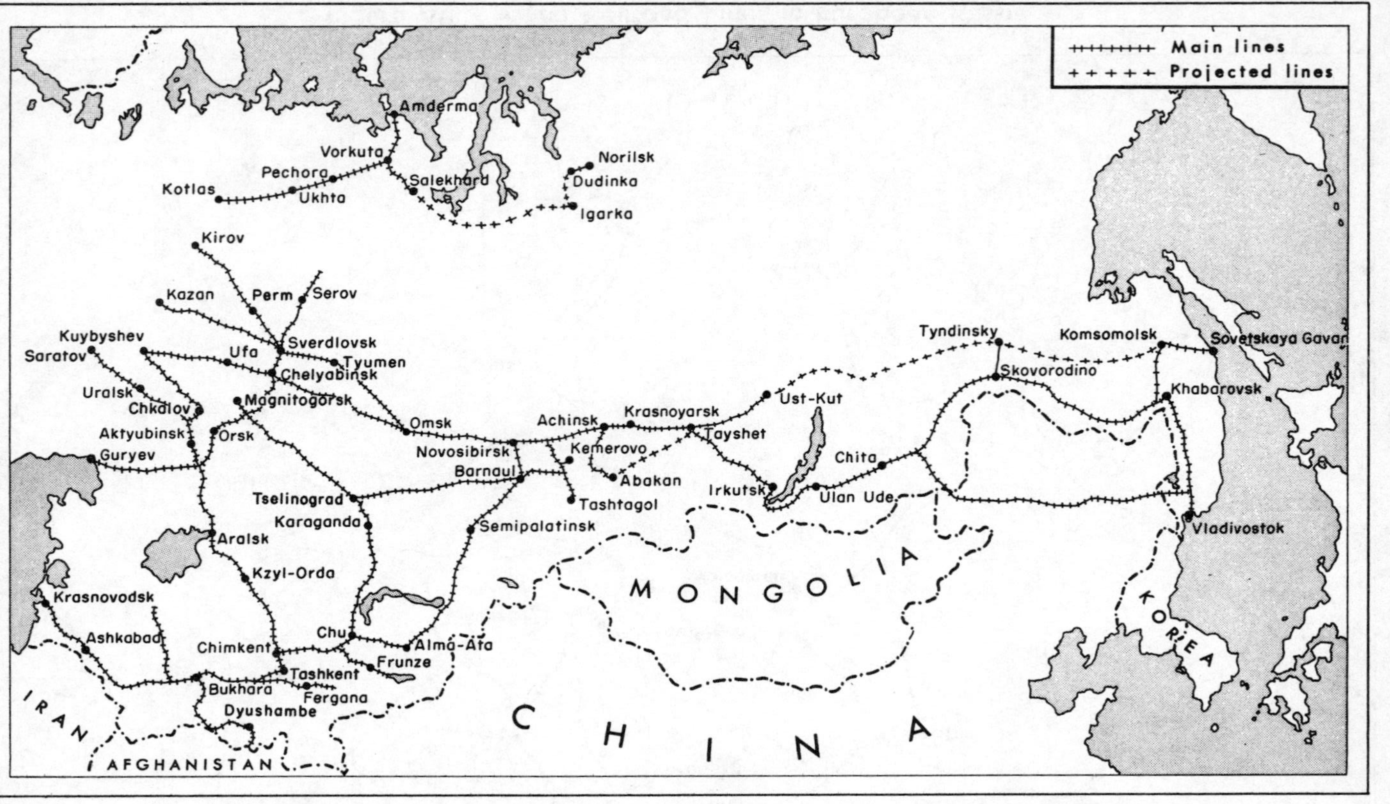

Figure XIV. Main Railroad Lines in the Urals, Siberia, and Central Asia

conflict is another debatable point. If the conflict were of long duration, the loss of bridges, main lines, and switching yards would have a seriously adverse effect on Soviet industry, especially as there are no alternative means of transportation. Whether these targets would be worth the risks incurred and the weapons expended would have to be determined at the time. If the conflict were of short duration, railroads would hardly be a prime target. Also to be considered is the fact that the Soviets showed great skill at restoring operations on damaged or demolished railroads in World War II. Soviet railroads cannot be counted upon to provide a convenient Achilles' heel in the Soviet ability to conduct a war.

WATER TRANSPORTATION

The Soviet Union possesses some of the world's greatest rivers, many of which are navigable. But most of the transportation needs of the country lie in a lateral, east-west direction, and the large rivers run north-south. Furthermore, some of the greatest of the Soviet rivers, such as the Ob-Irtysh system, the Yenisei, Lena, and Kolyma, flow northward into the Arctic Ocean, which is frozen for the greater part of the year. The northern geographic position of the U.S.S.R. also hinders water transportation. Even the southerly Sea of Azov, across which iron ore is hauled from the Kerch Peninsula to the Ukrainian ferrous-metallurgical plants, is frozen during much of the winter. Farther to the north, the length of the navigational seasons declines radically. Each March and April, *Vodnyy Transport,* the newspaper published by the ministries of the Sea and River Fleets, announces the various dates for the opening of navigation on the Don, the Volga-Don Canal, and the lower Volga. For example, the issue of March 20, 1958, contained the following announcement:

> Navigation on the lower Volga, from Stalingrad to Astrakhan, has begun. The early opening of navigation in this section was helped by the icebreaker *Volga.* On March 16, the first fuel was shipped from Astrakhan to Stalingrad.

In 1913, river transportation handled about 25 per cent of all

Russian freight and around 40 per cent of transportation. By 1917, these figures had dropped more than one-half. In February, 1918, a decree of the Council of People's Commissars, signed by Lenin, nationalized all river and sea transportation. In 1919, the newly nationalized fleet, some 2,188 ships in all, carried about 8 million ton-kilometers of freight, and gradually the total rose until by 1926, it reached 33 million ton-kilometers.

The first two Five-Year Plans (1928–37) provided for the construction of the White Sea-Baltic Canal (the Stalin Canal) and the

TABLE 12

DISTRIBUTION OF FREIGHT OVER THE VARIOUS FORMS OF SOVIET TRANSPORTATION *
(In Percentage of Ton-Kilometers)

Year	*Railroad*	*Maritime*	*River*	*Truck*	*Oil Pipelines*
1913	57.4	17.4	24.8	0.1	0.3
1940	85.1	4.9	7.4	1.8	0.8
1955	83.3	5.9	5.8	3.7	1.3
1960	79.8	7.0	5.3	5.2	2.7
1961	78.4	8.0	5.3	5.3	3.0
1962	77.8	8.2	5.2	5.3	3.5
1963	76.0	9.8	5.0	5.2	4.0

* *Narodnoe Khozyaystvo SSSR v 1963 Godu,* p. 373.

Moscow-Volga Canal. Port facilities along the river and sea routes were improved and mechanized. During World War II, river transport carried around 200 million tons of freight and contributed importantly in supporting Stalingrad and in maintaining the lifeline across Lake Ladoga during the siege of Leningrad. But the Germans seriously damaged the facilities along the Dnieper and the Stalin Canal, and it was not until the end of the Fourth Five-Year Plan (1950) that these routes were restored to their prewar condition.

According to the *Great Soviet Encyclopedia,* river transportation in 1955 hauled 36.7 per cent of the lumber, 21.5 per cent of the petroleum and its products, 6 per cent of the building materials, 1.7 per cent of the coal, and 9 per cent of the wheat of the Soviet Union. The real deficiency in river transport is that it cannot be used to haul coal; the rivers do not run from the coal fields to the steel centers.

It was not until the mid-1930's that Soviet river transport got back to the 1913 level in freight turnover. Since then, there has been a slow, but steady, rise in the quantity hauled. Even the 1963 total of 114.5 billion ton-kilometers, however, is only a small fraction of the 2,301.7 billion ton-kilometers hauled by all types of Soviet transportation in 1963. (See Table 13.)

TABLE 13

River Transport: Length of Waterways and Freight Turnover *

Year	*Length of Waterways Open to Steam Navigation (Kilometers)*	*Freight Turnover (Billions of Ton-Kilometers)*
1928	71,600	15.9
1940	107,300	36.1
1950	130,200	46.2
1960	137,900	99.6
1962	139,800	109.9
1963	140,700	114.5

* *Narodnoe Khozyaystvo SSSR v 1958 Godu*, pp. 564–65; *Narodnoe Khozyaystvo SSSR v 1963 Godu*, p. 395.

Much emphasis is being given to the future of river transport in the Soviet economy. The opening, in 1952, of the Volga-Don Canal (the Lenin Canal), which connects the Caspian and Black seas, signified the completion of a network of waterways linking these two with three other seas—the Baltic, the White, and the Sea of Azov. The hydroelectric station constructed at Volgograd (Stalingrad) in connection with the Lenin Canal is only the first of a new series of great hydroelectric installations to be constructed on the rivers of the country, installations such as the recently opened Kuybyshev Dam and the others projected on the Volga, Angara, and Great Stony rivers.

PIPELINES

The Soviet economy has been extremely slow in utilizing the advantages to be gained by using pipelines to transport oil and gas. About a fifth of the oil and oil products is hauled by river transport, and much of the rest by railroads. Transporting these products by pipeline would be much cheaper and more reliable, and would ease the burden of the already heavily laden railroads and river fleets.

Until recently, however, the expansion of pipeline facilities was slow indeed. The first pipeline (for kerosene) was built in 1907 from Baku, on the Caspian, to Batumi, on the Black Sea—a distance of 515 miles. By 1940, the total length of pipelines was only 2,750 miles.

Two facts lie behind this lag. First, as long as the main supply of Soviet oil came from Baku, water transport was easily available through the Caspian Sea and up the Volga, and a pipeline ran from Baku to Batumi on the Black Sea. Second, both the steel and the facilities to manufacture the pipe for pipelines were in relatively short supply until the 1950's.

The opening of the "Second Baku" oil fields in the area between the Volga and the Urals in the 1950's made the use of pipelines more imperative. Rivers just did not flow laterally across this area. Also, by this period, the available steel and pipe-manufacturing facilities were in being. Shortly after the death of Stalin, the Soviet planners decided to shift toward oil and natural gas as fuels.

By 1955, pipelines were carrying 10 per cent of Soviet oil. Early in January, 1956, the greatest oil pipeline in the U.S.S.R. was officially opened, the Tuimazy-Ufa-Omsk line, 850 miles long. The Sixth Five-Year Plan (1956–60) called for a sixfold jump in oil-line tonnage, utilizing a series of new lines: Omsk-Irkutsk, Almetevsk-Gorky, Almetevsk-Molotov, Gorky-Ryazan-Moscow, Gorky-Yaroslavl, and several others. Under the Seven-Year Plan, new thermal electric-power plants, diesel locomotives, and enlarged truck and air transport were all based on the use of petroleum and natural gas. The Soviets claimed that they moved

204 million tons of oil and oil products through 23,900 kilometers of pipeline in 1963 and that in 1964 the total was increased by 15 per cent, to 234 million tons.[4]

AUTO TRANSPORT

According to the *Great Soviet Encyclopedia,* "twice as much freight is hauled by truck as by railroads and river transport combined, but over much shorter distances. Therefore, the freight turnover of auto transport in comparison with railroads is still very small." The "much shorter distances" mentioned are indeed very short. There is practically no intercity highway transportation because of the lack of decent roads and most trucking is confined to urban areas—short hauls from railroad to plant or from plant to plant within a metropolitan area.

Auto transport in the Soviet Union suffers from a shortage of both vehicles and highways, the latter deficiency being by far the more serious. On the eve of World War II, vehicle production in the U.S.S.R. consisted of about 150,000 motor vehicles a year, chiefly trucks. During the war, truck production slowed to a standstill, and the United States supplied Soviet requirements in that field—probably the most valuable single item in the Lend-Lease Program as far as the Soviets were concerned. After the war, the production of automobiles increased rapidly, and by 1950, it had risen to 362,900 a year, still heavily weighted in the direction of trucks. Production rose to 445,300 vehicles in 1955, of which 329,000 were trucks. One authority estimated that there were about 2.5 million automobiles of all types in the Soviet Union in 1956.[5] By 1964, automobile output was up to 603,000, with 418,000 in the truck/bus category.[6] The agricultural segment of the economy is a heavy user of trucks, and its total park of trucks in 1963 was 922,000.[7]

Roads have always been a Russian headache and, in the case of invasions, a blessing. According to Guderian, the main handicap his panzer divisions faced in their drive on Moscow, in 1941, was the bottomless mud tracks humorously called roads by the Russians.

The Soviets claimed to have a total of slightly over 825,000

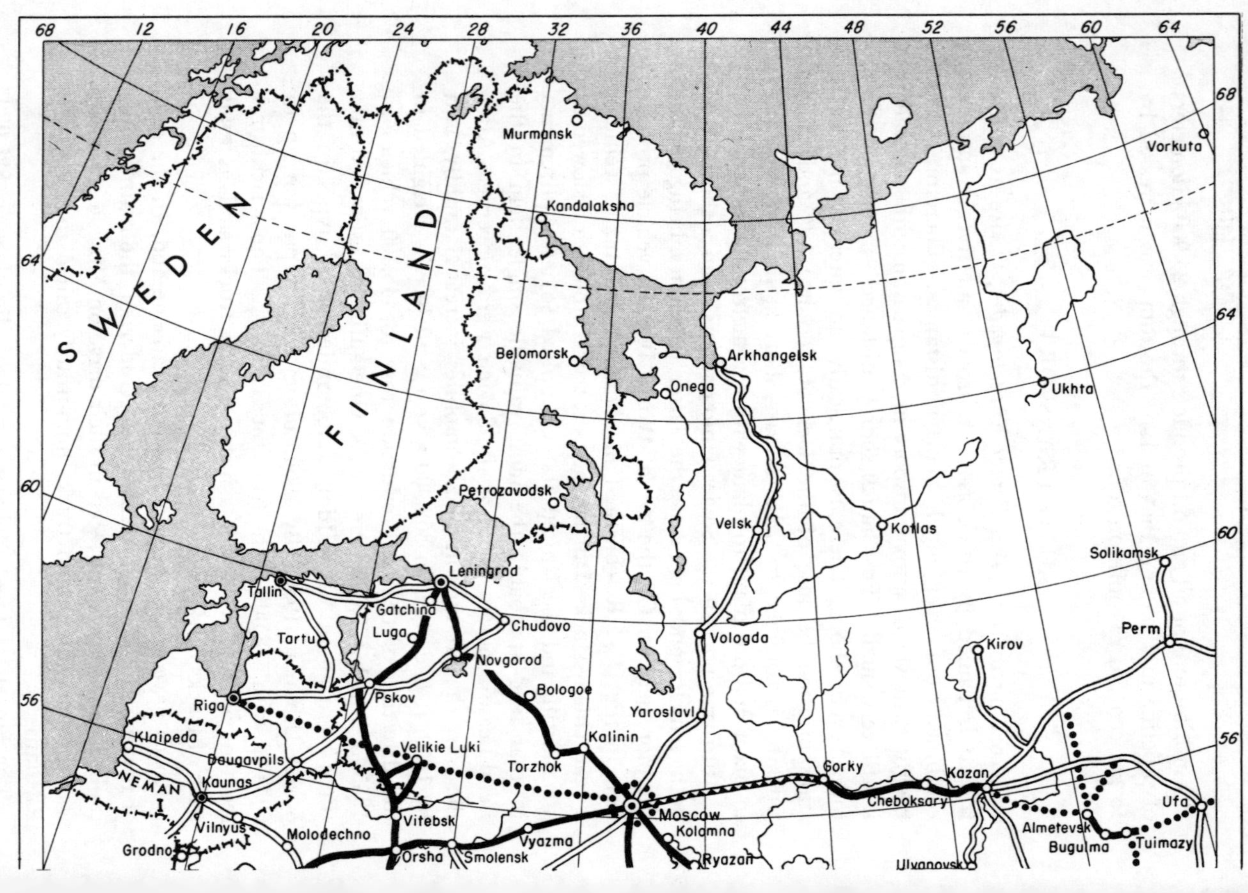

SWEDEN
FINLAND
NEMAN
Murmansk
Kandalaksha
Vorkuta
Belomorsk
Arkhangelsk
Onega
Ukhta
Petrozavodsk
Velsk
Kotlas
Solikamsk
Leningrad
Tallin
Gatchina
Chudovo
Luga
Tartu
Novgorod
Vologda
Perm
Kirov
Riga
Pskov
Bologoe
Yaroslavl
Klaipeda
Kalinin
Daugavpils
Velikie Luki
Torzhok
Gorky
Kazan
Kaunas
Cheboksary
Moscow
Ufa
Vilnyus
Vitebsk
Kolamna
Almetevsk
Molodechno
Vyazma
Bugulma
Tuimazy
Grodno
Orsha
Smolensk
Ryazan
Ulyanovsk

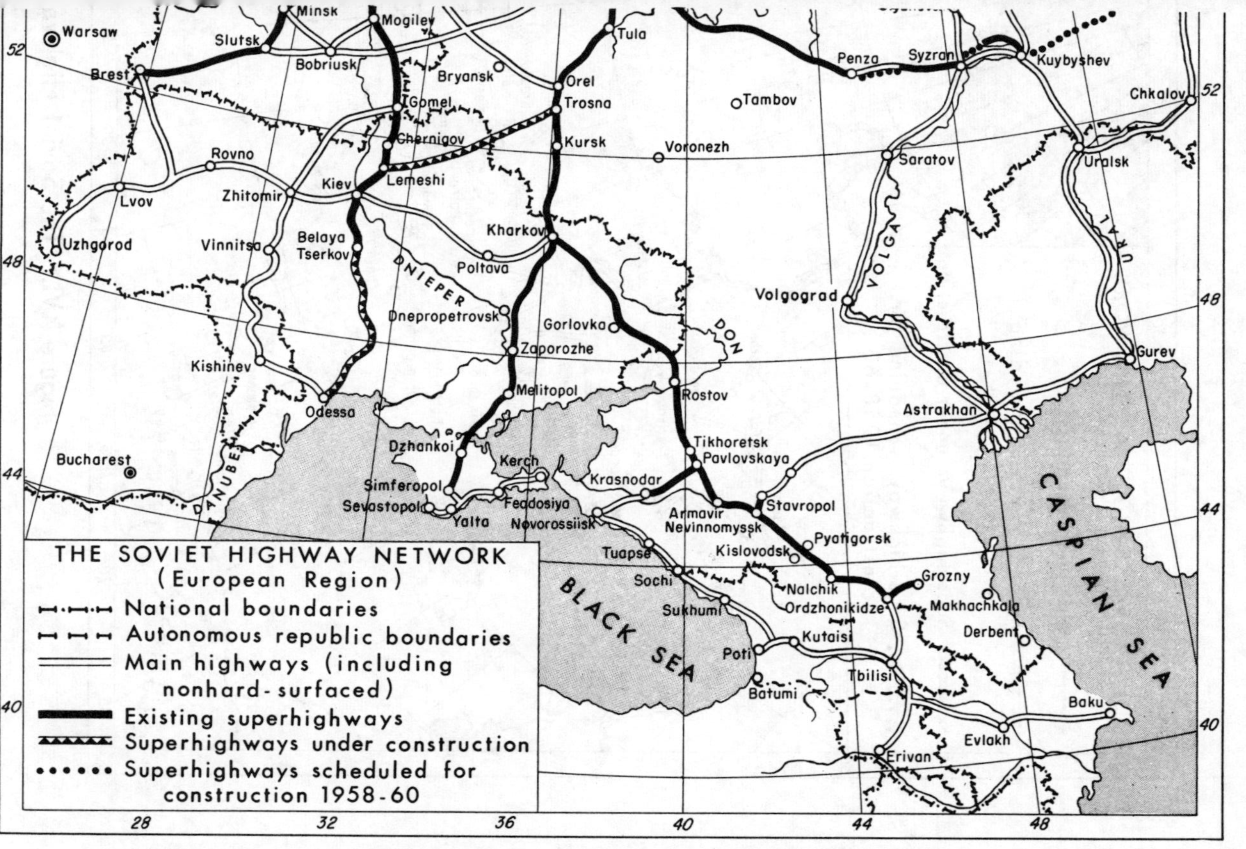

Figure XV. The Soviet Highway Network (European Region)

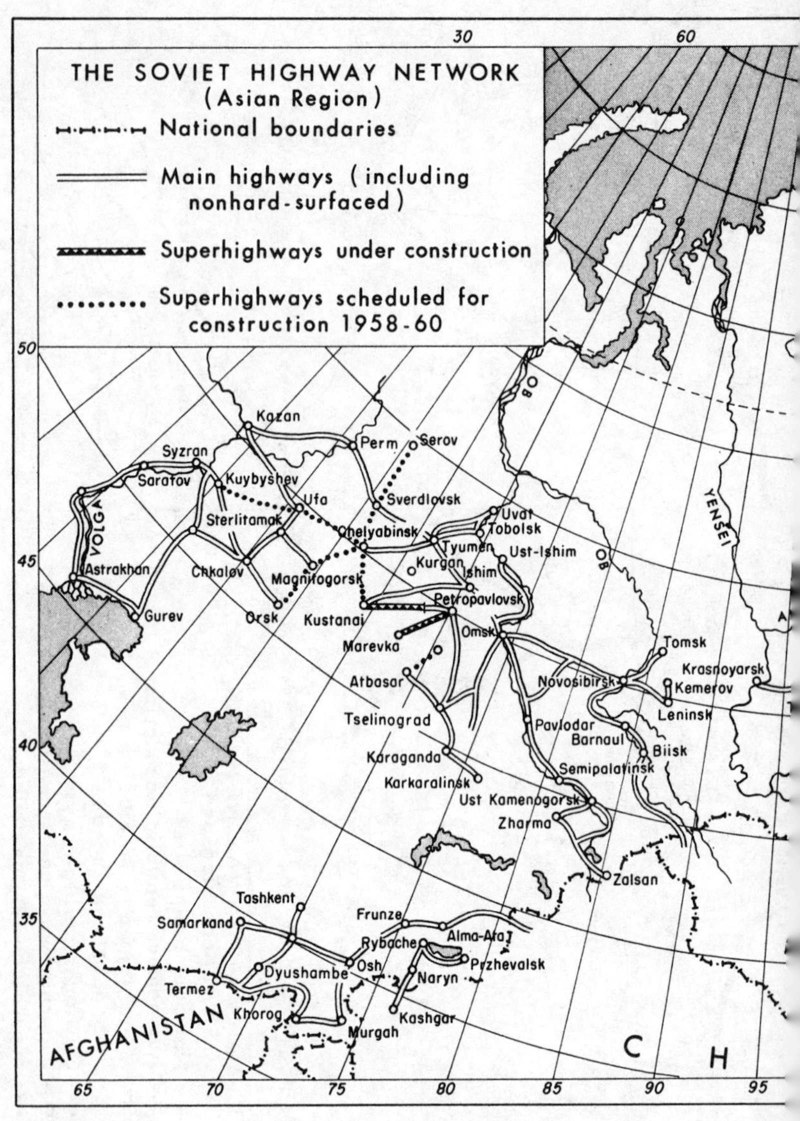

Figure XVI. The Soviet Highwa

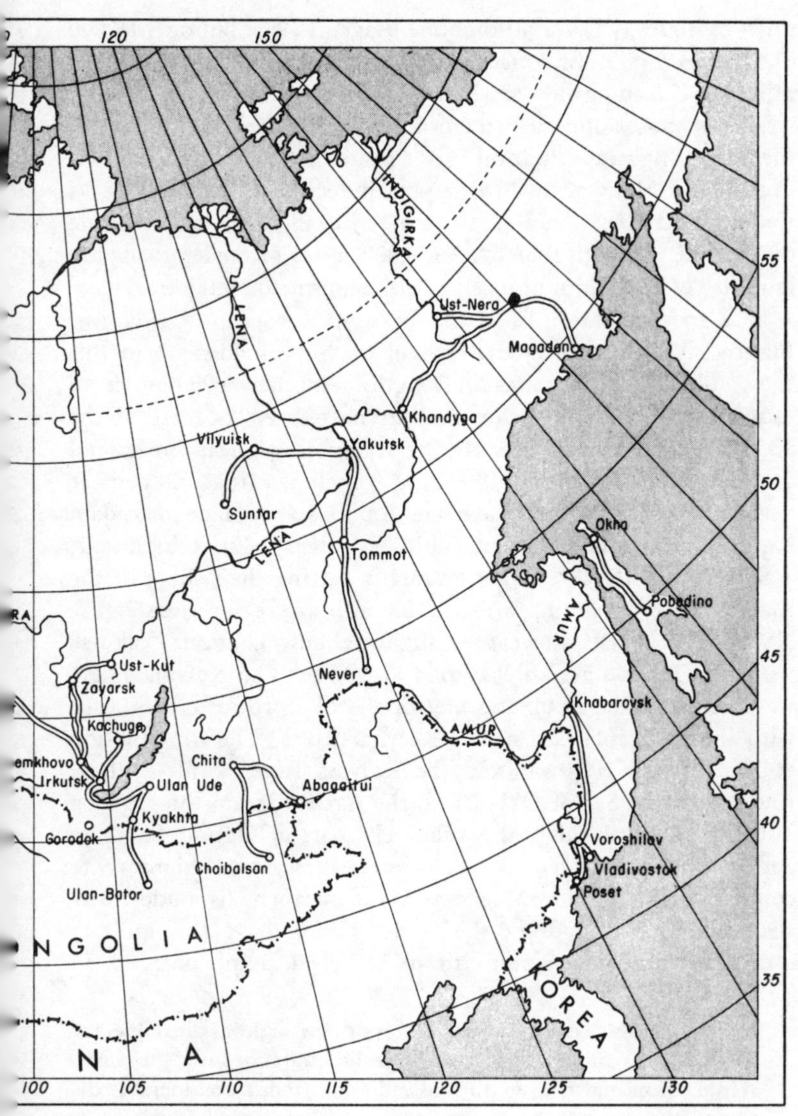

etwork (Asian Region)

miles of highway fit for automobile usage in 1963, but only 67,000 of this was asphalt or concrete. Contrast this with the 3.6 million miles of U.S. highways in 1962.[8] Inasmuch as the nonsurfaced roads are almost useless throughout extended periods in the year, the Soviet highway situation is not conducive to a rapid increase in trucking. Many of the "roads" are, indeed, only the mud tracks that connect the thousands of small villages. This fact is borne out by the estimate that over 750,000 miles of Soviet roads are labeled "of local importance," a euphemism for mud tracks.

The road situation is at its best in European Russia (see Figure XV); there is even a system of "superhighways" in this area, totaling 4,520 miles in length.[9] Another 3,960 miles of "superhighways" were scheduled to have been opened up by 1960. The author rode over the "superhighways" near Simferopol and near Leningrad in 1959 and concluded that they more nearly approximated the average American two-lane macadam highway than anything that could be called a "superhighway."

Siberia and the Arctic are gradually getting their share of the road-building program, probably for military reasons (see Figure XVI). A 760-mile all-weather highway now connects Yakutsk with the Trans-Siberian Railroad at Never. The Kolyma Highway connects Magadan, the metropolis of northeastern Siberia, with the navigable part of the Kolyma River. The combination of the Kolyma Highway and the Kolyma River forms a direct route from the Sea of Okhotsk to the Arctic Ocean, thus cutting out the route through the relatively narrow Bering Strait to get around the Chukotski Peninsula. A seasonal highway to connect Yakutsk with Magadan via Churapcha is under construction. Other roads in the Soviet Union have this military aspect, as a one-time Soviet citizen, A. Lebed, points out:

> It is noticeable that the construction of new highways is influenced by military strategy. The two large highways crossing the Soviet Union from north to south and radiating from a considerable distance to form a possible springboard for military operations are cases in point. They do not link up the industrial centers, they duplicate the railroads operating in these areas, and it can hardly be argued that they are needed for tourists, if only for the simple reason that Soviet citizens do not possess motor vehicles. The com-

> pleted superhighway Moscow-Minsk, the two parallel meridional superhighways now under construction which will probably continue in the direction of Zhitomir-Rovno-Lwow, and a projected third superhighway to Riga are undoubtedly primarily strategic in purpose. The continuation of these roads further eastward, to Gorky and Kuibyshev, centers of industrial regions chiefly engaged in military production, supports this view.[10]

Since the advent of the new regime in October, 1964, there has been a growing awareness in the Soviet Union that something drastic needs to be done about truck transport. In March, 1965, the Chairman of the Council of Ministers, Aleksei Kosygin, told the U.S.S.R. State Planning Committee that the types of trucks being turned out in the Soviet Union were "economically inefficient." [11] They have not been manufactured in the West for a long time, he said. "There, trailer trucks are produced that have greater capacities than our trucks. They carry loads of 15 to 20 tons and have very high speeds." Furthermore, Kosygin said, on a recent trip to East Germany, while driving along the Autobahn from Leipzig to Berlin, he had noticed that 90 trucks out of every 100 were loaded. But, when riding along the Moscow Belt Highway, he had counted 70 empty trucks out of every 100 he passed. To quote Kosygin: "These are shocking facts."

In May, 1965, two engineers, N. Khartseyev and G. Baz'ylenko, wrote an article in *Pravda* on the same topic.[12] They pointed out that truck transport accounted for less than 6 per cent of the total volume of Soviet freight tonnage. The reasons for this sad state of affairs were multiple, but the main ones, according to the authors, were the small size of Soviet trucks, too many different models (which increased repair costs), low economies of scale in manufacturing trucks (because of the plethora of different kinds), too many small manufacturing plants, and the lack of good highways. Although motor-vehicle production is scheduled to be doubled in the Seventh Five-Year Plan (1966–70), this in itself will not make truck transport profitable. What is needed is a standardization of truck types with fewer, but heavier, models. There is an especially urgent need for multiple-trailer assemblies of 5 to 20 tons for dirt roads and up to 40 tons for asphalt and concrete highways.

Even the new emphasis on increased agricultural output is to some degree dependent on more and better trucks. But more important is the need for better roads—truck transport on and between farms is all but immobilized in the spring.

AIR TRANSPORT

In much of the Soviet Union, the construction of railroads and highways is a difficult task because of the lack of stone and gravel in many areas and the prevalence of permafrost in others. Thus, air transport seems to be made to order in many of these cases. But even air transport has far to go before it can adequately serve the entire U.S.S.R. Tremendous as the Soviet need for air transportation may be, in 1963 only .0004 per cent of Soviet freight turnover was by air. In passenger turnover the picture was a bit brighter; air transport in 1963 accounted for 25 billion passenger-kilometers (almost 8 per cent) out of a total of 318 billion.[13]

From the very birth of the Soviet state, its leaders have recognized the potentialities of the aircraft in solving the problem of the vast distances in the U.S.S.R. As early as 1918, when Lenin had been in power for less than a year and was fighting for his political life, he acceded to the plea of Zhukovskiy to establish TsAGI (Central Aero-Hydrodynamic Institute). While some of the scientists at TsAGI immediately began to design aircraft (for example, Tupolev), the main effort of the institute was directed toward basic research. Zhukovskiy saw Soviet autonomy in aircraft production as the over-all goal of the institute.

In 1921, a Russian trade delegation signed an agreement with a group of Germans to operate a joint German-Soviet airline. This airline, called Deruluft (Deutsch-Russische Luftverkehrsgesellschaft), had a capital of 300,000 marks. Deruluft maintained regular air routes between Berlin and Moscow, and from 1928, between Berlin and Leningrad, with stopping points at Danzig, Königsberg, Kovno, Riga, and Tallin. In 1922, Deruluft planes flew 92,500 miles on scheduled flights, carrying 388 passengers and 40,124 lbs. of freight. Deruluft operated until 1937, when Soviet-German friction led to the dissolution of the company.

The first wholly Soviet airline on a regular schedule was

inaugurated in 1923 with the 260-mile route from Moscow to Nizhni Novgorod (now Gorky). But until the First Five-Year Plan (1928–33) had built up the Soviet Union industrially, the limited civil aviation then in existence was operated largely by aircraft with foreign-built frames, engines, and equipment.

From 1923 to 1930, the development of civil aviation in the Soviet Union was pushed entirely by Dobrolet (Voluntary Society of the Civil Air Fleet). It organized airlines for carrying passengers, mail, and freight, carried out ice reconnaissance for the Committee for the North Sea Route, fostered air-rescue work, and in 1929, even flew cargoes of young herring from the Caspian Sea to stock the Aral Sea. The growth of civil aviation was steady, as can be seen from these figures: Dobrolet planes flew 92,500 miles in 1922, increasing to slightly over 625,000 miles by 1925; air cargo of mail and freight increased from 40,000 lbs. in 1922 to almost 200,000 by 1925; the number of passengers rose from 300 in 1922 to 4,400 in 1925. By 1925, regular airline routes connected about ten major cities, with Moscow as the focal point, except for a special line between Tbilisi and Baku.

A closer look, however, shows that Soviet civil aviation was a shoestring operation in those years. In 1929, Vodopyanov (later to become one of the patriarchs of polar aviation, but then having only six months' experience as a pilot), was selected by the Assistant Director of Dobrolet to take a single airplane to the Far East for the purpose of setting up and operating a new airline from Khabarovsk to Sakhalin Island.

In 1930, the Council of People's Commissars abolished Dobrolet and established the State Organization of the Civil Air Fleet to coordinate and control the activities of civil aviation. This organization, which had taken over the funds and property of the defunct Dobrolet, was reorganized, in 1932, into the Chief Administration of the Civil Air Fleet (Glavnoe Upravlenie Grazhdanskogo Vozdushnogo Flota, abbreviated to GVF). GVF supervised all types of aviation except the air fleet of the Red Army. In 1935, the Council of People's Commissars promulgated the Air Code of the U.S.S.R., which defined and regulated the activities of Soviet civil aviation.

According to the figures given in the *Great Soviet Encyclopedia,*

Murmansk
Vorkuta
Arkhangelsk
Pechora
Ukhta
Petrozavodsk
Syktyvkar
Helsinki
Leningrad
Stockholm
Tallin
Vologda
Cherepovets
Kirov
Perm
Izhevsk
Tyumen
Riga
MOSCOW
Gorky
Sverdlovsk
Copenhagen
Kazan
Danzig
Smolensk
Chelyabinsk
Kurgan
Omsk
Arzamas
Ufa
Petropavlovsk
Ulyanovsk
Magnitogorsk
Kustanai
Minsk
Kuybyshev
Kokchetav
Berlin
Warsaw
Penza
Atbasar
Kursk
Balashev
Chkalov
Voronezh
Saratov
Uralsk
Tselinograd
Prague
Kiev
Aktyubinsk
Lvov
Kharkov
Karaganda
Paris
Stanislav
Chernovtsy
Voroshilovgrad
Vienna
Dnepropetrovsk
Volgograd
Uzhgorod
Zaporozhe
Donetsk
Budapest
Rostov
Kishinev
Nikolaev
Balkhash
Aralsk
Odessa
Kherson
Astrakhan
Simferopol
Krasnodar
Kzylorda
Belgrade
Mineralnye Vody
Bucharest
Adler
Sukhumi
Makhachkala
Turkestan
Frunze
Sofia
Kutaisi
Nukus
Chimkent
Batumi
Tbilisi
Tirana
Tashkent
Baku
Krasnovodsk
Leninabad
Erivan
Samarkand
Chardzhou
Dyushambe
Ashkhabad
Termez
Kabul
AEROFLOT AIR ROUTES
Aeroflot Routes
Other Airlines

Figure XVII.

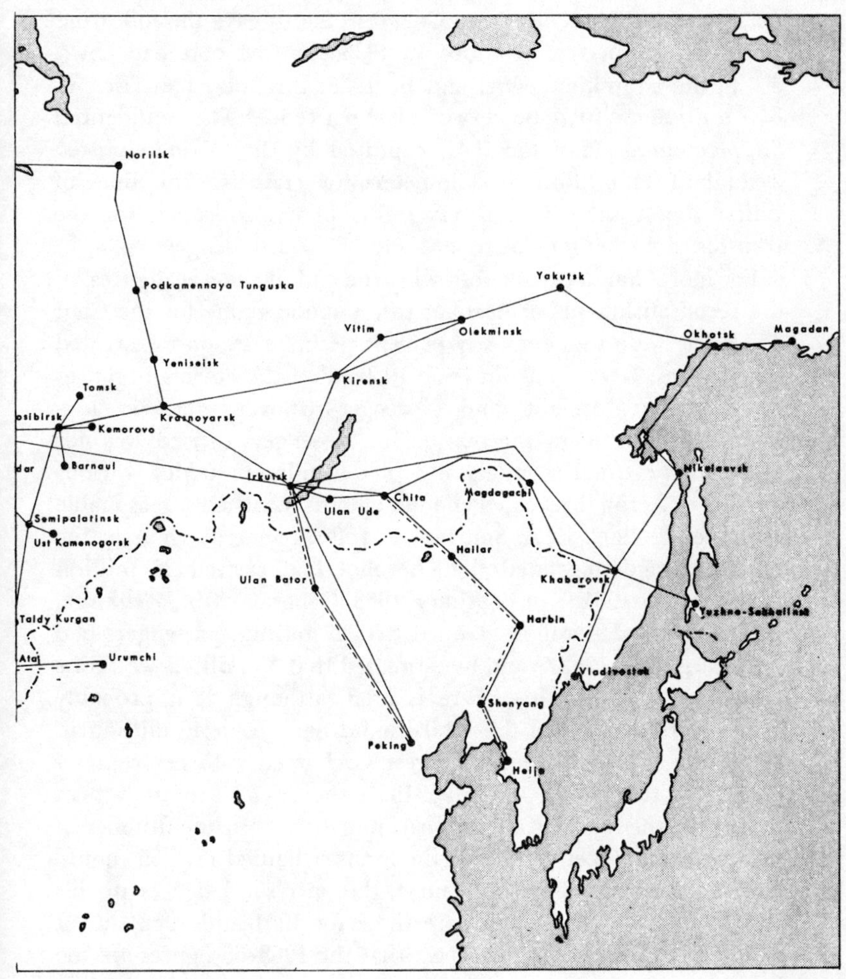

Aeroflot Air Routes

by 1928, U.S.S.R. air routes covered 6,750 miles; 1932 mileage was 22,650; and the 1937 figures jumped to 58,300 miles.[14] In 1939, at the Eighteenth Party Congress, Stalin gave the following information on civil aviation: In 1933, air transport had flown 3.1 million ton-kilometers, and by 1938, this total had risen to 31.7 million, an increase of over 1,000 per cent.[15] The confidential Supplementary Plan for 1941, captured by the Germans, listed a total of 44 million ton-kilometers for civil aviation lines of union importance in that year; this plan also called for the transfer of 40,000 tons of freight and 387,000 passengers.[16]

For more than a decade following the end of the war, figures on the accomplishments of Aeroflot (the popular name for the Civil Air Fleet) were vague, mostly percentage increases on unrevealed base figures. It was not until the 1960's that the Soviets began to give Aeroflot's freight- and passenger-turnover totals in ton-kilometers. Although the number of passengers carried was not given in the usual manuals and plan-fulfillment tables, various officials of Aeroflot revealed enough data to construct a reasonable estimate. In 1962, E. A. Smirnov, Aeroflot's general agent in the United Kingdom, stated that Aeroflot had carried 22 million passengers in 1961.[17] In February, 1963, General M. B. Bachkirov, deputy head of Aeroflot, claimed that 27 million passengers had been carried in 1962,[18] and he estimated that 35 million would be hauled in 1963. If this figure is used, although it is probably overly optimistic, then the total should have been 40 million in 1964, since the published plan results claimed a 15 per cent increase for that year.[19] In July, 1965, the Soviets, in their plan results for the first half of the year, put the rise in the number of passengers at 25 per cent, thus the number hauled in 1965 should have been 50 million.[20] Of course, the only solid figures in this conglomeration of estimates are those for 1961 and 1962, and it would seem reasonable to suspect that the 1963–65 figures are too high.

But even the estimate of 50 million passengers for 1965 is far below the rosy quotas set for the Seven-Year Plan (1959–65). Colonel General Y. F. Longinov, head of Aeroflot, in an interview for *Interavia* early in 1962, said that Aeroflot would annually carry 200 million passengers by 1980, which calls for a yearly increase of around 10 million a year.[21] He also stated that Aeroflot would fulfill the Seven-Year Plan's goal of a 600 per cent increase in passenger-kilometers. Actually, using the Soviets' own figures, the increase has been only 420 per cent. In August, 1964, however, Longinov was more circumspect and estimated that Aeroflot would carry 45 million passengers in 1965.[22]

TABLE 14

AEROFLOT DURING THE SEVEN-YEAR PLAN *

Year	*Freight Shipment (Billions of Ton-Kilometers)*	*Passengers (Billions of Passenger-Kilometers)*
1959	440	9.1
1960	560	12.1
1961	800	16.4
1962	890	20.3
1963	910	25.3
1964	1,030	30.8
1965	1,290	38.5

* *Narodnoe Khozyaystvo SSSR v 1963 Godu,* pp. 373–74; *Pravda,* January 30, 1965, p. 2; *Pravda,* July 26, 1965, p. 2.

During the "Great Fatherland War," as World War II is termed in Soviet parlance, civil aviation proved its worth as a backup for the military effort. It was immediately incorporated into the over-all military structure—not a difficult task in the highly centralized Soviet Union. The article on "Air Transport" in the *Great Soviet Encyclopedia,* summarizes the role of civil aviation in World War II as follows:

> In the years of the Great Fatherland War (1941–45), the activity of civil aviation was directed at helping the front. During the war, fliers of the civil air fleet flew more than 3.5 million hours. They carried over 2.3 million passengers, as well as around 300,000 tons of freight. Some 40,000 flights were made behind the enemy lines for contacts with partisans and for airdrop operations. Weapons, ammunition, medicine, food, etc. were delivered to the partisans, and the children and wounded flown out. By flying in food and munitions and evacuating wounded, they were of enormous help to the heroic cities, Leningrad, Odessa, and Sevastopol.[23]

In addition, civil aviation flew key personnel and vital equipment to the evacuated plants that were being re-established far to the rear.

From its earliest existence, Soviet civil aviation had an extremely varied inventory of aircraft. A. N. Tupolev, working at TsAGI, contributed a whole series of ANT's (named from his initials) ranging from small, single-engine craft to the huge eight-engine *Maxim Gorky* of 1934. A miscellany of single- and twin-engine aircraft, including the LI-2, PO-2, and ShchE-2, provided the backbone of the civil-aviation inventory during and immediately after World War II. For example, from 1940 to 1945 Lend-Lease supplied over 700 LI-2's (or PS-84's), which is the Russian designation of the Douglas DC-3. In 1946, the IL-12 was flown and soon became civil aviation's pet plane. This and its brother, the IL-14, were the work horses of civil aviation until 1955. In that year, the Soviet Union entered the age of jet transport with an aircraft that startled the West, the TU-104. This plane was demonstrated at the summer Tushino Air Show, and it entered regular Aeroflot service in September of 1956. In 1957, a four-engine turboprop transport, the AN-10, was introduced, and in the next year the Soviets unveiled two more large transports: the four-engine turboprop IL-18 and the enormous four-engine turboprop TU-114. Thus, by 1958, Soviet civil aviation was being rapidly equipped with a fleet of modern jet aircraft. Since then, the Soviets have produced the AN-24, the TU-124, and the IL-62.

Large Aeroflot Transports

AN-10: four-engine turboprop; 85 passengers
AN-24: twin-engine turboprop; 46 passengers
IL-18: four-engine turboprop; 70 to 100 passengers
IL-62: four-jet, rear-mounted; 182 passengers
TU-104: four-jet; 100 passengers
TU-114: four-engine turboprop; 120 to 220 passengers
TU-124: twin-engine turbofan; 40 to 60 passengers

Although the exact number of aircraft being used on Aeroflot lines is unknown, estimates put it well above 2,000. There are probably 500 to 600 TU-104's, several hundred IL-18's, sizable numbers of TU-124's, AN-10's, and AN-24's, and a few TU-114's and IL-62's.

The surprise of the Le Bourget Air Show in June, 1965, was the arrival of the gigantic Soviet AN-22 (Antaeus), which is capable of carrying 720 passengers. It is powered by four 15,000-horsepower turboprops, can cruise at 375 miles per hour at 36,000 feet, and can land (it is claimed) on a 900-foot grass runway. When this "air bus" comes into service on Aeroflot lines, it should bring down the cost of passenger travel considerably.

Aeroflot not only provides air transport service over scheduled routes but also supplies aircraft and operators for medical work, for agriculture (fertilizing, spraying, sowing, etc.), for forestry work, for geological surveying, for prospecting, for construction work—any job in which light fixed-wing aircraft or helicopters can be used. This type of service makes up about half of Aeroflot's operations. The AN-2 is the fixed-wing work horse in these operations, and a large fleet of helicopters—ranging from the Mi-2, which can lift a ton of fertilizer, to the Mi-6, with the capability of carrying 12 tons or 70 to 80 passengers—gives Aeroflot flexibility in this area of its work.

10

Education

In the unofficial contest between the United States and the Soviet Union for world leadership, the technological lead of the United States seemed unassailable. But in October, 1957, the Soviet "first" in launching its Sputnik into orbit shocked most Americans and jolted American scientific prestige around the world. There has been an agonizing reappraisal going on ever since, and the focal point of this national stocktaking is education. A sea of ink has been used in thrashing out the pro's and con's of American education versus the Soviet system. Even the formerly impregnable bastions of the educators have been shaken. The assumption that American education is the best in the world may be true, but under the hammering blows of irate critics the educators are being asked to prove their claim. The mere reiteration of their boast is no longer sufficient.

This chapter is concerned with a brief description of the Soviet system of education. Comparisons between the American and Soviet systems, when necessary, will be largely quantitative, not qualitative. The main reason for this is insufficient information upon which to judge the quality of Soviet education.

Soviet education has two main goals: First, to instill in the student those values and outlooks encompassed in the term, the "new Soviet man," or from the viewpoint of Soviet leaders, the development of good citizens. Second, to provide training in those subjects which best advance the economic and military interests of the state. However, the Soviet leaders do not want a generation of citizens trained to act and think independently and prepared to evaluate the Communist system.

THE DEVELOPMENT OF SOVIET EDUCATION

The Czarist regime in the latter part of the nineteenth and early years of the twentieth centuries was not very interested in universal education, particularly among the peasants, the largest group in Russia. But the picture of Czarist education was not as dark as the Communists have painted it. For instance, Czarist higher education was excellent, and to some extent the Soviet regime enjoyed that inheritance until recently. As early as 1864, the supervision of local schools was entrusted to zemstvos, local groups in charge of such things as health, statistics, and scientific agriculture. By 1914, there were around 50,000 zemstvo schools. Furthermore, there were plans for universal education by 1922.

Lenin's father, Ilya Nikolaevich Ulyanov, managed to graduate from the University of Kazan. Ilya Nikolaevich, the son of a tailor, became a teacher and later an inspector of the schools in Simbirsk Province. His elevation to the nobility well rewarded him for his arduous labor. It is true that Ilya Nikolaevich was an unusual man, but his career refuted the extremely dark picture painted by the Bolsheviks.

By 1914, the educational situation was improving steadily. At least half of the eligible children were in primary schools. Illiteracy among the peasants was very high, but the future was bright. Even budgetary plans had been made for a rapid expansion of the educational system. All this, of course, was a casualty of World War I and the following revolutions.

For the first ten years of Bolshevik rule, Soviet education was in a state of chaos. The seven years of war and revolution had torn the social fabric of Russian society to tatters, and the leaders of the country were determined to make a new society divorced from its Czarist heritage. It was a wild period of experimentation in which all kinds of theories—good, bad, and crackpot—were tried. Classroom discipline disappeared, and the teacher resembled a referee in the midst of unruly pupils. In a morbid attempt to get away from the traditional and authoritarian method of education, emphasis was placed on group action, brigade work, and social adjustment.

By the early 1930's, Stalin had consolidated his control of the state, inaugurated the First Five-Year Plan, and realized that the new industries needed many scientists, engineers, and technicians, as well as a literate labor force. He began to bring some order into the chaotic educational system, ending the era of experimentation. Moreover, the authoritarian Stalin saw nothing wrong with the traditional Russian educational methods. The teacher again became the classroom dictator who stressed memorization, rote recitation, and heavy homework. Stalin needed many technically trained people, so he tailored the school system to educate them.

The biggest problem was the shortage of competent teachers. All kinds of solutions were attempted, such as accelerated courses to train teachers, the use of industrial scientists and engineers as part-time teachers, and even the use of upper-grade students to teach those in the lower grades. These expedients, however, were marginal at best and in many cases simply disastrous. Finally, Stalin reverted to the slower, but more effective, system of training large numbers of teachers by requiring four or five years of higher education. The best graduates in each higher school were reinvested, so to speak, by making them into teachers. By the end of the 1930's, the Soviet educational system was turning out enough well-trained teachers to meet its needs.

Theoretically, the Soviet system provided education for all, from the nursery for ten-week-old infants to the schools for adults. But obtaining an education was not as simple as that. Many Soviet citizens found getting their share of education rather difficult, especially if they lived in rural areas, were not quite as intelligent as their comrades, or had intellectual bents that did not coincide with the state's objectives. In spite of these drawbacks, the Soviet Union developed an enormous public-school system, in many respects similar to that of the United States.

Until 1959, the Soviet educational system was organized into four-, seven-, and ten-year groupings in the general-education schools, often called, respectively, primary, incomplete secondary, and complete secondary schools. The pupil entered the primary, or four-year, school at the age of seven, and then went on to the incomplete secondary, or seven-year, school. All children were supposed to go through at least the seven-year school, although in many rural areas this was merely an aim, and not a reality, as the facilities were lacking for seven-year education. Upon graduation from the seven-year school, the student had three choices: he could work, enter a specialized technical school, called a technicum, or attend the ten-year school in preparation for higher education. If he elected to go to the ten-year school—grades eight through ten—he would carry a heavy college preparatory load. Upon graduation from the ten-year school, the pupil was eligible to take the entrance exams for college.

In the years between 1928 and 1958, the number of schools and the students attending them increased very rapidly. The number of general-education schools was almost doubled, the number of technicums tripled, and the number of universities quintupled.

TABLE 15

NUMBER OF SOVIET SCHOOLS AND STUDENTS *

Schools	*1940/41*	*1958/59*	*1960/61*	*1962/63*	*1963/64*	*1964/65*
Kindergartens	24,000	36,800	43,600	52,700	57,600	
General education	198,800	215,200	228,000	227,000	221,000	
Primary and secondary	191,500	199,700	199,200	197,600	195,500	
Working and rural youth	7,300	15,500	25,200	29,096	25,647	
Technicums	3,753	3,346	3,328	3,521	3,626	3,718
Higher education	817	766	739	738	742	754
Students (In Thousands)						
Kindergarten	1,171	2,357	3,115	4,171	4,813	
General education	35,600	31,500	36,187	42,442	44,682	46,700
Primary and secondary	34,800	29,000	33,400	38,500	40,500	42,000
Working and rural youth	800	1,900	2,769	3,960	4,203	4,700
Technicum	974	1,875	2,060	2,668	2,983	3,300
Extension and correspondence	187	750	969	1,358	1,509	1,700
Higher education	811	2,178	2,396	2,944	3,261	3,600
Extension and correspondence	253	999	1,240	1,657	1,878	2,000

* *Narodnoe Khozyaystvo SSSR v 1963 Godu,* pp. 555–66; *Pravda,* January 30, 1965, p. 2; *Pravda,* July 26, 1965, p. 2; *SSSR v Tsifrakh v 1964 Godu,* pp. 125–29.

The number of students increased even faster. The enrollment in the general-education schools rose from around 11 million in 1928 to over 31 million in 1958. The number of students in the technicums increased from about 200,000 in 1928 to 1,875,000 in 1958, and the total number of university students rose from 176,000 to 2,178,000 in the same period (see Table 15).

Since 1959, a great deal of confusion has developed in the general-education system. Khrushchev, in September, 1958, presented a speech to the Presidium of the Central Committee entitled "On the Strengthening of the Ties Between School and Life and on the Further Development of Public Education." After considerable discussion, Khrushchev's theses were approved by the Supreme Soviet in December, 1958.

Under the new scheme, the seven-year incomplete secondary school and the ten-year complete secondary school became, respectively, eight-year and eleven-year "general-education labor polytechnical schools with production training." The goal was compulsory education for all through the eight-year school; education in grades nine through eleven was for most Soviet citizens to be by extension and evening schools. Up to 80 per cent of those accepted in the institutions of higher education had to show evidence that in addition to completing their secondary education, they had also worked at least two years or had served in the armed forces. The other 20 per cent admitted were to be talented students who had been allowed to continue through secondary school without working.

"The ties between school and life" were to be strengthened by including a good deal of "polytechnical" education in the new program. Although the Soviet educationalists tried to put the "polytechnical" aspect on a high plane, it really boiled down to vocational training in industrial and agricultural production.

Why did Khrushchev decide to alter the Soviet general-education system so profoundly? The Soviet propagandists had pointed proudly to their schools as models of socialist efficiency. For several years, the announced goal had been a ten-year education for all by 1960, and the steadily increasing number of secondary-school graduates made the accomplishment of that aim even more probable. The apparent reasons behind Khrushchev's new look were weighty.

The first reason, and one agreed upon by most scholars, was demographic: A decrease in the birth rate and the high infant mortality rate during World War II were beginning to affect the industries, farms, and armed forces. The annual crop of eighteen-year-olds badly needed in the labor force began to shrink in 1957 and continued to decline. This deficit in young people was to remain a severe problem until 1965, the year in which the Seven-Year Plan was scheduled to end. One figure from the 1959 census shows the essence of the problem: There were only 8.2 million in the age group of ten- to fifteen-year-olds, compared with 14.9 million in 1939, a drop of 40 per cent.[1] Thus at the time the Seven-Year Plan called for a steady expansion of industry, the young people needed in industry were in short supply. Khrushchev's answer was to cut down on the length of the educational period so that more young people could enter the labor force, on the theory that muscles today are more important than skilled minds tomorrow. In the dilemma between the nonfulfillment of the Plan and the short-changing of education, the Plan had been chosen.

Nicholas DeWitt, an outstanding authority on Soviet education, contends that a conflict has been steadily growing between state planning and the option of the individual to develop his own potential.[2] If every child is allowed to decide whether he shall complete his secondary education and go on to higher education, the plans demanding large numbers of unskilled and semiskilled workers may be jeopardized. The Soviet leaders have always used such devices as examinations, quotas, and, at times, sheer compulsion to keep trained cadres flowing into the desired channels. But they have also held out the carrot that the individual could develop himself to the limits of his own capability. The goal of a ten-year education for all was a step in that direction. Nevertheless, the promise contained in Article 121 of the 1936 Constitution, that any citizen could get as much education as he was capable of absorbing, was changed by inserting the weasel words that education should be "based on the principle of the tie between education and life and production." This amendment was passed in 1958 in line with Khrushchev's new look.

There can be no doubt that the curriculum of the complete secondary school solely prepares students for higher education.

The graduates are not trained in manual skills. For years there has been agitation for more "polytechnization"—to use the word derived from the Russian—that is, more manual skills, a closer connection between, on the one hand, industry, agriculture, and transport and, on the other, the educational system. When the number of students completing the ten-year school was about equivalent to the vacancies in higher-educational institutions, the problem was easy. But when the number of graduates grew until there were three or four applicants for every vacancy in the universities and institutes, trouble developed. For example, in the autumn of 1959 the higher-educational institutions accepted around 229,000 full-time students in their day divisions, and in the spring some 1.4 million persons received their diplomas from the complete secondary schools.[3] This meant that there were about six applicants for every vacancy in the higher-educational institutions, or to put it another way, five out of every six graduates had to go to work, enter a technicum, or wait a year to take the entrance examinations again. The problem of "waiting a year" irritated Khrushchev very much. These one-year loafers, living off their families, were contemptuous of manual labor, and Khrushchev resented their attitude toward "socially useful labor." The government, however, tried to correct this situation by emphasizing previous employment as a prerequisite for admission to higher-educational institutions. In the autumn of 1959, of those accepted in the day divisions of higher-educational institutions, 122,000, or 49 per cent, had worked at least two years after graduation from the ten-year schools.

Another reason for the revolution in secondary education was Khrushchev's wish to weaken the power of the managerial elite, as opposed to the Party bureaucracy. The managerial elite had been able to perpetuate itself because the children of its members were getting the best education in the Soviet Union. A "gilded youth" had developed not only a contempt for manual labor but also for the classes that performed it. If the Party was to retain control, the managerial elite could not be allowed to dominate the educational system.

Just how enthusiastic the educationalists were about Khrushchev's so-called reforms is hard to say—the Soviet system does not encourage frank opposition to the leader's pet ideas. The President of the Academy of Sciences did point out that the most productive years in scientific training were precisely those during which, under the new system, the student might be forced to put in a two-year stint driving a tractor or running a drill press. Needless to say, the managerial elite did not look with pleasure upon this treatment of their children, whom Khrushchev referred to as *byeloruchki*, "white-handed ones." Soviet sociologists came up in 1965 with the statistic that the son of a white-collar worker is about eight times more likely to get into an institution of higher learning than the son of an agricultural worker. Thus, 89 per cent of the *byeloruchki* who want to go on to higher education do so, while only 13 per cent of the children of agricultural workers are able to fulfill their ambitions.[4] It would seem that the managerial elite had managed to circumvent Khrushchev's "reforms."

On August 13, 1964, the Central Committee of the CPSU and the U.S.S.R. Council of Ministers announced that beginning September 1, 1964, the eleven-year system would revert to the old ten-year system.[5] The increased vocational training in the eleven-year system had failed. By and large, the on-the-job training had been expensive and useless. Factory managers had either gone to great expense to train apprentices, most of whom never came back after graduation, or else provided menial jobs that included no adequate training. Thus, on the eve of Khrushchev's ouster. his educational reforms were being openly attacked.

ORGANIZATION OF THE SOVIET PRIMARY AND SECONDARY SCHOOLS

The Soviet educational system is organized in an ascending order, from the nursery to postdoctoral work in the Academy of Sciences. According to law, education is compulsory through the incomplete secondary, or eight-year, school. Beyond that point there is rigorous selectivity, and there is nothing automatic about further eduction. However, all propaganda is aimed at creating a desire for further education, and tempting rewards are held out to encourage the student to go on.

Preschool Education

The Soviet Union has a rather elaborate preschool system, mainly because it takes two salaries to sustain the average Soviet family, thus making it mandatory for most mothers to work. Therefore, the preschool system vitally affects the family budget and also makes recruiting the necessary labor force for the state much easier. As a result, the preschool institutions operate on an all-year basis.

In most plants, under the supervision of the Ministry of Health, a system of nurseries (*yasli*), or crèches as they are often called, is operated for the care of the very young children, from ten-weeks to three years of age. The nurseries have no educational function, but merely care for the child while the mother works. The children from three to seven years of age attend kindergartens, if one is available. The usual preschool methods are used, namely, supervised play and some training in drawing and music. A good deal of controversy exists among Soviet educators on the advisability of teaching the alphabet and the rudiments of reading in the kindergartens. However, the main function of the kindergarten, as in the case of the nursery, is to take care of the child so that the mother can work.

Primary, or Four-Year, School

The Soviet child begins his schooling at the age of seven, usually in one of the general education schools. The primary school is not necessarily located in a separate building; it is usually in a building in which all eight grades are housed. In the rural areas, however, the primary school may be the only educational institution within easy reach.

The primary, or four-year-school, is mainly concerned with teaching the pupil to read, calculate, and gain an elementary knowledge of the natural sciences through the reading program. The pupil usually has the same teacher for the first four years. In this way, the teacher becomes acquainted with the child and his parents, which may help in the evaluation of the pupil's strengths and weaknesses by allowing an evaluation of how the home environment affects the pupil's behavior. Judging from the textbooks used in the primary schools, the Soviet pupil is not pampered. Memorization and repetition are stressed, and homework is usual. As prescribed by law in 1952, the teacher may assign one hour a day in the first grade and as much as two hours a day in grades three and four. The pupil goes to school six days a week, so the homework may be rather heavy. Articles appearing in the Soviet press have discussed the merits of reducing or even eliminating homework.

Incomplete Secondary, or Eight-Year, School

Since the educational changes in 1959, all Soviet children are supposed to go through the eight-year school. Whether this state edict is being better observed than was the edict on compulsory seven-year education is unknown. What little evidence is available, however, seems to point to a fulfillment of the goal.

In the eight-year school, the subjects become more specialized, and each subject is handled by a teacher. Natural sciences are taught individually, and geography and history are introduced as separate subjects. Foreign languages are also introduced in the fifth grade, and the pupil elects one language to study for the next five or six years. The choices are English, German, French, and Spanish, although not all schools have teachers for these languages.

Graduation from the eight-year school means an interruption in education for a large number of Soviet children. At this point many young people go to work and continue their education either in extension schools or through correspondence courses.

Complete Secondary, or Ten-Year, School

The complete secondary school prepares the student for higher education. He continues his courses in history, natural sciences, foreign languages, Russian language and literature, and mathematics. At the end of the tenth grade he must pass a series of examinations to be eligible for graduation. The examinations are either written or oral, or a combination of the two. They are administered by a board made up of teachers, the director of the school, and representatives of the educational administration. If the student passes the examinations, he is granted a certificate of maturity and is eligible to take the entrance examinations for one of the higher-educational institutions. Despite the 1964 decision to abandon the eleven-year system, the old ten-year system has not been universally re-adopted, and many schools still go through the eleventh grade.

Curriculum of the General-Education Schools

The determination of the curriculum in the general-education schools is left to the individual republics, so that curriculum varies, for example, between the Armenian and Latvian republics. Because of the enormous size and population of the R.S.F.S.R., the curricula of the other republics have closely followed that of the R.S.F.S.R. The main difference is that the other republics teach the native languages. Russian is studied as a second language.

Soviet elementary and secondary education differs from the American system in many ways, but two differences are especially evident. First, the entire system of a republic is highly centralized and uniform standards obtain for the entire republic. For example, the same textbooks, teaching methods, and examinations are used from Leningrad to Vladivostok as in the R.S.F.S.R. Although such rigid standardization may have drawbacks, it does allow the Soviet planners to assume that the graduates of secondary schools within a republic will meet certain minimum standards. Second, the stress on mathematics and sciences is much greater in the Soviet elementary and secondary schools than it is in American schools. Out of slightly more than 10,000 hours of instruction in the ten-year system, 2,000 hours are spent in mathematics. Only the Russian language and literature are given greater emphasis. Soviet educators do not believe in "general" courses, such as general science. The motto is "learn the fundamentals" of each science. Biology is taught in the fourth grade through the ninth grade; while physics is introduced in the sixth grade and continues through the tenth grade; chemistry is taught in the seventh grade through the tenth grade; and a course in astronomy is given in the tenth grade.

The curriculum for the general schools vividly demonstrates the Soviet view that education is primarily for the development of the state, not the individual. The whole program is aimed toward shaping an individual who is imbued with an appreciation of the value of Marxist-Leninist society and who will be useful in the technological development of the national economy. Over 40 per cent of the curriculum is devoted to science and mathematics, and the humanities heavily stress Marxist doctrine. For example, all history courses from ancient to modern times reflect Marx's theories of the evolution of social institutions.

On the other hand, the Soviet pupil gets a consistent survey of history from the earliest times to the present, with emphasis on chronology, names, geography, and facts. Soviet pedagogy does not regard the child's memory as a fragile instrument to be protected from use. Even in the first grade, mathematics is treated as one of the facts of life, something that cannot be avoided and does not need to be sugar-coated in its presentation. Therefore, all graduates of the tenth grade have mastered arithmetic, algebra, plane geometry, and trigonometry. The study of foreign languages is mandatory through the upper grades.

Schools for Working Youth and Rural Youth

These schools were organized during World War II as a means to educate young people who had been drafted into the State Labor Reserve and those whose education had been terminated because of the wartime demand for labor. The schools were so successful that they became a permanent part of the Soviet educational system. In 1958, almost 2 million students were enrolled in them. After 1959, Khrushchev's new look in education made these schools even more important. These institutions are charged with the task of providing extension education for the eight-year-school graduates who desire to continue their secondary education while working. Some 4.7 million students were enrolled in the schools for working and rural youth in the 1964/65 academic year.

Boarding Schools

At the Twentieth Party Congress, in February, 1956, it was announced that a system of polytechnical boarding schools (*shkola-internat*) would be established. The reasoning behind this step was well expressed by Khrushchev: "It will rear and educate the new Communist Man. . . . Its teachers will be the engineers of the souls of the rising generation." [6] The schools were originally intended for the children of widows and parents who were not able to care for them properly. The fees were based on the parents' ability to pay, and the children were to live in the schools the year round.

Some 300 schools were opened in the fall of 1956; by 1961, 700,000 children were being housed and reared in boarding schools. In 1964, the figure was 2.4 million, but this total included the pupils in extended day schools, which discharge their pupils at the end of each day and do not board them over the weekend. Probably only half of the 1964 total referred to boarding-school pupils.[7]

The Seven-Year Plan envisaged 2.5 million children in boarding schools by 1965, but it is unlikely this goal was reached. Khrushchev even spoke of eventually educating all children in boarding schools, and while many of Khrushchev's pet schemes have been derided and even abolished since his fall from power, the new leadership seems intent on keeping the boarding schools and even improving and extending the program.

Special Schools

Artistically gifted children are often sent at an early age to special schools. A child who shows a special aptitude for dancing may be sent to one of the fourteen ballet schools in the U.S.S.R.; or if the talent is music, he is sent to a school specializing in music. The artistic phase of education is in addition to the regular academic curriculum. Upon graduation, the student may go to a conservatory or art institute for further training, or go directly into concert work. The state regulates the number of artists according to the cultural plan—the circuses to go with the bread. A desire to "go on the stage" makes little difference in the Soviet cultural world.

Physically or mentally handicapped children are educated in schools for the blind, deaf, and mentally retarded. The classes are taught by teachers who took special courses in the pedagogical institutes. These teachers usually receive extra pay.

Closed Secondary Military Schools

According to the official Soviet description, the closed secondary military educational institutions are designed to train students for entry into military schools. The cadet schools were established in 1943/44 to train the sons of Soviet officers killed in combat. Two types of cadet schools are the Suvorov schools, which train cadets for the army schools, and the Nakhimov schools, which prepare cadets for naval training. The naming of the schools after Suvorov, a great general during the era of Catherine the Great, and Nakhimov, an admiral in the Crimean War, is indicative of the rise in Russian nationalism. The Suvorov and Nakhimov schools are equivalent to the Soviet complete secondary schools, but with a much greater emphasis on military studies, riding, dancing, and the traditions associated with the officer corps. The number of students enrolled in the cadet schools is not tabulated in the official Soviet educational statistics.

Specialized Secondary Schools, or Technicums

One of the most important classes of schools in the Soviet Union is the so-called specialized secondary schools, usually referred to as technicums (*tekhnikumy*). The technicums have some of the characteristics of the secondary schools, and in some ways resemble the higher-educational institutions. Therefore, it is fitting that the programs, methods, and curricula of the technicums are under the administration of the Ministry of Higher and Specialized-Secondary Education. The financing and some of the administration were formerly carried out by the ministries that used the services of the technicians educated in these schools. But the decentralization of industry in 1957 and its horizontal organization under regional Economic Councils led to the eradication of a large number of all-union and union-republic ministries. In all probability these councils, not all of which were abolished by the general recentralization of power in 1963, have the job of financing the technicums.

Graduates of the eight-year schools are eligible to take competitive examinations for entrance into the technicums. The usual course lasts three to four years, depending upon the speciality. In the late 1950's, the large number of graduates from the ten-year schools who could not get into the higher-educational institutions overcrowded the technicums. The technicums in turn cut to two or two and a half years the courses attended by ten-year-school graduates. This problem is being resolved, since education for many Soviet youths terminates with the eight-year school. Only the selected students are allowed to enter the complete secondary schools without having put in a labor stint. In the 1964/65 academic year, there were 3.3 million students enrolled in technicums; about half (1.7 million) of them, however, were studying in the evening and correspondence divisions.[8]

The technicums train technicians and specialists for all fields of industry, transport, agriculture, education, medicine, physical culture, and even art. The graduates are subprofessionals, so to speak. They are not trained to the level of engineers and doctors, but are able to handle jobs just below the professional level. The industrial technicums are somewhat analogous to the American technical institute, but this type of institution in the United States accounts for less than 60,000 students. Much of this type of training in America is given in the school of business administration at colleges, in nursing courses, and in dental technician courses. American industry must supply its own technical training in many cases, and the armed forces also help supply technically trained men to private industry.

Since the First Five-Year Plan (1928–32), Soviet planners have set goals varying from one and a half to four technicians for every engineer. In 1959, according to Soviet figures, the specialized secondary institutions graduated 530,000 students of whom 260,000 were technicians for industry, construction, transport, and communications. Inasmuch as they trained 106,000 engineers in the same year, the ratio is about two and a half to one.[9] In 1964, more than 550,000 specialists were turned out by the technicums, while some 133,000 engineers were graduated from the higher-educational institutions.[10] Probably no more than half of the technicum graduates were specialists in industry, construction, transport, or communications. Therefore, the ratio was about the same as in 1959.

HIGHER-EDUCATIONAL INSTITUTIONS

Under the heading of "Higher-Educational Institutions," the *Great Soviet Encyclopedia* accurately defines the mission of Soviet higher education as follows: "Higher-educational institutions in the U.S.S.R. are educational institutions that train qualified specialists for the various branches of the national economy and culture." [11] The writer might well have added the word "military" to the words "economy" and "culture." The key word, however, is "specialist." The average Soviet student in a higher-educational institution devotes far more time to an extremely narrow field than does his counterpart in the United States. There is no equivalent to the American liberal-arts program, not in the forty Soviet universities, nor yet in the 700 or so more specialized institutes. In the 1964/65 academic year, there were 742 institutions of higher education in the Soviet Union, with a total enrollment of 3.6 million. But over half of them (2 million) were in the extension and correspondence divisions, i.e., part-time students.[12]

An outstanding characteristic of Soviet higher education, as in secondary education, is its extreme emphasis on natural sciences and engineering. At the University of Moscow, in the academic year 1955/56, there were 9,182 students in sciences and only 6,362 in all other fields. A quick look at the top elite of the Soviet educational system—the academicians of the Soviet Academy of Sciences, which includes the humanities—bears out this extreme emphasis on natural sciences and engineering, for the ratio is four to one against the humanities.

TABLE 16

STATE UNIVERSITIES IN THE U.S.S.R., 1960/61*

University	*Location*	*Number of Students*
Azerbaidzhan	Baku	8,750
Bashkir	Ufa	4,000
Byelorussia	Minsk	6,800
Central Asia	Tashkent	6,200
Chernovtsy	Chernovtsy	5,000
Dagestan	Makhachkala	3,400
Dnepropetrovsk	Dnepropetrovsk	5,000
Far East	Vladivostok	3,300
Gorky	Gorky	3,100
Irkutsk	Irkutsk	4,600
Kabardino-Balkar	Nalchik	2,800
Kharkov	Kharkov	8,300
Kiev	Kiev	10,500
Kirgiz	Frunze	5,000
Kishinev	Kishinev	6,600
Kazakh	Alma-Ata	11,650
Kazan	Kazan	6,000
Latvia	Riga	5,000
Leningrad	Leningrad	13,700
Lvov	Lvov	8,400
Mordovia	Saransk	4,500
Moscow	Moscow	23,650
Novosibirsk	Novosibirsk	600
Odessa	Odessa	8,200
Perm (formerly Molotov)	Perm	5,700
Petrozavodsk	Petrozavodsk	
Rostov	Rostov-on-Don	6,000
Saratov	Saratov	5,800
Tadzhik	Dushanbe (formerly Stalinabad)	4,350
Tartu	Tartu	4,500
Tbilisi	Tbilisi	8,900
Tomsk	Tomsk	
Turkmen	Ashkhabad	
Urals	Sverdlovsk	5,100
Uzbek	Samarkand	6,500
Uzhgorod	Uzhgorod	4,700
Vilnyus	Vilnyus	
Voronezh	Voronezh	
Yakutsk	Yakutsk	
Yerevan	Yerevan	5,700

* *Kul'turnoe Stroitel'stvo SSSR*, pp. 218–29; *Directory of Selected Scientific Institutions in the U.S.S.R.* (Columbus, Ohio: Charles E. Merrill Books, 1963), *passim.*

The system of higher education in the Soviet Union can be divided into two basic types: universities and institutes. The chief mission of the estimated thirty-six universities is to supply a large number of the theoricians and teachers for the higher-educational institutions, and to some extent, the secondary schools. Each union republic has at least one university, but the real concentration of students—over 50,000—can be found in the universities of Moscow and Leningrad. The size of the universities varies with the population of the republics, ranging from five faculties in the universities of the smaller republic to twelve faculties in the universities of Moscow and Leningrad. A faculty is a broad division, such as a faculty for history, a faculty for biology-soils, or a philological faculty, which includes languages and literature. The faculty in turn is broken down in subdivisions called *kafedry* (literally, "chairs"), which are similar to the departments of American universities. In the academic year 1955/56, the Soviet universities had a total of 248 faculties.

The university course usually runs five years, and the graduate receives a certificate instead of a formal degree. The entrance examinations are stiff, and the number of students admitted is far less than the number of applicants. In late years, preference has been given to those who have proof of at least two years of work, or have been recently discharged from the armed forces.

The term "institute" is generic for a variety of higher-educational institutions, such as forestry schools, technical schools, and conservatories of music. Any higher educational institution can be classified as a VUZ (*vysshee uchebnoe zavedenie*), the initial letters of the Russian words for "higher-educational institution." Of the more than 700 institutes, over 200 are technical institutes that train specialists for industry, transport, construction, and communications. An institute of this type is called a VTUZ (*vysshee tekhnicheskoe uchebnoe zavedenie*), or "higher-technical-educational institution." Most of the higher-education institutions are integrated under the Ministry of Higher and Specialized-Secondary Education, a union-republic ministry that has jurisdiction over them in all respects—administrative, academic (setting scholastic requirements), financing, and so forth.

Each university is headed by a rector; each institute, by a director. The faculty is under a dean, and each department (*kafedra*) has its own head. Each institution has an academic council made up of the deans, the department heads, representatives from the Komsomol and Party organizations in the school, as well as from the plants associated with the school.

The close integration of the entire Soviet educational system differentiates it radically from that of the United States. The top officials of the Ministry of Higher and Specialized-Secondary Education are in constant contact with their counterparts in the other ministries and branches of the government, and thus the needs and demands of the state—military and economic—are well known to them. The foremost scholars of the Academy of Sciences often wear several hats. In addition to their teaching and research activities at the Academy, they may be serving as teachers at the leading universities and institutes, as high-ranking military officers, and as advisers to various industrial-planning groups. For example, a leading designer of aircraft is at the same time a member of the Academy of Sciences, a consultant to the Ministry of Aviation Industry, and a teacher at the air force's Zhukovskiy Academy. His activities can be directed and coordinated at several levels, thus allowing scarce talent to be fully utilized.

Although the qualitative aspect of Soviet education is difficult to estimate with any accuracy, there seems to be agreement among scholars that it compares very favorably with that of the United States. The solid training in mathematics and basic sciences given in the secondary schools, the incentive to avoid the draft by enrolling in higher education, and the ample rewards for proficiency in the technical fields provide the higher-educational institutions with a more than adequate supply of well-trained candidates to select from. This has brought about a stiffening of the entrance examinations as well as more exacting standards for the courses given in the higher-educational institutions.

During the first two years in a VTUZ, the student takes courses primarily in the basic sciences, mathematics, and nonspecialized engineering. In the next two years, he specializes to a much greater degree. His fifth year is largely taken up with his diploma project, which is similar to a master's thesis under the American system. Over 15 per cent of the Soviet student's time is earmarked for physical and military instruction and for courses in Party doctrine. DeWitt has prepared a time-percentile breakdown of the Soviet engineering curriculum: nonscientific and political courses, 6 to 8 per cent; general sciences, 26 to 30 per cent; nonspecialized engineering, 22 to 28 per cent; physical training and military instruction, 6 to 10 per cent.[13] The rest of the time is devoted to specialization.

In addition, the Soviet engineering education is very closely tied to the actual production line. During the summer after the second year, the student spends four weeks at a plant associated with his special field. Eleven weeks of the third summer are spent observing more closely the industrial process of his specialty, and finally the summer between the fourth and fifth years is devoted to an eleven-week tour as an actual administrator in a plant dealing with his specialty. Obviously, this practice reduces the amount of on-the-job training between graduation and productive work. Furthermore, it provides the student with practical material for his diploma project in his fifth year.

Higher degrees in the Soviet Union are fewer and harder to obtain than in the United States. In 1963, the total number of persons holding higher degrees in the Soviet Union was 127,900, of which 12,700 held doctorates and 115,200 held the candidate degree.[14] The best students of the higher-educational institutions can apply for graduate, or *aspirantura,* training for the candidate (*kandidat*) degree. The three-year training consists of about one and a half years of reading and seminar work and one and a half years devoted to a dissertation. The candidate degree falls somewhere between the master's and doctor's degrees of the United States. Students obtaining a candidate degree may be permitted to work for a doctor's degree. Applicants for doctorates are required to submit a list of their published and unpublished works, a plan of research, and evidence of competence in foreign languages. At the end of the training, the candidate must submit a dissertation and demonstrate an ability to handle scientific literature in three foreign languages.

Both the candidate and doctor's degrees must be confirmed by the Supreme Attestation Committee (VAK), a division of the Ministry of Higher and Specialized-Secondary Education. Higher degrees can be, and have been, awarded without strict adherence to the steps outlined above, but the practice is fast disappearing. Dissertations for advanced degrees in the Soviet Union are likely to be worthwhile in the scientific fields, especially in engineering, physics, mathematics, and chemistry. But they are usually of little value in the nonscientific fields, particularly in modern history and other areas that impinge on the present and past political actions of the Party and its leaders.

The entire Soviet educational system has one goal: the production of specialists for service to the state. Ever since the beginning of the intensified industrialization of the First Five-Year Plan and the military buildup that accompanied it, there has been a shortage of trained manpower in the Soviet Union. This has led to the extreme emphasis upon engineering and science that has already been discussed. In the early 1930's, Stalin attempted an accelerated program for training a large number of engineers, but the quality was so poor that it was necessary to return to more fundamental training. As a result, in the last two decades a very large percentage of Soviet students have been trained as teachers, the essential basis for the production of engineers.

THE ACADEMY OF SCIENCES

At the very top of the Soviet scientific world stands the Academy of Sciences. A Soviet scholar can aspire to no higher honor than to become a member of this august body. The Academy, founded in 1724 by Peter the Great, was intended to be the nation's highest authority on academic matters. To this end, it was to carry out scientific research, to solve practical problems, to advise the government, and to oversee the nation's higher education. Its role is more or less the same today, except that carrying out scientific research is of much more importance now than it was in 1724. In 1934, the Academy was moved from Leningrad to Moscow.

Since 1930, the Academy's work has been closely integrated in the national economic planning, and each member spends at least two months a year fitting his work into the over-all plan that has been approved by the Council of Ministers. The Academy plays a major role in Soviet technological research. It has also been involved in a tug of war with the Party and government. The latter have continually urged more emphasis on the practical application of science to production, while the academicians have tended to stress basic research. As a result, a good deal of governmental interference with the Academy's internal affairs has taken place during the last thirty years.

The Academy is made up of full members, or academicians, and corresponding members, both of whom are elected to membership by the members of the Academy. Thus, it is a self-perpetuating body. In 1963, there were 520 academicians and corresponding members, the cream of the Soviet scientific community.[15] The members constitute the General Assembly of the Academy, but they elect a Presidium to function as administrator between sessions of the General Assembly. They also elect the President of the Academy. In addition, there is a Chief Scientific Secretary, the chief representative of the Party apparatus.

Below the Presidium and Chief Scientific Secretariat, authority descends through councils, functional departments, and other organs to the research institutes controlled by the Academy. In 1935, to improve integration of the Academy's mission with the over-all state plans and to insure that applied science was given proper emphasis, the Academy was put directly under the control of the Council of Ministers.

The U.S.S.R. Academy of Sciences is the director and coordinator of the fourteen Republic Academies of Sciences, the Lenin Academy of Agricultural Sciences, the Academy of Medicine, the Academy of Pedagogical Sciences, the Academy of Art, and of 192 scientific institutes. It has 22,119 scientific workers on its payroll.[16]

The Academy was reorganized in the spring of 1961, following an announcement from the Presidium of the Supreme Soviet, on April 9, of three decrees that affected the Academy's coordination of scientific research. One decree abolished the State Scientific and Technical Committee of the Council of Ministers, an organization working closely with the Academy. The second decree established a new State Committee for the Coordination of Scientific

Research Work, and the third decree named M. V. Khrunichev as head of the new committee and as Deputy Chairman of the Council of Ministers of the U.S.S.R.[17]

Three days later, an article in *Pravda* briefly explained the position of the government.[18] It pointed out that the Soviet Union had built up a vast network of scientific-research institutions which employed more than 350,000 scientific workers. For this reason, a radical reorganization of the methods of supervising this enormous structure had been necessary. Better coordination of the planning of scientific research was essential in order to avoid duplication of effort. Furthermore, the Academy of Sciences had had too much administrative work because of its association with so many scientific institutions. The administrative work had prevented the Academy from resolving its long-range problems in science. The new committee, therefore, had been established to carry out the necessary coordination. In order that the Academy might have enough time for its own research, it had been instructed to relinquish control of a number of scientific institutions hitherto under its supervision and to give up control of its affiliates as well.

Beneath this rationalization loomed the fact that Khrushchev was dissatisfied with the overemphasis on "pure" science and the underemphasis on applied science. Warnings in previous years indicated that the "pure" research people were not getting enough scientific achievements into industrial production fast enough. The appointment of Khrunichev, an experienced production man, and upon his death in June, 1961, his replacement, K. N. Rudnev, showed that this move was intended to put industry in a driving position above the scientific establishments. In other words, this part of Khrushchev's educational reforms of 1958/59 injected the factory into the schoolroom at the top level.

By the spring of 1963, it had become evident that the 1961 decentralization of scientific research was not working out any better than was the 1957 decentralization of the economy. M. V. Keldysh, President of the Academy, called for more centralization and coordination in determining the basic directions of research throughout the Soviet Union, and shortly thereafter another reorganization took place, reversing that of 1961. The Academy was re-established as the mainspring of the Soviet scientific endeavor. The Academy, hitherto divided into eight divisions, was now reorganized into fifteen divisions: mathematics, general physics, nuclear physics, physical-technical problems of energy, earth sciences, mechanics and control processes, general chemistry, physical chemistry, biochemistry, physiology, zoology, history, philosophy and law, economics, and languages and literature.[19] It is uncertain to what extent the new reorganization will improve Soviet scientific research. As James M. Swanson has pointed out: "The essentially bureaucratic belief that a reshuffling of organizational structures and administrative responsibilities produces effectiveness in operation is characteristic of Soviet institutional philosophy." [20]

THE TEACHER

The Soviet educational system, like any other, is about as good as its teachers. When Stalin began to emphasize the need for "trained cadres" in the early 1930's, the first obstacle was the shortage of competent teachers, especially in the higher-educational institutions where more teachers were to be trained. In addition, there is the continuous problem of reconciling sound education with Party control; many of the teachers were not, and are not, Party members. The solution of this problem has been to place Party members in key positions in the school administration.

The Soviet Government has worked hard over the last thirty years to produce an adequate number of teachers and to improve their quality. In 1928, there were 349,000 teachers in the general-education school; by 1955, the figure had risen to 1.7 million; [21] and in the 1963/64 school year there were 2.3 million.[22] One criterion of effective education is a low ratio of students to teachers. In 1931, the ratio was nineteen students per teacher; by 1947, it was less than ten to one. Then it began to climb and was seventeen to one by 1956.[23] By the 1963/64 school year, with 2.3 million teachers in the general-educational schools and a student body of 44.7 million, the ratio was about nineteen to one.[24] Of course, the fact that many teachers are in special areas with small classes, and that many more are administrators, accounts for visitors' reports of classes of well over thirty to a teacher.

Teachers in higher-educational institutions and scientific-research institutions are fairly well paid, by Soviet standards, but not so well paid in the general-education schools. Their salaries in 1965 ran under a hundred rubles a month (approximately $110 and less).

THE TECHNOLOGICAL RACE

In the decade of Khrushchev's ascendancy, 1955–64, a good deal was said about various races, between the Soviet Union and the United States, in economic growth rate, in general technological development, and especially in the conquest of space. Khrushchev's "peaceful coexistence" policy seemed to be based on the assumption that the Soviet Union was destined to win the races, although his missile gambit in Cuba, in 1962, did not seem to be of a piece with that assumption.

The Soviet leadership, first under Stalin, and then under Khrushchev, has always recognized the central role of education in the technological race, and there can be no argument that the output of skilled personnel between 1930 and the present has been impressive. The heavy emphasis, of course, has been on scientific and technical training. According to Soviet statistics, in the year 1963 there were 4,595 scientific institutes in the U.S.S.R., of which 1,976 were scientific-research institutes. These institutes employed some 326,800 scientific workers; in addition, 196,800 scientific workers were employed in higher-educational institutions.[25] This score is indeed impressive when contrasted to the total of 162,500 scientific workers in 1950. Another impressive figure is the 133,000 engineers graduated in 1964.[26]

In the fine art of persuasion, the Soviet leadership has been particularly successful. The materialistic basis of Communist ideology gives the Soviet state an initial advantage in the training of scientists and technicians. Science has assumed the aura of religion, and Soviet youth has almost been persuaded that science can provide the answer to all problems. Everything from the explanation of history to the building of an ideal future is credited to science; Soviet youth can aspire no higher than to enter the ranks of so dedicated a calling.

Another motivation toward technical training is provided by the vast and well-organized paramilitary society for Soviet youth, the DOSAAF (All-Union Voluntary Society for Assistance to the Army, Air Force, and Navy). Since 1951, this is the new name for the old Osoaviakhim (Voluntary Society for Assistance in Defense, Aviation, and Chemistry), which was formed in the late 1920's. This society, embracing over 15 million young people, sponsors all kinds of military training and the development of skills that will be useful to the armed forces. Thus the DOSAAF members learn to drive trucks and tractors, build and repair radios, use and maintain various types of automatic weapons, and engage in other activities that acquaint them with technological matters.

In addition to the Communist adulation of science and the social pressure to participate in the activities of DOSAAF, there is a new surge of patriotism in the Soviet Union. This is partly the result of the constant barrage by all the Soviet organs of propaganda, and partly the result of the victory over the Germans in World War II. One manifestation of the extreme nationalism has been the ridiculous series of "firsts" claimed as Russian inventions and technical discoveries. But beneath this childish disregard for truth lies a pride in Soviet achievement and a determination to advance Soviet science and technology further and faster in the future.

The output of scientists and engineers in the next decade will depend largely on the interests and capabilities of the students now in elementary and secondary schools. An adequate number of trained students presupposes an adequate number of well-trained teachers in the precollege schools, and it is precisely here that the United States is lagging. Of the Soviet teachers trained in pedagogical institutes, around 50 per cent are majors in science and mathematics. These graduates are now science teachers in the Soviet educational system. Not only is there a smaller percentage of mathematics and science majors in the total output of trained teachers in the United States, but a staggering number of these never become science teachers, or do so for only a short period of time. Many are attracted to the better-paying jobs in industry.

One frequently noted weakness of the Soviet educational system is the extreme concentration of higher-educational institutions in the two areas of Moscow and Leningrad. Moscow has ninety such institutions, with almost 300,000 students; Leningrad has fifty, with 150,000 students. This would imply a waste of much potential talent in the vast extent of the Soviet Union, even granting that many of the students in the Moscow and Leningrad areas are imported. The Soviets seem to be acutely aware of this problem, and many recent articles in the Soviet press have discussed the need for expanding rural-school facilities, for raising the standards of the outlying universities and higher-educational institutions, and, in general, for decentralizing education somewhat.

Another aspect of the race for production of technically trained manpower is the effort to evaluate the numbers themselves. The Soviet statistics seem accurate enough as far as they go, but it is likely that some of the students are censored out of the totals. Statistics are not available on the number of Soviet engineers turned out by military schools. We know that there are a large number of Soviet military schools, both secondary and on the higher levels, but the number of graduates is not given. When Stalin presented the figures for higher education to the Communist Party Congress of 1939, he pointed out that he was not including the military figure. The *Narodnoe Khozyaystvo SSSR* for 1956 omits military schools in its otherwise comprehensive compilation of statistics. Furthermore, many educational institutions under the various ministries have military-engineering sections under "special faculties," and their figures are not given. Engineers involved in the production of special weapons are not counted in any breakdown, nor is there any tabulation of the graduate students working in such establishments. Gorokhoff suggests that some idea of the magnitude of this group can be obtained from a study of the atomic-energy system of the United States and the number of engineers engaged in it.[27] The only approach to this problem is to assume that a rather sizable group of engineers is being trained and to recognize that figures on this group are never included in published Soviet statistics.

As with most aspects of the Soviet Union, accurate evaluations and estimates in the educational field are difficult due to the outright suppression, or, in some cases, partial censorship, of information. Furthermore, comparisons are not always easy. How does one compare an MIT-trained engineer with his Soviet counterpart? The Soviet engineer seems to be far more narrowly trained in his field of specialization, but on the other hand there are so many more Soviet engineers being trained that the state may feel it can afford this degree of specialization. It may safely be asserted, however, that the current direction and velocity of Soviet education seem adequate for the immediate needs of the state in the scientific and technical fields. In the humanities, the picture is far more gloomy.

11

The Armed Forces

In the present bipolar world, when enormous forces in being are regarded as the *sine qua non* for all great powers, some understanding of the origins, growth, and present state of the Soviet armed forces is essential in an evaluation of the U.S.S.R. The Bolsheviks came to power during the violence of World War I and attained that power by the use of force. To maintain their minority control of Russia, they built the Red Army, some 5 million strong by 1921. Although the Red Army had a checkered existence during the NEP period, it became one of the chief beneficiaries of the forced industrialization under the Five-Year Plans. It defended the homeland adequately during World War II, and became an instrument for conquest after the war. After 1953, the army played an important role in contest within the "collective leadership" for Stalin's mantle, and the support of the army was one of the important factors in Khrushchev's victory. Once the dictatorship was firmly re-established, the army was forced back into its subservience to the Party; but no leader is immortal, and any power struggle on the top echelon of the Party may bring the army into politics again. Both within the U.S.S.R. and on the world scene, the Soviet Army looms large, and there seems to be little chance of a diminution of its importance in the immediate future.

ORIGINS OF THE RED ARMY

The outstanding feature of the revolution of March, 1917, was its spontaneity; it occurred with a suddenness that left a power vacuum at the top of the huge, sprawling empire still engaged in a major war. From March until October, a number of leaders tried to curb the revolution, but it moved relentlessly toward the Left. The war-weary, land-hungry mass of peasants, both in and out of uniform, wanted peace and land, but the leadership of the Provisional Government, plagued more and more by the rival government of the Soviets, was pledged to continue the war and had no clear-cut plan for the land problem.

In April, 1917, the Germans permitted Lenin to go through Germany en route to Russia. They hoped his activities would undermine the battered Russian Army. The correctness of their calculations was amply demonstrated when Lenin took Russia out of the war in February, 1918. On his arrival in Petrograd, Lenin promptly took command of the confused Bolshevik Party, infused a new spirit into his followers, and laid down a definite program. A fundamental part of that program was either to win over, or at least to neutralize, the peasants and soldiers and to destroy the Russian Army as a bulwark of the Provisional Government.

Although Lenin had the Marxist's distrust of the peasant, he had come to realize by 1917 that the Bolsheviks could not gain power without peasant allies. When the peasants had seized the land, or were in the process of doing so, their opposition to the group that had urged the seizure would be weakened. He saw, too, that this program would directly weaken the army, for the overwhelming mass of Russian soldiers were peasants in uniform, and once they heard that land was being distributed at home, no power could hold them in ranks. When Lenin urged immediate peace, he did so with the expectation of winning the army's peasants to his side.

In April, the Bolsheviks established a propaganda group, the Military Organization, to carry the slogan of "Bread, Peace, and

Freedom" to the soldiers. It printed newspapers, dispatched agitators to the front, and, in general, undermined army discipline. By July, the Military Organization had 26,000 agents organized in forty-three front and seventeen rear organizations. It should be kept in mind, however, that Lenin was not active from pacifist principles; the undermining and destruction of the army was aimed at clearing the road for the Bolshevik seizure of power.

That the Bolsheviks did not confine themselves to a strictly negative attitude toward force can be seen in their revival of the Red Guard, a factory militia that had its roots in the 1905 revolution. In September, 1917, the Commander in Chief of the Russian Army, Kornilov, attempted a Rightist coup, and in the crisis, Kerenski called on the Red Guard for assistance. Kornilov failed, but the Red Guard obtained a large supply of arms. By November, when the army had "voted for peace with its legs," as Lenin put it, and the Bolsheviks had gained control of the Petrograd Soviet, the Red Guard was strong enough to carry the Bolsheviks to power. Looking back on the events of the October Revolution, it seems amazing that the Bolsheviks could have taken over the control of a major nation with such a small force. The Red Guard probably numbered no more than 20,000 partly trained factory workers, and it was supplemented by a few detachments of regular soldiers and some Baltic sailors.

The Bolsheviks soon found that the power so easily obtained was going to be much harder to retain. Having destroyed the Russian Army, the new government was left naked in a world that had little respect for those lacking the instruments of military power, for although the Red Guard had been strong enough to oust a bankrupt government, it was woefully inadequate to cope with the mounting anti-Bolshevik pressures. Even after the Treaty of Brest Litovsk, the Germans were pushing into the Ukraine and the Caucasus; General Kaledin had raised a White Army in the Don region at the time the Bolsheviks were taking over, and soon White armies were pushing in from all four points of the compass. The British in the north and the French in the south were intervening on the side of the

Whites, and toward the end of May, 1918, the Czech troops, who were being moved to France via Vladivostok, took over the Trans-Siberian Railroad from Kazan to the Pacific. The Bolsheviks needed an army, a big one, and in a hurry.

To meet the situation, the Sovnarkom (Council of People's Commissars), on January 28, 1918, set up the machinery for building an army, the Red Army. It was to be a volunteer army formed around the nucleus of the 35,000 Red Guardists. By the end of April, the Red Army totaled just over 100,000 men, which was very slow progress toward the goal of 3 million that Lenin had set for the spring of 1919. It was obvious that stiffer tactics were called for, and on April 22, the Central Executive Committee issued a decree subjecting the entire male population from eighteen to forty years of age to the draft. By the end of 1919, the goal of 3 million men had been attained, and by 1921, over 5 million men were in the Red Army.

The Red Army celebrates its birthday on February 23. There seems to be no reason for this particular date other than that on February 23, 1918, a small Soviet force repulsed some German detachments at Pskov and Narva—the first "victory" of the new state over a foreign enemy.[1]

The Reds won the Civil War. They had several advantages in the conflict besides their numerical superiority. They had internal lines of communications and were able to coordinate their activities much more effectively than could the White armies on the periphery of the country. They had inherited most of the military equipment of the Czarist regime, and they could emphasize the patriotic motif because of the foreign intervention on the side of the Whites. In addition, they won over a large percentage of the peasants, who felt that the Whites might restore the confiscated land to its former owners.

Contrary to Stalin's historians and their custom-built history, the guiding spirit of the Red Army during the Civil War was Trotsky, the Commissar of War. Trotsky gave short shrift to the egalitarian notions with which the Bolsheviks had undermined the army of the Provisional Government. He abolished the election of commanders, and to attain a state approximating efficiency, he drafted some 48,000 former Czarist officers into the Red Army. These "military specialists" could handle large bodies of men, read a map, and cope with logistical problems. But their use aroused the ire of many Bolsheviks, partly because they feared treachery on the part of these class enemies, and partly because they wanted the command posts for themselves. Trotsky countered the possibility of treachery by attaching a political commissar to each military specialist to countersign his orders.

A doctrinal battle of monumental proportions, the only open doctrinal struggle in Soviet military history, ensued at the end of the Civil War. In the process of fighting the war, the Red military leaders had developed many new ideas, or thought they had. A group led by Mikhail Frunze, a self-taught military genius, and including Tukhachevski, Voroshilov, and Stalin, asserted that the new proletarian state needed a new military doctrine. Trotsky and most of the former Czarist officers who had joined the Red Army held that the new army had all it could do for the time being to assimilate the best of the foreign military doctrines.

According to Frunze, the whole character of a nation's army—its organizational structure, training, tactics, and strategy—flowed automatically from the class character of the state, above all, from its economic structure. The military doctrine of the newly fledged proletarian state should include the following: The main emphasis should be upon the offensive, especially in anticipation of the aid to be expected from the proletariat of the enemy bourgeois state. Armies should be made up of small units and have a minimum of cumbersome centralization, thereby stressing maneuverability. Preparation should be made for carrying on guerrilla warfare in the probable theaters of war within the Soviet Union. And great emphasis should be put on the cavalry because of its mobility (later, mechanized forces replaced the cavalry in this concept). This doctrine obviously reflects the horror of emulating the costly positional warfare of World War I on the Western Front and a fondness for the guerrilla warfare of the Russian Civil War.

Trotsky and his professionals hit this doctrine in its weakest spot, its derivation solely from the strategy of the Civil War.

Trotsky pointed out that the strategy of maneuverability was followed by both the Reds and Whites and thus did not flow automatically from the class character of the proletarian state. In truth, as a result of the enormous areas of the combat theaters, the relatively small numbers of combatants engaged, and the poor communications, the strategy of maneuverability had been inevitable. Furthermore, the poor officer material was the cause of the many advances and retreats that made it necessary to fight two or three times over each area. Trotsky also argued that extreme emphasis on the offensive was out of the question for some time to come; the backbone of the army was the peasant, and he was less moved by doctrinal exhortations than by the threat to Russian soil. (In 1941, Stalin found this analysis was still valid. He based his appeal in the desperate days of the war on patriotism as more compelling than Party devotion.)

Intertwined with the Marxian convictions of the Frunze group were a number of political considerations. If Trotsky's emphasis on historic military art were accepted, the ex-Czarist officers would be in the ascendancy. Not knowing Clausewitz, Jomini, or even Suvorov, the new group had little choice but to opt for a military doctrine based on the experience of the Civil War and Marxian theory. In the power struggle developing between Stalin and Trotsky, Stalin, speaking through Frunze, was able to put Trotsky in the position of defending bourgeois military doctrine and being *ipso facto* a reactionary.

At the end of the Civil War, the regime had to decide what type of army it wanted, or could get. The Red Army was war-weary, the population in general objected to feeding a large army, and the nucleus of ardent Communists turned to civilian careers. Most of the professional officers wanted a large, regular army, both for career reasons and in their belief that the Bolshevik offensive doctrine required it. But the economic plight of the country made the cost of maintaining a huge regular army unfeasible, and the lack of heavy industrial production compounded the difficulty. The political leaders favored a militia army, but in 1921, the country was seething with peasant rebellions; supporting a militia under such circumstances was tantamount to arming the enemies of the regime.

The leaders compromised. They established a regular Red Army, the so-called "Cadre Army," and a militia, the "Territorial Army," and spread the militia training over a five-year period. In the first year, the recruit had two months' service in the barracks and, in the following years, spent six weeks a year in camp or on maneuvers. The recruits formed into territorial units permitted a minimum dislocation of the nation's economic life. From 1923 to 1934, 74 per cent of the Red Army was territorial militia.

INDUSTRIALIZATION AND THE RED ARMY

Although Frunze's attempt to develop a consistent Marxian military doctrine was somewhat naïve, he did leave another and more potent legacy: the concept of the complete integration of all the elements of power within the state so that leaders of the state could exert the entire strength of the nation toward any goal they chose. In a speech to the Red Army Academy in 1924, he stated that "future work must be concentrated on planning for the mobilization of the economy of the country . . . it must militarize all our Soviet work from economy to education." In his essay "The Front and Rear," Frunze asserted that the Soviet state needed a strong military force both to defend itself and to carry the Revolution abroad. He insisted with equal vehemence that the rear was just as important as the front, perhaps even more so in modern warfare, and the industrial build-up of the rear must precede a war, as matériel in being would probably be a decisive factor.

When Stalin began to carry out his development of "socialism in one country" at the end of the 1920's, Frunze's ideas came into their own. The economic objectives of the Five-Year Plans put a high priority on the needs of the military. The development of heavy industry, the heart of the new industrialization, gave the Red Army a chance to attain technological parity with West European armies, and its primacy over the consumer-goods industry has endured. By 1934, the results of the new industrialization made it possible to convert the Red Army into a predominantly regular army by reversing the old ratio of three-quarters militia and one-quarter cadre. The weapons and supplies were now available to increase the effectiveness of the regime's most favored arm.

Indulging the military in all its requirements has not, apparently, guaranteed its unswerving obedience. Ever since Trotsky dragooned a number of former Czarist officers into the Red Army, it has been deemed necessary to have political commissars within the army to ensure the loyalty of the troops to the regime. The commissars were the eyes and ears of the Communist Party within the army, as well as its mouth; they were both spies and propagandists. As the officer corps became more professionalized, it came to resent these political intruders. This has been a continuous problem for the professional in all walks of Soviet life. The director of an industrial enterprise thinks that the Party watchdog in the plant is a drag on production; the scientist resents the Party's narrow outlook on his specialty; and the army officer objects to the time his political officer wastes on propaganda.

In the case of the officer corps, part of the trouble may have sprung from its close ties with the German *Reichswehr*. The German military made an agreement with their Soviet counterparts in the early 1920's to swap their professional know-how in exchange for Soviet territory in which to develop and train those components of their army outlawed by the Versailles Treaty. They built an aircraft plant at Fili, near Moscow, an airfield at Lipetsk, and an armored-car school near Kazan. In return, Red Army officers attended the general-staff courses that were given in the *Reichswehr* Ministry. It is hard to believe that Soviet general-staff officers could have been exposed to such training without taking on some of the "above politics" professional characteristics of their German teachers.

By 1937, Stalin had come to believe that the officer corps of the Red Army was not reliable, and he attacked them ruthlessly in the Purge of 1937–38. When it was over, the Red Army had lost three marshals, including Tukhachevski, most of its Supreme Military Council, about 90 per cent of the officers above the rank of colonel, about 80 per cent of its colonels, and some 30,000 officers of lower rank. Whether this hurt the Red Army in the long run is a moot point. It has been claimed that the poor showing in the Finnish War, in 1939–40, was due partly to the lack of competent officers. On the other hand, Stalin's Purge rid the Red Army of an overage, fossilized upper echelon of officers.

Stalin's distrust of the professional officer, rising to a crescendo in 1937–38, resulted in the restoration of an all-powerful system of political commissars. The system permeated the army from the very top down to the *politruk* who was co-equal in authority to the company commander. The Communist commanders were now as closely watched as the ex-Czarist "military specialists" had been in the Civil War; but apparently the Communists were less trustworthy than the ex-Czarists, for in 1939, it took some 34,000 political officers to do the job that 6,000 had done in an army of comparable size during the Civil War.

No nation can be a great military power in the modern world without some popular support, especially from the youth. It must have a reservoir from which to draw the personnel to man its air force, armored forces, and other branches demanding technologically literate youngsters. Throughout Soviet history, this task has been allotted to paramilitary organizations, at first genuinely voluntary, and later government sponsored and controlled.

As early as 1920, a Military-Scientific Society (VNO) was organized to augment the military training of Red Army personnel. A series of other groups came into being during the 1920's, culminating in 1927 in an amalgamated organization, Osoaviakhim—the Voluntary Society for Assistance in Defense, Aviation, and Chemistry. The consolidation of the independent paramilitary societies into the single Osoaviakhim again demonstrated how the Soviet state was gradually gathering every segment of the citizen's life under its wing.

Through a network of clubs, Osoaviakhim met a major objective: to train young people in the technological aspects of military life, especially in aeronautics, communications, and the repair and handling of machinery. Its millions of members, male and female, were, for the most part, either peasants or newly come from that status, and things mechanical, taken for granted in the more technologically advanced countries, were mysteries to them. Since the technical equipment the new industrialization provided for the Red Army was not for the heavy-handed, untrained peasant, Osoaviakhim served to make Soviet youth technologically literate before induction into the armed forces. Osoaviakhim provided potential fliers who had done most of their primary training, mechanics, radio operators, and other technicians who had at least learned the rudiments of their trades. It is doubtful if the Red Army could have been converted from a militia force of infantry into a modern military force without having had the benefit of the widespread activities of Osoaviakhim.

The subsequent changes in the organization of Osoaviakhim are indicative of the Soviet passion for reorganization. In January, 1948, a decree of the Council of Ministers of the U.S.S.R. divided Osoaviakhim into three independent societies: DOSAV, All-Union Voluntary Society for Assistance to the Air Force; DOSARM, All-Union Voluntary Society for Assistance to the Army; and DOSFLOT, All-Union Voluntary Society for Assistance to the Navy. In August, 1951, another decree of the Council of Ministers unified DOSAV, DOSARM, and DOSFLOT into a single organization, DOSAAF, All-Union Voluntary Society for Assistance to the Army, Air Force, and Navy.[2]

THE RED ARMY IN ACTION

In spite of the conviction of inevitability in Communist pronouncements on world revolution and the imminent decline of capitalism, the Soviet leaders showed a hardheaded realism in their estimates of the world situation after November, 1917. They made mistakes; but on the whole their moves were tailored to the forces available, and when miscalculations were made, they showed an ability to cut their losses before being involved in the use of means not commensurate with the value of the objective. Probably the outstanding mistake of the early years was the Soviet invasion of Poland; even the most realistic Communists of that period became enthusiastic about Tukhachevski's chances of carrying the revolution into Western Europe. The lesson of that disastrous campaign was learned well, and no such mistake was made again—at least up to the Korean War.

The best example of the cautious use of Soviet force is to be seen in the Soviet policy of opposing Japanese expansion in the Far East in the 1930's. The Japanese invasion of Manchuria, in 1931, alerted the Soviets to a new danger from the east and resulted in a build-up of their armed forces, industry, and communications in the Soviet Far Eastern areas in an effort to overcome the deficiencies inherent in depending for supply on a single railroad line, the Trans-Siberian. But at the same time, they were determined to keep the situation from deteriorating into a full-scale war with the Japanese. In 1934, they even went so far as to sell their interest in the Chinese Eastern Railroad to the Japanese to avoid that point of friction. Between 1931 and 1938, there were over 2,000 separate incidents along the Soviet border, and the situation worsened after the Japanese joined the Anti-Comintern Pact, in 1936, which meant the possibility of a two-front war. Finally in 1938, the "cold war" became hot when the Japanese attacked the Soviet forces at Changkufeng (a point where the boundaries of Korea, Manchuria, and the U.S.S.R. come together at the Pacific, not far from Vladivostok). This Battle of Lake Khasan lasted from July 29 to August 11, 1938, and involved at least two Soviet divisions with 200 tanks and 100 aircraft, while the Japanese used an even larger number of troops, although fewer tanks and aircraft. This was a sizable engagement in the pre-World War II period. The Soviet commander, Grigori Stern, describing the battle a year later in *Pravda,* explained that he had to make a frontal assault on the entrenched Japanese in order to keep the fighting limited to the Lake Khasan area. He succeeded, but it was very costly.

A year later, war broke out along the Khalka River, which divides Outer Mongolia from Manchuria for a short distance. The war lasted from May 4 to September 16, 1939. It was a fully mechanized war, involving hundreds of aircraft and tanks, and the Japanese later admitted 18,000 casualties. When the big

Soviet push came, on August 28, Zhukov won his spurs by administering a sound defeat to the Japanese. Behind the desultory pace of the Soviet war effort—from May 4 to August 28—lay a political explanation: Stalin in this period was angling for a pact with Japan's Anti-Comintern Pact partner, Germany, and wanted to keep the conflict as small as possible. With the signing of the Molotov-Ribbentrop Pact, on August 23, the Soviets took the wraps off their forces, and the Japanese were defeated in short order.

During the period of German-Soviet collaboration—from August 23, 1939, to June 22, 1941—the Red Army shared the spoils of Hitler's victories. As soon as Hitler had defeated Poland, the Red Army raced in to get the Soviet share of the corpse. The threat of force was sufficient to bring Estonia, Latvia, and Lithuania into the Soviet empire, and Romania yielded Bessarabia rather than face the Red Army. Finland, alone, proved recalcitrant and resisted the Red Army. It took three and a half months of very hard fighting to bring the Finns to heel, and even then, the result was a negotiated peace. The Soviet command had badly underestimated both the Finns and the difficulties of fighting over rough terrain under severe winter conditions.

On June 22, 1941, Hitler's Nazi legions came crashing over the Soviet borders, fanned out into a four-pronged offensive, and made a shambles of the Red Army and Soviet military doctrine. In spite of all the theorizing about a new doctrine, Soviet strategy and tactics in "the Great Fatherland War" differed little from those of their German opponents. The course of the war validated Trotsky's contention that the laws of strategy were universal; it became obvious to the Soviet command that the so-called backward bourgeois military doctrine was still full of vitality. Once the Soviet command had recovered from the shock of the blitzkreig, it began to exploit its superiority in manpower ruthlessly. Even the Frunze-Tukhachevski dictum of avoiding positional warfare went by the board; the only places where the Soviet armies could stop the German onslaughts in 1941–42 were fortified positions such as Leningrad, Moscow, and Stalingrad. The Red Army gradually gained some sophistication in the use of armored forces, but its use of air power demonstrated no originality whatsoever. Luckily, the Germans did not use air power very imaginatively, either. The Soviet leaders retreated to the traditional strategy of the Czarist generals—the use of vast quantities of cannon fodder and metal to gain victory.

The Soviets also found that another of Trotsky's arguments was valid: The Russian peasant was not willing to fight to the death for Communism, and the mass surrenders of 1941 were frightening. Quickly, a switch was made toward a patriotic appeal: "The Motherland was being violated by the Fascist beast!" The Nazis, for their part, did their best to make "the Fascist beast" of the slogan a reality. The victories at Moscow, in December, 1941, and at Stalingrad, in February, 1943, helped swell the patriotism of the Russian population, and restored confidence in the regime's ability to win.

For all intents and purposes, the Germans were on the defensive after the fiasco at Stalingrad. Hitler's decision to fight to keep every inch of occupied territory took the flexibility out of German strategy and put an intolerable burden on his generals to maintain the line from Leningrad to the Crimea. As the Red Army grew rapidly in superiority of manpower and equipment, its leaders were able to concentrate enormous forces for breakthroughs in the German line of defense. Because the Germans had to spend most of their energies shuttling their numerically inferior forces from one weak spot to another, they could not regain the initiative. The last major German offensive took place near Kursk in the summer of 1943, but the Soviets absorbed the blow with relative ease and then counterattacked when the German force had spent itself. By 1944, the Red Army had such overwhelming superiority that it struck almost at will along the overextended German line, and "Stalin's ten destructive blows," as Soviet historians used to call them, rolled the Germans back to Hungary, the Vistula, and East Prussia. In 1945, the Soviets, after a breathing spell in order to consolidate their gains and regroup, made a final assault on the Reich. During this last stage of the war, the Soviet ability to mass enormous amounts of artillery, planes, and tanks on relatively narrow fronts made the defense of Germany suicidal.

Although the Soviet military doctrine of the 1920's was a casualty of World War II, the Frunze-Stalin concept of rapid industrialization with a high priority to military requirements had paid off. This was especially true of the decision to move some industry to the east. The Magnitogorsk-Kuznetsk *kombinat* may not have seemed a good investment in the 1930's, but it proved to be invaluable when the Ukraine fell to the Germans, in 1941. The German Air Force's lack of a strategic striking force, or even the concept of one, enabled the Soviets to move hundreds of industrial plants out of the reach of the enemy. Although Soviet rail lines jammed with loaded trains carrying this equipment to the rear in 1941 offered easy targets for bombings, they went unscathed. All through the war, Russian industry was almost untouched by the German Air Force. The combination of Lend-Lease supplies from the United States and Great Britain and their own ever-increasing industrial output enabled the Soviets to attain an overwhelming superiority over the Germans in planes, tanks, and guns.

On the other hand, the Soviet victory also owed much to the primitiveness of the country. Red soldiers were able to get along on a very minimum of life's amenities and needed little beyond bread and ammunition during the long advances. The primitive roads, deep in dust in the summer and bottomless tracks of mud in the spring and fall, reduced the effectiveness of the German blitzkrieg in 1941 and 1942. Guderian's dash toward Moscow in the fall of 1941 might have had a different ending if his tanks, and especially his wheeled supply vehicles, had not had to cope with the Russian roads. In addition, the Germans were not prepared for the rigors of the Russian winter, the everyday environment of the Russian muzhik.

Partisan warfare rose to new dimensions in "the Great Fatherland War." The German *Untermenschen* policy in the occupied areas forced many Russians to join the partisan bands, which also gained valuable recruits from the remnants of the Red Army formations broken up by the rapid German advance in 1941. Through the use of aircraft and radio communications, it was possible to supply and direct these bands and coordinate their activities with the strategical and tactical needs of the Red Army.

The wildness of the terrain and the toughness of the population were also great assets in making partisan warfare successful.

The last stages of the war found the Red Army in control of much of Eastern Europe and the Balkans. The sheer momentum of pursuing the Germans had brought it into such countries as Romania, Hungary, Poland, and Czechoslovakia, but in other areas, such as Bulgaria, the Red Army marched in to help the Communists set up regimes favorable to Moscow. The Red Army was now converted from a force defending the homeland into an agent for Communist imperialism. By the end of 1945, the Soviet troops had become a gendarmery to enforce the Communization of the Soviet Union's satellite empire.

Into each country it overran, the Red Army brought a group of nationals to help take over the government. These Eastern Europeans and Balkans had been trained in Moscow as subservient agents, and their only allegiance was to the Kremlin. But they would have been helpless in their new jobs if they had not had the bayonets of the Red Army at their disposal.

STALINIST MILITARY DOCTRINE

As soon as the war was over, Soviet propaganda media began attributing the victory to Stalin and the Party. The outstanding hero of the war, Zhukov, was quickly hidden in the provinces, and "Operation Rewrite" went all-out in the glorification of Stalin as the greatest military genius of all time, the creator of a military doctrine that had guided the Red Army to victory. The old tiger had not shed his stripes, and just as in 1924 he had backed the doctrine that derived its tenets entirely from the Civil War, now he evolved a doctrine based solely on Soviet experience in "the Great Fatherland War." He decided there was no need to look at the strategies of the Americans and the British, for they had played only a minor role in the victory.

Consequently, from 1945 to 1955, a whole decade during which the instruments of warfare were undergoing their most rapid evolution, Soviet doctrine seemed at a standstill. Even more strangely, the Soviets themselves were developing weapons systems that cried out for new doctrine—jet fighters, nuclear weapons, and long-range jet bombers. Despite the existence of radically new weapons systems at home and abroad, the theorists kept discussions within the confines of Stalin's five "permanently operating factors for victory": stability of the rear, morale of the army, quantity and quality of army divisions, armaments of the army, and organizational and leadership ability of the command personnel. These factors were neither original with Stalin and the Russians nor, certainly, the sole property of the Communist world.

But was Stalin's doctrine quite as backward and obtuse as has been generally assumed? An examination of the actual situation from 1945 to 1953 reveals that the Soviet Union had few nuclear weapons and no real delivery capability during this period. Furthermore, toward the end of the war, the main Soviet objective was to occupy as much of Europe as possible. They were extremely successful, but the appetite grew with the eating, as their moves in Greece, Turkey, and Iran indicated. Having obtained this huge territory and needing time to digest it, did the Soviets need a new doctrine? Their main goal was to keep control of the newly acquired regions until they could incorporate them solidly within their orbit. Large land forces and a preponderantly tactical air force were the ideal instruments for accomplishing this task. Even after Stalin's death, the uprisings in East Germany, Poland, and Hungary were best put down by masses of hard-hitting, highly mobile troops.

Were Stalin and his close advisers quite as stagnant even in their preparations for modern war as their public doctrine implied? This question poses the perpetual pitfall in assessing Soviet doctrine—the difference between public expression and secret action. If Stalinist thinking was stagnant and his doctrine backward-looking, why did the Soviets commit so much money, resources, and scarce technical personnel in the research and development of weapons not encompassed in the Stalinist doctrine? Official answers are nonexistent. A possible answer is provided by Lieutenant Colonel G. A. Tokaev, an aeronautical engineer, who was engaged in the Soviet counterpart of our own Operation Paperclip (the rounding up of German technicians and scientists). He states that while he was reporting on this project to the Politburo in 1947, Stalin interrogated him very closely on the Sänger Project. This concerned a German engineer's plan for an aircraft with better than intercontinental range. According to Tokaev, Stalin said that if the U.S.S.R. could build a Sänger-type aircraft, discussions with Mr. Truman would be easier.[3]

At a meeting with Malenkov and Khrunichev (the Minister of Aviation Industry), Tokaev says Malenkov asked Khrunichev how rocket development was coming along. Khrunichev replied that perhaps they had made a mistake in undertaking to develop the V-2.

"I agree with you," said Malenkov. "I paid a visit recently to Noginsk [this is where the work on the Soviet V-2 was going on] and I was most dissatisfied. You don't seem to make any progress at all—it's still only the same old V-2. What are you thinking of, Comrade Khrunichev? We are not going to fight a war with Poland; we have got to remember there are vast oceans between ourselves and our potential enemy."[4]

This is certainly dubious evidence, but when it is juxtaposed with Soviet weapons developments, the spirit, at least, seems correct.

The actual hardware development in the Soviet Union since 1945 refutes those who label the 1945–53 period as one of Stalinist stagnation. By 1949, the Soviets had an atomic device, and by 1953, they were in the thermonuclear business. We know from our own experience that such programs are not initiated, developed, and successfully concluded without the diversion of enormous sums of money, hordes of scientists and technicians, and a large segment of material from the other facets of national production. And this took place in a Soviet Union that was trying to recover from the hideous damages of World War II and that even today has far less national income than the United States. In this same period, the main line of aircraft development was jet interceptors—understandable for a power confronted by SAC. But even more to the point, sometime in the late 1940's during Stalin's regime, plans were developed for long-range bombers such as the Bison, Badger, and Bear. These did not come into being in a day, even if we give the Soviets credit for a much more rapid development from concept to production than we have, and I think we have already sufficiently exaggerated their agility in this field. Lastly, the state of Soviet missile development in the past few years is positive proof that missile planning and development must have been making good progress under Stalin.

Does it not appear, then, that the "permanently operating factors for victory" of Stalinist doctrine were merely clichés for popular consumption and hardly the basis for an imaginative use of the new weapons in development or in being? Stalin seems to have operated far more wisely under the façade of this doctrine than has been generally assumed. He obviously devoted a great deal of material and personnel to the development of new weapons at a time when both were extremely scarce in the Soviet Union. For the military needs of the 1945–53 period, the Stalinist doctrine was very adequate.

The really important legacy that Stalin handed on to his successors was the highly integrated political-economic-military unit called the Soviet Union. He had carried to the ultimate Clausewitz' dictum that war is a continuation of politics by more forceful means. Stalin's concept was that a state should have an integral strategy; all the elements of power should be so compounded in a state as to facilitate their concentration in carrying out the objectives of the state with the least possible confusion and friction. This integral strategy took the whole of Soviet industrial production, education, propaganda media, and diplomacy and welded them into a well-synchronized political-military machine obedient to the direction of the leader.

THE SOVIET ARMED FORCES TODAY

Facts and figures on the present state of the Soviet military structure are, of course, highly classified, and the Soviet Union is much stricter about military secrets than is any other great power, save maybe Communist China. Anything bearing on the military aspect of the Soviet Union is carefully omitted from their otherwise quite copious statistics, and the Western observer who does not have access to classified information must be satisfied with the large picture, a picture, however, that is probably not very distorted.

In one six-year period, the Soviets announced the following series of cutbacks in their armed forces: 640,000 men in August, 1955; 1.2 million in May, 1956; 300,000 in January, 1958; and 1.2 million in 1960. When the Berlin crisis flared up in the summer of 1961, this trend was sharply reversed—if, in fact, the cutbacks were ever carried out on the scale announced. But new weapons, new strategical concepts, and a severe shortage of young people in industry made some reductions, at least, probable. If they had planned to reduce their forces by the magnitude claimed, it points up how large they must have been under Stalin. In January, 1960, Khrushchev announced that the 1.2 million cut for 1960 was one-third of the total Soviet forces of 3.62 million, which would have brought the total of the Soviet armed forces to 2.42 million.[5] Marshal Sokolovsky, former Chief of the Soviet General Staff, claimed in February, 1961, that the reduction in manpower had been completed. He went on to assert that the addition of newly developed nuclear and rocket weapons had more than compensated for the reduction in manpower.[6] By 1965, a more widely accepted figure for the size of the Soviet armed forces was 3.3 million men.[7]

The Ground Forces

About two-thirds of the military manpower, well over 2 million men, are in the ground forces, organized in about 140 divisions. This question of how many divisions the Russians have is fraught with thorny problems. Sokolovsky, in his book, *Soviet Military Strategy,* points out that there are three degrees of combat readiness in the Soviet divisions. This probably accounts for the figure of sixty to seventy divisions that has been so prevalent of late. But that figure may apply only to the divisions in Category 1, those ready to go. The twenty divisions in East Germany, the four in Hungary, and the two in Poland are undoubtedly in that category. Some forty or fifty divisions within the Soviet Union itself are probably also in that state of readiness. The rest are in either

Category 2 or 3; in other words, sixty to ninety days would be needed to make them ready for action.

The Soviet division is smaller than the American division. A Soviet motorized rifle division, for example, probably runs under 10,000 men, while a tank division is even smaller. Both the motorized rifle and the armored divisions are well supplied with tanks, armored personnel carriers, artillery, and tactical-missile support. The Soviet ground forces, commanded by Marshal of the Soviet Union Vasili I. Chuikov, have been undergoing intensive training under simulated nuclear attacks. Because dense concentrations of troops are such excellent targets in nuclear war, the traditional Russian reliance on huge groupings of manpower and enormous quantities of artillery has been abandoned, and greater reliance placed on smaller, semi-autonomous units. Naturally, the authority of lower-echelon commanders has increased because of this necessity of keeping the forces dispersed.

The ground forces have at their disposal a fairly wide range of missiles, including tactical missiles with ranges from 10 to 450 miles, ground-to-air missiles, and antitank missiles. In addition, it should be kept in mind that the Soviet Frontal Aviation (Tactical Aviation) is closely integrated with, and under the command of, the ground forces.

The Navy

Although Russian naval traditions go back to Peter the Great, this branch of the services has never played a decisive role in Russian military history. The geographical position of Russia, a nation expanding over, and defending, a great plain, made the army supreme. Nowhere was this geographical determinism better demonstrated than in the Russo-Japanese War, in 1905, when the Baltic Fleet, under Admiral Rozhdestvenski, sailed almost around the world to get at the Japanese fleet and then was blown to bits in the Battle of Tsushima Strait. Even before Rozhdestvenski's fleet got out of the North Sea, it caused an international incident by firing on an English fishing fleet on the Dogger Bank—a somewhat ignominious error.

The fact that the exits from the Black and Baltic seas are

controlled by non-Russians has hampered Russian naval development throughout the centuries. Even the Russian ports with direct access to open water—Murmansk and those of the Far East—are handicapped. To use Murmansk effectively, at least for surface ships, control of the long Norwegian coast is mandatory, and Japan lies athwart most of the Far Eastern ports. The Soviets have spent enormous amounts of energy and capital in the development of the Northern Sea Route across the top of Siberia, and it is now possible to sail from Murmansk and Arkhangelsk to the Pacific during the summer months. Even in this case, the narrow Bering Strait is a decided disadvantage.

The four main fleets of the Soviet Navy are located in the Black, Baltic, and White-Barents seas and in the Pacific Ocean. Exit from the Black and Baltic seas means going through narrow waters controlled by Turkey and Denmark, respectively—both NATO powers. Surveillance of the Far Eastern ports is possible from Japan and Korea, and egress from the White-Barents area is through the North and Norwegian seas, i.e., through NATO patrols.

Because of these harsh geographical realities, the Soviet Navy has concentrated upon the defensive as far as its surface vessels are concerned. It has 20 cruisers, around 100 destroyers, and some 2,000 other smaller craft. The main responsibility of the surface fleet is the protection of the Soviet coastline and support of the ground forces.

The Soviet Navy has received a new lease on life in the last decade. Technological advances in the submarine and missile fields furthered the importance of Soviet submarines in two ways: First, the Soviet Navy was enabled to circumvent some of its geographical disadvantages; second, when the development of the U.S. submarine threat made it mandatory that the Soviets do something to counter it, the improved Soviet submarines were the natural weapon for the job. Estimates vary on the size of the underwater fleet, but the generally accepted figures range between 400 and 450. Some thirty to forty are nuclear-powered subs, and one guess is that they are being produced at the rate of ten a year. About two-thirds of the Soviet submarine fleet are ocean-going and many can fire either guided or ballistic missiles. These capabilities are one of the real strategic punches in the Soviet military posture.

The Soviets have no aircraft carriers, a decided handicap in fighting limited wars in distant areas; but given the geography of the U.S.S.R., one can understand their reluctance to invest in carriers. The navy does, however, have an air force made up of 400 to 500 bombers and 400 other aircraft. Primarily, its mission is to provide antisubmarine defense.

The Air Force

The Soviet Air Force is divided into the following categories:

1. Tactical, or Frontal, Aviation (VVS—*Voenno-vozdushnye sily,* or FA—*Frontal'naya aviatsiya*)
2. Fighter Aviation of the Air Defense Forces (IA-PVO—*Istrebitel'naya aviatsiya—Protivovozdushnaya oborona*)
3. Long-Range Aviation (DA—*Dal'naya aviatsiya*)
4. Aviation of the Airborne Troops (A-VDV—*Aviatsiya-Vozdushnodesantnye voyska*)
5. Naval Aviation (A-VMF—*Aviatsiya-Voenno-Morskoy Flot*)

Frontal Aviation is merely a new name for the old VVS-KA (Army Air Forces of the Red Army of World War II and before). By far the largest number of Soviet aircraft are in Frontal Aviation, which is designed solely to provide tactical support of the Soviet ground forces. Frontal Aviation is organized in about twelve Frontal Air Armies, which are assigned to Fronts, or Army Groups. In peacetime, Fronts are usually the same thing as military districts. Frontal Air Armies are under the direction of Air Force Headquarters for most purposes, but they are operationally subordinate to the ground commander of the Front they are assigned to.

PVO (Air Defense) is divided into two parts: PVO *Strany,* i.e., PVO of the country, which is concerned with the defense of the nation as a whole, and PVO of the armed forces, which is concerned with the defense of the various military units. PVO has several types of surface-to-air missiles, conventional antiaircraft artillery, and several thousand interceptor aircraft, mostly of recent vintage. The PVO interceptors are directly controlled by the Commander in Chief of PVO, Marshal V. A. Sudets, through his deputy for PVO Aviation, Colonel General of Aviation I. D. Klimov.

Long-Range Aviation comprises three or four Air Armies that have a total of 200 turboprop Bears (TU-95) and four-jet Bisons, plus some 700 or 800 twin-jet Badgers (TU-16). Only the Bears and Bisons have the legs to get to the United States without elaborate refueling procedures. A new aircraft, the twin-jet Blinder, has been coming into the inventory of Long-Range Aviation in the last couple of years. This aircraft has a supersonic-dash capability. The Soviets now have several types of stand-off air-to-surface missiles that give their bombers added striking power.

Aviation of Airborne Troops, which fulfills the mission of transporting Soviet airborne and parachute forces, has an air-transport fleet of around 500 aircraft, but it can also call upon Aeroflot for assistance. Aeroflot, with its 700 to 800 jet and turboprop aircraft, is really on loan to the civil government and can be immediately integrated into the military air force at a moment's notice.

The Soviet Air Force has a rather weird organizational setup. Marshal K. A. Vershinin, Commander in Chief of the Air Force, exercises administrative control over almost everything that flies, but operational control over nothing. Long-range Aviation is controlled directly by the Minister of Defense, Marshal R. Ya. Malinovsky; the commander of PVO, Marshal Sudets, controls IA-PVO and is outside the command of Marshal Vershinin; while the various units of Frontal Aviation are under the control of the ground commanders of the various Fronts to which the air units are assigned.

All told, the Soviet Air Force has 11,000 to 12,000 first-line aircraft. Almost three-quarters of these are the fighters and light-bombers of PVO and Frontal Aviation, while the rest belong to Long-Range Aviation, the Navy, and Aviation of Airborne Troops.

Missile Force

The dimensions of Soviet capability in the missile field have been widely analyzed and heatedly discussed in the United States. Various figures cited during Congressional hearings have served to bewilder more than to enlighten the layman. Soviet performance in orbiting men, launching artificial satellites, lunar probes, and even photographing the hind side of the moon has been outstanding, and it would be extremely risky to assume that such a capability could not be transferred to military weapons—if it did not originate in that quarter.

The Soviets probably had between 250 and 300 operational ICBM's (Inter-Continental Ballistic Missiles) in 1965. Of the total number at present, some must be second-generation missiles with storable liquid fuel, which makes it easier to conceal them. How many are in hardened sites is not known to the author, but there can be little doubt that every effort is being made to insure the safety of the ICBM's.

The Soviets are much wealthier in MRBM's (Medium-Range Ballistic Missiles) and IRBM's (Intermediate-Range Ballistic Missiles), of which types they probably have 800 or more. The MRBM's, with ranges of 700 to 1,100 miles, can take out most of the strategic targets in Western Europe. The IRBM's, with ranges of slightly over 2,000 miles, can get at targets in the Near East, the Middle East, and the entire Mediterranean Basin.

In May, 1960, Khrushchev announced a new branch of the Soviet armed forces—the Strategic Missile Force (in Russian it reads "Rocket Forces of Strategic Designation")—which was given control of all Soviet strategic missiles. The first chief of the new force, Marshal M. I. Nedelin, was killed in October, 1960, when an experimental nuclear-fueled missile blew up on the test stand. He was succeeded by Marshal K. S. Moskalenko. In April, 1962, Marshal S. S. Biryuzov, a Khrushchev protégé, became chief of the missile force, but when he became Chief of the General Staff, in March, 1963, Marshal U. I. Krylov took over. Knowledge on how the Strategic Missile Force is organized and on the extent of

Krylov's operational authority, as well as on other details, is lacking. It seems certain, however, that he has control of all the ICBM's and IRBM's, and some of the MRBM's.

The other dozen or so types of missiles are under the operational control of the ground forces, PVO, and the Navy. In July, 1961, Marshal Malinovsky stated that tactical-missile units—units capable of operating independently—were being organized, thus insuring more flexibility. But he said nothing about how they were to be organized. In 1962, on February 23, Soviet Army Day, Marshal A. I. Yeremenko, Inspector General of the Ministry of Defense, boasted that nearly 2,000 Soviet rocket units were operational and able to "hit the target with excellent precision." He must have been including every missile-equipped vessel (surface and underwater), all missile-carrying aircraft, the surface-to-air-missile units in PVO, and the tactical missiles possessed by the ground forces. In the case of ICBM's, he must have counted every missile as a unit. The fact that he was trying to impress the West, however, is not left to doubt.

12

Foreign Policy

On November 8, 1917, the Bolsheviks, under the aegis of the All-Russian Congress of Soviets, set up a new government to rule Russia, and like most other governments of that period, it had a cabinet. Unlike the others, however, the Bolshevik cabinet was called the Council of People's Commissars, or Sovnarkom. Trotsky took over the Commissariat of Foreign Affairs and proposed an immediate armistice with repudiation of all annexations and indemnities, published the secret agreements of the Czarist government with its allies, and, some time later, unilaterally annulled the foreign debts of the former regime. In February, 1918, Trotsky capped his brief but stormy career as Commissar of Foreign Affairs by disdainfully refusing the German terms at Brest Litovsk and then advancing the novel thesis that the Soviet Government was in a state of "neither war nor peace." A new era in diplomacy seemed to have arrived, and the Bolsheviks appeared intent on alienating all the major powers in the world.

Three years later, in March, 1921, the Soviets concluded a trade agreement with the world's archcapitalist nation, Great Britain, and thus gained *de facto* recognition. A year later, Soviet delegates went to the Genoa Conference, and failing to win concessions from the major Versailles powers, they signed an agreement with Germany at the neighboring town of Rapallo. Thereby they gained *de jure* recognition from Germany, not the most esteemed of the major powers at that time, but even a back-door entry into respectability was a far cry from Trotsky's attitude early in 1918.

These events illustrate the two strands that run through the history of Soviet foreign policy and are present today. One strand is the foreign relations "natural" to any great power, which cannot avoid certain constants deriving from its geographical and political position in the world. The other strand is the influence of Marxist-Leninist philosophy, which colors the glasses through which the Soviet leaders view the world around them. Sometimes the two strands can easily be distinguished; and at other times they seem inextricably tangled. For example, in the 1920's, Chicherin, by then Commissar of Foreign Affairs, seemed to be pursuing a conventional foreign policy, while Zinoviev, through the Communist International, was urging foreign Communist Parties into actions that thwarted Chicherin at every step. By the late 1920's, however, Stalin had secured his position of primacy, and the divergent strands were merged. The Communist International became merely a branch of the Commissariat of Foreign Affairs, and during the 1930's, the non-Russian Communist leaders had to gyrate like dervishes in order to follow the twists and turns of Soviet foreign policy.

Another constant of Soviet foreign policy is its dedication to expansion. This may be considered both a continuation of the historical Russian expansion that began with the Muscovite Grand Dukes, and a result of the Communist compulsion toward world domination. Some of the present aspirations of the Soviet foreign office have an exceedingly long history. Ever since the rulers of Kiev attacked "Czargrad" in the tenth century, the Russians have been trying to find some way of controlling the Straits and gaining free access into the Mediterranean. Control of the Straits became an obsession with Russian rulers from Catherine II to Nicholas II, and geography being a fixed element, it is no surprise that Stalin had the traditional yearning to make the Bosporus and Dardanelles a Russian canal.

When, however, Soviet foreign policy concerns itself with a revolution in Guatemala, or urges an anti-American policy upon a Castro, or suddenly finds a deep interest in Yemen, Laos, or the Congo, then it has departed from the traditional Russian objectives and is clearly engaged in its crusade to expand Communism.

Such a difference must seem rather academic to a Hungarian shut up behind the Iron Curtain, or even to a Soviet diplomat. But in the present Cold War, it may make a vast difference in a nation's response to know whether the opponent's primary motive is merely to bolster a weak point in his *defensive* posture, or whether his attempt to push a whole area into chaos is a step toward ultimate world conquest.

THE SEARCH FOR RECOGNITION

Lenin and his lieutenants were confident that their success in Russia was merely the opening gun in the world revolution. In the early years of the Revolution, no one thought that the new Communist state could stay alive unless there were socialist revolutions in some of the leading industrial countries of Europe. Lenin, in urging the unpalatable Treaty of Brest Litovsk on his comrades, argued that the world revolution, which was just around the corner, would obliterate all territorial boundaries anyway, so little importance need be attached to the onerous conditions of the treaty. The establishment of a Communist regime in Hungary, under Béla Kun, the various attempted coups in Germany, and the general confusion in a war-weary Europe kept up the Bolshevik hope for an expansion of the revolution. In March, 1919, the Soviets took the lead in setting up the world-wide machinery for carrying out the world revolution —the Communist International, or Comintern. Finally, having defeated the Whites and discouraged the intervention of France, England, Japan, and the United States, the Red Army took the offensive against the Poles. Under the leadership of a brilliant General, Tukhachevski, the Reds drove the Poles out of the Ukraine and back to Warsaw. Even the cautious Lenin hailed this as the first step in carrying the revolution throughout Europe on the bayonets of the proletarian Red Army.

The successful Polish resistance at Warsaw and the consequent headlong retreat of Tukhachevski's forces in August, 1920, cooled the Bolshevik ardor for spreading the revolution by bayonet.

Early in March, 1921, the Kronstadt revolt in Petrograd, a revolt in the name of the original promises of the Bolsheviks, shocked the Bolshevik faithful. These events, combined with the return to "normalcy" in Western Europe, dimmed hope for an immediate world revolution. Lenin realized that a breathing spell was necessary, and at the Tenth Party Congress, later in March, 1921, he shifted to his New Economic Policy (NEP).

Soviet diplomacy reversed its field and now sought recognition and trade instead of immediate world revolution. Almost simultaneously with Lenin's announcement of the New Economic Policy, the age-old Russian differences with Turkey were resolved and a treaty signed with Kemal Ataturk, who was as anti-Versailles as the Soviets. At the same time, the Soviets concluded the trade agreement with Great Britain that gained them *de facto* recognition, and shortly thereafter they obtained *de jure* recognition from Germany with the Treaty of Rapallo. This treaty between the two major anti-Versailles nations placed the other powers in an awkward position and strengthened the Kremlin's hand considerably. Having broken the ring of isolation, the Soviet Government was recognized by most of the major powers in the next few years.

The effects of the NEP on Soviet domestic and foreign policies have been well summarized by E. H. Carr as follows:

> The change of front carried out by Moscow in March 1921 affected the climate in which Soviet foreign policy henceforth operated rather than the substance of that policy. It did not mean, in domestic affairs, the abandonment of the goal of socialism and communism or, in foreign affairs, of the goal of world revolution. But it meant a recognition of the necessity of a certain postponement in reaching these goals, and in the meanwhile of building up the economic and diplomatic strength of Soviet Russia by all practicable means, even if these means were in appearance a retreat from the direct path to socialism and world revolution. The new foreign policy had been adopted, in the words used by Lenin of NEP, "seriously and for a long time." It was the relative durability thus imparted to expedients hitherto invoked only as short-time practical manoeuvres which, more than anything else, changed the character of Soviet foreign policy after 1921.[1]

Between 1921 and 1928, Soviet foreign policy reflected the internal situation of the country. There was confusion at the top as Stalin and Trotsky fought for Lenin's crown, and foreign Communist Parties were equally confused. Life was getting better in the Soviet Union, food production was getting back to its pre-Revolutionary levels, and under the "mixed" economy, even steel production was approaching its 1913 output. Although Soviet diplomacy found it hard to resist targets that represented opportunity, it restricted itself chiefly to agitation, except in China. Because official diplomacy and Comintern policies were not synchronized, there were many embarrassing blunders.

By 1928, Trotsky was out, and Stalin was free to discard the idea of immediate world revolution. He pressed for "socialism in one country," the building of the Soviet Union into an impregnable fortress, a self-sufficient major power able to hold its own against capitalist attacks. To do this, it was necessary to industrialize at a forced tempo and to collectivize agriculture so that it could support the needs engendered by the rapid industrialization.

Building a self-sufficient Soviet Union required, at least during the initial stages, a cautious foreign policy that would not endanger its success. Furthermore, the Red Army had been reduced to a cadre of 562,000 men since 1924 and was in no position to carry on any full-fledged war with a major power. The Soviet-dominated Comintern, holding its Sixth Congress, in Moscow in 1928, paid its usual lip service to the world revolution and then took as its main concern the defense of the Soviet Union. The Commissariat of Foreign Affairs of the Soviet Union directed the Party faithful throughout the world in the implementation of its defensive policy, and the Comintern became a tool of Soviet foreign policy, which put the defense of the U.S.S.R. above all else.

The Soviet leaders continued a verbal attack on France and Great Britain as the "capitalist military threat," but they soon recognized that the real threat came from the East; Japan was on the rampage in Manchuria. By early 1932, Manchuria had been transformed into the Japanese puppet Manchukuo. In line with their policy of avoiding conflicts, the Soviet leaders agreed to sell their share of the Chinese Eastern Railroad to Japan; however, they were fully aware that this concession relieved, but did not settle, the Japanese problem.

COLLECTIVE SECURITY

Hitler came to power in January, 1933, and the Soviet leaders were soon disabused of the idea that it was going to be easy to topple the Nazi regime by a German Communist revolution. By 1934, the threat of Japan in the East and Hitler and Mussolini in the West caused the Soviets to set up a "united front," a working coalition among Communists, socialists, and any other anti-Nazi groups that could be enticed into joining. The Popular Front in France demonstrated the speed with which Moscow's orders could be carried out by the Party faithful abroad.

In the search for collective security, the Soviet Union signed nonaggression pacts with every neighbor they could convince: first, Poland, Estonia, Latvia, and Finland; later, Czechoslovakia and France. Then the Soviets took the final step by joining that "bourgeois conspiracy" the League of Nations, and the Soviet Commissar of Foreign Affairs, Maxim Litvinov, gained pre-eminence as an advocate of all-out disarmament. The Seventh Congress of the Comintern, in 1934, came out for a "united front" with democratic groups, parties, and governments. Soviet obeisance to democracy was made more convincing in 1936 by the publication of the new Constitution, which seemed to grant a variety of liberties. In it, the devices nullifying with one hand what was given with the other were largely hidden, and the Soviet "new look" helped in cementing collective security abroad.

The collective-security policy received a severe jolt in 1938, when France and Great Britain capitulated to Hitler's demands at Munich. The Soviet alliance with Czechoslovakia demanded action *only if France decided to act*. Angered by the exclusion of the Soviets from the negotiations at Munich, Stalin, at the Eighteenth Party Congress, on March 10, 1939, hinted at a new policy when he accused Great Britain and France of abandoning collective security in an attempt to engender a German-Soviet conflict. He also stated that Germany had no designs on the Ukraine. Germany, as we know now, acted on the hint, and the way was opened for immediate German-Soviet negotiations.[2]

In the meanwhile, Great Britain and France were pursuing objectives that diverged radically from the U.S.S.R.'s and made negotiations with her difficult. Great Britain, hesitantly followed by France, wanted more flexibility in dealing with Germany; the Soviet Union wanted a tight alliance that would protect the countries on its western border. Furthermore, Poland feared Soviet aid as much as German aggression, and the British were inclined to overrate the Polish military capacity. As a result, Great Britain and France proposed a three-power declaration of mutual aid if they were drawn into war by a German attack on either Poland or Romania.

THE GREAT REVERSAL—THE SOVIET-GERMAN PACT

While sparring with Great Britain and France, the Soviets had been putting out secret feelers to Germany. The first definite event pointing toward a change in policy came on May 3, when Litvinov, a symbol of collective security, was ousted to make way for Molotov. This shift, combined with increasing German truculence toward Poland, stimulated French and British efforts to obtain a mutually satisfactory agreement with the Soviet Union. They sent military missions to Moscow.

In the light of the evidence in the documents on Nazi-Soviet relations and the Nuremberg trials, published by the U.S. State Department, it would seem that Great Britain and France would have had to take heroic steps after May 3 to stop the Nazi-Soviet *rapprochement*. Voroshilov was stalling for time with the British and French military missions until Stalin and Molotov could complete negotiations with Hitler. The refusal of the Poles to allow Soviet troops on their soil, even to repel a German attack, gave the Soviets an excuse to end the talks with the military missions. On August 21, collective security, as far as the Soviets were concerned, came to an end. Two days later, Ribbentrop and Molotov signed a nonaggression treaty providing that neither party would commit an act of aggression against the other, and that if either party should become engaged in war, the other would provide aid of all kinds.

This treaty gave Germany two advantages: First, the war could be held to a single front once Poland was knocked out; second, the economic provisions of the treaty nullified Great Britain's chief weapon, the blockade. An added bonus that accrued to Hitler was that Communism's huge international propaganda machine was directed toward putting the onus for the war on the Allies. This worked to Germany's advantage, especially in France.

For the Soviet Union, the secret protocol was even more important; it gave the territorial guarantees the Allies had been reluctant to grant. The protocol stated that in the areas belonging to the Baltic states (Finland, Estonia, Latvia, and Lithuania), the northern boundary of Lithuania was to represent the boundary of the spheres of influence of Germany and the U.S.S.R. On any division of Poland, the line formed by the Narew, Vistula, and San rivers was to delimit the respective spheres of influence. Finally, Soviet interests in Bessarabia were conceded by Germany.

With the Soviet Union showing favorable neutrality, Germany attacked Poland on September 1, 1939, and World War II was under way. German superiority in air power, mechanization, and organization enabled her to pulverize Polish defenses in a very short time. By September 17, the Red Army, with German approval and encouragement, marched into Poland and delivered the *coup de grâce*. On September 28, a treaty was signed that extended the German sphere of influence slightly to the east and gave Lithuania to the Soviets.

Having destroyed Poland and fixed her eastern boundaries with the Soviet Union, Germany was now free to throw her entire military might against the West. Economically the Soviet alliance worked well: In the first twelve months, the Soviets were to deliver almost 1 million tons of oil, 100,000 tons of cotton, 500,000 tons of iron ore, 300,000 tons of scrap iron, 2.5 tons of platinum, as well as manganese, timber, and oil seeds. Although the Germans were very often behind in their payments of manufactured goods, the Soviets usually maintained their end of the bargain. Moscow also acted as a broker in buying strategic materials abroad and transshipping them through her own territory to Germany. All in all, the economic arrangements resulting from the nonaggression pact of August 23 were very favorable to Germany.

As soon as the Soviets had seized their share of the Polish booty, they put pressure on the Baltic countries to sign mutual-assistance pacts and to allow Soviet military contingents within their territories. By October 10, 1939, Estonia, Latvia, and Lithuania had signed. Finland, however, steadfastly refused to lease any territory on the Gulf of Finland to the Soviet Union. On November 29, 1939, the Soviet Union broke off relations with Finland and attacked. The Russo-Finnish War, which lasted until March 12, 1940, revealed many weaknesses in the Soviet military machine, but ultimately the Soviets won concessions. The Finnish border was moved in some seventy-five miles, and the Hangö Peninsula was leased to the Soviet Union for thirty years. Although rearming feverishly, the U.S.S.R. made no further territorial strikes until June, 1940.

While the Soviets were publicly cheering the German victories, the fantastically rapid conquest of France caused serious misgivings in the Kremlin. Almost immediately, the three Baltic states that had signed mutual-assistance pacts were incorporated within the Soviet Union. The Soviets also seized Bessarabia in July, 1940. It was no coincidence that the Baltic countries and Bessarabia were occupied in the three weeks following the collapse of France; the Russians were trying to build a bulwark against the rapidly expanding empire of Hitler.

Hitler now began to look suspiciously at Russian penetration of the Balkans, especially when the Soviets demanded Bucovina as well as Bessarabia. In an effort to keep the Soviets out, on August 30, 1940, Germany compelled Romania to cede much of Transylvania to Hungary and the southern Dobruja to Bulgaria, offering in return a guarantee of the new Romanian frontier. Moscow bitterly objected to this unilateral action, regarding it as a violation of the secret protocol of August. In retaliation, the Soviets began to negotiate for trade and navigation agreements with Bulgaria and Yugoslavia. Hitler now wanted to prevent the Soviet Union from further encroachment in Europe at any point—which explains his pro-Finnish attitude in September, 1940, and his refusal to grant Lithuania a free port at Memel, in August, 1940. The Three-Power Pact signed by Germany, Japan, and Italy on September 27, 1940, was aimed chiefly at England, but it also put the Soviet Union in a precarious position. An attack on Germany would leave the Soviet rear exposed to Japan. As a final step, Hitler decided to go after the Balkans himself.

German troops were sent into Romania in October, ostensibly to protect the oil fields but, in reality, to get the jump on the Soviets. Mussolini, trying to assert his strength in the face of Hitler's growing power, attempted to outwit his Axis partner with a *fait accompli:* He launched his ill-fated attack on Albania and Greece—an action that greatly complicated the Balkan situation.

In November, 1940, Molotov came to Berlin in an effort to solve, or at least to clarify, the situation. He asked three questions: Would Germany recognize the Soviets' full liberty of action in Finland and withdraw German troops from the country? Did the German guarantee of Romanian boundaries apply to the Soviet Union? Would Germany look with favor on the establishment of Soviet bases in the Dardanelles? Hitler tried to evade such blunt and detailed questions by holding out global bribes. He proposed that the Soviets join the Three-Power Pact and thus gain a free hand in expansion toward India and Iran. This attempt to steer the Soviets eastward failed to impress Molotov, and he stuck stubbornly to his original demands: concrete terms on Finland, the Balkans, and the Straits. Forced to answer, Hitler conceded that he regarded any war in the Baltic over Finland as inadmissible, and expressed the opinion that as far as the Straits went, Russia should be satisfied with a revision of the Montreux Convention. The Berlin talks revealed that Germany and the Soviet Union were heading for a collision of interests, and Hitler became convinced that war was inevitable.

The Soviet Union and Germany now entered an open race to control the Balkans. Mussolini's reverses in the Greek campaign, plus the Yugoslav *coup d'état* of March 25, 1941, forced the Germans to accelerate their consolidation of the Balkans. These two operations left the Germans with their right flank protected and Romanian oil secured.

Virtually the only advantage the Soviet Union obtained in the last few months before the German attack was the declared neutrality of Japan—a result of the pact signed in April, 1941. At least the Soviet Union would have a war on only one front.

THE GRAND ALLIANCE

After the Nazi invasion of the Soviet Union, in June, 1941, an uneasy alliance came into being between the Soviet Union and Great Britain. This developed into a tripartite alliance when the United States entered the war. Throughout the succeeding four years of the struggle against the Axis, the leaders of the three great Allied powers were in almost constant contact with each other and, in spite of friction now and then, worked together effectively at their main task of defeating Germany.

The points of concern and discussion were many, but three problems stood out. Of immediate importance was the matter of military and economic aid to the Soviet Union from Great Britain and the United States. Another was the question of military cooperation, which involved essentially the Soviet demand for an immediate second front in France and Allied insistence upon adequate preparation. And, finally, there was the need for decisions on the fate of Germany and the small countries on Russia's western border, territorial settlements, and the creation of a world organization at the end of hostilities—in short, politics.

As soon as Churchill learned of the Nazi invasion of the Soviet Union he stated that Great Britain would give whatever help it could, and on the following day, the United States also pledged economic aid and military supplies. Although some

Soviet industry had been established or relocated in the east, it had suffered a calamitous loss when the German armies swept across the Ukraine in 1941.

The negotiations were simple in comparison with the problems of getting the goods to the Soviet Union. Three routes were available: by sea to Murmansk, by sea to Iran and overland from there, and through Siberia. The Murmansk route was the easiest, but by 1942, the Germans held bases in Norway from which they were able to dispatch submarines and aircraft that destroyed much of the shipping along this route. Because of the inadequacies of the Trans-Siberian Railroad, the Siberian route was not very satisfactory. Although the route through Iran was long, it was the safest. American and British engineers built up the transport facilities along this route, and by 1943, it was the main highway for Lend-Lease aid to the Soviet Union. During the entire period, the Russians had been irascible and unreasonable, refusing to consider the difficulties faced by the Allies and constantly demanding the promised deliveries. Four protocols were negotiated during the war, and these covered a stupendous amount of armaments, raw materials, foods, etc. Probably the most important item was the number of trucks sent to the Soviet Union—trucks that enabled the Red Army to supply its rapidly advancing forces after the victory at Stalingrad.

During the entire period from May, 1942, until the carrying out of Operation Overlord, in 1944, Stalin's pressure for a second front was a constant irritant in Soviet-Allied relations. It haunted the Moscow conference of October, 1943, and was a major topic at Teheran, in November, 1943. Stalin's demand may have reflected his defensiveness. He had negotiated the pact with Hitler in August, 1939, in the expectation of watching Germany and the Allies exhaust themselves. Now the Allies had him in a similar vise. But, seemingly, there was a sincere conviction on the part of the Soviets that the invasion of Europe was a simple operation.

At the time of Molotov's trip to Washington in June, 1942, the Soviets were asking for an immediate second front, and Molotov believed it could be managed that same year. Roosevelt, Hopkins, and Marshall were in favor of an early attempt to land in Europe, but Churchill and the British were much more reluctant. When Churchill went to Moscow in August, 1942, he was coolly received. The Russians were convinced that the Allies were stalling and bluntly said as much during the next two years.

Political negotiations between the Soviets and the Allies began almost as soon as the Nazis invaded Russia. The Anglo-Soviet agreement of July 12, 1941, stated that neither party would negotiate or conclude an armistice or treaty of peace with Germany except by mutual agreement. In December, 1941, Eden went to Moscow to survey tentative war and peace aims. Stalin asked for recognition of the Soviet boundaries of June 22, 1941; and for a check on Germany by the creation of a separate Austria, the annexation of East Prussia to Poland, and the possibility of an independent Rhineland and Bavaria. Churchill regarded these requests as fair enough, but negotiations ended when the United States refused to discuss territorial arrangements before the defeat of Germany.

The idea of negotiating terms with Germany was definitely dropped with Roosevelt's demand at Casablanca for "unconditional surrender." Churchill concurred in this. There can be little doubt that Roosevelt, being in the midst of the Giraud–De Gaulle squabble, contemplating the divergent aims of Great Britain and the Soviet Union, and having to consider Chinese desires in the Far East, felt that the doctrine of "unconditional surrender" was necessary to bring about harmony among the Allies. But this declaration made negotiations with the Axis impossible. At Teheran, in November, 1943, Stalin pointed out to Roosevelt that "unconditional surrender" had the disadvantage of keeping the Germans united; specific terms would make surrender easier.

At the time of the Teheran Conference, it was apparent that the defeat of Germany would leave a vast power vacuum all along the borders of the Soviet Union from Bulgaria to Finland. An immediate and critical question was the fate of Poland, now that the Germans were about to evacuate it. Churchill inclined toward dividing the whole area into separate spheres of influence, but the United States vehemently opposed this. It seemed as though the ghost of Wilsonian self-determination still haunted American statesmen. Roosevelt assumed that if he gave Stalin security and asked for no guarantees, the problem would be solved. The net result was that very little was accomplished at Teheran.

By the time of the next Big Three meeting, at Yalta, in February, 1945, the Soviet armies were already occupying the vacuum of the Balkans and Central and Eastern Europe. The Soviet armies held most of Poland, East Prussia, and had moved as far as the Oder at some points; they also had troops in Romania, Bulgaria, Hungary, and eastern Czechoslovakia. The American and British troops, on the other hand, were just recovering the ground lost in the Battle of the Bulge and had not yet crossed the Rhine. From a military viewpoint, therefore, Roosevelt's goal at Yalta was to gain concessions from Stalin, not give them.

The toughest problem at Yalta was to get a settlement of the Polish question. The Russians held the country and had recognized their own group, the Lublin Committee, as the legal government. Both Roosevelt and Churchill disagreed with Stalin on this issue; they maintained that the Lublin group did not represent more than a fraction of the Poles and that the Polish Government in Exile, in London, should have representatives in any new government. Roosevelt would have to account to 6 million Polish-Americans at home if he gave in to the Soviet Union on this issue. The three heads of state agreed upon the Curzon Line as the eastern boundary of Poland, but no agreement could be reached on a western demarcation. The Russians were demanding the Oder-Neisse Line, and Churchill warned them that "it would be a pity to stuff the Polish goose so full of German food that it gets indigestion."

The resolution of the Polish question looked very good on paper. It called for a reorganization of the Lublin Committee "on a broader democratic basis with the inclusion of democratic leaders from Poland itself and from Poles abroad." The new government was to be called the Polish Provisional Government of National Unity and was "pledged to the holding of free and unfettered elections as soon as possible on the basis of universal suffrage and secret ballot."

After much disagreement over the amount of reparations to be required of Germany, a Declaration on Liberated Europe was published in an effort to bring about a solution for the numerous problems that had not been adequately discussed. The substance of the Declaration was an agreement by the three powers to assist the peoples liberated from the Axis in solving their pressing economic and political problems "by democratic means." The three powers were pledged to consult together when problems arose in those areas and "to act jointly" in their solution.

Toward the end of the Yalta Conference, terms were agreed upon by which the Soviet Union was to enter the war against Japan. Briefly summarized, the Soviet Union won these concessions: recognition of the *status quo* in Outer Mongolia, control over the southern part of Sakhalin Island, a lease on Port Arthur as a naval base, ceding of pre-eminent rights in Dairen, joint control with China of the Chinese Eastern and South Manchurian railways, and possession of the Kurile Islands. The Soviet Union was to recognize the full sovereignty of China in Manchuria. It is evident that the concessions made at Yalta showed Roosevelt's eagerness to get Russia into the Japanese conflict; his military advisers had given him some dour prognostications on the difficulties involved in the Pacific theater—especially because the Japanese Kwantung Army was largely intact—and the atomic bomb was still in the future.

BUILDING THE SOVIET EMPIRE

At the time of the German capitulation, the Soviet position in Europe was excellent. The negotiations at Teheran and Yalta had given them a good legal position in respect to the penetration of the Balkans and Eastern Europe, especially in view of the new definition of "democracy" to be evolved by the Russians. The Red Army was in physical control of Poland, the eastern part of Germany, some of Czechoslovakia, and all of Romania, Hungary, and Bulgaria. The regimes of Yugoslavia and Albania were Communist and looked reliable from Moscow's point of view. To say that a "confused situation," so dear to the hearts of the Soviet leaders, existed in Eastern Europe and the Balkans in 1944 and 1945 is an understatement. The situation was made even more favorable for the Russians by the decisions, or lack of decisions, or by the ambiguity of the decisions, at Teheran and Yalta.

In taking advantage of this confusion to seize and control the countries now called the satellites, the Soviets followed one general pattern of procedure. The name given to the states that became satellites of the Soviet Union—"people's democracies"—was not originated in 1945 by the Politburo. It had been given to the People's Republic of Outer Mongolia in the early days of the Revolution. There, over a thirty-year period, the Soviet Union had been developing a technique for ruling a "captive country" absolutely and yet allowing it to keep a façade of autonomy. Thus, in 1945, the Soviet Union already had the name for the new satellites and the technique for their seizure and control.

To govern the satellites, the Politburo in Moscow had for years, with great foresight, been training a group of Communist refugees from these regions. Almost as part of the equipment of the occupying Red Army, these Party members entered the newly established satellites to serve as Soviet proconsuls. G. A. Tokaev, an expatriated Soviet engineer, refers to this group as the "Kremlin Column" gang. Some became notorious in their rise to power—Mátyás Rákosi in Hungary, Ana Pauker in Romania, Georgi Dimitrov in Bulgaria, Boleslaw Bierut in Poland. While the Americans and British were still concentrating on the military victory, the Soviets had already set the stage for one of the biggest territorial seizures in history.

The dozen countries seized or threatened by the Soviet Union fall into four groups: First, the Baltic group—Estonia, Latvia, and Lithuania—incorporated into the Soviet Union by August, 1940, and promptly reincorporated following the German exodus in 1944–45. The second group was made up of those countries in which a civil war raged either while they were under Axis control or immediately following their so-called liberation, namely, Yugoslavia, Albania, and Poland. (In Poland, the civil war was imported by the Russians.) The third group—Romania, Bulgaria, and Hungary—was occupied swiftly and completely by the Red Army, and Sovietization followed. In the fourth group —the "periphery states" of Greece, Finland, and Iran—the Soviet Union was unsuccessful. And, finally, there was Czechoslovakia, which deviated from the general pattern in the first stage of subjugation.

In Yugoslavia and Albania, the Axis forces smashed the social structure of the country and tried to fill the gap with quislings. The Communists in the resistance movements in these countries not only fought the Axis forces and their quislings, but also waged civil war against the more conservative resistance movements—Draža Mikhajlović in Yugoslavia and the pro-monarchy Zogists in Albania. In both these countries, with the downfall of the Axis, a full-fledged Communist leader emerged—Tito in Yugoslavia and Enver Hoxha in Albania.

In Poland, the situation was much more complex. There was a well-organized, strong, and dedicated underground, the Homeland Army, in constant courier and radio communication with the Polish Government in Exile. The Communists were extremely weak in the resistance movement. The Soviets' stab-in-the-back of 1939, the Katyń Forest massacre of Polish officers, and the deliberate Soviet sabotaging of the Warsaw uprising had inflamed the traditional anti-Russianism of the Poles. The Soviet Union realized that the establishment of a subservient government in Poland would necessitate the smashing of the Homeland Army. This it proceeded to do directly by means of the Red Army and the Lublin Committee and indirectly by the inaction of the Red Army while the Germans smashed the Warsaw uprising.

Romania, Bulgaria, and Hungary had experienced fairly stable regimes during the period of Axis control. The Red Army invaded and occupied these countries swiftly, and there was little opposition to their liquidation of the pro-Axis regimes. It is in these three countries that we see a definite pattern of

Sovietization emerging. The pattern developed in three stages: (1) genuine collaboration, (2) bogus collaboration, and (3) the establishment of the monolithic regime.

In the first stage, the Communists cooperated with the independent nonfascist parties of these countries in purging the fascists and in beginning a reform program. The length of this stage varied from country to country. In Bulgaria, it lasted only from September, 1944, to January, 1945. At that time the Communists forced the resignation of Dr. G. M. Dimitrov of the Agrarian Union. In Romania, Vyshinsky forced King Michael to appoint a stooge, Petru Groza, as head of the government in March, 1945. In Hungary, the Soviets moved slowly, and the first stage ended in February, 1947, with the arrest of Béla Kovács.

The second stage, bogus collaboration, saw the non-Communists still in the government, but these men were hand-picked by the Communists. The independent parties in this stage were driven into opposition, and more and more restrictions were placed upon their freedom of activity. Newspapers were severely censored and denied supplies of paper, and their printers were controlled by the Communists. Opposition meetings were broken up by gangs of thugs, and non-Communist leaders were jailed. This stage lasted in Romania and Bulgaria from early 1945 until the fall of 1947; in Hungary, from the spring of 1947 to the spring of 1948, with the arrest of Cardinal Mindszenty. Poland went through a similar stage from 1945 to the autumn of 1947.

In the third stage, the establishment of the monolithic regime, all political activity was concentrated in one party. Opposition came to a halt or was driven underground. The opposition leaders were arrested and tried as agents of Anglo-American imperialism—with the exception of those who escaped abroad, as did Ferenc Nagy of Hungary, and Stanislaw Mikolajczyk of Poland. In this final stage, the satellites became pawns of Soviet politics.

In Greece, Turkey, and Iran, the Soviet drive failed, but in these cases, the Soviets had restricted themselves to the limited application of force and subsequently withdrew with only a minor loss of face. In Greece, the British managed to land forces in October, 1944, and were successful in breaking up the attempt of the Greek Communists, the EAM, to take over the country. The EAM was never able to regain the initiative, although civil war continued until late 1949. United States aid to Greece under the Truman Doctrine kept the anti-Communist government alive, and in July, 1949, Tito closed the Yugoslav-Greek border in retaliation for his ejection from the Communist camp, in 1948. This deprived the Greek Communists of their base of supplies and sanctuary, and defeat was inevitable.

In Iran, the Soviets had troops in the northern area, Iranian Azerbaidzhan, in 1945. These troops, by treaty, were to be evacuated by March, 1946, six months after the cessation of hostilities. But the Soviets used these troops to back up the Tudeh (Communist) Party, and established an autonomous Azerbaidzhanian state within Iran. An Iranian appeal to the United Nations, the first one to reach it, pressure on the U.S.S.R. by the United States, and clever maneuvers by the Iranians frustrated this Russian scheme.

In Turkey, the Soviets tried a combination of methods to gain some historic objectives in the confusion following the war. First, they tried to blackmail the Turks by threatening to drop the 1921 Friendship Treaty unless granted both Soviet bases on the Straits and the fortified towns of Kars and Ardahan. Twenty-five Soviet divisions were stationed on the eastern border of Turkey, and the Soviet press and radio launched an anti-Turkish propaganda campaign. Two Georgian professors advanced bases for Soviet claims to Turkish territory, and the Soviets pressured the Bulgarians into pushing their Turkish minority over the border faster than the Turks could take care of it. All that saved Turkey from the synchronized effort was the aid provided under the Truman Doctrine and the age-old Turkish hatred for the Russians.

The Western powers were becoming more and more disillusioned about Stalin. The Truman Doctrine, in 1947, was a firm step toward halting Soviet expansion in one area. The Soviet take-over of Czechoslovakia, in February, 1948, and the Berlin Blockade, in June of the same year, killed the last hope that

Stalin was amenable to reasonable negotiations. The result was a coalescence of the Western powers and the formation of the NATO alliance of 1949. Stalin had reached the limits of expansion in Europe and the Middle East.

THE SOVIET UNION AND THE FAR EAST

As the confusion resulting from the collapse of the Nazi empire facilitated Soviet expansion in Europe, the chaos in the Far East following Japan's defeat was even more promising for the spread of Communism.

At the Yalta Conference, it was obvious to Stalin that if he were to gain anything in the Asiatic theater, he would have to commit the Soviet Union in the war with Japan. Roosevelt, believing the Japanese to be still a formidable force, wanted to have Soviet help as soon as possible. Capitalizing on the eagerness of the United States, Stalin drove a hard bargain and obtained exorbitant rewards for Soviet participation. He agreed that the Soviet Union would come into the Pacific war not later than three months after the cessation of hostilities against Germany. It is debatable whether the Russians would have complied with this time schedule if their intelligence in Tokyo had not warned them that the end was near for Japan. However that may be, on August 9, 1945, the Soviet Union declared war on an already beaten Japan and was able to qualify for a share in the spoils of the Japanese Empire.

Part of the Russian booty was control of Manchuria, which meant control of the Chinese Eastern and South Manchurian railways, a naval base at Port Arthur, and predominant interests in Dairen. All of this was concurred in by Chiang Kai-shek, but in all fairness, the Generalissimo had been presented with a Hobson's choice. The Chinese extracted a few concessions in their negotiations at Moscow in July, 1945—among them, a pledge that Chinese sovereignty in Manchuria would be respected and that the Soviets would withdraw their troops three months after the defeat of Japan.

The Soviets, however, decided to support Mao and the Communists in China. They followed two policies: One was to exert constant pressure on Chiang to accept "democratic" (Communist) elements into his government; the other, to hand over all the Japanese equipment possible to Mao's forces. Occupying Manchuria, the Soviets had at their disposal the tremendous arsenal of the Kwantung Army, little of which the Japanese had ever had a chance to use. Manchuria was also the most highly industrialized area of China. By calculated obstruction, the Russians were able to keep the Nationalist forces from getting into Manchuria in time to stop the Communist infiltration of the territory.

Immediately upon declaring war on Japan, the Russians were able to move into Korea. At Potsdam, it was decided that for temporary administration the Russians would control Korea north of the Thirty-eighth Parallel, and the United States the territory south of that line. The Russians hastened to set up Communist-controlled committees in South Korea, but General Hodges made short work of this system when he arrived with American troops.

Once the Nationalists began to fail in Manchuria in 1947, the rout grew progressively. In 1948, they lost Mukden. In January, 1949, the Nationalist capital, Nanking, fell, and the great commercial ports of Shanghai and Hankow followed in May. The Nationalists were forced back to their wartime capital, Chungking, and by the middle of 1950, the disaster was complete except for Formosa.

By May, 1948, the relations between the two regimes in Korea had deteriorated to the extent that the North Koreans cut off all electric power going to South Korea. The United Nations Commission finally began preparations for an election, but only in South Korea; and on July 17, 1948, in the name of both Koreas, the newly elected assembly met, promulgated a constitution, and named Syngman Rhee as President. About the same time, a government was established in North Korea that also claimed to represent the entire country. It was modeled closely on the government of the Soviet Union.

The United States withdrew its troops in 1949 and took an

ambiguous stand on backing Korea militarily. Probably encouraged by U.S. wavering, the North Korean regime sent troops across the Thirty-eighth Parallel on June 25, 1950. The United States immediately called the U.N. Security Council into session and, as the Soviet Union was then boycotting the Security Council, got unanimous condemnation of North Korea's action. The North Koreans, with Soviet armament and Soviet advice, almost succeeded in occupying all South Korea. But soon the forces of the United States, with their U.N. allies, were able to roll the Communists back, almost reaching the Yalu River by the end of October, 1950. One month later, the Chinese Communists stepped in, and again the battle line moved south. In mid-1951, after months of bitter fighting and heavy losses, truce negotiations began when the battle line hovered around the Thirty-eighth Parallel. An armistice was finally signed at Panmunjom on July 27, 1953.

The signing of the armistice took place a few months after the death of Stalin, and in this case, *post hoc, ergo propter hoc* is probably applicable. The armistice talks had been stalled for a year on the question of voluntary repatriation of prisoners, and the fact that the Malenkov regime yielded on this point was an indication of the change in Soviet foreign policy. Many of the nonessential, but extremely irritating, aspects of the Stalinist foreign policy were discarded. The new regime realized that the bellicose Stalinist policy only welded the opposition more closely; the Truman Doctrine, NATO, and the U.N. operation in Korea were prime examples. The new approach aimed at transforming the world-image of the Soviet Union. In place of the dour, belligerent Stalinist Russia, a Russia now emerged that advocated peace and coexistence. The non-Communist world was urged to relax; the Soviet Union no longer presented a clear and immediate danger, and alliances and pacts could become less binding, and armament expenditures could be curtailed.

SOVIET POLICY IN THE UNDERDEVELOPED AREAS

Soviet foreign policy was now directed toward wooing the uncommitted nations, especially those in the underdeveloped areas of the world. The Stalinist policy of seeking complete control of an area now gave way to a policy of merely removing an area from the influence of the Western powers. Stalin had been very suspicious of revolutionary movements he could not control completely. His bitter experience with Chiang Kai-shek and the Kuomintang in 1927 and 1928, as well as his differences with Tito in 1948, made him reluctant to cooperate with leaders and groups that were not entirely under his control. He never believed that the newly independent India, Burma, Indonesia, and Ceylon were anything but puppets of their former masters. Stalin's successors, however, concluded that by inciting small Communist forces that had no chance of gaining power against such leaders as Nehru, U Nu, and Sukarno, they could succeed only in driving these would-be neutrals into the Western camp. This does not mean that the architects of the post-Stalin policy had lost interest in the eventual Communization of the uncommitted areas, but it does mean that they were aware of the revolutionary situation that had developed in these regions since World War II and felt that collaboration with the nationalist movements would pay large dividends in the years to come. Khrushchev emphasized this new policy in 1955 by touring some of the Asian countries.

Khrushchev's first major reversal of Stalin's policy was his pilgrimage to Belgrade in 1955 to resume relations with Tito. An attempt was made to blame the original rupture on the dead Beria, but Tito's lack of response made that line unprofitable. Khrushchev, therefore, used the ultimate argument when he stated in his anti-Stalin "Secret Speech," at the Twentieth Congress, in February, 1956, that Stalin was to blame for the break with Tito. In April, 1956, the Cominform, the main weapon in the attack on Tito, was abolished, and in June, Tito went to Moscow for a hero's welcome. Rákosi, the boss of Hungary and Tito's archenemy, was replaced by Ernö Gerö in July. In other words, everything was done to bring Tito closer to Moscow.

The Middle East had been more or less neglected in Soviet foreign policy during the last years of the Stalin regime. The Communist faithful worked assiduously in most of the Middle

Eastern countries, but most of the Parties—with the exception of the Syrian group—were small and not very effective. The news of the arms deal between Nasser and the Communist bloc came as a surprise to the Western powers. Nasser's explanation—that he had to turn to the Communist bloc because the Western powers had been laggard in supplying him with arms—did not make Western statesmen any happier. Seldom had Soviet diplomats bought so much trouble for the West so cheaply.

REVOLT IN THE SATELLITES AND SUEZ

The Khrushchev policy seemed to be moving smoothly throughout 1955 and most of 1956. Following the denigration of Stalin, there had been a relaxation of controls in the satellites known as the "thaw." There was also something called the "Spirit of Geneva," which had resulted from the Khrushchev-Eisenhower talks at the "summit." It is true that trouble seemed to be brewing in Poland; first, the Poznań riots in June, then the reinstatement to the Party of Wladyslaw Gomulka, who had been jailed during the Stalinist regime as a Titoist. On October 19, Gomulka was elected to the Central Committee of the Polish Communist Party. This brought Khrushchev to Warsaw on the same day, but Gomulka faced him down, even obtaining the dismissal of the Kremlin-appointed Defense Minister of Poland, Marshal Rokossovsky, and on October 21, Gomulka was elected First Secretary of the Party.

In Budapest, student demonstrations in favor of the Poles broke out on October 23 and continued the next day. The Hungarian secret police (AVH) fired on the students, and a full-scale revolt broke out. But the Hungarian Army refused to fire on the revolutionists, and many soldiers went over to the side of the rebels. Imre Nagy became premier, refused to ask for Soviet help, and even withdrew from the Warsaw Pact. It looked as though Hungary had won its revolution. Then, on November 4, Soviet mechanized and armored detachments smashed into Budapest and put down the revolt by sheer force. The Western powers protested, but kept their objections far short of any physical commitment.

The Western powers faced a crisis of their own in another area. In July, 1956, the United States informed Nasser that it would not take part in the financing of the Aswan High Dam, and the British and the World Bank took a similar position. Within a week, Nasser retaliated by nationalizing the Suez Canal. Relations between Nasser and the main users of the canal, Great Britain and France, deteriorated steadily throughout the next three months. Finally, on October 29, Israeli troops invaded the Suez peninsula and the English and French attacked the canal area.

Nothing could have so effectively helped the Soviets with their Hungarian problems. While Soviet tanks were smashing the Hungarian revolution, the Soviet diplomats in the U.N. were pointing an accusing finger at the "colonialists" and describing the heinous crimes being committed by the British and French in Egypt. To make matters even more confused, the United States found itself on the Soviet side of the debate and opposed to its NATO partners. The Soviets threatened to send "volunteers" to Egypt and hinted at the use of ballistic missiles against England and France.

The result of the events of October and November, 1956, was a boost for Soviet prestige in the Middle East and a neutralization of Western participation in the Hungarian question. There can be no doubt that the Hungarian affair had an adverse effect on the Communist-inspired image of the U.S.S.R. as the purveyor of peace and coexistence, but probably not so permanent a staining of the image as the Western powers thought. Moreover, notice had been served on the satellites that the Soviet Union would tolerate no more revolutionary activity; they had used naked force against a satellite, and they were prepared to use it again. Any good will that had emanated from the summit in 1955 was dissipated by the Suez and Hungarian affairs, and Khrushchev's messages to the West were couched in belligerent language for most of 1957.

By 1958, however, the Soviets were well launched on a new peace offensive. In February of that year, they asked for a discontinuance of nuclear testing, a renunciation of the use of nuclear weapons, and a nonaggression pact between NATO and the Warsaw Pact countries. The Rapacki Plan for a denuclearized zone in Central Europe, presented to the U.N. in October, 1957, was refurbished and resubmitted in February, 1958. In March, the Soviets announced a unilateral suspension of nuclear tests, having just finished their own series of tests. Strangely enough, in June, in the midst of this new peace offensive, the Soviets aroused hostile feelings throughout Europe by announcing the execution of Imre Nagy and other Hungarian revolutionists.

Khrushchev's peaceful-coexistence policy really flourished in 1959. In that summer, Vice President Nixon visited Moscow for the opening of the American Exhibition, and even the "kitchen debate" between Nixon and Khrushchev did not dampen the latter's enthusiasm. In September, Khrushchev came to the United States and, at the conclusion of his tour, met with President Eisenhower at Camp David. By early 1960, there was much hope that the summit conference to be held in Paris in May would lead to a lessening of the tensions of the Cold War.

SOVIET FOREIGN POLICY (1959–64)

The story of Khrushchev's foreign-policy moves in the 1959–64 period, however, is one of rapid oscillations between violent missile rattling and endeavors to arrange a *détente* with the West. Some observers have seen in Khrushchev's actions a Pavlovian technique to demoralize the West, but most students regard his moves as so many desperate attempts to gain a diplomatic victory that might have shored up his sagging reputation as a dynamic leader on the world scene. A quick review of his policies in that period will point up the capriciousness of his essays into world politics.

The coexistence policy was at its warmest stage in the fall of 1959, when Khrushchev visited the United States and held his talks with Eisenhower at Camp David. The time-limit aspect of the Berlin "ultimatum" was suspended, and Khrushchev and Eisenhower agreed that resolution of the problem should not be prolonged indefinitely. The groundwork was completed for a summit meeting in Paris in the spring of 1960, at which Khrushchev apparently thought he could get some kind of agreement with the United States on the Berlin problem.

Early in 1960, however, Khrushchev seemed to grow less optimistic about the prospects of obtaining a favorable deal on Berlin from Eisenhower at the scheduled summit conference, or else he wanted to needle Eisenhower into a receptive mood, because he began to bring up the Berlin issue with monotonous regularity. In a speech delivered in Moscow on January 14, 1960, he threatened to make a separate peace treaty with Ulbricht, and while on a visit to Indonesia in February, he stated that a treaty with the East German regime would mean an immediate end to all Allied rights in Berlin. On April 3, while on a trip through France, he repeated his threat of a separate treaty, and at Baku, on April 25, he brought the subject up again, this time promising to back the East Germans with force. No doubt he was trying to build up enough pressure on Eisenhower to get a favorable decision on Berlin at the summit, but even the irrepressible Khrushchev must have realized by the end of April that he was not going to get his way at Paris.

The shooting down of the U-2, on May 1, was made to order, and on May 16, Khrushchev used the incident to torpedo the summit conference. The awkward U.S. cover story and Eisenhower's acceptance of responsibility for the U-2 flights allowed Khrushchev to wax indignant and even rescind the invitation he had extended to Eisenhower to visit the Soviet Union. The last vestiges of the Camp David spirit seemed to have gone down the drain.

But Khrushchev, despite his histrionics at the Paris summit, was in no position to end his peaceful-coexistence policy entirely, for his erstwhile partner in the East, Mao Tse-tung, was becoming more and more obstreperous. To be pressed between an actively hostile West and an aggressive China was a situation to avoid at all cost.

Russia's rulers have always feared a simultaneous squeeze from the East and West. Stalin's China policy from 1928 until well into the 1940's was based on maintaining a strong China to offset Japan, and when a German attack loomed in the days of the Ribbentrop-Molotov Pact, Stalin made every effort to insure Japan's neutrality. In Khrushchev's case, Sino-Soviet relations had become so strained by mid-1960 that he pulled his technicians, and their blueprints, out of China, and almost all Soviet aid to China came to an end. Thereafter, as relations with the United States went from bad to worse, Khrushchev had to keep looking over his shoulder at the East.

In retrospect, it seems extremely doubtful that Khrushchev was ever serious in his threats to sign a separate treaty with East Germany, or at least one that would allow Ulbricht to control access to Berlin. Such a treaty would, in effect, give Ulbricht the power to bring on World War III, an abdication of responsibility no Soviet statesman could even contemplate. So, in spite of his disappointment over Berlin in 1960, Khrushchev stated that he would again discuss the issue after the election of a new President in the United States.

Early in June, 1961, the new President, John F. Kennedy, met Khrushchev in Vienna. A very inconclusive conference resulted, and a few days later, June 15, Khrushchev stated that a Soviet peace treaty with East Germany could no longer be postponed. Finally, on August 13, the East Germans, with the help of Soviet divisions, erected the Berlin Wall. This helped Khrushchev in his relations with the East Germans, for the East German regime was being badly hurt by the massive migration of skilled workers and professionals to the West. In fact, the flow of refugees through West Berlin was the constant irritant that had forced Khrushchev to look so desperately for a solution to the Berlin problem. The Wall, to some degree, was a loss of face for the Communist world, but pacifying Ulbricht was worth that.

Of all the problems Khrushchev faced in the 1959–64 period, the growing gulf between Moscow and Peking was by far the worst. Not only was the "monolithic" solidarity of the Communist bloc being split into Soviet and Chinese camps but the Soviet satellites in Central and Eastern Europe, taking advantage of the split, were paying less heed to admonitions from the Kremlin. One of Khrushchev's boasts in his January, 1960, speech to the Supreme Soviet concerned the impregnability of the Soviet Union because of the "consolidation and growth of the mighty socialist camp." Six months later, the socialist camp had become very unconsolidated indeed. Furthermore, Kremlin leadership in the world Communist movement was threatened. In June, 1960, Khrushchev made a brutal attack on the Chinese at the Romanian Party Congress in Bucharest and was answered in kind by P'eng Chen, the Chinese delegate.[3] Then, for two months, November and December, 1960, the delegates from eighty-one Communist Parties met in Moscow to iron out the differences between Moscow and Peking. They issued a statement that tried to ignore the widening split between the two Communist giants. Any unity that may have been created in December, 1960, was completely shattered at the Twenty-second Party Congress, held in Moscow in October, 1961, when Khrushchev threw the Albanians out of the Soviet bloc. Chou En-lai, the Chinese delegate to the Congress, took umbrage at the treatment meted out to Peking's only European client, Enver Hoxha, and left the Congress to return to Peking, where the whole top level of the Chinese Government turned out to meet him, to show Khrushchev they supported Chou's action. In 1962, Moscow's fiasco in Cuba, plus its tacit condemnation of the Chinese policy on the Indian border late in the year, did nothing to improve Sino-Soviet relations.

In 1963, Khrushchev decided to draw nearer the West, a move bound to alienate the Chinese even more. They were already furious over the Soviet pro-Indian stand, and skirmishes along the Sino-Soviet border resulted. There is even some evidence that the Soviets were fomenting trouble in Sinkiang. Khrushchev's resumption of a warmer coexistence policy was probably prompted by his desire for greater economic cooperation with the West. He was pushing a major buildup of the Soviet chemical industry, especially in plastics, artificial fibers, and fertilizers, and needed long-term credits to buy equipment from the industrialized nations of the West. Only a *détente* in the Cold War would make this project feasible.

In July, 1963, Khrushchev, in token of the new spirit, agreed to a treaty banning nuclear tests above ground. In the same month, the Chinese were in Moscow, ostensibly to settle the dispute between the two states. Nothing came of the meeting, but the test-ban treaty increased the fury of the Chinese, if that were possible.

Although Khrushchev's ever worsening relations with Mao, his growing feud with Gheorghe Gheorghiu-Dej of Romania, and his flirtation with West Germany were all reasons for his fall, the main causes were undoubtedly domestic. His successors have had no more luck with Peking than he had. Romania, even with its new leader, Nicolae Ceausescu, has continued to go its own way, with little respect for the word of the Kremlin. And, even with the escalation of the war in Viet Nam, coexistence is still the basis of Soviet foreign policy. It was Khrushchev's style in foreign policy more than the content of his policies that alienated his Kremlin associates.

FOREIGN-POLICY MACHINERY

Superficially, the machinery for conducting Soviet foreign policy is similar to that of most powers. The Ministry of Foreign Affairs is responsible for establishing and maintaining diplomatic relations with other countries. It also does most of the negotiating with other powers (Khrushchev, of course, often decided to use some of his personal diplomacy instead). There is a small group at the top of the Ministry, the collegium, which is composed of the Minister, the six Deputy Ministers, and some division chiefs. This group is the nerve center of the Ministry; it decides the way in which policy is to be carried out, assigns tasks to subordinate agencies, and advises the Minister.

Below the collegium there are fourteen geographic offices that supervise the activities of Soviet missions in specific areas. The geographic offices also receive and analyze reports from the field and pass significant information on to the collegium. There are also a number of special agencies to handle protocol, treaties, press relations, and other technical and housekeeping matters.

The number of Soviet missions has steadily grown in the last forty years from a few nonaccredited representatives to fifty-three embassies and four legations. Soviet diplomats, like most diplomats, have little authority to make policy. The speed of modern communications enables the home-based leaders to confer with the negotiators at each stage of the conference. The most important task of a Soviet diplomat is gathering information on the country to which he is assigned. His yearly report to Moscow is used by the Ministry of Foreign Affairs to help formulate future policies. Soviet diplomatic establishments abroad, compared with those of other nations, are unusually large; they include military attachés and representatives of the various trade committees and the Ministry of Foreign Trade, as well as chauffeurs and other low-ranking individuals assigned for the purpose of espionage and subversion. Many of these representatives, although ostensibly subordinate to the Soviet ambassador, actually report directly to their superiors in Moscow.

All this formal structure is necessary for the execution of policies, for breaking down policy directives into assignments. The actual policies are probably decided at the level of the Presidium-Secretariat of the Party, coordinated through the Presidium of the Council of Ministers, and then passed on to the Ministry of Foreign Affairs.

In the last years of his reign, Khrushchev made foreign policy one of his main concerns. He was inclined to conduct foreign relations on a leader-to-leader basis, and there was a steady stream of heads of state arriving in Moscow, receiving the red-carpet treatment, and then engaging in personal talks with Khrushchev. Unlike Stalin, Khrushchev showed no reluctance to travel, either within Russia or abroad, and he was out of Moscow frequently and for considerable lengths of time.

The new leadership, which has not yet had a chance to display a unique style in foreign policy, does seem disinclined to interfere more than is necessary in the day-to-day operations of the Foreign Ministry. This relatively "inactive" foreign policy will probably last until one leader, either Kosygin or Brezhnev, gains the upper hand in the policy-making process.

13

International Communism

The Soviet Union is more than a state in the conventional sense; it is also the center, the heart, of a militant secular religion, Communism. Every Soviet agent sent abroad—diplomat, technician, or artist—is a missionary for the faith, and the old adage "The end justifies the means" is part of his moral baggage. Consequently, it has been extremely difficult to deal with the Soviet Union on the traditional plane of foreign politics ever since November, 1917.

The Soviet Union in the 1920's and early 1930's, a relatively weak country occupied in trying to solve its agricultural and industrial problems, was more a nuisance than a real threat in the eyes of Western statesmen. The situation today is vastly different. The Soviet Union is now the nucleus of an imposing empire, encompassing a large part of Europe, with tentacles extending far into Asia and containing almost a billion people. The power center of the empire, the U.S.S.R., is now the world's second greatest industrial and military nation.

Communist missionaries now represent a religion that is growing at a prodigious rate—from a few thousand in 1917 to the control of almost a billion people by 1949. Probably most of these are reluctant members of the faith, but the magnitude of the expansion undoubtedly gives the Communists confidence that history is on their side. The growth of the Communist empire has not, at least up to the present time, aided the Communists in proselytizing the "proletariat" of the industrially advanced nations, although traditional Marxism considered that class the most amenable to conversion. Long before the advent of the present Communist campaign in the underdeveloped areas, however, Lenin taught that capitalism's weakest link lay precisely there. The "revolution of rising expectations" in those areas has made them much more fertile fields for conversion than they were in Lenin's time.

Communist converts in nations outside the U.S.S.R. have played various tactical roles in the last forty years, but the over-all strategy has been constant: the preservation of the fortress of Communism—the Soviet Union—and the expansion of the faith.

ORIGIN AND GROWTH OF THE COMINTERN

During World War I, Lenin became increasingly pessimistic about the value of the Second International as an instrument for the advancement of the world Communist movement. He was severely jolted when the German Social Democrats in the Reichstag voted for the war budget in August, 1914, and his disillusionment grew stronger as the socialist parties, one after the other, put patriotism above revolution. As early as September, 1914, Lenin advocated turning the war into a social revolution and stressed the importance of the defeat of the Russian monarchy. Two months later, the Central Committee of the Bolsheviks (a tiny group at that time) issued a manifesto calling for the transformation of the imperialist war into a civil war, and urging the proletariat to turn their guns on their imperialist masters. Lenin took this slogan to the Zimmerwald conference (September 5–8, 1915), a meeting of international socialists opposed to the war. But even this select group felt that Lenin was too far to the Left; only six of the thirty delegates joined Lenin's "Zimmerwald Left." In April of the following year, another conference was held, this time in another Swiss town, Kienthal, but Lenin still commanded a very small minority. Lenin became more determined than ever to have his own International. On his return to Russia, in 1917, he issued his "April Theses," the tenth of which was a call for a revolutionary International.

In January, 1919, the Bolsheviks sent out invitations for a meeting to create a new International, and early in March, about fifty delegates, representing nineteen countries, gathered in Moscow. Eberlein, the German delegate, represented the only important Communist Party aside from the Russian one, and he came instructed to torpedo the conference if it gave indications of becoming a permanent organization. The Germans, correctly, as it turned out, feared Russian control of any international organization that might be set up in Moscow. On March 4, 1919, the conference became the First Congress of the Communist International (usually abbreviated to Comintern), and Eberlein abstained from voting. The Congress elected an Executive Committee of the Communist International (the infamous ECCI) to act between Congresses, and Grigori Zinoviev became the first President of the ECCI. The Congress elected Karl Radek Secretary, although he was then in jail in Berlin.

The first accomplishment of the Comintern was to issue an appeal "To the Workers of All Countries," which urged them to rally to the aid of the Soviet regime. At its very birth, the Comintern reflected the two strands of Soviet foreign policy: to defend the Soviet fortress of Communism and to spread the faith throughout the world. From its inception, the Comintern was firmly under Russian control and its effectiveness was dependent upon the strength of the Soviet Government. In this early period, it even worked closely with Chicherin and the People's Commissariat of Foreign Affairs, the Narkomindel.

In 1919, the year the Comintern was born, Communist affairs everywhere looked black: The Communist coup in Bavaria collapsed in May; Béla Kun's Communist regime in Hungary fell in August; and the White Armies of Yudenich, Denikin, and Kolchak were pushing in from the west, south, and east, respectively. With the exception of the German Party, no real Communist Party had yet been established abroad. In short, the Comintern was isolated in Moscow and had no effective tools with which to work outside Russia.

The Second Congress of the Comintern met in Moscow, in July, 1920, and was attended by 200 delegates from thirty-five countries. This Congress was held under much rosier conditions than the first one: The Red Army was now on the offensive, even to the extent of carrying the war into Poland. The Second Congress, therefore, stressed the defense of the new Soviet state much less than had its predecessor and put a great deal more emphasis on carrying the revolution abroad. In addition, the Congress laid down stringent rules for the admission of foreign Parties—the famous "twenty-one conditions," tailored along the Leninist theory that a small, well-organized, doctrinally pure group was more effective than an eclectic, amorphous larger organization. The "twenty-one conditions" put absolute control of all Communist Parties in the hands of the Comintern, and since the Comintern was controlled in turn by Moscow, eventually under the rule of the Soviet leaders or leader. A brief listing of some of the conditions will indicate the degree of control. Each member Party of the Comintern had to urge the proletarian revolution and the dictatorship of the proletariat; to remove all reformists; to create underground organizations and combine legal and illegal activities; to conduct propaganda in the armed forces; to denounce colonial exploitation; to obey the principle of democratic centralism and carry out periodic purges within the Party; to submit the Party program to the ECCI for confirmation; and to expel any member who voted against the acceptance of these conditions.

Russian control was ensured not only by the location of the Comintern headquarters in Moscow and its dependence upon Russia as the only Communist state, but also by the provision that five members of the twenty-one-man ECCI should come from the country in which the ECCI was located, and no more than one from any other single country. This gave the Russians the only solid bloc in the Executive Committee. The rest of the organizational structure of the Comintern was modeled closely on that of the Bolshevik Party, and centralized control channeled all power to the Kremlin.

The Third Congress of the Comintern met in June–July, 1921. The revolutionary optimism that had marked the Second Congress was moderated by 1921. The political situation in Western Europe was stabilizing, the attempts at Communist coups outside of Russia had all failed ignominiously, and Russia herself needed a breathing spell in which to repair the damages of six years of war and revolution. The time was not conducive to overt revolution-making. For example, in September, 1920, at the Congress of Eastern Peoples held in Baku, every effort had been made by the Russians to whip up sentiment against British imperialism. Nine months later, at the Comintern Congress, this was scarcely mentioned because the Russians had just signed a trade agreement with the British. Lenin had announced the NEP, and the Russians hoped to obtain goods and services from the very capitalist powers at whom the Comintern had raged in 1920. A slowdown was applied also to the implementation of the "twenty-one conditions," by which the Second Congress had intended "to split" out small, pure Communist Parties from the large socialist parties. The pure Communist Parties were so small as to be ineffective, and the call now went out to enlarge them, even at the cost of some compromise. The slogan of the Third Congress became "To the Masses." One step in that direction was the creation, in July, 1921, of the Red International of Trade Unions (usually abbreviated to Profintern). This was an attempt to seize the initiative in the labor-union movement and to wrest the unions away from the International Federation of Trade Unions, which the Comintern referred to as the "yellow Amsterdam International." In December, 1921, the ECCI even promulgated a "United Workers' Front," but included enough reservations to keep the purity of the Communist Parties intact. But it did lead to trouble with the Italian, French, German, and British Parties, and the ECCI had to pressure them into conformity.

The Third Congress demonstrated beyond a doubt that the Comintern's role was primarily to bolster the foreign policies of the Soviet state. There was even some protest among the delegates to the Congress that the particular interests of Soviet Russia did not always coincide with the general interests of the world revolution or the needs of the various national Communist Parties.

The Fourth Congress, in November, 1922, was even less concerned than its predecessor about the imminence of world revolution. But a new factor had entered the picture: Soviet Russia was now an established major power, and the Treaty of Rapallo had confirmed its entrance into the community of world powers. As the hope of world revolution faded, as the Russian state gained authority, the subservience of the Comintern to Soviet dictation became more evident. The duty of the members of the Comintern was openly stated at the Fourth Congress as being that of strengthening Soviet power. The Narkomindel was to dictate policies from now on, and the Comintern was to use its resources to back those policies. Even the organization of the Comintern was made to conform with that objective. The members of the ECCI were no longer to be elected by national Party Congresses, but by the world Congress. A Presidium of the ECCI was established, and it in turn appointed an organizational bureau. The Comintern structure was now slavishly modeled on that of the Communist Party in Soviet Russia and was controlled by it. Whoever controlled the Communist Party of the Soviet state would control the Comintern.

THE COMINTERN IN STALIN'S HANDS

Stalin had little to do with the Comintern while Lenin was alive. Stalin's inability to handle any of the Western languages, especially German, was a major handicap in the early, internationalist heyday of the Comintern, and his lack of knowledge about conditions in Western Europe would have put him in a ridiculous position if he had tried to compete with Zinoviev, Radek, Trotsky, Bukharin, and other leaders who had spent most of their lives in Western Europe. Stalin, moreover, had little respect for, or confidence in, the efficacy of the Comintern, even in the early days of its existence.

The recognition of Soviet Russia by many of the major powers in the years immediately after the Treaty of Rapallo, the stabilization of the political situation in Europe, and the economic recovery of Soviet Russia under the mixed economy of the NEP all gave help to Stalin in his struggle with Trotsky and the "internationalists" of the Comintern. Stalin's advocacy of "socialism in one country" and temporary "coexistence" with capitalism appealed both to the patriotism of the Party members and to their desire for a somewhat less taxing foreign policy than Trotsky's "permanent revolution" promised. This downgrading of the role of the revolution abroad was reflected in the decline in the frequency of the Comintern Congresses under the aegis of Stalin. The Fifth Congress, in 1924, served two purposes: It backed Stalin against Trotsky and gave even more complete control to the ECCI. The next Congress did not meet until 1928, and another hiatus ensued, which lasted until 1935. In Lenin's era, the Comintern met every year; in the Stalin period, it met only three times in the nineteen years prior to its dissolution, in 1943. To Stalin, the Comintern was merely an instrument of Soviet foreign policy. The Soviet-dominated ECCI and organizational bureau could handle Comintern affairs without the various considerations raised by countless delegates from foreign Parties that made up a Congress.

The Chinese situation provided Stalin with his first experience in trying to control a foreign Communist movement, and the lessons learned there confirmed his objections to foreign revolutions not entirely controlled by subservient Communist Parties. On the other hand, it is doubtful if any Moscow policy—Stalin's or Trotsky's—could have won out in the Chinese maelstrom of the 1920's.

There was an embryonic Communist Party in China as early as the spring of 1918, and Marxist study groups increased in number throughout 1919. The Comintern sent Voitinsky to Peking in June, 1920, to organize a Communist Party, but he achieved little success. The First Congress of the Chinese Communist Party (the CCP), held in Shanghai, in July, 1921, likewise produced little hope for a future organization. In the meanwhile, the Narkomindel was trying to establish some type of regular relations with China. Chicherin was still collaborating closely with the Comintern and was willing to deal with both Peking and with Sun Yat-sen's Nationalists in the south of China. The consolidation of Soviet control of Outer Mongolia by the treaty of November, 1921, alienated the Peking Government, and the Soviet representative, Paykes, was thrown out. This forced the Soviets to turn to Sun Yat-sen's group. At the Fourth Congress of the Comintern, in November, 1922, the Chinese delegate stated that the CCP was in a united front with Sun Yat-sen's Kuomintang. Early in 1923, Joffe, a leading Soviet diplomat, who had again tried to talk to Peking, found that Outer Mongolia was still a bone of contention, and he went south to see Sun Yat-sen. They agreed that China needed "unification" above all, and the Outer Mongolian issue was quietly ignored.

By 1923, the Kuomintang and the CCP were running in tandem, although who was ahead of whom was a moot point. Sun even sent Chiang Kai-shek to Moscow in August to ask for military assistance and to discuss affairs with Trotsky, Lenin, and Chicherin. Mikhail Borodin became the liaison man between Moscow and the Kuomintang in September, 1923, and worked assiduously at reorganizing it nearer to the format of the Russian Communist Party. Early in 1924, Borodin, with Soviet funds, helped to establish a military training academy for the Kuomintang at Whampoa in Canton harbor, and Chiang Kai-shek became the commandant.

If there had been a confused situation in China up to this point, that of the next few years was decidedly more so. Chiang in 1924 sided with the Left Kuomintang, but from 1925 on, he began to fear Communist control of the organization. In 1926, the Kuomintang and Borodin agreed that it was necessary to unify China before anything else of a lasting nature could be done, and the Northern Expedition was agreed upon. But while Borodin was in the north trying to persuade Feng Hu-hsiang, the "Christian general," to join hands with the Kuomintang to facilitate the Northern Expedition, Chiang brought about a coup in Canton against the Russians and the CCP, hitting them hard. When Borodin got back, however, he and Chiang patched up their differences. This *mariage de convenance* did not last long, and in early 1927, while the Kuomintang forces were moving north, the CCP-Russian bloc and Chiang came to a parting of the ways. Borodin was forced out of the picture in July, 1927.

This was the skeleton of events in 1923–27, but what about the thinking back of the Chinese policy in Moscow? Stalin and his wing of the Party controlled policy from 1924 on, and they decided to work with the Kuomintang. In spite of the model of the October Revolution in Russia, they still held out for a national bourgeois revolution first, and the socialist upheaval to follow. As late as November, 1926, Stalin was preaching that the CCP could not operate effectively without a close alliance with the Kuomintang and that to organize peasant soviets to fight the Kuomintang Government would be folly. In brief, Stalin still considered the Chinese proletariat as the backbone of the CCP and regarded the peasants as mere allies of the workers. But although Russia had had a small proletariat to carry the Revolution, the proletariat in China was minute. Furthermore, throughout this period, Trotsky was prophesying that Stalin's policy of cooperation with the Kuomintang would lead to disaster. After the break with Chiang Kai-shek in the summer of 1927, Stalin did change his strategy; but when a Communist coup was attempted in Canton in December, it was a debacle, with over 20,000 Chinese Communists slaughtered. Stalin became very reluctant to cooperate with national-liberation movements as a result of this Chinese rout, and his Chinese experiences go a long way toward explaining his stiff, unimaginative policies toward the newly liberated colonies such as India, Burma, and Indonesia in the late 1940's.

Stalin directed a radical shift to the Left in Comintern policy at the Sixth Congress, in 1928. The failure of the "cooperation policy" in China plus the anti-NEP attitude at home were the root causes of the shift. Communist Parties abroad were now to fight social democratic parties as social-fascist movements—a policy that led to dramatic results in Germany. The German Communist Party, on orders from Moscow, treated the Social Democrats as worse than the Nazis, and thus split the strength of German labor. Stalin underestimated Hitler badly in the early 1930's, just as he did in the late 1930's.

By 1934, Stalin realized that Hitler was no interim *papier-mâché* dictator to be tumbled easily before the onward march of the Communist revolution but was, on the contrary, a dynamic leader with an ability to arouse demonic emotions in the Teutonic soul. Stalin was forced to look for allies to offset the rising power of Germany, a Germany that had a nostalgic yearning to expand toward the East, the traditional *Drang nach Osten*. It was not surprising that the Seventh Congress of the

Comintern, in 1935, witnessed another radical policy shift. The defense of democracy now became paramount, and Communists were ordered to work closely with social democrats, liberal parties of varying hues, and even conservatives if they were anti-Nazi. This was the era of the united front. The Bulgarian Dimitrov, fresh from his spectacular performance at the Reichstag-fire trial in Germany, took over the leadership of the Comintern in 1935, and Litvinov coordinated Soviet foreign policy with the new line. The about-faces of Comintern policies in 1928 and 1935 were vivid demonstrations of Stalin's absolute dominion over the so-called International.

After the Soviet-German pact of August, 1939, the foreign Communist Parties again had to reverse themselves. Now the official line termed Hitler the victim of "imperialist aggression," and there occurred the strange phenomenon of French, Yugoslav, Polish, and other Communist brethren mouthing justifications for the Nazi rape of their homelands. The strains within the Comintern were almost unendurable during this period, and many who were Stalinist stalwarts up to August, 1939, found the new line impossible to accept.

Stalin continued to underestimate Hitler, however, and the Nazi attack on the Soviet Union, in June, 1941, necessitated another reversal of the Communist line. The American Communists' switch from the slogan "The Yanks Aren't Coming" to the slogan "The Yanks Aren't Coming Too Late" vividly exemplified the newest gyration of Communist strategy. International Communism was again playing the familiar tune of defending the Soviet Union above all else, and there was no thought of turning the imperialist war into a proletarian revolution during this period.

The outworn Comintern was allowed to die on May 22, 1943. But even in its death, it served a purpose for Soviet foreign policy by acting as a token of the Soviet Union's new line of solidarity of democracies. The Comintern had long been a dummy organization. Orders from Moscow to the foreign Communist Parties were transmitted through the Soviet foreign missions or else sent by special couriers. The pretense that the Communist Party of the Soviet Union was merely another member of an international organ had been so punctured by the Soviet-serving policy reversals of 1928, 1935, and 1941, that by 1943, the Comintern's demise was long overdue.

THE ROLE OF KREMLIN AGENTS IN SOVIET POSTWAR EXPANSION

Although the Comintern expired with great fanfare in 1943, the Soviet determination to extend the area controlled by Communism was more adamant than ever by late 1944 and early 1945. An extremely tempting power vacuum was developing all around the periphery of the U.S.S.R. Iran had been thoroughly shaken up by the three-power occupation. Greece looked ripe for falling into the hands of the Communist-controlled resistance group, and all the rest of the Balkans and Eastern Europe was in a confused political, economic, and social condition because of the sudden collapse of the Nazi empire. The "revolutionary situation," so dear to the hearts of all Communists, was virtually forcing the Kremlin into action.

The areas on the periphery of the Soviet Union varied in the degree of their penetrability. Some, such as the Baltic countries, Poland, and Romania, were overrun by the Red Army and isolated from any contact with the West. Others, like Bulgaria, Hungary, and East Germany, were occupied by Soviet troops, but their incorporation into the Soviet empire called for more subtle handling. However, the main instrument of Soviet policy in all these countries was Soviet armed might.

In Albania, Yugoslavia, and Czechoslovakia, a different set of conditions prevailed. The Red Army control was weak, and contact with the West was possible. To send the Soviet armed forces into these areas to establish a military occupation would be to alert an already suspicious West. It was felt best to work through the local Communist leaders: Enver Hoxha, Tito, and Klement Gottwald.

Finally, in Iran and Greece, the Kremlin had no option but to work through the local Communist faithful. Greece had been more or less thrown to the British as part of their sphere of influence, and there were treaty obligations to move Soviet troops out of Iran within six months of the cessation of hostilities with Germany. The Greek EAM (Greek Liberation Front), with its ELAS (Greek People's Liberation Army), was a tool ready at hand to use against the British occupation and the re-establishment of a democratic Greek government. In Iran, the Communist-controlled Tudeh Party was available, and the Soviet forces occupied Iranian Azerbaidzhan and had a strong following among the Kurds of the area. Although Soviet expansion in these two countries had to be accomplished by indirect means, the prospects were not too unfavorable.

The Kremlin, moreover, had another tool to use in its expansionist program, a tool it had developed and elaborated within the Comintern—a faithful, well-indoctrinated band of nationals from each of these countries. Many of these nationals had been in Moscow since the 1920's, and most of them had held jobs in the Comintern. Although they were, or had been, citizens of the various countries now marked for inclusion in the greater Soviet empire, their first loyalty was to the Communist leader of the Soviet Union. These agents of Soviet imperialism have been variously labeled as the "Kremlin Fifth Column Gang," or the "Muscovites"—both accurate designations. They came into the future satellites along with the invading Red Armies and immediately set about resurrecting the moribund Communist Parties or establishing the nuclei of new ones. Former Nazi Storm Troopers provided a ready source of supply to build up the muscles of the new Parties. The Muscovites had been well trained during their years in Moscow, they knew the tactics and strategies expected of them, and they were responsive to any shifts in the Kremlin line. In the countries under Red Army administration, their job was fairly easy. A certain decorum was expected of them, but if brute force was necessary, it was available. Grotewohl and Pieck in Germany, Rákosi in Hungary, Pauker in Romania, and Dimitrov in Bulgaria were typical examples of Muscovites sent in to erect the façade of legality in satellites thoroughly cowed by Red Army bayonets.

In Czechoslovakia, the use of native Communists restricted the speed of Sovietization. In the May, 1946, elections, the Communists secured 38 per cent of the popular vote, and

Gottwald, the head of the Communist Party, became Premier. The Soviets had two advantages in Czechoslovakia: The Czechs still resented the Munich betrayal, and the peasants were grateful for the Communist-inspired postwar land reform. By early 1948, however, the reservoir of good will was drying up, and the Communists resorted to a *coup d'état* to gain full control of the government. A combination of internal subversion and the pressure of Soviet armed might on the outside forced Beneš to capitulate in February, 1948. Czechoslovakia was rapidly converted into a full-fledged satellite.

The Soviet movement to the south was not successful. Turkey had no domestic Communists to lend support, and the government stood firm in withstanding Soviet pressures from the outside. In Greece, the EAM-ELAS tried to set up a Communist-dominated regime, but the landing of British forces almost immediately after the Nazi withdrawal in October, 1944, threw the Greek Communists off stride and allowed the non-Communist government to get a foothold. In Iran the native Communists, the Tudeh Party, looked very formidable in early 1946, when they had the backing of the "government" at Tabriz under Peshavari, but Allied pressure, Iranian stubbornness, and the appeal to the U.N. jointly thwarted Stalin's gamble for access to the Persian Gulf. Stalin tried again in 1951–53 to make headway in Iran by working through Mossadegh and the Tudeh, and again failed. Apparently, these countries lacked the necessary requirements for a Communist take-over: They had relatively weak domestic Communist Parties (or none); they were independent nations and had no national-liberation movement to be exploited; and, finally, they were backed by the Western powers and were not isolated from Western aid.

The resistance movements that sprang up in the Western European countries occupied by the Nazis were powerful forces in the postwar readjustments of those countries. The best disciplined of these resistance movements, after June 22, 1941, of course, were those led and controlled by the Communists. They also provided the nuclei of strong Communist Parties in some Western European countries after the war, especially in France and Italy, and probably gave the Kremlin strategists exaggerated ideas of the "revolutionary situations" available for exploitation. Conditions were somewhat reminiscent of those prevailing in Germany in the years immediately following World War I; but, as in Germany of that era, the majority of the industrialized and sophisticated populations of France and Italy were not amenable to Communist revolution, either by *coup d'état* or by the ballot box. The Communists have still not yet taken over a single industrialized country by internal subversion alone. Czechoslovakia and East Germany were under the Soviet guns when they became satellites. In a letter to the apostate Tito in 1948, Stalin admitted that Soviet troops were a necessity in converting an industrialized state to Communism. Tito had made some belittling remarks about the lack of success of Togliatti in Italy and Thorez in France, and Stalin reminded Tito that, after all, Soviet troops had not been able to get on the soil of Italy and France.

STALIN, TITO, AND THE COMINFORM

The Tito case pointed up the necessity of getting Soviet forces firmly in control of a country if it was to be successfully incorporated into the Soviet empire. A state with its own armed forces and geographically separated from the Soviet Union was in a position to exert its own nationalism vis-à-vis that of the Soviet Union. Tito, a Croatian whose real name is Josef Broz, was a well-trained Kremlin agent with an impeccable record of subservience to the Comintern line before the war. Because of geography, he was forced to win his own Communist revolution in Yugoslavia with little help from Moscow. Moscow could do very little for Tito during the war other than providing advice, often worse than useless because of the Soviets' lack of knowledge about conditions in Yugoslavia. Tito's partisans were dependent upon the Western Allies for supplies and assistance, especially those from the British. It was late in the war, in October, 1944, when Marshal Tolbukhin captured Belgrade and linked up with Tito and his partisans. Thus Tito emerged from the war with a tight control over the Yugoslavian Communist Party and its armed forces, and in the process, he had been developing a strong sense of nationalism. He moved swiftly, and by late 1946, he was in total control of Yugoslavia, now a "monolithic" Communist country.

Stalin, accustomed to the effectiveness of Soviet control in the other satellites, expected to dominate Yugoslavia in a similar fashion. He tried to impose the usual trade agreements, overwhelmingly favorable to Moscow, and to check on Tito's Communization of Yugoslavia through Soviet police agents. Tito had his own police and felt that the large number of Soviet agents was an infringement on his regime. He probably had no intention of breaking with the Kremlin, but Stalin pushed the issue. The newly established Cominform (Communist Information Bureau), a successor to the defunct Comintern, denounced Tito in June, 1948, as a heretic, and a test of strength was on between Stalin and Tito. Under the cover of charges that Yugoslavia was not collectivizing agriculture at a sufficient speed (untrue) and that Tito was running the Yugoslavian Party in too dictatorial a fashion (humorous, emanating from Stalin), the Kremlin tried to persuade the Yugoslavian Communists to depose their boss. Tito, an apt pupil of the Soviet *vozhd,* moved quickly: Hebrang, Moscow's chief supporter in Belgrade, was arrested along with some of his cohorts, and Tito appealed to the Yugoslavian nationalists by posing as their David against the Russian Goliath. Stalin was enraged at this display of insolence, and the entire resources of the Cominform group were enlisted to crush Tito.

The break having become irreparable, Tito now proceeded to do those things Stalin had accused him of doing before the break: He allowed himself to be courted by the West and accepted aid from the "imperialists"; he slowed down the collectivization of agriculture in an effort to woo peasant support; he relaxed pressures on the workers through "decentralization"; and, finally, he accused Moscow of deviation from the true Marxist-Leninist doctrine. The resulting correspondence between Moscow and Belgrade provided the West with the unusual spectacle of two Communist leaders washing their dirty linen in public.

Nationalism of the Tito type could be a threat to the new

Soviet empire and Stalin apparently realized it. One of Tito's early crimes had been his attempt to work with Georgi Dimitrov of Bulgaria toward the formation of a South-Slav Federated Republic—an idea repugnant to the Soviets, as the very concept of blocs of satellites was a threat to Soviet control. Whether other satellite leaders had any intention of even faintly emulating Tito is debatable, but Stalin had been stung and he reacted in his characteristic manner—by purging any *potential* deviators. In 1949, Dimitrov of Bulgaria died in Moscow, Koci Xoxe of Albania, Traicho Kostov of Bulgaria, and László Rajk of Hungary were executed as "deviators," and Clementis of Czechoslovakia and Gomulka of Poland were purged from the Party. Only the most abject servants of Moscow were permitted to head satellite governments. Native Communists were suspect unless they continually demonstrated their absolute obedience to the Soviet line. In Stalin's concept, a foreign Communist Party was one that had no life of its own, one that was merely an extension of the strictly controlled Party of the Soviet Union.

Stalin's rage at Tito's "deviation" can be explained only by religious analogy: Tito was a heretic, and he threatened the monolithic structure of the doctrine as laid down by the head of that faith, Stalin. Heresies, such as Tito's, would lead to other heresies; the deviation of Djilas, Tito's deputy, seemed to bear out this thesis. If these heresies went unchecked, they might well spread throughout the satellite empire and even to the Communist Parties of other lands.

One peripheral benefit fell to the West as a result of Tito's excommunication; he then closed his borders to the Greek Communist guerrillas. The Greek guerrilla movement was already in a parlous state, and the loss of its Yugoslavian base was the *coup de grâce*.

COMMUNISM AND THE UNDERDEVELOPED AREAS

The Communist Parties in the colonial and newly liberated areas had undergone a bewildering era of tactical and strategic shifts from 1924 on. The swerves and reversals from 1939 through 1945 had been debilitating, especially for the Communists in

India, Burma, and Indonesia. This allowed the nationalist parties to gain in popularity because of their steadfast opposition to the Western countries in control of them. The position of the local Communists was further weakened when Stalin directed the Party faithful in India, Burma, and other newly liberated nations to attack the new regimes as stooges for the imperialists. Apparently his ill-fated collaboration with the nationalist Kuomintang in the 1920's still rankled. Zhdanov's hard-line "two camp" thesis, promulgated at the first meeting of the Cominform in September, 1947, left the foreign Communist Parties with no choice of tactics, let alone strategy. The *Great Soviet Encyclopedia* spoke of the necessity of national-colonial problems being solved only under the leadership of the Communist Parties, which meant little chance of revolution, in view of Stalin's lack of confidence in the ability of local Communist Parties to carry out revolutions without the aid of Soviet armed strength. The chief value of the national Communist Parties was to act as snipers harassing the opponents of the Soviet Union, and as such, they were expendable.

Near the end of Stalin's reign, there was a noticeable change in Moscow's attitude toward the colonial and newly liberated peoples. Mao Tse-tung's success in China may have been partly responsible for the new outlook on the problems raised by the burgeoning nationalism in most of the underdeveloped areas. Mao was exploiting the nationalism dormant in the overwhelming majority of the Chinese population, the peasants. But he was also careful not to alienate the other classes more than necessary. Even the bourgeoisie was allotted a niche in Mao's scheme of things. By this time, Stalin's lieutenants were coming to see the futility of forcing the local Communists to oppose the new national leaders of the stature and popularity of Nehru, for one. Nationalism and national-liberation movements in Asia, Africa, and the Middle East were springing into life, and the new leaders were riding into power by taking advantage of the new dynamism in areas hitherto mainly noted for the lethargy of the masses. If the Communists either fought against, or disregarded, the new trend, they were simply ignoring the facts of life.

Stalin's death, in 1953, freed his successors of the incubus of the Stalinist notion that neutrals were automatically in the pay of the capitalist nations. Khrushchev and his advisers promptly developed a new "Leninist" policy that regarded the national leaders as opponents of the imperialist powers and, therefore, potential friends of the Soviets to be wooed assiduously. The attitudes of these national leaders toward their own local Communists were their own business and had little bearing on their relations with the Soviet Union. The world now saw the leaders of many newly liberated countries receiving Soviet largess with one hand, while they crushed the native Communists with the other; Nasser's activities are a prime example.

Soviet flexibility on the foreign front developed to the point where no nation was too "feudal" or "reactionary" to be unworthy of Soviet friendship. Feudal Yemen now became a Soviet protégé, and Haile Selassie received the red-carpet treatment in Moscow in July, 1959. The Soviet leaders had only one requirement in picking their new friends: They had to have some potential hostility toward the West.

It was obvious that by the 1950's, the Soviet leadership had come to recognize the facts of life in the underdeveloped segments of the world. Through bitter experience, they had finally realized that the newly formed nations were highly nationalistic and that the leaders who had brought these nations into being were popular with their peoples. They also learned that the weak Communist Parties in these countries, victims of a quarter of a century of rapid Kremlin policy reversals, had no chance of seizing power by themselves, but that they could join the nationalists and help whip the anti-Western sentiments to an even higher pitch. This new approach was cold *Realpolitik* and showed a clear appreciation of the actual situation prevailing in these countries.

Communists, however, would not be Communists if their every act was not buttressed by ideological justifications. The Communist theorists, as usual, came forth with scriptural quotations to justify the new approach. It has been almost impossible to read a Soviet journal in recent years without coming across at least one article on Lenin's approach to the colonial and newly liberated nations. This flood reached its crest in the spring of

1960, during the celebration of the ninetieth year of Lenin's birth. Typical of the ascriptions of a Leninist framework to the new doctrine is the following:

> The movements which are transforming the face of the world are a real triumph of the idea of Leninism, of his whole revolutionary concept, which is based on the scientific analysis of the line up of class forces in the modern world. . . . When capitalism achieved its imperialist stage, it retarded the development of democratic processes throughout the world. The further development of bourgeois-democratic revolutions has become impossible other than as a struggle against imperialism. . . .
>
> Among the new forms and methods of colonialism are the military-political blocs of the SEATO and CENTO type, the so-called economic "aid" of the imperialist powers to the underdeveloped countries, the preservation of foreign occupation forces and military bases on foreign territories, the "common market" of six European countries, in which are included many African countries, and a number of other methods. "An especial danger for the peoples of Asia, Africa, and Latin America," emphasized N. S. Khrushchev in a speech to the deputies of the Indonesian Parliament on February 26, 1960, "are the various forms of collective colonialism." [1]

Although these are random quotes from an article picked at random, nevertheless they illustrate the method of creating new dogma. Stalin is in disrepute, so Lenin has to be resuscitated as the great authority. An apt quotation or two is abstracted from Lenin's voluminous writings, they are applied to a current situation, and then Khrushchev is quoted to put the seal of authority on the discussion. This game of evolving eternal truths on demand is now played *ex post facto,* and is used only to back up a policy determined by the real situation. Thus it is an aid, not a detriment, to Soviet foreign policy; a change in the situation followed by a change in strategy could easily be supported by new "truths" dredged up from the inexhaustible well of Leninist lore.

Once the Soviets had decided to ride the tide of nationalism in Asia, Africa, and the Middle East, they were faced with the problem of how best to influence these countries to their side, or at least keep them neutral, i.e., out of Dulles' numerous multiple alliances. The answer was obvious—economic and technical assistance. Most of the nations in question have populations that are outrunning the increase in food production, and living standards are declining from already extremely low levels. The leaders and an ever-increasing number of their followers are convinced that the only solution to the problem posed by this age-old cycle of population increase and starvation is industrialization. There is a strong probability that several years before the U.S.S.R. itself attempted such a venture, Soviet diplomats were impressed with the popularity won through aid to the underdeveloped areas—starting with Truman's Point Four Program, in 1949. But the output of Soviet industry in 1949 was hardly adequate to allow for sending much in the way of machinery and technicians into underdeveloped areas. At that time, there were many "have-not" areas within the Communist bloc itself.

It was not until 1952–53 that the Soviets were in a position to do something more than characterize American aid to the underdeveloped areas as "economic imperialism." In 1953, they made their first move by offering to contribute 4 million rubles to the U.N. Technical Assistance Program, and in the same year, Soviet trade delegations began to seek business in the underdeveloped areas. In 1954, the Soviets were supplying a mere $11 million in aid, but by 1958, this had jumped to $1 billion. In 1961, there was a sharp curtailment in the Soviet aid program. It was probably caused by a number of factors, but two stand out: The rate of Soviet economic growth was slowing and the satellites were becoming resentful of the funds sent abroad. By late 1963, however, the Soviets were again vigorously engaging in the foreign-aid game, with a $280 million loan to Egypt and $226 million to Algeria. Cuba was the recipient of several hundred million dollars a year—just keeping Castro's economy from going under has been a severe drain on the Soviet aid program. All told, the Soviets expended a total of $3.5 billion on foreign aid in the 1954–64 decade.[2]

Soviet aid is accurately pin-pointed and not scattered, and the number of recipients is quite small in comparison with the number of nations involved in the U.S. foreign-aid program. The U.A.R., India, and Cuba were the major beneficiaries in 1965, although Iraq, Algeria, and Indonesia have received large-scale Soviet aid during the last decade. The Soviet aid programs in Latin America and Africa are as much anti-Peking as "anti-imperialist," and many of the new states find two Communist groups fighting for their affections.

The Soviets have several advantages in this field, and some liabilities. They are untainted by any connection with the old colonial powers, they have achieved a startling rate of development in heavy industry, which they advertise widely in the non-industrialized areas, and they have given their recipients a very free hand in choosing the type of development they want sponsored. Furthermore, for the first time, these new nations have a choice of from whom they will take their aid. The Soviet loans have generous interest rates, 2–2.5 per cent, payable in local currencies and native products. Lastly, the Soviet Union has no political ties with the NATO nations, many of which are, or have been, colonial powers; the Soviets can, therefore, exploit quarrels and disputes among the Asian, African, and Latin American countries with impunity. Egypt and the Suez issue, Castro and Cuba, and the Arab hostility to Israel are examples of this advantage.

However, lack of experience in dealing with foreign countries, especially with tropical countries, has been a liability in the Soviet aid program. The piles of bagged cement on the docks of Rangoon solidifying under the tropical rains is an oft-cited example. The Soviets, who have a lot to learn in the art of packaging their exports, have also made a mistake in building too many magnificent stadiums, luxury hotels, and other spectaculars where they should have invested in economic activities that would eventually generate the funds with which to pay back the Soviet low-interest loans. In addition, the Soviets had to learn the hard way, as the Americans did, that the acceptance of aid does not guarantee the friendship of the recipient, nor support of the giver's foreign policies. This fact of life has been dramatically demonstrated in Iraq, Indonesia, and Guinea.

The numerous Soviet technicians and administrators who accompany Soviet aid and technical assistance give the Soviets an opportunity to get their agents into the new nations at influential levels, and the thousands of students going to the Soviet Union and other bloc countries for technical training provide an opportunity to influence potentially important leaders with the Communist point of view. Accurate figures are hard to obtain, but it is estimated that there are about 5,000 Communist technicians at work outside the Communist bloc, and that over 3,000 foreign technicians have been trained within the bloc. The new University of Friendship of Peoples in Moscow for training students from Asia, Africa, and Latin America is another step in this direction.

POLYCENTRISM

One of the crucial problems in the Communist world today is how to keep some degree of unity without a center of ultimate authority. In the period from the middle of the 1920's until 1948, when Tito was denounced as a heretic, Moscow was the acknowledged source of doctrine, strategy, tactics, and discipline. Any Communist Party that failed to follow the Party line as enunciated in Moscow was automatically guilty of deviationism, i.e., heresy, and the leadership of that Party was doomed. The rapid spread of Communism after World War II brought with it a new problem: How could the national Communist leaders be made to toe the Party (Soviet) line if force could not be used? The Tito affair dramatized the problem. Then came Mao Tse-tung's victory in 1949 and the problem became even more complicated, for here was a Communist country with a population three times greater than that of the U.S.S.R.

In the summer of 1956, the leader of the Italian Communist Party, Palmiro Togliatti, coined a new word, polycentrism, to describe this disintegration of Moscow's hitherto absolute power. Late in 1961, Togliatti became more specific and pointed out that "the spread of Communism to distant countries, and the great objective differences in the methods and conditions of work, made polycentrism absolutely necessary." [3] The events of 1956 in Poland and Hungary, followed by the open split between Moscow and

Peking, gave impetus to the development of polycentrism. The once monolithic Communist bloc no longer had a center. Instead, there were two major centers and several minor ones. The Communists now claim to be a "world system" of fourteen countries (the number varies, depending upon who is doing the counting) and well over eighty nonruling Communist Parties. But there is no generally accepted system to govern the international relations in this "world system."

Although the Sino-Soviet split has done much to accelerate polycentrism, the dispute is by no means the sole cause. The cultural heritage and national peculiarities of each nation that has a Communist government are bound to influence the Party ideology. Even the Communist Parties in nations not under Communist control seem to be succumbing to national or regional deviations. Thus the once pure faith is being Africanized, Asianized, or Latinized in the underdeveloped world, and conflicts are caused even between the Italian and French Communist Parties because of national differences.

It would seem that the leaders of the various national Communist Parties have eaten of the fruit of the tree of knowledge and now know the sin of polycentrism. One might facetiously describe the present Sino-Soviet relationship as the "peaceful coexistence" of two countries with different ideological systems. But the rest of the Communist world is busy taking advantage of the acrimonious dialogue of the two giants—in order to further polycentrism. Once the infallibility of the Communist pope in Moscow might be questioned with impunity, the satellite churches were bound to assert some degree of independence. The question is: How much independence?

14

Current Trends

The American reading public has been thoroughly deluged with predictions on the future of the U.S.S.R.—ranging from cheerful predictions of its imminent collapse to dour prophecies that the U.S. is approaching senility, while the Soviet Union is forging ahead in the full vigor of its youth. Scholars, on the other hand, have largely contented themselves with spelling out the broad trends of the past.

Unfortunately, in an age in which boldness and resolution of leadership in the democracies must be based to a large extent on an informed public opinion, scholarly descriptions of the Russian-Soviet past do little to educate the public about the dangers of the present.

By limiting the discussion to current trends, it may be possible to avoid not only the dangers inherent in making predictions but also the overcautiousness of sticking exclusively to the past. Current trends, however, are inextricably tied to both the past and the future. The problem of Soviet agriculture is a case in point. Khrushchev tried desperately to solve the problem, but the difficulties he faced were products of a long past and his attempted solutions were restricted by the basic tenets of Communist ideology. He left behind for his successors an unavoidable challenge—by promising so much to the Soviet consumer, Khrushchev nearly eliminated the possibility of returning to the "consumer starvation" strategy of the Stalinist period. The new leadership must attempt to fulfill the aroused expectations of the consumers.

Much of this chapter will be a review of the developments

of the last forty years, developments whose course in the future is generally obvious. The evolution of the U.S.S.R. from a predominantly agricultural economy in 1917 to a huge industrial power in the 1960's is one such trend. With its leadership driven by a desire to see a Soviet Union bristling with huge factories and studded with large cities, there can be no doubt about its further industrialization and urbanization. Another broad trend has been the consolidation of the Party's power, the development of a hierarchy of command with orders flowing from the top to the bottom; this system now has the sanction of tradition. The ill-starred attempt to operate the Soviet Union under a "collective leadership," but using tools that Stalin had forged for a dictatorship, reinforces the probability that the Soviet state will again be under one-man control. There will be interregna, and the source of the dictator's power may change, but the system demands a *vozhd*. The expansion of the Communist faith has been phenomenal in the past half-century, and although the rate of expansion may slow down in the future, it would be a bold man who would state that *none* of the newly emerging states will adopt the Communist system.

Some of the trends in the Soviet Union are measurable—to a greater or lesser degree. The economy can be measured by means of the Soviet Union's own published figures. Not always completely reliable, often biased to prove theory rather than accomplishment, these statistics are, nevertheless, accurate enough to measure magnitudes of economic progress. The geographical expansion of the Soviet empire is certainly measurable, although the consolidation of Soviet power therein is less certain. Soviet military power is known to some extent, but there are lacunae in our information in the very fields where the offensive threat is greatest.

Some Soviet trends can be classified as imponderables. The influence of public opinion on policy decisions is a particularly sticky one. There have been no Gallup polls in the Soviet Union —at least, none available to Western observers. Attempts have been made to poll Soviet escapees, but there are built-in factors that militate against using them as indicators for the Soviet population as a whole. Much has been, is, and will be, said about automatic changes brought about by urbanization and industrialization. This process demands a managerial elite, well-educated at least in technological matters, and it seems axiomatic that constant preoccupation with industrial efficiency and technical achievement must eventually weaken the ideological fervor of a large segment of the elite. There are other imponderables, such as the attitudes of the national groups in the U.S.S.R. toward Russian domination, the ability of the Party to confine the artist to the treadmill of socialist realism, and the maintenance of Soviet imperialism in the satellites by something less than brute force. The status of the Moscow-Peking axis is an imponderable in a class by itself.

ECONOMIC TRENDS

The most measurable, and the most measured, trend in the Soviet Union is its economic growth. Since 1956, when the Soviets first published a collection of statistics entitled *Narodnoe Khozyaystvo SSSR (The National Economy of the U.S.S.R.),* there has been a flood of Soviet statistics on industry, agriculture, and transportation, mostly in actual physical outputs instead of percentage increases based on an unstated figure in some previous year. The observer still has to be wary of biased figures and still finds himself looking in vain for some hard figures in important categories, but on the whole, he has entered the era of statistical plenty.

Khrushchev's repeated boasts that the Soviet Union was going to overtake and surpass the United States in gross national product (GNP) and even in per capita production converted the Cold War into a planetary endurance race. The first lap of the race, according to Soviet rules, was the fulfillment of the Seven-Year Plan (1958–65), and having triumphantly completed that lap the Soviet Union would begin to run neck and neck with the United States in the middle 1970's. Khrushchev's boasting was based on two assumptions: (1) the U.S.S.R. would maintain the rapid economic growth rate of the middle 1950's, and (2) the United States would continue to creep along at less than half the Soviet rate. Neither assumption held. The Soviet growth rate slowed down in the early 1960's and the U.S. rate shot ahead. By 1965, the gap between the two GNP's was wider than it had been at the beginning of the Seven-Year Plan.

How will this affect Soviet policies in the immediate future? For one thing, the Soviet expenditures on their military structure, a relatively fixed ratio of the budget, is already a strain on their economy. If U.S. military spending continues at its present ratio to GNP, the Soviets will be even harder pressed to match U.S. military growth during the next few years. In the early 1960's, Khrushchev entered upon one of his bitterest debates with his marshals when he insisted on cutting into military spending by reducing the size of the Soviet conventional forces. The marshals, however, dragged their feet, and the new leadership faces the same problem. The U.S. build-up in Viet Nam is not easing their task.

The economic prosperity of the United States and the somewhat dour economic picture in the Soviet Union tends to dull the edge of a valuable Soviet propaganda tool in the underdeveloped areas of the world. This is especially true of agricultural propaganda. How can the Communists brag about the virtues of collectivized agriculture when they are buying enormous quantities of wheat from their capitalist rivals?

Although the Soviets have economic troubles at the moment, the future may bring some relief. The first and foremost element in their favor is the determination of the leadership to continue rapid economic development. The problem now under debate is how to do this. The economy is doing very well in heavy industry and in fuels, especially oil and natural gas, and is making headway in the chemical and plastic industries. The big problems are consumer goods and agriculture.

The Soviet emphasis on the training of scientists and technicians is another advantage. Beginning with Stalin's push to produce technicians and scientists in the middle 1930's, the Soviets have continued to invest liberally in the education of this necessary element in the increase of the technological level of their industry. The present output of engineers, scientists, and technicians would seem more than adequate for a continued improvement in all phases of the Soviet economy. The Soviet educational system makes no pretense at being other than a training system to provide the human resources needed by the state, nor does it deny its elitist character; higher education is not wasted on inferior students.

Although planning techniques and industrial administrative practices have come a long way since the rough pencil-and-paper estimates of the First Five-Year Plan, at the end of the 1920's, there is a great deal of speculation, both in the Soviet Union and outside, that the whole idea of highly centralized economic planning is in need of an agonizing reappraisal. The Soviet economy is too large and too complex to be efficiently controlled from Moscow. Professor Yevsei Liberman and his followers advocate greater autonomy for the plant manager, and without openly saying it, they are really suggesting a change to a market system with profits as the main incentive to better management. Their opponents, the advocates of more and better centralized planning, argue that electronic computers and better statistical devices will enable Gosplan to solve the problem.

The outcome will probably be a compromise: a little more autonomy for the local managers, a rapid increase in the use of computers, linear planning, and input-output analysis in the Moscow headquarters, and a continuing headache for the leaders as they balance ideological costs against economic good sense.

Finally, the extremely rich natural resources of the U.S.S.R. provide a solid basis for further economic expansion. The intensive geological exploration of the Soviet Union has continually revealed hitherto untapped underground resources. The Soviets have progressed in the last decade from an oil shortage to an ability to export. This was partly because of the discovery of new oil fields, and partly the result of a growing capability to produce the pipe, machinery, and trained manpower to exploit the new discoveries. Newly discovered iron-ore and copper deposits in Kazakhstan, industrial diamonds in Yakutsk, and other resources in hitherto unexplored regions are all now, or soon will be, contributing to Soviet economic growth.

Most of these positive factors are offset by negative ones. The most serious threat to the continued rapid growth of heavy industry is the pressure for more and better consumer goods and a more varied diet. While heavy-industrial goals were largely attained in the Seven-Year Plan, consumer goods were way off target (see Table 17).

TABLE 17

SELECTED SEVEN-YEAR-PLAN TARGETS

	Actual 1958	*Actual* [a] *1965*	*Planned 1965*
Steel (million metric tons)	54.9	89.8	86–91
Oil (million metric tons)	113.2	236.0	230–240
Coal (million metric tons)	496.0	631.0	670
Electric power (billion K.W.H.)	235.4	492.0	500–520
Fertilizer (million metric tons)	12.4	25.2	35
Cloth (million square meters)	5,800.0	5,440.0	8,000
Shoes (million pairs)	356.4	482.0	515
Meat (million metric tons)	9.0	8.1 [b]	18
Milk (million metric tons)	58.7	63.1 [c]	115
Sugar (million metric tons)	6.0	9.0	11

[a] Actual figures for 1965 are based on the outputs for the first six months, as given in *Pravda,* July 26, 1965.

[b] Figure for 1964, as given in *Pravda,* January 30, 1965.

[c] Figure for 1964, as given in *SSSR v Tsifrakh v 1964 Godu,* p. 82.

The most galling shortage has been, and still is, in housing. For decades, the Soviets lived off their Czarist heritage and expenditures for housing were very limited. At the present time, a large-scale housing program is under way throughout the Soviet Union, particularly in the large urban centers. There can be little doubt that this step was forced on the government; the situation had become unbearable. However, there are some good economic and social reasons for the present building program. For one thing, the shortage of manpower in industry makes it desirable to attract rural youth to the cities, but the unsatisfactory housing conditions work against this. Bad as the housing may have been on the kolkhoz, in most cases it was as good if not better than in the cities. Secondly, the building of huge new plants demands a concomitant construction of housing for the workers. Thirdly, the urban population has shown a slow rate of increase, partly because of crowded housing.

Another negative factor is the necessity of replacing worn-out capital equipment. More investment will have to be diverted into the repair and replacement of buildings and equipment, which, in turn, takes funds away from new capital goods. This is especially true of plants and equipment constructed one or two decades ago, not to speak of equipment in the consumer-goods field that has been handed down from Czarist times. This factor, however, is not entirely negative, for the new equipment will probably be far more productive and far less demanding of scarce manpower.

The Soviet situation in natural resources is not quite so cheerful as the Soviet press would have it. The cream has been skimmed off many formerly rich deposits, and it is now necessary to use inferior grades of raw materials, which entail expensive preliminary preparations. Iron ore is a good example of this problem. The rich ore of Magnitogorsk has been used up, and the plant is now relying on ores that are hauled over some distance. Krivoi Rog ore has to be beneficiated, and even the taconite ore of the belt known as the Kursk Anomaly is beginning to be exploited. There are new sources of most raw materials in Siberia, Kazakhstan, and other recently explored areas, but the utilization of these resources involves either long hauls over an already overloaded transportation system or capital investment to build plants and housing in the vicinity of the raw materials.

The Soviet Union is also restricted by a shortage of manpower. The main reasons for this shortage are the backwardness of Soviet agriculture, which requires almost 50 per cent of the labor force, the heavy losses in World War II and the concomitant drop in the birth rate, and the low productivity of labor in many sectors of the economy. At the present time, the 1941–46 baby shortage is about to work itself out, but the high percentage of workers in agriculture and the low productivity of labor in many branches of industry are still problems to cope with. In the face of these problems, there was something of unreality in Khrushchev's promise of a shorter work week for all in the near future.

Khrushchev's promise to increase the quantity, quality, and variety of food will be a burden on the new leaders for some time to come. Agriculture is the weakest sector of the Soviet economy.

Stalin permitted only a minimal investment in agriculture and, at the same time, exploited the peasants as a source of capital for the forced industrialization of the nation. The result was an agriculture in shambles by the early 1950's, and although Khrushchev managed to raise total production temporarily by plowing up millions of acres of new land and raising incentives through higher prices for farm products, agriculture slipped backward in the early 1960's. Output per acre in the new lands fell precipitously in the last few years, the emphasis on raising corn was a mistake, and even higher prices did not engender enough enthusiasm to overcome the built-in liabilities of collectivized agriculture.

The Soviet diet was not the only reason for Khrushchev's beneficent attitude toward agriculture. Almost half of the Soviet population is engaged in farming—an extremely high proportion for an industrial country. The main reservoir from which industrial manpower was obtained was the underemployed rural population, and with the industrial sector of the economy literally crying for more workers, Khrushchev had every reason to raise the productivity of farm labor. His successors must face up to the same problem. One solution is to expand capital investment in machinery and fertilizer, to develop intensive farming instead of relying on the traditional expansion of the amount of sown land. The gross waste of manpower in Soviet agriculture is notorious, but it has been diminishing very slowly.

Khrushchev's tactic of raising prices for farm products, freeing the farmer from taxes on the products of his personal plot, and, in general, trying to improve living conditions on the kolkhoz had one specific drawback: It tended to retard the flow of labor from the farm to the factory. Why put up with crowded housing, several hours of shopping every day, and the eternal pressure to reach planned output if things are going to get better down on the farm? Khrushchev's successors will have to steer carefully between the Scylla of a too-contented peasantry and the Charybdis of removing peasant incentive.

The root of the trouble is the peasant's distaste for the kolkhoz and sovkhoz. The leadership in the Soviet Union, however, has always feared the independent farmer tilling his own soil—he is the little bourgeoisie on the make. A return to private ownership in agriculture, which is improbable, would probably cause temporary chaos in the Soviet economy as a whole. Willy-nilly, the new leadership has no choice but to find ways to raise outputs by making the present system work better. More machinery, more artificial fertilizers, insecticides, and herbicides, and higher prices may help. There was some evidence that the state intended to put $6 billion of additional investment in the agricultural sector in 1965.[1] However, in 1963 and 1964 the output of these necessities increased only moderately in some cases, and hardly at all in others. For example, tractor output was 325,000 in 1963 and 329,000 in 1964 [2]—hardly a startling growth rate. A hollow ring might even be heard in the cheery announcement that milk yield per cow in 1965 was up to 1,011 kilograms a year, the best yield in the last five years,[3] for that is only about one-third of the U.S. average and is way below the Soviet yield in 1958.

The relaxation of restrictions on private plots, an encouragement of private enterprise via the back door, may help fill in the shortages of fruit, vegetables, dairy products, eggs, and meat in the next few years. There are even suggestions that in some areas it might pay to break up the big collectives into smaller farms that would each be operated by a half-dozen peasant families which would be granted a good deal of autonomy.[4] A bit of Libermanism in agriculture.

The fact that more than eighty Soviet clothing factories and some fifty shoe factories are now operating on the Liberman Plan, i.e., basing their production on actual consumer demand and not a Gosplan quota, is one of the most startling trends in recent Soviet economic developments. Other changes are not out of the range of probability. Soviet leaders and economists are speaking in restrained tones these days, and there can be little doubt that recent downward trends in the economic growth rate are inducing some serious rethinking of the basic structure of the Soviet economy. It would be a bold prophet indeed who would predict just how the economy might be changed in the next few years.

POLITICAL TRENDS

The current political trends in the Soviet Union, unlike the economic ones, do not lend themselves to measurement. During the period of "collective leadership," when various aspirants to Stalin's mantle were jockeying for advantageous positions, a good deal of information leaked out to foreign observers; when a leader was tumbled from power, relatively accurate guesses could be made about which one of the four power blocs in the Soviet Union went down with him. Beria's fall knocked out the secret police as a primary source of power; Malenkov's forced abdication was a blow to the managerial elite; and the clean sweep in June, 1957, that sent the "anti-Party group" to Siberia and Outer Mongolia removed another large obstacle to Khrushchev's domination of the Party. Of course, there was still the army, and Marshal Georgi Zhukov's assistance in the expulsion of the "anti-Party group" seemed to presage an increased role for the army. Whatever role Zhukov was playing in the Presidium ended abruptly in October, 1957. Khrushchev seemed to have drawn all Stalin's power into his own hands.

There was one un-Stalinist aspect in Khrushchev's rise to power: None of the deposed leaders was executed. (Beria and his entourage had been sent to the block by the entire "collective leadership.") It may be argued that Khrushchev was more humane than Stalin, but his role as Stalin's hatchet man in the Ukraine in the late 1930's would seem to refute that assumption. Another theory is that Khrushchev could not emulate Stalin's tactics after so vigorously denouncing them in his "Secret Speech" to the Twentieth Party Congress, and, with more vigor, to the Twenty-second. But Stalin also protested at the thought of shedding Bukharin's blood only a few years before the horrors of the *Yezhovshchina*. Perhaps the explanation of Khrushchev's apparent leniency is the simple fact that he did not have the power to rid himself permanently of his rivals. Stalin based his power on the secret police, and it was not until the police were all-powerful that he ventured into the all-out use of terror in the late 1930's; the KGB of the 1960's is a far cry from the NKVD of the era of the Great Purge. Stalin, like Khrushchev, relied on control of the Central Committee and the Secretariat to gain ascendancy, but it is doubtful that Stalin could have murdered the overwhelming majority of the Central Committee with only Party support. An all-powerful police was the foundation of Stalin's absolute power. Khrushchev's power rested on his control of the Party machinery. When ousted by a majority of the Presidium members in 1957, he turned to the Central Committee, which overrode the Presidium decision. A precedent had been established, however, and in October, 1964, Khrushchev's opponents in the Presidium appealed to that same Central Committee to ratify their ouster of the chief.

The events of the last decade point up the difficulty involved in handing on political power in the Soviet Union. During a quarter of century of power, Stalin, utilizing the "democratic centralist" organization created by Lenin, built up a totalitarian governing machine with all the levers of power in the hands of the *vozhd*. The system was tailored for a dictator. The death of the *vozhd* in 1953 left the machine without its most important part, the boss. The flounderings of Malenkov and the frenetic activities of Khrushchev did not enable either to seize complete control of the machine. Periodical reversions to "collective leadership" have proven to be unsatisfactory interim solutions to a permanent problem. Sooner or later someone must put together a winning combination and become the sole leader, the *vozhd*. Since a single leader is unlikely ever to gain the absolute control once exercised by Stalin, the new *vozhd* no doubt will have to mingle persuasion with dictation. If he were to try to build up a Stalin-type police force that would make him independent of the Party and the armed forces, he would probably unite those two power blocs in an effort to unseat him.

The problem of the transference of power, or the succession problem, as it is usually called, is of more than mere academic interest. The problem has arisen three times in the history of the Soviet Union, and in each case the law of the jungle seemed to be the only code of action available to the contestants for supreme power. Stalin eventually wiped out the Leninist wing of the Party, and Khrushchev hung the dead albatross of Stalinism around the necks of his rivals. Stalin took some fourteen years (1924–38) to eliminate his rivals, while Khrushchev had only a decade in which to consolidate his grip—too short a period, it would seem. But even Stalin could not name his successor, or, at least, make his choice stick. Khrushchev was given no chance to do so.

The Soviet Union, now almost half a century old, has become a status society, and has the urge to become respectable. Continual dog-eat-dog struggles among the leaders threaten both the stability and the respectability of the nation. As long as the locus of power remains the Party, aided by the secret police, there is no way of avoiding vicious struggles for control of the Party machinery. Under the present system, it is hard even to imagine how succession to leadership could be legitimized. All the Party leaders, from the lowly secretaries on the bottom echelons up to the members of the Presidium, are selected from above, and it seems inevitable that a dictator has to be at the top of this ever-narrowing pyramid to begin the whole cooption process. The greatest danger to the political stability of the Soviet Union probably lies in a future situation where two aspirants for the top job are backed by nearly equal forces and might tear the state apart before one succumbed.

The two great non-Party forces in the Soviet Union today are the managerial elite and the armed forces. The leaders of both are chiefly concerned with the protection of their status and with doing their jobs efficiently, which means they are automatically in conflict with the Party—political officers interfere with military-training time and Party watchdogs in plants make managers nervous. Moreover, any new *vozhd* will have to strive to keep both groups reasonably happy unless he obtains the capability of using terror in the manner of Stalin, which seems improbable. Fulfillment of Khrushchev's promises to raise the living standards of the whole population, promises difficult for the new leadership to shirk, is possible only by reducing funds in some other sector of the economy, such as heavy industry, or by curtailing military expenses. These are dangerous alternatives, for any attempt to tamper too cavalierly with such vested interests could be explosive.

In their first year of power, the duumvirate, Brezhnev and

Kosygin, have demonstrated little, if any, ability to lead vigorously. At a time when the Communist world is riven with deviations and heresies, the double-headed leadership seems much like a caretaker regime in charge of warming the Kremlin until a real leader comes along. The new leaders are not even pale replicas of the Stalin-type dictator. Brezhnev has the bases of power in the Party through his positions as First Secretary of the Party, head of the Bureau of the R.S.F.S.R., and a member on the Presidium of the Supreme Soviet. Stalin ruled with no more than that. Kosygin heads the government as Chairman of the Council of Ministers. Competition for these top posts is undoubtedly furious, but because of the veil of secrecy that conceals the Kremlin struggles for power, the Western observer can only guess at what is going on. No candidate, so far, seems able to put together a winning combination and oust the present incumbents, nor does one of the incumbents seem able to oust the other. Suslov is apparently satisfied to work behind the scenes, a sort of Soviet *éminence grise*. Shelepin, who is young, ambitious, and exudes the aura of the executive, will be well worth watching. Polyansky, Shelest, and Mazurov also appear to be up among the contenders. But whether Brezhnev and Kosygin can be unseated, and if they are, who will do it, is a puzzle for the Kremlinologists. It may be some time before the succession problem is resolved. Following the serious illness of Lenin in 1922, there was a "collective leadership" for four or five years; after Stalin's death, the "collective leadership" lasted again for four or five years. Thus, we may have another four or five years of the present "collective leadership" ahead of us.

TRENDS IN MILITARY POWER

To assess the current Soviet military strength with any degree of accuracy, one must be a highly trained specialist, and it is hoped that the information specialists glean from reconnaissance, espionage, Soviet defectors, and research in open sources is adequate for the grave responsibilities that have been given to them. On the other hand, it is also hoped that they are adequate to utilize fully the information available. The nonspecialist must be satisfied to deal in magnitudes and generalities, basing his judgments upon open sources and that which the intelligence community sees fit to release. The paucity of accurate military information available in Soviet open sources must wring a reluctant respect for their skill in concealing vital data.

The advent of nuclear weapons, long-range aircraft, guided and ballistic missiles, and far-flung radar networks has resulted in an astronomical rise in defense budgets. It is estimated that the Soviet armed forces are allotted 25 per cent of the gross national product. Although the Soviets have difficulty in levying this huge tribute on their people, they have the advantage of doing it by fiat from the top. A democratic government has to raise its defense funds with the consent of a majority of its citizens, and the taxpayers demand evidence that the huge sums are really necessary. They have to be shown a convincing Soviet threat. This puts a democratic government on the horns of a dilemma: To overestimate the Soviet threat could cause a clamor for a hysterical defense build-up that might wreck the budget, yet an underestimation of the threat might produce a fatal degree of complacency and penny-pinching. Of the two, complacency and penny-pinching would seem to be the more dangerous; nations have survived outrageously unbalanced budgets, but it is problematical whether it is possible to survive an all-out nuclear attack.

The average citizen, long satisfied to leave things military to the professional soldiers, has, of late, been forced to concern himself with national strategy. His taxes and his survival are both at stake. Probably to his amazement, he has found the experts at odds with each other, often miles apart, on what constitutes a proper strategy. At the outset, the civilian is awed by apocalyptic terms such as "the end of civilization" and "mutual suicide," or by such vivid figures of speech as "two scorpions in a bottle" and "nuclear stalemate." If he persists beyond these ringing phrases, he finds bitter disputes raging between groups in the Pentagon, Congress, and the White House over whether the Soviets have a missile lead, and if so, how great it is, the probable effectiveness of their strategic-bomber attack, their ability to nibble us to death in limited wars, and other controversies that seem to generate more heat than information. The citizen's first impulse is to flee this Babel of conflicting views, and only the fact that his survival is in great jeopardy compels him to take sides in the debates.

The Soviet citizen may be equally troubled about his nation's strategy, maybe even more so, as he had a foretaste of all-out destruction in World War II, but he cannot participate in the formulation of strategy. The creation of Soviet strategy is the prerogative of the very top elite. The national objectives, the weapons systems, the balance of forces, and the amount spent on armaments are all decided upon by a small group of men in the Presidium and Secretariat. How much influence the military leaders have on these decisions is not known, but they must certainly influence the decisions to the extent that the Kremlin leaders, too, are dependent upon their specialists. In some fields, the military leaders may even have a decisive voice.

Any attempt to describe the military strategy the Soviet Party and military leaders may have arrived at is bound to be largely conjectural. There are some knowns in the problem, but there are even more unknowns. The number of Soviet aircraft, missiles, and submarines can be estimated, and probably not too inaccurately, but their intentions are really an unknown. Even more important, what do they think our intentions are, and how much reliance do they put on our public utterances? The present situation has some of the characteristics of a global poker game in which bluff may be as important as good cards if it is carried out with iron nerves.

Khrushchev, as early as 1960, decided upon the ballistic missile as the main offensive weapon, and he proceeded to belittle the bomber and naval surface craft on numerous occasions—even to the extent of referring to the bomber as a museum piece. The Soviet successes in their space program after 1957 may have made Khrushchev overoptimistic about Soviet superiority in the missile field. In his speech in January, 1960, he even called for a cut of over a million men in the conventional forces, stating that the increased firepower of nuclear weapons and missiles made this possible.

The Soviet military strategists, while under the threat of the United States SAC and bereft of any adequate retaliatory weapon, had a long period in which to contemplate all the nuances of surprise, counterblows, and pre-emptive attacks. It was probably in this period of being have-nots in the field of strategic weapons that they decided to put their emphasis on ballistic missiles. The advent of the relatively light thermonuclear warhead, which could be so easily married to the ICBM, was their long-sought answer. In a single leap, the awesome SAC lead was overcome, and although SAC could not be ignored, it could, at least, be matched as a threat. Stalinist military doctrine had held that surprise could not be a decisive factor in the outcome of a war, but Soviet military leaders began to throw off this incubus by 1955. How decisive they now think that surprise can be is not clear.[5] It would probably be evaluated on the basis of how secure the enemy's retaliatory forces were.

In the present situation, Soviet military strategists contemplating a surprise, pre-emptive, or "preventive" all-out nuclear attack on the West must take into consideration what they can accept in the way of retaliation. This problem of acceptable losses is intimately tied up with the psychology of the Soviet leaders, military and political: What sacrifice would be considered reasonable for an expansion of Communism? But in addition to the psychological unknown, there are some known advantages that accrue to the Soviet Union in this matter of acceptable losses. First, as Raymond L. Garthoff has pointed out, the Soviets' experience in World War II gives them the advantage of having actually undergone something like total destruction in large areas of the U.S.S.R. Second, the Soviet Union has the advantage of being a backward nation in some respects: More than 50 per cent of its population still lives in rural areas, and the urban population could easily be evacuated to the rural villages, especially in the event of a Soviet surprise attack, where the time of retaliation could be forecast accurately. The large metropolitan centers are separated by long distances in most cases; the Soviet Union has nothing resembling the huge urban area of the United States that stretches from Boston to Richmond. Finally, what the Kremlin strategists might regard as "acceptable losses" might be totally unthinkable to the men in the Pentagon.

It would appear from Soviet sources that most of the Soviet marshals disagreed with Khrushchev's new military doctrine and strategy, which he promulgated in 1960. The Berlin crisis and the resulting build-up of the U.S. military forces caused the Soviet marshals to procrastinate in carrying out the Khrushchev-directed cuts in military manpower. In September, 1962, a stir was created by a book written by fifteen military theorists, mostly generals and colonels, who had worked under the over-all direction of Marshal Vasily D. Sokolovsky, Chief of the General Staff between 1955 and 1960.[6] The book was the first full-dress exposition of Soviet military strategy and doctrine since A. Svechin's *Strategiya,* published in 1926, and the Sokolovsky work has been trumpeted in both the Soviet Union and in the Western press as the ungarbled word on the subject. Even a cursory reading of the book, however, reveals the word to be still quite garbled.

The authors, along with their director, seem to have worked both sides of the street in an attempt to please Khrushchev as well as their military consciences. The result was a compromise on many important aspects of Soviet doctrine and strategy. One authority, Thomas W. Wolfe,[7] has described in some detail the difficulties the authors faced in steering their course through the straits formed by Khrushchev's "new strategy," as enunciated to the Supreme Soviet in January, 1960, and Malinovsky's "rebuttal," given at the Twenty-second Party Congress, in October, 1961. Wolfe divides the participants in the struggle over Soviet doctrine and strategy into the "radicals," who, like Khrushchev, see the ICBM and the supermegaton warhead as the main ingredients of the Soviet strategical posture, and the "traditionalists," who regard the new weapons as simply another component of the combined forces. Both views are advocated in the book, thus awkwardly arriving at a compromise that is really an agreement to disagree.

The analysis of the U.S. strategic capabilities in the Sokolovsky book betrayed a growing realization that the U.S. military strategists were no longer taken in by the so-called missile gap. Confidence in the U.S. strategic superiority was growing rapidly in the West, and Soviet influence seemed to be waning by mid-1962. How much this had to do with Khrushchev's decision to plant

MRBM's and IRBM's as well as IL-28 bombers in Cuba is hard to prove; the chapter and verse are lacking, in the conventional scholarly sense. But the move did seem to be engendered by a desire on Krushchev's part for a quick adjustment of the strategic balance.

When the United States discovered the weapons, Khrushchev blustered momentarily, but when President Kennedy stated clearly that any nuclear launches from Cuba would be treated as an attack by the Soviets on the United States requiring a full retaliatory response on the Soviet Union, Khrushchev pulled his gadgets out of Cuba. Khrushchev's "new strategy" was based on his missiles and big nuclear weapons, but in the crisis of October–November, 1962, it was precisely U.S. superiority in long-range aircraft and ICBM's that forced him to back down. His marshals were undoubtedly humiliated and his mystique as a strategist, if he ever had one, was badly bruised. There are many facets to the Cuban crisis, but the damage to Khrushchev's reputation as a military savant is indisputable. The crisis led to a growing dialogue between him and his marshals in the last two years of his reign, and the marshals seemed to grow bolder and bolder in their criticism of his military role.

Khrushchev's fixation on reducing the military sector of the national budget, especially the part allocated to conventional forces, further exacerbated his relations with the marshals. Just as the United States was gaining in flexibility, Khrushchev seemed determined to reduce his marshals' options to one—missiles with nuclear warheads. As if chanting a litany, Khrushchev made plea after plea for new cuts in the military budget. At the December, 1963, plenum of the Central Committee, he came out for a $46 billion expansion of the chemical industry and a cut in the military budget. In February, 1964, at another plenum of the Central Committee, he again called for a reduction in defense expenditures.

Then, in a two-part article that appeared in *Red Star* in August, 1964, Marshal V. D. Sokolovsky and Major General M. Cherednichenko, the authors of the article, forecasted that World War III would be either a short-lived missile-nuclear exchange or a protracted conflict involving the combined forces on an enormous scale.[8] But, they warned, since it is impossible to know beforehand which of the two ways the war might go, a country must prepare for both. The authors thus came up with important missions for every branch of the service: There would be vital roles for huge fleets of bombers, fighters, and interceptors, for tank, infantry, and airborne forces, for both the surface and the underwater branches of the navy, and even for airlift.

Khrushchev did not take this lying down. In September, 1964, he told a gathering of international youth in Moscow that he had just been at some maneuvers in which tanks were used in large numbers. Those tanks would be melted before they got to the battle line in any future war, said Khrushchev, and it made him sick to his stomach to see such a waste of good rubles so badly needed elsewhere.[9] He was now hitting the "traditionalists" hard—but one suspects that even many of the "modernists" were not willing to go to the extreme of calling *tanks* useless weapons. In this way, Khrushchev actually broadened the base of the opposition to his strategy, and when he failed his real ordeal in October, 1964, probably few high-ranking military men were inclined to mourn his passing.

Brezhnev and Kosygin are heirs to a thorny situation in the military. The top ten in the military leadership have an average age of sixty-five, and to say that they are set in their ways is an understatement. The new, complex weapons, such as nuclear subs, ICBM's, and antimissile missiles, are extremely expensive, and if they are to be produced in large numbers, either the military share of the budget must be raised, or the conventional forces reduced. But even if the reluctance of the World War II-trained marshal to cut his conventional forces is disregarded, which it cannot be, there is still the argument that conventional forces are necessary to maintain flexibility. The 5,000-mile frontier with Communist China, and China's 700-million population, must be uppermost in the Soviet strategist's mind. Whichever way the duumvirate turns, they face the same dilemma that made Khrushchev's relations with his marshals so bitter in the last years of his tenure in office.

TRENDS IN FOREIGN POLICY

A discussion of current Soviet foreign policy ought to be confined largely to tactics, since the Soviet leaders probably regard their strategic goals as immutable. Of course, the successes or failures of the various tactics undoubtedly influence their strategic goals, not so much as to objectives as in timing. For example, the strategic objective of Soviet domination of the Middle East may be slowed by the obduracy of Iran, or speeded up by Nasser's clash with the West and a revolutionary situation in Iraq. Even the best-laid plans of the Kremlin can go awry because of a Hungarian revolt; and they can veer off in a new direction at the appearance of a target of opportunity such as the Castro regime in Cuba.

At the present time, the Soviets are finding their best targets in the uncommitted and underdeveloped areas of the world, and their worst problems in Europe. The defense of the free world is anchored in Europe—in NATO—and Soviet efforts to split the NATO powers have been unsuccessful thus far. No sooner had the Soviets succeeded in living down the Stalinist legacy of hard-boiled diplomacy illustrated in the Berlin Blockade and the Korean War, than the brutal suppression of the Hungarian Revolution revealed the indelible Stalinist stain. Furthermore, Soviet attempts to create a world image of a benign Khrushchev holding aloft a Picasso dove of peace were not helped by the Chinese aggressions against Tibet and India and the on-and-off bombardment of Quemoy and Matsu.

The key to Soviet policy in Europe is the German problem, especially Berlin. The Soviets have tried tactic after tactic to find a crack in the NATO position on this problem, and all have failed. A reunited non-Communist Germany is absolutely unacceptable to the Soviets, and a Communist Germany is just as abhorrent to the West. The West refuses to get out of West Berlin, and the Soviets fear that forcing the West out might mean all-out war. In the German problem, time is not on the Soviet side. The increasing prosperity of capitalist Western Germany is an embarrassing contrast to the limping economy of its Eastern brother. The movement of refugees from the East—a daily flood now held to a trickle since the erection of the dividing wall, on August 13, 1961—was more than merely an irritant. Many of the escapees were young and well-trained, and their loss was a blow to the economy of East Germany. It was probably this factor, as much as the over-all propaganda impact or the long-range effects on NATO, that prompted the sealing in of East Berlin. Violent attacks by the Soviet press on West Germany seemed to be a constant in Soviet foreign policy until 1964, when Khrushchev suddenly began to woo Bonn. He even sent his son-in-law, Alexei I. Adzhubei, to investigate the possibility of a *détente* with the West Germans—to no avail, for there seems to be no way to solve the German problem without someone losing badly. Poland is adamantly set against the return of the Oder-Neisse lands to Germany, and the Poles find it hard to visualize a united Germany not devoted to accomplishing just that. Czechoslovakia will not willingly surrender the Sudeten area, and the Czechs likewise fear loss of their land to a unified Germany. Both these satellites are solidly behind the Soviet opposition to a German reunification; they would also back the Soviet Union in the repulse of any German aggression. It would seem that the German problem will be with us for some time to come.

NATO, long the target of Soviet attacks and blandishments, began to generate its own fissures as General de Gaulle pulled farther and farther away from involvement in the organization. The good general seems to grow more obstinate as he gets older, and he was about as manageable as a bramble bush when at his most amenable. Luckily for the West, Soviet fortunes in the international sphere have been at their lowest during this period of befuddlement in NATO. Many would say, however, that it is a matter of cause and effect: Soviet weakness makes the NATO partners feel relatively independent and thus they become cantankerous.

Outside of Europe, Soviet foreign policy finds greener pastures. The postwar crop of newly independent nations in Asia and Africa, and the underdeveloped countries in those two continents plus Latin America, are facing severe problems: extremely low standards of living, burgeoning populations, and an ever-growing demand by their peoples that something be done to solve these problems. Most of the new nations are intensely nationalistic, and Soviet policy in recent years has been directed at heightening this nationalism, while the Soviet press deplores the "imperial" policies of the Western powers. But Soviet policy has a fertile field in this rampant nationalism, which has to feed on outside threats, and the old colonial powers are the easiest targets. The effort of the Western powers to keep the situation stable is a much more difficult task than the Soviet objective of creating confusion.

The Soviets, however, do have a positive policy in a number of underdeveloped countries. In some cases, they support the whole economy, and in others they undertake construction of a "demonstration" project. Buttressing Cuba's creaking economy is an example of the first, while finishing the Aswan Dam illustrates the second. To some extent these arrangements are quicksand-like. Once a huge amount is invested, there is little choice but to protect the investment with further aid. With the exception of Cuba, the Soviets do not seem to have good prospects for Communizing the chief recipients of their funds. Nasser belabors the domestic Communists with one hand while he takes Soviet aid with the other; India has a rather small, as well as a split, Communist Party, and the Chinese forays on the Tibetan border have not made Communism any too popular. About the best the Soviets can hope for in the short run is to keep these nations uncommitted and thus outside any alliance controlled by the United States.

The major problem in Soviet foreign policy during the last decade has been the relations with the Peking regime of Mao Tse-tung. The Chinese comrades not only have threatened the Kremlin leadership of the world Communist movement but have tried to dictate Soviet military strategy.[10]

Although the roots of the Sino-Soviet split reach back to the 1920's, or even to the territorial grabs of the nineteenth century, the issues in dispute, having been intensified during the post-Korean War era, came to a head in the 1958–59 period. The situation was, and is, complex, but the main points can be outlined as follows:

1. The Soviet Union, in order to keep China in the Korean War, between 1950 and 1953, had to supply the Chinese with modern weapons and to train them in the use of the weapons. This accelerated the development of the PLA (People's Liberation Army) into a professional army with a professional officer corps, which caused Mao some trouble, for the professional officers grew steadily less enamored of Mao's military doctrine. Only the heavy preponderance of old guerrilla leaders in the upper echelons of the army and the government prevented the scuttling of these doctrinal ideas.

2. Khrushchev promised at some point—probably in 1954–55, when he needed all the assistance he could get in his fight for power—to help the Chinese create a base for an indigenous nuclear capability. In October, 1957, according to the Chinese, the Soviets made some definite promises regarding this help.

3. In 1958 (exact time unknown), the Russians began to tie conditions to any nuclear weapons supplied to the Chinese. Alice Langley Hsieh has made the following comments on the situation:

> . . . it would appear that some time in the course of 1958 Moscow sought to bring certain aspects of China's military establishment under Soviet control. Soviet proposals, as some commentators have suggested, may have been for a joint naval command in the Pacific and integrated air defense arrangements (Crankshaw, 1961; Garthoff, 1963, p. 87). Or they may have included a Soviet bid for bases in China and joint Sino-Soviet control of nuclear weapons and advanced delivery systems on Chinese territory, or even for close military cooperation across the board.[11]

The Chinese balked; they wanted a nuclear capability, but not at the price of putting China's military and foreign policies under Soviet control. In any event, Soviet behavior in the Formosa Strait crisis of 1958 made the Chinese doubtful of the value of the Soviet nuclear shield. In fact, the Chinese could see that the shield might not even be raised if they were to adopt foreign policies at some variance with Soviet objectives.

4. Sometime in the 1958–59 period, the Chinese opted for a "go-

it-alone" policy. At this point (September, 1959), Marshal P'eng Teh-huai (a member of the Politburo, head of the Military Affairs Committee of the Central Committee, and Minister of National Defense) and General Huang K'o-ch'eng (member of the Central Committee and of the Military Affairs Committee and Chief of the General Staff of the PLA) were dismissed. Why? The evidence seems to indicate that P'eng and Huang represented the professional officer corps, which was against the "go-it-alone" policy in weapons production, and that they represented their colleagues too vociferously. They saw the military and political implications of such a policy. There is some possibility that an understanding existed between P'eng and Khrushchev.

5. In mid-1959, according to the Chinese, the Soviets welched on the 1957 agreement. The Chinese claim that Khrushchev did this in order to foster the spirit of Camp David.

6. During 1959, Soviet aircraft deliveries to China were cut back. In mid-1960, the Soviets ordered their economic and military advisers and technicians to return home. By the end of 1960, the Chinese were on their own.

7. Since 1960, Mao has had a free hand to carry out China's foreign policy, the main points of which are: to get the United States out of the waters of the Western Pacific, to get a favorable (to him) solution to the Formosan problem, to expand into the rice bowl of Southeast Asia, to get domination of Outer Mongolia, and to put enough pressure on India to cause her to lose face in Asia. But Mao does not have the tools to bring these policies to fruition. Even the explosion of two nuclear devices in 1964–65 has not helped much. China needs many more nuclear weapons than it has at present, plus a decent delivery capability. While the Soviets could go far toward providing these, their price, in terms of controls over China's military and foreign policies, is too high for Mao to pay. Ironically, however, the lack of Russian backing in the military field means that the Kremlin is to some extent actually dominating Mao's foreign policies. An analogy might be made between General de Gaulle's "go-it-alone" nuclear policy within NATO and Mao's within the Communist world. De Gaulle objects to sole United States control over the only tools that make a foreign policy meaningful today—nuclear weapons. The Suez

crisis, in 1956, was probably a turning point in De Gaulle's thinking along this line. Mao, for his part, objects to having China's foreign policy dependent upon the nuclear weapons of the Soviet Union. His "Suez" was probably the Formosa Strait crisis of 1958. Both the United States and the Soviet Union have been willing to provide their partners with promises of adequate nuclear protection, but the partners in both cases feel the price is too high.

8. Mao has now declared the Chinese Communist take-over as the model for all "people's wars" in the underdeveloped areas of Asia, Africa, and Latin America. The "people's war" in China established the universal law of the development of people's struggles everywhere. In early September, 1965, Lin Piao, the Communist Chinese Minister of Defense, published a long article in which he summarized the latest in Maoist thinking on "people's wars." The new ingredient was the extension of Mao's "encirclement of the cities by control of the countryside" to global dimensions. To quote Lin Piao:

> Taking the entire globe, if North America and Western Europe can be called the "cities of the world," then Asia, Africa, and Latin America constitute "the rural areas of the world."
>
> Since World War II, the proletarian revolutionary movement has for various reasons been temporarily held back in the North American and Western European capitalist countries, while the people's revolutionary movement in Asia, Africa, and Latin America has been growing vigorously. In a sense the contemporary world revolution also presents a picture of the encirclement of cities by the rural areas.[12]

Lin Piao then went on to accuse the Soviets of failing to back the wars of liberation. He was very specific in his accusations:

> The Khrushchev revisionists have come to the rescue of U.S. imperialism just when it was most panic-stricken and helpless in its efforts to cope with the people's war. Working hand in glove with the U.S. imperialists, they are doing their utmost to spread all kinds of arguments against the people's war, and wherever they can, they are scheming to undermine it by overt or covert means.[13]

There seems little chance of a Sino-Soviet rapprochement after accusations such as these.

The next decade will be tremendously important in determining the balance of power between the free world and the Communist bloc, and policy-makers will have to rely to some extent on guesswork if they hope to come out on top, or even stay abreast, of the opposition.

The world is going through three simultaneous revolutions: the scientific revolution throughout the entire world, a combined industrial-scientific revolution in the underdeveloped regions of the world, and a "revolution of rising expectations" among the masses of the have-not nations. The balance of power between the free world and the Communist bloc may well tilt in favor of the side that can win over most of the uncommitted third of mankind. Both the leaders and the masses in this uncommitted third of the world now have a choice: the managerial society of the Communist bloc, or the open, democratic society of the free world. Even if the leaders of the new nations are emotionally in favor of the more humane way of the open society, they may be forced by the urgency of their problems to try the short cuts promised by the managerial society. If they do not produce results, they will be pushed aside by those who promise quicker solutions. For example, most of the new nations need capital. The Russian and Chinese method of collectivized agriculture may not be appealing from a humanitarian standpoint, but it is one method of sweating capital out of a predominantly agricultural society.

How well adapted is the Communist society to cope with the scientific revolution? On the surface, at least, one is tempted to answer in superlatives. The Soviet Union resembles a huge corporation in many ways. Its management can determine where the nation's capital is to be invested and, within certain limits, can disregard immediate returns in favor of long-range objectives. Its educational system is centrally directed, and the flow of skilled personnel can be channeled into the areas that seem most essential. The three decades of education designed to supply the planned economy have produced a large corps of "organization" men, men dedicated to the national corporation. The hope that education will lead this class to question the ideological aims of their society may have some basis, but the technologically oriented education of the U.S.S.R. seems more likely to produce conformists than dissenters. As C. P. Snow points out, engineers are conservative almost to a man.[14] Although it may seem paradoxical, a conservative in the Soviet Union is one who stands for the *status quo,* i.e., the Communist-controlled state. The elite in the Soviet Union has been trained in both Party ideology and the technological disciplines, and as long as the Party maintains a favorable milieu in which the engineer can operate, there seems little hope of much opposition from the elite. Although we may not approve the aims of Soviet leadership, the fact remains that it does set up definite goals, definite challenges, and there is a sense of order and organization for the future that appeals to the "organization" man. The official ideology states that the past was bad, the present is only an interim, and the future is both certain and good. Thus, it is an innately optimistic ideology, an ideology that regards the physical world as something to be remade by man, and as there is nothing except the physical world in the Communist philosophy, the future is man's. There is no intellectual group in the Soviet Union that questions the values of the new technological world of the future—at least no overt group. Y. I. Zamyatin's *We,* a forerunner of Orwell's *1984,* could not even be published in the Soviet Union in the relatively free 1920's, let alone today. As long as the Soviet leaders can keep the main emphasis in education on technology, there seems little hope that the elite will question the values of Communism.

What is the present status of the arts and the artists? About a year after Stalin's death, Ilya Ehrenburg published a novelette, symbolically entitled *The Thaw,* in which he discussed such *verboten* topics as the *Yezhovshchina,* the anti-Semitism of the "Doctors' Plot," and the asininity of the Stalinist aesthetic norms. A year or so later, a young author, Vladimir Dudintsev, came out with his *Not by Bread Alone,* a novel in which he criticized the backwardness of plant managers and the bureaucraticism of the local Party chiefs. The Khrushchev "de-Stalinization" speech in February, 1956, seemed to encourage greater freedom in the arts, but events in Poland and Hungary in the autumn of 1956 led to a freeze. However, Khrushchev's decisive victory over the "anti-

Party group," in July, 1957, so filled him with confidence that he eased up a little on the artists.

The last decade has been one of ups and downs as far as freedom in the arts is concerned. The "downs" have been the result of two forces: The reluctance of the old guard—the artistic hacks who have controlled the arts for the last three decades—to let go, and the Party's concern lest the artists undermine the Communist faith by criticizing ideological fundamentals.

Nevertheless, in the late 1950's and in the first half of the 1960's, the cultural atmosphere in the Soviet Union has been far more exhilarating than at any time since the 1920's. A number of young poets have come to the fore, though they may be less interesting as poets than as free spirits. Yevgeny Yevtushenko, for example, has won world renown for his daring as much as for his poetry, and has traveled widely outside the Soviet Union as an advertisement of the new Soviet artist. His *Babi Yar* brought the subject of Soviet anti-Semitism into the open; his *Stalin's Heirs* warned of the Stalinism that lurked in the background just waiting for an opportunity to reassert itself. Some of the other young poets, such as Robert Rozhdestvensky, Andrei Voznesensky, and Vasily Aksenov, have been thrilling large crowds of Soviet young people with public poetry readings, sometimes given in stadiums to satisfy the great demand for seats.

In prose, the situation is ambivalent. The sad saga of Boris Pasternak is probably best known. His novel, *Dr. Zhivago,* was published in Italy—apparently Pasternak took the 1956–57 thaw more seriously than he should have. The regime hit him hard, and when the Nobel Prize for Literature was offered to him, in 1958, the Party made things so nasty that he turned it down. (Mikhail Sholokhov, who was given the Nobel Prize for Literature in 1965, was in good standing with the regime and could accept the award.) Pasternak was thrown out of the Union of Soviet Writers, and that is equivalent to cultural death in the Soviet Union. Although *Dr. Zhivago* is still unpublished in the Soviet Union, much of Pasternak's poetry has been issued since his death —a sort of posthumous rehabilitation.

While the Pasternak uproar was still reverberating, Khrushchev himself ordered the publication of the very controversial *One Day in the Life of Ivan Denisovich,* by Aleksandr Solzhenitsyn. Probably the difference in Khrushchev's approach was caused by the fact that Pasternak's novel attacked the Soviet Union as a whole and Solzhenitsyn's novelette attacked only the Stalin regime, one of Khrushchev's favorite targets. An even stranger event was the publication of a long short-story by Fyodor Abramov. Entitled "Round and About," it was published in the literary journal *Neva* in early 1963. Abramov's description of a day in the life of a collective farm manager in the Leningrad area was a devastating criticism of the collective farm.

In the fields of painting and sculpture, matters are worse than in literature. This is a peculiar twist; most often the written word is considered more dangerous than the graphic arts. But socialist realism, the Soviet aesthetic canon, is very hard on the "unrealistic" in painting—thus the "calendar" art of the entire Soviet period. There were signs of a break-through in the late 1950's and early 1960's, but in December, 1962, after visiting an exhibit of "modern art" in Moscow, Khrushchev rose to new heights of profanity and vulgarity in his descriptions of the art and the artists. Little was heard after that about abstract, modern, or any other kind of art that violated the dictates of socialist realism.

The events of the last decade seem to indicate merely that the struggle for freedom of expression in the Soviet arts will continue. The Party needs the artist; it is art that makes the propaganda at least palatable. But the artist cannot publish much or display his paintings without the cooperation of the Party. Thus the Party must give in a little, and each time it does, the artist will be quick to exert his creativity above and beyond the restrictions of socialist realism.

The other custodian of traditional values, the Church, seems to be barely alive in the Soviet Union. How large the religious ground swell beneath the surface is in the Soviet Union is not ascertainable. Again, as with the artist, the state has control of the channels through which a viable religion must flow. It restricts the number of priests and rabbis through control of the theological schools, and it also controls the number of churches. But even more effective, those who turn to religion are penalized by having desirable careers shut to them. When Hobbes described the state as a Leviathan, he had no idea of the omnipotence of the governmental whale once it was harnessed to modern technology.

Is all so black in the immediate future? Some observers of the Soviet scene feel that there is hope in the fact that the Soviet Union has become a status society. The "organization" men, unlike their revolutionary forebears, now have something to lose. They are, this argument goes, bound to become nervous about adventurous policies that threaten the destruction of all they have built up so painfully. They are bound to become less enthusiastic about the ideology and will come to regard the enormous Party machinery as a block to progress. The industrial administrators may come to believe that they can proceed with their job faster and better without the Party and its eternal preachments.

The Party seems aware of this danger and seems to feel that its salvation lies in a bellicose foreign policy. The spread of the Communist faith on one hand, and the image of the ravening capitalist wolves threatening the Communist fold on the other, provide a valid *raison d'être* for the Party. If this is a reasonable assumption, then the most fervent hope of the free world, the weakening of the Party within Russia, is also the free world's greatest danger, for if the Party should feel its control slipping, its most likely course would be an even more violent foreign policy.

The next decade will probably see a continuation of Soviet economic development at something like its present rate, and with the emphasis on heavy industry. Regardless of the maneuvering at the top, the Soviet political system will remain dictatorial. The present ratio of around a quarter of the GNP will be expended on the military structure, although the new weapons systems may allow further reductions in manpower. In spite of temporary periods when "coexistence" will be urged, the Soviets will continue to probe the free-world defenses for weak spots, and move swiftly if any are discovered. The most probable targets in the next decade will be the new nations; sowing confusion in Asia, Africa, and Latin America will cost the Soviets little but may bring large returns. Furthermore, the example of the rapid industrial growth of Russia, plus aid and trade to the underdeveloped nations, promises trouble for the free world. If ever a Toynbee "challenge and response" situation held promise or disaster, it is the situation the free world faces in the next decade.

Notes

Notes

Chapter 1: THE PHYSICAL SETTING

1. Admiral Peltier, "Servitudes de l'Économie Soviétique," *Revue de Défense National,* XXV (October, 1957), 1471.

Chapter 2: THE PEOPLE

1. The chief sources for the figures used in this chapter are the following: *Narodnoe Khozyaystvo SSSR v 1958 Godu (The National Economy of the U.S.S.R. in the Year 1958)* (Moscow: State Statistical Publishing House, 1959); *SSSR: Administrativno-Territorial'noe Delenie Soyuznykh Respublik na 1 Yanvarya 1958 Goda (The U.S.S.R.: Administrative-Territorial Divisions of the Union Republics on January 1, 1958)* (Moscow: Publishing House of "Izvestia of the Soviet of Workers' Representatives of the U.S.S.R.," 1958); *Pravda,* February 4, 1960, pp. 1–2.

2. *Communist Manifesto: Socialist Landmark,* ed. Harold J. Laski (London: George Allen & Unwin, 1948), p. 149.

3. Quoted in A. Pankratova, *Velikiy Russkiy Narod (The Great Russian People)* (Moscow: State Publishing House for Political Literature, 1948), p. 4.

4. "Natsionalnaya politika Kremlya v SSSR" ("The Nationality Policy of the Kremlin in the U.S.S.R."), *Fourth Conference of the Institute for the Study of the History and Culture of the USSR* (Munich: Institute for the Study of the USSR, 1954), pp. 141–48.

5. *Ibid.,* pp. 148–50.

Chapter 3: A BRIEF HISTORY

1. *Current History,* XXV, No. 144 (August, 1953), 65.

2. *Pravda,* March 27, 1965.

Chapter 4: COMMUNIST IDEOLOGY

1. *Sochineniya (Works),* XXI, 34, as quoted in *Kratkiy Ekonomicheskiy Slovar,* ed. G. A. Kozlov and S. P. Pervushin (Moscow: State Publishing House for Political Literature, 1958), p. 162.

2. *The Theory and Practice of Communism* (New York: The Macmillan Company, 1958), p. 13.

3. *Capital: A Critique of Political Economy,* ed. Friedrich Engels; trans. S. Moore and Eleanor Aveling (3 vols.; Chicago: Charles H. Kerr & Co., 1912), I, 836–37.

4. *Selected Works* (New York: International Publishers, 1943), II, 14.

5. *New York Times,* September 4, 1965, sec. C, p. 2.

Chapter 5: THE GOVERNMENT

1. *The New Class* (New York: Frederick A. Praeger, 1957), p. 45.

Chapter 6: THE LEADERSHIP

1. *Selected Works,* II, 47.

2. *Ibid.,* p. 147. Lenin's italics.

3. *Ibid.,* p. 62. Lenin's italics.

4. *Ibid.,* p. 149. Lenin's italics.

5. *Ibid.,* p. 155.

6. Merle Fainsod, *How Russia Is Ruled* (Cambridge, Mass.: Harvard University Press, 1953), p. 230.

7. *Mastering Bolshevism* (New York: Workers Library Publishers, 1937), p. 36, as quoted in Fainsod, *op. cit.,* p. 178.

8. Boris Meissner, *The Communist Party of the Soviet Union,* ed. and with a chapter on the Twentieth Party Congress by John S. Reshetar, Jr. (New York: Frederick A. Praeger, 1956), p. 10.

9. *Ibid.,* p. 68.

10. "The Kremlin in Transition," *Christian Science Monitor,* August 10, 1965.

Chapter 7: AGRICULTURE

1. *Narodnoe Khozyaystvo SSSR v 1958 Godu,* p. 345.
2. *Narodnoe Khozyaystvo SSSR v 1963 Godu,* pp. 356, 359.
3. *Ibid.,* p. 341.
4. *Ibid.,* pp. 168, 332.
5. *Ibid.,* p. 311; Roy D. Laird, "Agriculture Under Khrushchev," *Survey,* No. 56 (July, 1965), pp. 111–12; *Current Economic Indicators for the U.S.S.R.* (Washington, D.C.: Government Printing Office, 1965), p. 58.
6. *SSSR v Tsifrakh v 1962 Godu,* p. 249, quoted in Laird, *op. cit.,* p. 112.
7. *Narodnoe Khozyaystvo SSSR v 1963 Godu,* p. 141.
8. Lazar Volin, "Reforms in Agriculture," *Problems of Communism,* VIII, No. 1 (January–February, 1959), 39.
9. *Pravda,* June 18, 1958.
10. Decree of the Council of Ministers, *Pravda,* July 1, 1958.
11. *Pravda,* March 27, 1965, pp. 2–4.

Chapter 8: INDUSTRY

1. *Sobranie Sochineniy (Collected Works)* (3 vols.; Moscow: State Publishing House, 1927), II, 30.
2. *The Soviet Industrial Reorganization of 1957* (P-1569) (Santa Monica, Calif.: The RAND Corporation, December, 1958), p. 12.
3. *Pravda,* May 8, 1957.
4. *Ibid.*
5. *Works* (Moscow: Foreign Languages Publishing House, 1955), XII, 342.
6. *Aspects of the Informal Social Organization of Russian Industry* (Mimeographed; Maxwell Air Force Base, Ala.: Human Resources Research Institute, 1952), pp. 37–38.
7. *Krasnaya Zvezda* (*Red Star*), October 2, 1965, pp. 1–2.
8. P. E. Lydolph and T. Shabad, "The Oil and Gas Industries in the U.S.S.R.," *Annals of the Association of American Geographers,* December, 1960, p. 474; *Narodnoe Khozyaystvo SSSR v 1963 Godu,* p. 150.
9. V. Veyts, "Elektrifikatsiya SSSR za 40 let" ("The Electrification of the U.S.S.R. During the Last 40 Years"), *Voprosy Ekonomiki* (*Problems of Economics*), No. 10 (October, 1957), p. 40.

Chapter 9: TRANSPORTATION

1. *Promyshlennost SSSR: Statisticheskiy Sbornik (The Industry of the U.S.S.R.: A Statistical Collection)* (Moscow: State Statistical Publishing House, 1957), p. 9.

2. *Transport i Svyaz SSSR: Statisticheskiy Sbornik (Transport and Communications in the U.S.S.R.: A Statistical Collection)* (Moscow: State Statistical Publishing House, 1957), pp. 48, 52.

3. *Narodnoe Khozyaystvo SSSR v 1958 Godu,* pp. 624–25.

4. *Narodnoe Khozyaystvo SSSR v 1963 Godu,* p. 420; *Pravda,* January 30, 1965, p. 2.

5. A. Lebed, "The Development of Soviet Highway Transportation," *Bulletin,* Institute for the Study of the U.S.S.R., III, No. 12 (December, 1956), 24.

6. *Pravda,* January 30, 1965, p. 1.

7. *Narodnoe Khozyaystvo SSSR v 1963 Godu,* p. 332.

8. *Ibid.,* pp. 421–22; *World Almanac 1965,* p. 702.

9. Lebed, *op. cit.,* p. 26.

10. *Ibid.,* p. 30.

11. *Planovoye Khozyaystvo* (*Planned Economy*), No. 4 (April, 1965), pp. 3–10.

12. *Pravda,* May 18, 1965, p. 2.

13. *Narodnoe Khozyaystvo SSSR v 1963 Godu,* pp. 373–74.

14. *Bolshaya Sovetskaya Entsiklopediya* (*Great Soviet Encyclopedia*) (2d ed.; Moscow: State Scientific Publishing House, 1951), VIII, 523.

15. Quoted in *Bolshaya Sovetskaya Entsiklopediya,* VIII, 523.

16. *Gosudarstvenniy Plan Razvitiya Narodnogo Khozyaystva SSSR na 1941 God* (*State Plan for Developing the National Economy of the U.S.S.R. in the Year 1941*) ("American Council of Learned Societies Reprints," Russian Series No. 30 [Baltimore: Universal Press, 1951]), p. 478.

17. H. J. Coleman, "Aeroflot Changing to Rear-Jet Aircraft," *Aviation Week,* March 19, 1962, p. 43.

18. *Krasnaya Zvezda,* February 9, 1963, p. 2.

19. *Pravda,* January 30, 1965, p. 2.

20. *Ibid.,* July 26, 1965, p. 2.

21. *Interavia,* No. 2 (February, 1962), pp. 202–3.

22. *Ibid.,* No. 10 (October, 1964), p. 1496.

23. *Bolshaya Sovetskaya Entsiklopediya,* VIII, 529.

Chapter 10: EDUCATION

1. *Pravda,* February 4, 1960.
2. Nicholas DeWitt, "Upheaval in Education," *Problems of Communism,* VIII, No. 1 (January–February, 1959), 25–34.
3. *Pravda,* January 22, 1960.
4. *Christian Science Monitor,* July 24, 1965.
5. *Pravda,* August 13, 1964, p. 1.
6. Quoted in A. L. Weeks, Jr., "The Boarding School," *Survey,* No. 56 (July, 1965), p. 84.
7. *Ibid.,* p. 85.
8. *Pravda,* January 30 and July 26, 1965.
9. *Ibid.,* January 22, 1960.
10. *Ibid.,* January 30, 1965.
11. *Bolshaya Sovetskaya Entsiklopediya* (2d ed.; Moscow: State Scientific Publishing House, 1961), IX, 514.
12. *Pravda,* January 30, 1965.
13. Nicholas DeWitt, *Soviet Professional Manpower: Its Education, Training, and Supply* (Washington, D.C.: National Science Foundation, 1955), p. 119.
14. *Narodnoe Khozyaystvo SSSR v 1963 Godu,* p. 589.
15. *Ibid.,* p. 594.
16. *Loc. cit.*
17. *Pravda,* April 9, 1961.
18. *Ibid.,* April 12, 1961.
19. James M. Swanson, "Reorganization: 1963," *Survey,* No. 52 (July, 1964), pp. 37, 39.
20. *Ibid.,* p. 40.
21. *Narodnoe Khozyaystvo SSSR v 1956 Godu,* p. 222.
22. *Narodnoe Khozyaystvo SSSR v 1963 Godu,* p. 556.
23. Nicholas DeWitt, *Soviet Professional Manpower,* p. 176.
24. *Narodnoe Khozyaystvo SSSR v 1963 Godu,* p. 556.
25. *Ibid.,* pp. 588–89.
26. *Pravda,* January 30, 1965.
27. Boris Gorokhoff, *Materials for the Study of Soviet Specialized Education* (mimeographed; Washington, D.C.: National Research Council, 1952), pp. 31–33.

Chapter 11: THE ARMED FORCES

1. Boris N. Yakovlev and I. P. Barbashin, *Vazhneyshie Daty Geroicheskoy Istorii Vooruzhennykh Sil SSSR (Outstanding Dates in the Heroic History of the Armed Forces of the U.S.S.R.)* (Moscow: DOSAAF Publishing House, 1958), pp. 19–20.

2. B. L. Simakov and I. F. Shipilov, *Vozdushnyy Flot Strany Sovetov (Air Fleet of the Land of the Soviets)* (Moscow: Military Publishing House of the Ministry of Defense of the U.S.S.R., 1958), p. 455; Yakovlev and Barbashin, *op. cit.*, pp. 200–201.

3. G. A. Tokaev, *Comrade X,* trans. Alec Brown (London: The Harvill Press, 1956), p. 326.

4. *Ibid.*, p. 319.

5. *New York Times,* January 14, 1960.

6. *Ibid.*, February 20, 1961.

7. *The Military Balance: 1964–1965* (London: Institute for Strategic Studies, 1964), p. 3.

Chapter 12: FOREIGN POLICY

1. *A History of Soviet Russia: The Bolshevik Revolution, 1917–1923* (New York: The Macmillan Company, 1953), III, 304.

2. *Nazi-Soviet Relations, 1939–1941: Documents from the Archives of the German Foreign Office,* ed. Raymond J. Sontag and J. S. Beddie (Washington, D.C.: Department of State, 1948), p. 76.

3. G. F. Hudson, R. Lowenthal, and R. MacFarquhar, *The Sino-Soviet Dispute: Documented and Analyzed* (New York: Frederick A. Praeger, 1961), pp. 132–41.

Chapter 13: INTERNATIONAL COMMUNISM

1. G. Skorov, "Torzhestvo Leninizma i Narody Vostoka" ("The Triumph of Leninism and the Peoples of the East"), *Mezhdunarodnye Otnosheniya (World Economy and International Relations),* No. 4 (April, 1960), pp. 24–31.

2. M. I. Goldman, "A Balance Sheet of Soviet Foreign Aid," *Foreign Affairs,* XLIII, No. 2 (January, 1965), 349.

3. W. Z. Laqueur, "The Schism," in W. Z. Laqueur and L. Labedz, *Polycentrism: The New Factor in International Communism* (New York: Frederick A. Praeger, 1962), pp. 2–3.

Chapter 14: CURRENT TRENDS

1. *Christian Science Monitor,* July 13, 1965.
2. *SSSR v Tsifrakh v 1964 Godu,* p. 56.
3. *Pravda,* July 26, 1965, p. 2.
4. V. Zhulin, in *Komsomolskaya Pravda,* as cited in *Christian Science Monitor,* August 23, 1965.
5. This topic has been exhaustively discussed in Raymond L. Garthoff, *Soviet Strategy in the Nuclear Age* (Rev. ed.; New York: Frederick A. Praeger, 1962) and H. S. Dinerstein, *War and the Soviet Union* (New York: Frederick A. Praeger, 1959).
6. V. D. Sokolovsky (ed.), *Voennaya Strategiya* (*Military Strategy*) (Moscow: Voenizdat, 1962); *Military Strategy: Soviet Doctrine and Concepts* (New York: Frederick A. Praeger, 1963).
7. Thomas W. Wolfe, "A First Reaction to the New Soviet Book 'Military Strategy' " (mimeographed; Santa Monica, Calif.: The RAND Corporation, February, 1963).
8. "Voennoe Iskusstvo na Novom Etape" ("A New Stage in Military Art"), *Krasnaya Zvezda* (*Red Star*), August 25 and August 28, 1964.
9. *Pravda,* September 22, 1964.
10. G. F. Hudson, R. Lowenthal, and R. MacFarquhar, *The Sino-Soviet Dispute,* pp. 132–41.
11. Alice Langley Hsieh, "The Sino-Soviet Nuclear Dialogue: 1963," *Journal of Conflict,* VIII, No. 2 (June, 1964), 112. The Crankshaw article quoted in the Langley piece appeared in *The Observer,* February 12 and 19, 1961; the Garthoff article, entitled "Sino-Soviet Military Relations," appeared in *The Annals,* Vol. CCCXLIX (September, 1963).
12. *New York Times,* September 4, 1965, sec. C, p. 2.
13. *Loc. cit.*
14. C. P. Snow, *The Two Cultures and the Scientific Revolution* (New York: Cambridge University Press, 1959), p. 33.

Suggested Reading

Suggested Reading

Chapter 1: THE PHYSICAL SETTING

BALZAK, S. S.; VASYUTIN, V. F.; and FEIGIN, Y. G. *Economic Geography of the USSR.* American edition edited by CHAUNCY D. HARRIS. Translated by ROBERT M. HANKIN and OLGA ADLER TITELBAUM. New York: The Macmillan Company, 1949.

BARANSKY, NIKOLAI NIKOLAEVICH. *Economic Geography of the U.S.S.R.* Moscow: Foreign Languages Publishing House, 1956.

BERG, LEV SEMYONOVICH. *Natural Regions of the U.S.S.R.* (American Council of Learned Societies Translation Project.) New York: The Macmillan Company, 1950.

CRESSEY, GEORGE BABCOCK. *The Basis of Soviet Strength.* New York: McGraw-Hill Book Company, 1945.

FITZSIMMONS, T., *et al. R.S.F.S.R.: Russian Soviet Federated Socialist Republic.* 2 vols. New Haven, Conn.: Human Relations Area Files Press, 1957.

GREGORY, J. S., and SHAVE, D. W. *The U.S.S.R.: A Geographic Survey.* New York: John Wiley & Sons, 1946.

JORRÉ, GEORGES. *The Soviet Union, the Land, and Its People.* Translated by E. D. LABORDE. London and New York: Longmans, Green & Co., 1950.

KRYPTON, CONSTANTINE. *The Northern Sea Route and the Economy of the Soviet North.* New York: Frederick A. Praeger, 1956.

LYDOLPH, PAUL R. *Geography of the U.S.S.R.* New York: John Wiley & Sons, 1964.

MELLOR, ROY E. H. *Geography of the U.S.S.R.* New York: St Martin's Press, 1964.

MIKHAILOV, N. N., and POKSHISHEVSKY, V. *Soviet Russia; The Land and Its People.* Translated by G. H. HANNA. New York: Sheridan House, 1948.

MIROV, N. T. *Geography of Russia.* New York: John Wiley & Sons, 1951.

SHABAD, THEODORE. *Geography of the USSR: A Regional Survey.* New York: Columbia University Press, 1951.

SUSLOV, S. P. *Physical Geography of Asiatic Russia.* Translated by NOAH D. GERSHEVSKY. San Francisco: W. H. Freeman & Co., 1961.

THIEL, ERICH. *The Soviet Far East: A Survey of Its Physical and Economic Geography.* Translated by ANNELIE and RALPH M. ROOKWOOD. New York: Frederick A. Praeger, 1957.

Chapter 2: THE PEOPLE

ARMSTRONG, JOHN A. *Ukrainian Nationalism, 1939–1945.* New York: Columbia University Press, 1955.

ASPATURIAN, V. V. *The Union Republics in Soviet Departments.* Geneva: Droz, 1960.

BARGHOORN, FREDERICK C. *Soviet Russian Nationalism.* New York: Oxford University Press, 1956.

CAROE, SIR OLAF K. *Soviet Empire: The Turks of Central Asia and Stalinism.* New York: The Macmillan Company, 1953.

CONQUEST, ROBERT. *The Soviet Deportation of Nationalities.* New York: St Martin's Press, 1960.

DMYTRYSHYN, BASIL. *Moscow and the Ukraine, 1918–1953.* New York: Bookman Associates, 1956.

GOLDBERG, B. Z. *The Jewish Problem in the Soviet Union.* New York: Crown Publishers, 1961.

HOSTLER, CHARLES WARREN. *Turkism and the Soviets: The Turks of the World and Their Political Objectives.* New York: Frederick A. Praeger, 1957.

KAMENZADEH, F. *The Struggle for Transcaucasia, 1917–1921.* New York: Philosophical Library, 1951.

KOLARZ, WALTER. *The Peoples of the Soviet Far East.* New York: Frederick A. Praeger, 1954.

———. *Russia and Her Colonies.* New York: Frederick A. Praeger, 1952.

LORIMER, FRANK. *The Population of the Soviet Union: History and Prospects.* Geneva: League of Nations, 1946.

MANNING, CLARENCE. *Ukraine Under the Soviets.* New York: Bookman Associates, 1953.

MATTHEWS, W. K. *Languages of the U.S.S.R.* London: Cambridge University Press, 1951.

PARK, ALEXANDER G. *Bolshevism in Turkestan, 1917–1927*. New York: Columbia University Press, 1957.

PIPES, RICHARD EDGAR. *The Formation of the Soviet Union: Communism and Nationalism, 1917–1923*. Rev. ed.; Cambridge, Mass.: Harvard University Press, 1964.

SCHWARZ, SOLOMON M. *The Jews in the Soviet Union*. Syracuse, N.Y.: Syracuse University Press, 1951.

STALIN, JOSEPH. *Marxism and the National Question*. New York: International Publishers, 1942.

VAKAR, NICHOLAS PLATONOVICH. *Belorussia: The Making of a Nation—A Case Study*. Cambridge, Mass.: Harvard University Press, 1956.

ZENKOVSKY, SERGE ALEXANDER. *Pan-Turkism and Islam in Russia*. Cambridge, Mass.: Harvard University Press, 1960.

Chapter 3: A BRIEF HISTORY

CARR, EDWARD HALLETT. *A History of Soviet Russia: The Bolshevik Revolution, 1917–1923*. 3 vols. New York: The Macmillan Company, 1951–53.

———. *A History of Soviet Russia: The Interregnum, 1923–1924*. N York: The Macmillan Company, 1954.

CHAMBERLIN, W. H. *The Russian Revolution, 1917–1921*. 2 vols York: The Macmillan Company, 1935.

CLARKSON, JESSE D. *A History of Russia*. New York: Randor 1961.

CONQUEST, ROBERT. *Russia After Khrushchev*. New York: Praeger, 1965.

FLORINSKY, MICHAEL T. *Russia: A History and Interpr* New York: The Macmillan Company, 1953.

HARCAVE, SIDNEY. *Russia: A History*. 4th ed., rev. P Lippincott Company, 1959.

KENNAN, GEORGE F. *Soviet-American Relations* Princeton, N.J.: Princeton University Press,

KLYUCHEVSKY, VASILI. *History of Russia*. 5 v HOGARTH. New York: E. P. Dutton & York: Russell & Russell, 1960. (Klyuch is the best history of Russia up to century, but Hogarth's translation i

KORNILOV, A. *Modern Russian Histc*

the Great to the End of the Nineteenth Century. Translated by A. S. KAUN. New York: Alfred A. Knopf, 1943.

PARES, SIR BERNARD. *A History of Russia.* 5th ed. New York: Alfred A. Knopf, 1953.

PIPES, RICHARD EDGAR. *The Formation of the Soviet Union: Communism and Nationalism, 1917–1923.* Rev. ed.; Cambridge, Mass.: Harvard University Press, 1964.

REED, JOHN. *Ten Days That Shook the World.* New York: Boni and Liveright, 1919; New York: The Modern Library, 1935.

RIASANOVSKY, NICHOLAS V. *A History of Russia.* New York: Oxford University Press, 1963.

RUSH, MYRON. *Political Succession in the U.S.S.R.* New York: Columbia University Press, 1965.

SCHAPIRO, LEONARD. *The Origin of the Communist Autocracy: Political Opposition in the Soviet State: First Phase, 1917–1922.* New York: Frederick A. Praeger, 1965.

SETON-WATSON, HUGH. *The Decline of Imperial Russia, 1855–1914.* New York: Frederick A. Praeger, 1952.

SUMNER, B. H. *A Short History of Russia.* Rev. ed. New York: Reynal and Hitchcock, 1943.

TREADGOLD, DONALD W. *Twentieth Century Russia.* Chicago: Rand McNally & Company, 1959.

TROTSKY, LEON. *The History of the Russian Revolution.* Translated by MAX EASTMAN. (1st ed., 1932.) Ann Arbor, Mich.: The University of Michigan Press, 1957; Garden City, N.Y.: Doubleday & Company, 1959 (selections, paper).

VON RAUCH, GEORG. *A History of Soviet Russia.* Translated by PETER and ANNETTE JACOBSOHN. 4th ed.; New York: Frederick A. Praeger, 1964.

Chapter 4: COMMUNIST IDEOLOGY

DYAEV, NICOLAS. *The Origin of Russian Communism.* Translated by R. M. FRENCH. Ann Arbor, Mich.: The University of Michigan Press, 1960.

ARIN, NIKOLAI I., and PREOBRAZHENSKY, EVGENI A. *The ABC of ommunism.* Translated by EDEN and CEDAR PAUL. London: The mmunist Party of Great Britain, 1922.

IER, ISAAC. *The Prophet Armed. Trotsky: 1879–1921.* New York: ord University Press, 1954.

———. *The Prophet Unarmed. Trotsky: 1921–1929.* New York: Oxford University Press, 1959.

———. *Stalin: A Political Biography.* New York: Oxford University Press, 1949.

FAINSOD, MERLE. *How Russia is Ruled.* Rev. ed.; Cambridge, Mass.: Harvard University Press, 1963.

FISCHER, LOUIS. *Men and Politics.* New York: Duell, Sloan and Pearce, 1940.

———. *The Life of Lenin.* New York: Harper & Row, 1964.

GURIAN, WALDEMAR. *Bolshevism: An Introduction to Soviet Communism.* Notre Dame, Ind.: University of Indiana Press, 1952.

HAIMSON, LEOPOLD H. *The Russian Marxists and the Origins of Bolshevism.* Cambridge, Mass.: Harvard University Press, 1955.

History of the Communist Party of the Soviet Union (Bolsheviks): Short Course. New York: International Publishers, 1939.

HOOK, SIDNEY. *Marx and the Marxists: The Ambiguous Legacy.* Princeton, N.J.: D. Van Nostrand Company, 1955.

HUNT, R. N. CAREW. *The Theory and Practice of Communism.* New York: The Macmillan Company, 1951.

KELSEN, HANS. *The Political Theory of Bolshevism: A Critical Analysis.* Berkeley, Calif.: University of California Press, 1948.

LEITES, NATHAN. *A Study of Bolshevism.* Glencoe, Ill.: The Free Press, 1953.

LENIN, VLADIMIR I. "What Is to Be Done?," *Selected Works.* New York: International Publishers, 1943. II, 27–192.

MARCUSE, H. *Soviet Marxism: A Critical Analysis.* New York: Columbia University Press, 1958.

MEYER, ALFRED G. *Leninism.* Cambridge, Mass.: Harvard University Press, 1957; New York: Frederick A. Praeger, 1962 (paper).

———. *Marxism: The Unity of Theory and Practice.* Cambridge, Mass.: Harvard University Press, 1954.

SCHUMPETER, JOSEPH A. *Capitalism, Socialism and Democracy.* 3d ed. New York: Harper & Brothers, 1950.

SHUB, DAVID A. *Lenin.* Garden City, N.Y.: Doubleday & Company, 1949.

SIMMONS, ERNEST J. (ed.). *Continuity and Change in Russian and Soviet Thought.* Cambridge, Mass.: Harvard University Press, 1955.

SOUVARINE, BORIS. *Stalin: A Critical Survey of Bolshevism.* New York: Longmans, Green & Co., 1939.

STALIN, JOSEPH. *Problems of Leninism.* Moscow: Foreign Languages Publishing House, 1947.

TREADGOLD, DONALD W. *Lenin and His Rivals: The Struggle for Russia's Future, 1898–1906.* New York: Frederick A. Praeger, 1955.

TROTSKY, LEON. *Stalin: An Appraisal of the Man and His Influence.* Translated and edited by CHARLES MALAMUTH. New York: Harper & Brothers, 1946.

ULAM, ADAM B. *The Bolsheviks.* New York: The Macmillan Company, 1965.

WILSON, EDMUND. *To the Finland Station: A Study in the Writing and Acting of History.* Garden City, N.Y.: Doubleday & Company, 1953.

WOLFE, BERTRAM D. *Three Who Made a Revolution.* New York: The Dial Press, 1948; Boston: Beacon Press, 1955 (paper).

———. *Marxism: One Hundred Years in the Life of a Doctrine.* New York: The Dial Press, 1965.

Chapter 5: THE GOVERNMENT

ARMSTRONG, JOHN A. *The Politics of Totalitarianism: The Communist Party of the Soviet Union From 1934 to the Present.* New York: Random House, 1961.

CONQUEST, ROBERT. *Power and Policy in the U.S.S.R.: The Study of Soviet Dynastics.* New York: St Martin's Press, 1961.

DANIELS, ROBERT V. (ed.). *A Documentary History of Communism.* New York: Random House, 1960.

FAINSOD, MERLE. *How Russia Is Ruled.* Cambridge, Mass.: Harvard University Press, 1953.

FLORINSKY, MICHAEL T. *Towards an Understanding of the U.S.S.R.: A Study in Government, Politics, and Economic Planning.* New York: The Macmillan Company, 1951.

GRULIOW, LEO (ed.). *Current Soviet Policies.* Vol. I: *The Documentary Record of the Nineteenth Party Congress and the Reorganization After Stalin's Death.* Vol. II: *The Documentary Record of the Twentieth Party Congress and Its Aftermath.* New York: Frederick A. Praeger, 1953 and 1957.

GSOVSKI, VLADIMIR. *Soviet Civil Law.* 2 vols. Ann Arbor, Mich.: University of Michigan Law School, 1948.

HARPER, S. N., and THOMPSON, R. *The Government of the Soviet Union.* 2d ed. New York: D. Van Nostrand Company, 1949.

HAZARD, JOHN. *The Soviet System of Government.* Chicago: The University of Chicago Press, 1957.

KULSKI, WLADYSLAW W. *The Soviet Regime: Communism in Practice.* 3d ed. Syracuse, N.Y.: Syracuse University Press, 1959.

MEISEL, JAMES H., and KOZERA, EDWARD (eds.). *Materials for the Study of the Soviet System.* Ann Arbor, Mich.: George Wahr Publishing Company, 1953.

MEISSNER, BORIS. *The Communist Party of the Soviet Union: Party Leadership, Organization, and Ideology.* Edited with a chapter on the Twentieth Party Congress by JOHN S. RESHETAR, JR. New York: Frederick A. Praeger, 1956.

MOORE, BARRINGTON, JR. *Soviet Politics: The Dilemma of Power.* Cambridge, Mass.: Harvard University Press, 1950.

———. *Terror and Progress USSR: Some Sources of Change and Stability in the Soviet Dictatorship.* Cambridge, Mass.: Harvard University Press, 1954.

SCHAPIRO, LEONARD. *The Communist Party of the Soviet Union.* New York: Random House, 1960.

SCHUELLER, GEORGE. *The Politburo.* Stanford, Calif.: Stanford University Press, 1951.

TOWSTER, JULIAN. *Political Power in the U.S.S.R. 1917–1948: The Theory and Structure of Government in the Soviet State.* New York: Oxford University Press, 1948.

WOLIN, SIMON, and SLUSSER, ROBERT M. (eds.). *The Soviet Secret Police.* New York: Frederick A. Praeger, 1957.

Chapter 6: THE LEADERSHIP

ARMSTRONG, JOHN A. *The Politics of Totalitarianism: The Communist Party of the Soviet Union From 1934 to the Present.* New York: Random House, 1961.

BAUER, RAYMOND A. *The New Man in Soviet Psychology.* Cambridge, Mass.: Harvard University Press, 1952.

———; INKELES, ALEX; and KLUCKHOHN, CLYDE. *How the Soviet System Works: Cultural, Psychological and Social Themes.* Cambridge, Mass.: Harvard University Press, 1956.

BECK, F., and GODIN, W. *Russian Purge and the Extraction of Confession.* New York: The Viking Press, 1951.

BRZEZINSKI, ZBIGNIEW K. *The Permanent Purge: Politics in Soviet Totalitarianism.* Cambridge, Mass.: Harvard University Press, 1956.

CONQUEST, ROBERT. *Power and Policy in the U.S.S.R.: The Study of Soviet Dynastics.* New York: St Martin's Press, 1961.

DANIELS, ROBERT V. *The Conscience of the Revolution: Communist*

Opposition in Soviet Russia. Cambridge, Mass.: Harvard University Press, 1960.

DJILAS, MILOVAN. *The New Class*. New York: Frederick A. Praeger, 1957.

FRIEDRICH, CARL J., and BRZEZINSKI, ZBIGNIEW K. *Totalitarian Dictatorship and Autocracy*. Cambridge, Mass.: Harvard University Press, 1956; New York: Frederick A. Praeger, 1961 (paper).

INKELES, ALEX. *Public Opinion in Soviet Russia: A Study in Mass Persuasion*. Cambridge, Mass.: Harvard University Press, 1950.

KOESTLER, ARTHUR. *Darkness at Noon*. Translated by DAPHNE HARDY. New York: The Macmillan Company, 1941.

MONNEROT, JULES. *Sociology and Psychology of Communism*. Translated by JANE DEGRAS and R. REES. Boston: Beacon Press, 1953.

NICOLAEVSKY, BORIS I. (ed.). "The Crimes of the Stalin Era," *The New Leader*, Section II, July 16, 1956. The text of Khrushchev's "Secret Speech" at the Twentieth Party Congress with notes and commentary by Nicolaevsky.

PETHYBRIDGE, ROGER. *A Key to Soviet Politics: The Crisis of the "Anti-Party" Group*. New York: Frederick A. Praeger, 1962.

PISTRAK, LAZAR. *The Grand Tactician: Khrushchev's Rise to Power*. New York: Frederick A. Praeger, 1961.

ROSTOW, W. W., *et al. The Dynamics of Soviet Society*. New York: W. W. Norton & Company, 1953; New York: New American Library, 1954 (paper).

RUSH, MYRON. *The Rise of Khrushchev*. Washington, D.C.: Public Affairs Press, 1958.

SCHAPIRO, LEONARD. *The Origin of the Communist Autocracy: Political Opposition in the Soviet State, 1917–1922*. Cambridge, Mass.: Harvard University Press, 1955.

WOLFE, BERTRAM D. *Khrushchev and Stalin's Ghost*. New York: Frederick A. Praeger, 1957.

Chapter 7: AGRICULTURE

BELOV, FEDOR. *The History of a Soviet Collective Farm*. New York: Frederick A. Praeger, 1955.

DINERSTEIN, HERBERT S., and GOURÉ, LEON. *Communism and the Russian Peasant: Moscow in Crisis*. Glencoe, Ill.: The Free Press, 1955.

JASNY, NAUM. *The Socialized Agriculture of the USSR*. Stanford, Calif.: Stanford University Press, 1949.

LAIRD, ROY D. *Collective Farming in Russia: A Political Study of the Soviet Kolkhozy*. Lawrence, Kans.: University of Kansas Publications, 1958.

MAYNARD, SIR JOHN. *Russia in Flux*. New York: The Macmillan Company, 1946.

ROBINSON, GEROLD TANQUERY. *Rural Russia under the Old Regime*. New York: The Macmillan Company, 1949.

SANDERS, IRWIN T. (ed.). *Collectivization of Agriculture in Eastern Europe*. Lexington, Ky.: University of Kentucky Press, 1957.

SHOLOKHOV, MIKHAIL. *Seeds of Tomorrow*. Translated by STEPHEN GARRY. New York: Alfred A. Knopf, 1935.

VOLIN, LAZAR. *A Survey of Soviet Russian Agriculture*. Agriculture Monograph 5. Washington, D.C.: Department of Agriculture, 1951.

Chapter 8: INDUSTRY

ARAKELIAN, A. *Industrial Management in the USSR*. Translated by ELLSWORTH L. RAYMOND. Washington, D.C.: Public Affairs Press, 1950.

BAYKOV, ALEXANDER. *The Development of the Soviet Economic System*. New York: The Macmillan Company, 1947.

BERGSON, ABRAM. *The Real National Income of Soviet Russia Since 1928*. Cambridge, Mass.: Harvard University Press, 1961.

——— (ed.). *Soviet Economic Growth: Conditions and Perspectives*. Evanston, Ill.: Row, Peterson and Company, 1953.

BERLINER, JOSEPH S. *Factory and Manager in the U.S.S.R.* Cambridge, Mass.: Harvard University Press, 1957.

CAMPBELL, ROBERT W. *Soviet Economic Power: Its Organization, Growth, and Power*. Boston: Houghton Mifflin Company, 1960.

CLARK, M. GARDNER. *The Economics of Soviet Steel*. Cambridge, Mass.: Harvard University Press, 1956.

DALLIN, DAVID J., and NICOLAEVSKY, BORIS I. *Forced Labor in Soviet Russia*. New Haven, Conn.: Yale University Press, 1947.

DOBB, MAURICE. *Soviet Economic Development Since 1917*. New York: International Publishers, 1948.

GRANICK, DAVID. *Management of the Industrial Firm in the U.S.S.R.* New York: Columbia University Press, 1953.

———. *The Red Executive: A Study of the Organization Man in Russian Industry*. Garden City, N.Y.: Doubleday & Company, 1960.

HASSMAN, H. *Oil in the Soviet Union.* Translated by A. M. LEESTON. Princeton, N.J.: Princeton University Press, 1953.

HOLZMAN, FRANKLYN D. *Soviet Taxation: The Fiscal and Monetary Problems of a Planned Economy.* Cambridge, Mass.: Harvard University Press, 1955.

JASNY, NAUM. *Soviet Industrialization, 1928–1952.* Chicago: The University of Chicago Press, 1961.

JOINT ECONOMIC COMMITTEE, U.S. Congress. *Annual Economic Indicators for the U.S.S.R.* Washington, D.C.: Government Printing Office, 1964.

JOINT ECONOMIC COMMITTEE, U.S. Congress. *Dimensions of Soviet Economic Power.* Washington, D.C.: Government Printing Office, 1962.

NOVE, ALEC. *The Soviet Economy: An Introduction.* Rev. ed.; New York: Frederick A. Praeger, 1965.

NUTTER, G. W. *The Growth of Industrial Production in the Soviet Union.* Princeton, N.J.: Princeton University Press, 1962.

RICHMAN, BARRY M. *Soviet Management: With Significant American Comparisons.* Englewood Cliffs, N.J.: Prentice-Hall, 1965.

SCHWARTZ, HARRY. *Russia's Soviet Economy.* 2d ed. New York: Prentice-Hall, 1954.

———. *The Soviet Economy Since Stalin.* Philadelphia: J. B. Lippincott Company, 1965.

SCHWARZ, SOLOMON M. *Labor in the Soviet Union.* New York: Frederick A. Praeger, 1952.

SHAFFER, HARRY G. (ed.). *The Soviet Economy: A Collection of Western and Soviet Views.* New York: Appleton-Century-Crofts, 1963.

SPULBER, NICHOLAS. *The Soviet Economy: Structure, Principles, Problems.* New York: W. W. Norton & Company, 1962.

STALIN, JOSEPH. *Economic Problems of Socialism in the U.S.S.R.* New York: International Publishers, 1952.

VOZNESENSKY, NIKOLAI A. *The Economy of the USSR During World War II.* Washington, D.C.: Public Affairs Press, 1948.

WILES, PETER J. D. *The Political Economy of Communism.* Cambridge, Mass.: Harvard University Press, 1962.

Chapter 9: TRANSPORTATION

ARMSTRONG, TERENCE. *The Northern Sea Route: Soviet Exploitation of the North East Passage.* London: Cambridge University Press, 1952.

ESTEP, RAYMOND. *Transportation in the Soviet Union.* Maxwell Air Force Base, Ala.: Air University Documentary Research Study, 1951.

HUNTER, HOLLAND. *Soviet Transportation Policy.* Cambridge, Mass.: Harvard University Press, 1957.

———. *Statistics of Transportation in the USSR.* Washington, D.C.: Council for Economic and Industrial Research, 1955.

JANSE, RENÉE S. *Soviet Transportation and Communications: A Bibliography.* Washington, D.C.: Library of Congress Reference Department, 1952.

LEBED, A., and YAKOVLEV, B. *Soviet Waterways: The Development of the Inland Navigation System in the USSR.* Munich: Institute for the Study of the USSR, 1956.

Chapter 10: EDUCATION

ASHBY, ERIC. *A Scientist in Russia.* New York and London: Penguin Books, 1947.

COUNTS, GEORGE S. *The Challenge of Soviet Education.* New York: McGraw-Hill Book Company, 1957.

DEWITT, NICHOLAS. *Soviet Professional Manpower: Its Education, Training, and Supply.* Washington, D.C.: National Science Foundation, 1955.

Directory of Selected Scientific Institutions in the U.S.S.R. Columbus, Ohio: Charles E. Merrill Books, 1963.

Education in the U.S.S.R. Washington, D.C.: Department of Health, Education, and Welfare, 1957.

KLINE, GEORGE L. (ed.). *Soviet Education.* New York: Columbia University Press, 1957.

KOROL, ALEXANDER G. *Soviet Education for Science and Technology.* New York: John Wiley & Sons, 1957.

LEVIN, DEANA. *Soviet Education Today.* New York: Monthly Review Press, 1963.

MEDLIN, W. K., LINDQUIST, C. B., and SCHMITT, M. L. *Soviet Education Programs.* Washington, D.C.: Department of Health, Education, and Welfare, 1960.

MEDYNSKY, Y. N. *Public Education in the USSR.* Moscow: Foreign Languages Publishing House, 1950.

REDL, HELEN B. (ed. and trans.). *Soviet Educators on Soviet Education.* New York: Free Press of Glencoe, 1964.

ROSEN, S. M. *Higher Education in the U.S.S.R.: Curriculums, Schools, and Statistics*. Washington, D.C.: Department of Health, Education, and Welfare, 1963.

Soviet Commitment to Education: Report of the First Official U.S. Educational Mission to the U.S.S.R. Washington, D.C.: Department of Health, Education, and Welfare, 1959.

TRILLING, LEON. *Soviet Education in Aeronautics: A Case Study*. Cambridge, Mass.: Center for International Studies, Massachusetts Institute of Technology, 1955.

VUCINICH, ALEXANDER. *The Soviet Academy of Sciences*. Stanford, Calif.: Stanford University Press, 1956.

Chapter 11: THE ARMED FORCES

ALEXANDROV, VICTOR. *The Tukhachevsky Affair*. Englewood Cliffs, N.J.: Prentice-Hall, 1963.

ANDERS, W. *Hitler's Defeat in Russia*. Chicago: Henry Regnery Company, 1953.

BRZEZINSKI, ZBIGNIEW (ed.). *Political Controls in the Soviet Army*. New York: Research Program on the U.S.S.R.; Frederick A. Praeger, 1954.

CARELL, PAUL. *Hitler Moves East, 1941–1943*. Translated by EWALD OSERS. Boston: Little, Brown and Company, 1965.

CARR, E. H. *German-Soviet Relations Between the Two World Wars, 1919–1939*. Baltimore: The Johns Hopkins Press, 1951.

CLARK, ALAN. *Barbarossa: The Russian-German Conflict, 1941–1945*. New York: William Morrow & Company, 1964.

DALLIN, ALEXANDER. *German Rule in Russia, 1941–1945*. New York: St Martin's Press, 1957.

DENIKIN, A. I. *The White Army*. Translated by C. ZVEGINTSOV. London: Jonathan Cape, 1930.

DINERSTEIN, H. S. *War and the Soviet Union: Nuclear Weapons and the Revolution in Soviet Military and Political Thinking*. New York: Frederick A. Praeger, 1959.

ELY, L. B. *The Red Army Today*. Harrisburg, Pa.: The Stackpole Company, 1953.

EMME, EUGENE M. *The Impact of Air Power*. Princeton, N.J.: D. Van Nostrand Company, 1959.

ERICKSON, JOHN. *The Soviet High Command: A Military-Political History, 1918–1941*. New York: St Martin's Press, 1962.

FEDOTOFF WHITE, D. *The Growth of the Red Army*. Princeton, N.J.: Princeton University Press, 1944.

FISCHER, GEORGE. *Soviet Opposition to Stalin: A Case Study in World War II.* Cambridge, Mass.: Harvard University Press, 1952.

FULLER, J. F. C. *The Second World War, 1939–1945.* New York: Duell, Sloan and Pearce, 1949.

GALLAGHER, MATTHEW P. *The Soviet History of World War II: Myths, Memories, and Realities.* New York: Frederick A. Praeger, 1963.

GARTHOFF, RAYMOND L. *The Soviet Image of Future War.* Washington, D.C.: Public Affairs Press, 1959.

———. *Soviet Military Doctrine.* Glencoe, Ill.: The Free Press, 1953.

———. *Soviet Strategy in the Nuclear Age.* Rev. ed., New York: Frederick A. Praeger, 1962.

GUILLAUME, A. *Soviet Arms and Soviet Power.* Washington, D.C.: Infantry Journal Press, 1949.

INSTITUTE FOR STRATEGIC STUDIES. *The Soviet Union and the NATO Powers: The Military Balance.* London, 1960.

KENNAN, GEORGE F. *Russia, the Atom and the West.* New York: Harper & Brothers, 1958.

KILMARX, ROBERT A. *A History of Soviet Air Power.* New York: Frederick A. Praeger, 1962.

LEE, ASHER. *The Soviet Air Force.* London: Gerald Duckworth, 1950.

——— (ed.). *The Soviet Air and Rocket Forces.* New York: Frederick A. Praeger, 1959.

LIDDELL HART, B. H. *The German Generals Talk.* New York: William Morrow and Company, 1948.

——— (ed.). *The Red Army.* New York: Harcourt, Brace & Company, 1956.

SAUNDERS, M. G. (ed.). *The Soviet Navy.* New York: Frederick A. Praeger, 1958.

SOKOLOVSKY, MARSHAL V. D. *Military Strategy: Soviet Doctrine and Concepts.* New York: Frederick A. Praeger, 1963.

STOCKWELL, RICHARD E. *Soviet Air Power.* New York: Pageant Press, 1956.

TAYLOR, J. W. R. *Russian Aircraft.* London: Ian Allan, 1959.

VOROSHILOV, K. Y. *Stalin and the Armed Forces of the USSR.* Moscow: Foreign Languages Publishing House, 1951.

WERTH, ALEXANDER. *Russia at War, 1941–1945.* New York: E. P. Dutton & Company, 1964.

WOLFE, THOMAS W. *Soviet Strategy at the Crossroads.* Cambridge, Mass.: Harvard University Press, 1964.

WOLLENBERG, ERICH. *The Red Army.* London: Secker and Warburg, 1938.

Chapter 12: FOREIGN POLICY

BELOFF, MAX. *The Foreign Policy of Soviet Russia, 1929–1941*. 2 vols. London and New York: Oxford University Press, 1947–49.

———. *Soviet Policy in the Far East, 1944–1951*. London and New York: Oxford University Press, 1953.

BRZEZINSKI, ZBIGNIEW K. *The Soviet Bloc: Unity and Conflict*. Cambridge, Mass.: Harvard University Press, 1960. Rev. ed.; New York: Frederick A. Praeger, 1961 (paper).

COMMITTEE ON FOREIGN AFFAIRS, U.S. Senate. *United States Foreign Policy: U.S.S.R. and Eastern Europe*. Washington, D.C.: Government Printing Office, 1960.

DALLIN, ALEXANDER (ed.). *Soviet Conduct in World Affairs: A Selection of Readings*. New York: Columbia University Press, 1960.

———. *The Soviet Union at the United Nations: An Inquiry into Soviet Motives and Objectives*. New York: Frederick A. Praeger, 1962.

DALLIN, D. J. *The Rise of Russia in Asia*. New Haven, Conn.: Yale University Press, 1949.

———. *Soviet Foreign Policy After Stalin*. Philadelphia: J. B. Lippincott Company, 1961.

DEGRAS, JANE (ed.). *Soviet Documents on Foreign Policy*. 3 vols. London and New York: Oxford University Press, 1951–53.

FEIS, HERBERT. *The China Tangle*. Princeton, N.J.: Princeton University Press, 1953.

———. *Churchill—Roosevelt—Stalin: The War They Waged and the Peace They Sought*. Princeton, N.J.: Princeton University Press, 1957.

FISCHER, LOUIS. *The Soviets in World Affairs, 1917–1929*. 2 vols. Princeton, N.J.: Princeton University Press, 1951.

GRIFFITH, WILLIAM E. *The Sino-Soviet Rift*. Cambridge, Mass.: The M.I.T. Press, 1964.

KENNAN, GEORGE F. *Russia and the West Under Lenin and Stalin*. Boston: Little, Brown and Company, 1961.

LEDERER, IVO J. (ed.). *Russian Foreign Policy: Essays in Historical Perspective*. New Haven, Conn.: Yale University Press, 1962.

MACKINTOSH, J. M. *Strategy and Tactics of Soviet Foreign Policy*. New York: Oxford University Press, 1963.

MOSELY, PHILIP E. *The Kremlin and World Politics: Studies in Soviet Policy and Action*. New York: Vintage Books, 1960 (paper).

——— (ed.). *The Soviet Union, 1922–1962: A Foreign Affairs Reader.* Foreword by Hamilton Fish Armstrong. New York: Frederick A. Praeger, 1963.

Moore, H. L. *Soviet Far Eastern Policy.* Princeton, N.J.: Princeton University Press, 1945.

Nettl, J. P. *The Eastern Zone and Soviet Policy in Germany, 1945–1950.* New York: Oxford University Press, 1951.

Rossi, A. *The Russo-German Alliance, August 1939–June 1941.* Boston: Beacon Press, 1951.

Royal Institute of International Affairs. *The Soviet-Yugoslav Dispute.* London, 1948.

Seton-Watson, Hugh. *The East European Revolution.* New York: Frederick A. Praeger, 1956.

———. *Neither War Nor Peace: The Struggle for Power in the Post-war World.* New York: Frederick A. Praeger, 1960.

Schapiro, Leonard (ed.). *Soviet Treaty Series.* 2 vols. Washington, D.C.: Georgetown University Press, 1950–55.

Shulman, Marshall. *Stalin's Foreign Policy Reappraised.* New York: Atheneum Publishers, 1965 (paper).

Slusser, Robert M., and Triska, Jan F. *A Calendar of Soviet Treaties, 1917–1957.* Stanford, Calif.: Stanford University Press, 1959.

Snell, John L., *et al. The Meaning of Yalta: Big Three Diplomacy and the New Balance of Power.* Baton Rouge, La.: Louisiana State University Press, 1956.

Sontag, Raymond J., and Beddie, J. S. (eds.). *Nazi-Soviet Relations, 1939–1941: Documents from the Archives of the German Foreign Office.* Washington, D.C.: Department of State, 1948.

Wei, Henry. *China and Soviet Russia.* Princeton, N.J.: D. Van Nostrand Company, 1956.

Wolff, Robert L. *The Balkans in Our Time.* Cambridge, Mass.: Harvard University Press, 1956.

Chapter 13: INTERNATIONAL COMMUNISM

Berliner, Joseph S. *Soviet Economic Aid: A New Policy of Aid and Trade in Underdeveloped Countries.* New York: Frederick A. Praeger, 1958.

Black, Cyril E., and Thornton, Thomas P. (eds.). *Communism and Revolution.* Princeton, N.J.: Princeton University Press, 1964.

BORKENAU, FRANZ. *European Communism.* New York: Harper & Brothers, 1953.

———. *World Communism: A History of the Communist International.* New York: W. W. Norton & Company, 1939.

BRANDT, CONRAD; SCHWARTZ, BENJAMIN; and FAIRBANK, JOHN K. (eds.). *A Documentary History of Chinese Communism.* Cambridge, Mass.: Harvard University Press, 1952.

COLUMBIA UNIVERSITY, RUSSIAN INSTITUTE (ed.). *The Anti-Stalin Campaign and International Communism: A Selection of Documents.* New York: Columbia University Press, 1956.

DALLIN, ALEXANDER, *et al.* (eds.). *Diversity in International Communism: A Documentary Record.* New York: Columbia University Press, 1963.

DEGRAS, JANE (ed.). *The Communist International, 1919–1943: Documents.* 3 vols.; New York: Oxford University Press, 1956–.

DIMITROFF, GEORGI. *The United Front.* New York: International Publishers, 1938.

EBON, MARTIN. *World Communism Today.* New York: Whittlesey House, 1948.

EINAUDI, MARIO (ed.). *Communism in Western Europe.* Ithaca, N.Y.: Cornell University Press, 1951.

FISCHER, RUTH. *Stalin and German Communism.* Cambridge, Mass.: Harvard University Press, 1948.

GANKIN, OLGA HESS, and FISHER, H. H. *The Bolsheviks and the World War: The Origins of the Third International.* Stanford, Calif.: Stanford University Press, 1940.

GOODMAN, ELLIOT R. *The Soviet Design for a World State.* New York: Columbia University Press, 1960.

HUDSON, G. F.; LOWENTHAL, RICHARD; and MACFARQUHAR, RODERICK. *The Sino-Soviet Dispute: Documented and Analyzed.* New York: Frederick A. Praeger, 1961.

ISAACS, HAROLD R. *The Tragedy of the Chinese Revolution.* Stanford, Calif.: Stanford University Press, 1951.

KAHIN, GEORGE MCTURNAN. *Nationalism and Revolution in Indonesia.* Ithaca, N.Y.: Cornell University Press, 1952.

KAUTSKY, JOHN H. *Moscow and the Communist Party of India.* New York: John Wiley & Sons, 1956.

KENNEDY, MALCOLM D. *A History of Communism in East Asia.* New York: Frederick A. Praeger, 1957.

KRIVITSKI, W. G. *I Was Stalin's Agent.* London: Hamish Hamilton, 1939.

LAQUEUR, WALTER Z. *The Soviet Union and the Middle East.* New York: Frederick A. Praeger, 1959.

LOWENTHAL, RICHARD. *World Communism: The Disintegration of a Secular Faith.* New York: Oxford University Press, 1964.

MCLANE, CHARLES B. *Soviet Policy and the Chinese Communists, 1931–1946.* New York: Columbia University Press, 1958.

MCVICKER, CHARLES P. *Titoism: Pattern for Inernational Communism.* New York: St Martin's Press, 1957.

NOLLAU, GÜNTHER. *International Communism and World Revolution: History and Methods.* Translated by VICTOR ANDERSEN, with a Foreword by LEONARD SCHAPIRO. New York: Frederick A. Praeger, 1961.

NORTH, ROBERT C. *Kuomintang and Chinese Communist Elites.* Stanford, Calif.: Stanford University Press, 1953.

———. *Moscow and the Chinese Communists.* Rev. ed.; Stanford, Calif.: Stanford University Press, 1963.

POSSONY, STEFAN T. *A Century of Conflict: Communist Techniques of World Revolution.* Chicago: Henry Regnery Company, 1953.

ROY, M. N. *Revolution and Counterrevolution in China.*. Calcutta: Renaissance Publishers, 1946.

SCHWARTZ, BENJAMIN I. *Chinese Communism and the Rise of Mao.* Cambridge, Mass.: Harvard University Press, 1951.

SETON-WATSON, HUGH. *From Lenin to Khrushchev: The History of World Communism.* New York: Frederick A. Praeger, 1960.

SNOW, EDGAR. *Red Star over China.* New York: Random House, 1938.

SWEARINGEN, RODGER, and LANGER, PAUL F. *Red Flag in Japan: International Communism in Action 1919–1951.* Cambridge, Mass.: Harvard University Press, 1952.

TOMASIC, D. A. *National Communism and Soviet Strategy.* Washington, D.C.: Public Affairs Press, 1957.

TRAGER, FRANK N. (ed.). *Marxism in Southeast Asia: A Study of Four Countries.* Stanford, Calif.: Stanford University Press, 1959. (Burma, Thailand, Vietnam, and Indonesia.)

TROTSKY, LEON. *The Third International After Lenin.* New York: Pioneer Publishers, 1936.

ULAM, ADAM B. *Titoism and the Cominform.* Cambridge, Mass.: Harvard University Press, 1952.

ZINNER, P. E. (ed.). *National Communism and Popular Revolt in Eastern Europe.* New York: Columbia University Press, 1956.

Chapter 14: CURRENT TRENDS

BLAKE, PATRICIA, and HAYWARD, MAX. *Halfway to the Moon: New Writing from Russia.* New York: Holt, Rinehart & Winston, 1964.

COMMITTEE ON FOREIGN AFFAIRS, U.S. House of Representatives. *Sino-Soviet Conflict.* Washington, D.C.: Government Printing Office, 1965.

CONQUEST, ROBERT. *Russia After Khrushchev.* New York: Frederick A. Praeger, 1965.

DALLIN, ALEXANDER, *et al. The Soviet Union and Disarmament: An Appraisal of Soviet Attitudes and Intentions.* New York: Frederick A. Praeger, 1965.

HAYWARD, MAX, and CROWLEY, EDWARD L. (ed.). *Soviet Literature in the Sixties: An International Symposium.* New York: Frederick A. Praeger, 1964.

JOHNSON, PRISCILLA. *Khrushchev and the Arts.* Cambridge, Mass.: The M.I.T. Press, 1965.

JOINT ECONOMIC COMMITTEE, 89th Congress, 1st Session. *Current Indicators for the U.S.S.R.* Washington, D.C.: Government Printing Office, June, 1965.

LASKY, VICTOR. *The Ugly Russian.* New York: Trident Press, 1965.

LOWENTHAL, RICHARD. *World Communism: The Disintegration of a Secular Faith.* New York: Oxford University Press, 1964.

O'BRIEN, FRANK. *Crisis in World Communism: Marxism in Search of Efficiency.* New York: Committee for Economic Development, 1965.

STRUMILIN, S. G. *Man, Society, and the Future.* New York: Crosscurrents Press, 1964.

SWEARER, HOWARD R. *The Politics of Succession in the U.S.S.R.* Boston: Little, Brown and Company, 1964.

THORNTON, THOMAS P. (ed.). *The Third World in Soviet Perspective.* Princeton, N.J.: Princeton University Press, 1964.

Index